Popular Sovereignty in a Digital Age

Popular Sovereignty in a Digital Age

Lessons for the Global South and Working Classes

Edited by
AARON SCHNEIDER

Cover art designed by Andres Tencio, with credit to the original publisher, Instituto de Investigaciones Sociales – Universidad de Costa Rica

Published by State University of New York Press, Albany

© 2024 State University of New York

All rights reserved

Printed in the United States of America

No part of this book may be used or reproduced in any manner whatsoever without written permission. No part of this book may be stored in a retrieval system or transmitted in any form or by any means including electronic, electrostatic, magnetic tape, mechanical, photocopying, recording, or otherwise without the prior permission in writing of the publisher.

Links to third-party websites are provided as a convenience and for informational purposes only. They do not constitute an endorsement or an approval of any of the products, services, or opinions of the organization, companies, or individuals. SUNY Press bears no responsibility for the accuracy, legality, or content of a URL, the external website, or for that of subsequent websites.

For information, contact State University of New York Press, Albany, NY
www.sunypress.edu

Library of Congress Cataloging-in-Publication Data

Name: Schneider, Aaron, editor.
Title: Popular sovereignty in a digital age : lessons for the global south and working classes / Aaron Schneider.
Description: Albany : State University of New York Press, [2024] | Includes bibliographical references and index.
Identifiers: ISBN 9781438498850 (hardcover : alk. paper) | ISBN 9781438498867 (ebook) | ISBN 9781438498843 (pbk. : alk. paper)
Further information is available at the Library of Congress.

Contents

Acknowledgments	ix

1. Introduction   1
   Henrique Estides Delgado and Aaron Schneider

Future Histories

2. A Usable Past for a Democratic Future: How Looking
   Backward Can Help Us Navigate the Digital Revolution   19
   Lizzie O'Shea

3. Technological Innovations and Fake News: Democratic
   Challenges and What Is to Be Done   35
   Rafael R. Ioris

4. Computing Machinery and the Modern Triumvirate:
   State, Market, and Science   45
   Ivan da Costa Marques

Tech, Capital, and Collectivities

5. Evaluating Work in the Platform Economy: The Fairwork
   Project in Brazil and Latin America   65
   Claudia Nociolini Rebechi, Marcos Aragão de Oliveira,
   Tatiana López Ayala, Jonas C. L. Valente, Rafael Grohmann,
   Julice Salvagni, Roseli Aparecida Figaro Paulino, Rodrigo Carelli,
   Victória Mendonça da Silva, Ana Flávia Marques da Silva,
   Camilla Voigt Baptistella, Jackeline Cristina Gameleira
   Cerqueira da Silva, Helena Rodrigues de Farias, Mark Graham,
   and Kelle Howson

vi | Contents

6. The Role of Fake News in the Erosion of Brazilian Democracy   83
    Tássio Acosta, P. Locatelli, and Sílvio Gallo

7. A Conversation with Julietta Hua and Kasturi Ray:
    Feminism, AI, and Racial Technocapitalism in the Uber   99
    and Lyft Economy
    Neda Atanasoski

8. On Coding Democracy, Popular Data-Equity, and
    Algorithmic Action: Notes from Brazil   117
    Andre Isai Leirner

9. Participatory Institutions, Digital Technologies, and
    Democratic Crises   137
    Benjamin Goldfrank and Yanina Welp

10. Britain's Food Crisis: Capital, Class, Technology, and
     Alternatives   155
     Benjamin Selwyn

Digital States, Democracy, and Development

11. Global Capitalism after the Pandemic   173
     William I. Robinson

12. Building Digital Sovereignty in Middle Powers: The Role
     of Intended and Spillover Effects   185
     Vashishtha Doshi

13. Digital Economy Policies for Developing Countries   209
     Parminder Jeet Singh

14. The Chinese Digital Revolution: How Digital Transformation
     Is Shaping a New China   227
     Alessandro Teixeira Golombiewski and Zhenyu Jiang

15. Digital Futures and Global Power: Dynamics, Inequality,
     and Governance   255
     Marco Cepik and Pedro Txai Leal Brancher

Contents | vii

16. Conclusion 275
    Aaron Schneider

List of Contributors 281

References 287

Index 323

Acknowledgments

Portions of chapter 2 appeared first in Lizzie O'Shea, *Future Histories: What Ada Lovelace, Tom Paine, and the Paris Commune Can Teach Us about Digital Tech* (London: Verso, 2019). We are grateful to the publishers for their generosity in bringing this material to a new audience.

Chapter 11 appeared first in the journal *Race & Class* (copyright the Institute of Race Relations, London), W. I. Robinson, "Global Capitalism Post-Pandemic," *Race & Class* 62, no. 2 (2020): 3–13. We are grateful to the editors for the generous assistance in bringing this material to a new audience.

1

Introduction

HENRIQUE ESTIDES DELGADO AND AARON SCHNEIDER

The digital age represents an epochal shift in the operation of global capitalism. This volume seeks to place the current transition, called the "fourth industrial revolution" by some, in its historical context, as the latest in the series of epochal changes experienced by the world system over the last several hundred years. Each such transition provokes crises at the national and international levels, presenting both complicated and opportune moments to engage. The full implications of the current shift remain only partially visible, and social understanding, especially at the popular level and in the Global South, is not widespread though widely felt. Still, if popular sectors and developing countries do not actively struggle to define the terms of the digital transition, we will miss the opportunity to turn toward noncapitalist, deeply democratic, anti-imperial, socially inclusive, and ecologically sustainable forms of modernity. Such a future could be defined in this moment, and the first steps are to understand the current epochal shift, imagine utopian futures, and seek to build them.

This volume emerges from a series of lectures and seminars sponsored by the Instituto Lula in São Paulo from February to April 2022.[1] The series bore the title, "Popular Sovereignty in a Digital Age," and most of the contributors to this volume participated directly in the lectures and seminars.[2] It is worth reflecting on why a think tank bearing the name of the Brazilian president from 2003 to 2010 and candidate and eventual winner of the 2022 presidential election would be interested in the digital transition. As is well known, Luiz Inácio "Lula" da Silva was a shoeshine boy turned factory worker and labor leader who came to prominence in the Brazilian struggle for democracy of the 1970s and 1980s. He went on to lead the Workers' Party in opposition to neoliberal adjustment in the 1990s, won the presidency in 2002, and became a central figure in the Pink Wave of leftist governments coming to power across Latin America. He left power in January 2011 after two terms as the most popular president in the history of Brazil and became a global reference for critical, southern leadership at the international level.[3] After being blocked from the presidency in 2018 by trumped-up corruption charges to open the path for extreme-Right president Jair Bolsonaro (Arcary 2021), he returned to the presidency atop a campaign to restore democracy and development to Brazil.

The Instituto Lula sponsored the Popular Sovereignty in a Digital Age series in the first months of 2022, coinciding with the start of Lula's presidential campaign. The series targeted Workers' Party activists, students, scholars, and community activists eager to engage the topic. The course has to be understood as a platform to cultivate alternative visions at a critical moment in Brazilian politics and history. Lula's campaign sought to raise the level of debate, overcoming the simple arguments of Bolsonaro and the extreme Right, and approach global capitalist transition in terms of a modernity that is more democratic, more just, more ecologically balanced, and more inclusive of diverse identities and cultures.

The Digital Age

Digital technology has become central to the current manifestations of capitalism, altering the ways we work, consume, socialize, and communicate. It is also making incursions into the way we do politics. The rise of digital technology was driven at first by the search for new sources of accumulation after the collapse of the 2008–2009 financial crisis, buoyed by liquidity that central banks pumped into the international economy through quantitative easing and other policies. The onset of the COVID-19 pandemic only exaggerated the centrality of digital technologies, padding the profits of the biggest high-tech corporations and their owners even as millions were turned out of work, left their jobs, and suffered ill health from an ongoing health calamity (Varoufakis 2021). Such absurd wealth generated and accumulated in the midst of a global pandemic highlights crises of inequality brewing in economic, political, geopolitical, cultural, and ecological realms.

To resolve these crises, great powers and dominant corporations are attempting to set the rules for the oncoming digital age in ways that worsen inequality, undermine democracy, reassert international hierarchies, exclude large populations, and push the environment to its brink. Yet the future has not yet been written, and there is still time to articulate an alternative. This book takes a critical, historical view of the digital transition, placing digitalization in the context of historic transitions of capitalism, opening the debate on how traditionally exploited sectors, labor and the Global South, can define the digital age. To advance an alternative agenda, popular sectors must understand and be able to act, and developing countries must be able to assert sovereignty over their future. Before outlining the strategies of labor and the Global South, it is worthwhile to consider the other ways in which digitalization has been approximated to date.[4]

Most developed are important perspectives on the social impacts of digitalization, technical and technological aspects of digitalization, digitalization as a media and communications transformation, digitalization and its sociopolitical and economic impacts, digitalization and its impact on business, and digitalization in developed economies. With a focus on labor and the Global South, this volume fills a critical niche.

Some of the earliest observations coincided with the introduction of the internet in the 1990s, placing digitalization in the context of globalization, defining both in terms of increased social connections across distance. Manuel Castells described the "Network Society" (Castells 2015); others labeled it "the participatory condition" (Barney et al. 2016), "connectivity culture" (Van Dijck 2013), and "superconnectivity" (Chayko 2017). Contributions like these emphasized the communication and connections facilitated by new technologies, with implications for the fundamental relations among people, within groups, between individuals and firms, between state and society, and between humans and machines (González-Bailón 2017; Graham and Dutton 2014; Lindgren 2017). The most important aspect of these contributions was the focus on relations—the way in which quantitatively more connections of a qualitatively different type produced emergent outcomes (Graham and Dutton 2014).

Making sense of these connections required attention to core infrastructures, including technical details, perhaps appropriate to a field in which technological change lies at the heart (Athique 2013). This focus emphasized the infrastructure on which digitalization was built, emphasizing especially how quickly digital infrastructure continues to evolve, citing 3D printing (Hanna 2016), sensors and tracking (Dourish and Bell 2011), the internet of things (Bunz and Meikle 2017), cloud computing (Hu 2015), robotics (Ford 2015; Mosco 2017; Turkle 2011), and the algorithms driving platforms (Srnicek 2016; Cheney-Lippold 2017; Turow 2017). Various engineering "laws" describe the rapidity of change: Moore's law suggests that the processing capacity of computer chips doubles every eighteen months; Butter's law suggests that network communication speed doubles every nine months; Nielson's law suggests that connection speeds for home users double every twenty-one months; Kryder's law suggests that storage capacity doubles every thirteen months.[5]

A related approach emphasized digitalization as a media field, highlighting the interaction between social processes and the media through which they are filtered (Beyes, Leeker, and Schipper 2017; Dourish and Bell 2011). Changes to the media through which we interact create their own incentives, constraints, and possibilities, altering identity, group formation and behavior, socialization, and culture (Bauerlein 2011; Bennett, Chin, and Jones 2015; Berry 2015). For some, the ubiquity of online connections turned them invisible or habitual, masking their massive social impacts (Chun 2017). As Turkle (2011, 243) notes, "Facebook looks like 'home,' but you know that it puts you in a public square with a surveillance camera turned on."

At the core of digitalization is data, and increasing attention has been paid to the quantity, collection, storage, analysis, and power of big data (González-Bailón 2017; Graham and Dutton 2014; Lupton 2016; Rudder 2014). Innovations such as the internet of things and robotics incorporate sensors into everyday appliances, transportation, entertainment, workplaces, and accessories, turning virtually everything into a data-generation and capturing device. This multiplication of content creates endless possibilities for participation and collaboration but also leads to concerns about anonymity, privacy, surveillance, and control (Graham and Dutton 2014; Zuboff 2019; Barney et al. 2016; Bunz and Meikle 2017).

The ubiquity of data raises various questions about the relation between humans and machines (Latour 2004). The possibility of mining data with algorithms and artificial intelligence and the ubiquity of robotics places an additional distance between the ethics of society and the possibilities of science, conjuring science fiction cyborg fears as old as science itself (Beyes, Leeker, and Schipper 2017; Kember and Zylinska 2012; Mosco 2017). This has forced a rethinking of individual identity issues such as the changes involved in childhood (Turkle 2011), adolescence (James 2014), and emotional development (Kvedar, Colman, and Cella 2017). To manage these relations, guidelines have emerged on how to limit dependence on technology (Levy 2016), take advantage of technology (Rheingold 2012), evaluate our information "diet" (Johnson 2015), protect children (Steiner-Adair and Barker 2013), curate our online identities (White 2014; Cheney-Lippold 2017; Lindgren 2017), and protect ourselves (Schneier 2015).

The identities conjured by digitalization extend to groups, shaping and perhaps distorting the ways in which collective identities operate. While online contacts make connections quicker and easier, they also create an "illusion of intimacy" that masks distance and even prevents deeper solidarities (Turkle 2011). The nuances to collective identities are especially worrisome as there are explicit and implicit biases encoded in new technologies. This starts with the "digital divide" in terms of inequalities of access and use patterns (Graham 2014) and extends to racialized patterns of discrimination through biases built into algorithms, economic interests, and monopolistic platforms and media (Eubanks 2018).

A number of analyses focus on the ways digital technologies exacerbate existing social exclusions (Helsper 2012; Yates, Kirby, and Lockley 2015; Yates and Lockley 2018). By contrast, optimistic views celebrate the possibilities of digital activism and collective action impossible before online connections and the potential to evade official monitoring (Dey 2018; Fotopoulou 2017; Gordon and Mihailidis 2016). In part, judgments about the opportunities and pitfalls depend on understandings of "digital capital" and how it interacts with other forms of material and social capital (Ignatow and Robinson 2017; Gladkova and Ragnedda 2017; Ragnedda 2018; Ragnedda and Ruiu 2017).

These various observations motivate public policy attention, with increased information and connection offering presumed benefits for civic engagement (Gordon and Mihailidis 2016). Still, significant debate surrounds issues of regulation and legal frameworks, as technological change races ahead of the capacity of states to keep up (Graham and Dutton 2014). This extends to debates on whether local, national, or international bodies should regulate digitalization (Mueller 2010), questions of public or private provision (Hanna 2016), and regulations to protect privacy and govern access to data (Sonnier 2017), directing attention to possibilities

6 | Henrique Estides Delgado and Aaron Schneider

of abuse and questions of cybersecurity (Goodman 2015). While much is made of the green advantages of digital activity, there is increasing attention to the need for environmental policies related to the massive energy requirements of cloud computing and the toxic impacts of the materials mined to build and operate, and later be discarded by, digital networks (Cubitt 2016; Hu 2015; Mosco 2017). Environmental regulation has become even more pressing as we become aware of the differential impacts of digitalization on the ecosystems of developing and developed societies (Chan, Selden, and Ngai 2020).

Some work on collective identities has extended to the workplace, considering the ways in which digitalization has altered business organization. Frameworks to understand accumulation and surplus capture through digitalization include "value co-creation with consumers" (Gauthier, Bastianutti, and Haggege 2018; Hasselblatt et al. 2018; Rachinger et al. 2018); transition theory (Gorissen, Vrancken, and Manshoven 2016; Parida et al. 2015); platform theory (Cenamor, Sjodin, and Parida 2017; Eloranta and Turunen 2016); and a focus on entrepreneurs and entrepreneurship (Ehret and Wirtz 2017; Krotov 2017).

These analyses of production extend also to questions of work and the working class (Huws 2014). Many note that digitalization makes possible new business models and industries, such as through crowdsourcing (Bennett, Chin, and Jones 2015), the "gig" economy (Daley 2015), and commodifying daily activities mediated through data (Wu 2017), as well as fragmenting workplaces to be more dispersed and networked (Graham and Dutton 2014). The very separation between work and nonwork has blurred (Alter 2017; Schwab 2016), and there is increasing awareness and worry about the loss of jobs from labor-saving technology (Acemoglu and Restrepo 2019; Benavov 2019; Ford 2015; Tapscott and Tapscott 2018).

Macro-social analysis of digitalization has considered the institutional architecture in which digital innovations occur (Holmes et al. 2016), as well the timing of economic cycles and technological innovation (Mansfield 1983). Others note the particular ways in which producers in developing countries fit within global value chains (Luo, Sun, and Wang 2011; Buckley and Strange 2015), as well as the difficulty of catching up to the "world technology frontier" (Caselli and Coleman 2000). Some have identified opportunities for leapfrogging, using information and communication technology for development (Heeks 2017; Walsham 2017), while others emphasize global digital divides of various dimensions (Ragnedda 2017;

Van Dijk 2005), requiring policies for digital inclusion (Goraya, Light, and Yates 2012; Yates, Kirby, and Lockley 2015).

This book builds on these prior contributions by focusing on the form taken by the output of infinite digital relationships—data (Fuchs and Mosco 2016). As a commodity, data presents boundless potential, in part because it is nonrivalrous (it does not deplete as it is used), but it can be privatized (UNCTAD 2019). In this condition, the potential to generate surplus is practically boundless, giving great advantage to firms that can ring-fence the generation, storage, analysis, and commodification of data. This advantage is of central concern in the current volume for the power it gives capital over labor and the control it gives monopoly firms backed by great powers over developing countries. In the face of digitalization, the current volume asks two basic questions: (1) How can working classes and popular sectors claim a share of the immense surplus created by digitalization and a degree of dignity and control over their lives? (2) How can developing countries access the power and wealth generated by advanced technologies without deepening their dependence on monopolistic firms based largely in the Global North?

Popular Sovereignty in a Digital Age

For lower classes to participate in the terms of the digital age, setting limits on exploitation and securing a livable future for them and the planet, they must organize and struggle. Yet digital capitalism changes who is a worker and what is their relation to the production process, even as alienation continues, in the Marxian sense of being alienated from the product of their labor (Lohman 2021).

One view of the digital age lower class comes from Michael Hardt and Antonio Negri—a "multitude"—a relatively undifferentiated mass in terms of their relation to capital and exploitation (Hardt and Negri 2004). Indeed, one can observe a division of the 1 percent who own platforms, capturing surplus from everyone else, evident in the incredible wealth accumulating in the hands of the very few and rising inequality across the globe. Yet these inequities do not yet organize the 99 percent as a class, nor does it identify the relationship of workers to the production process in a systematic way. Even worse, inside the 99 percent various divisions are enhanced, created, and exploited by digitalization, opening

8 | Henrique Estides Delgado and Aaron Schneider

space for antipopular and antiworker feelings and practices even among classes that do not own the means of production.

One complication of class in a digital age is the blurring of boundaries. Between the proletariat and the reserve army of unemployed labor, some have identified the precariat, who are harder to organize and in a more tenuous relation to capital (Standing 2011). Additional blurring occurs between work and nonwork, as digital platforms make use of data from leisure time in "playbor" (Kücklich 2005), "microlabor" in the form of "crowd-work" and "crowd-sourcing" (Kittur et al. 2013) breaking work into miniscule per-click tasks, and data from consumption in "prosumption" (Fuchs 2010). One of the more striking innovations of digitalization is precisely this trick, incorporating into the production process the data generated from the unpaid but productive "free labor" of people spending time online (Terranova 2000). In the process of consuming, traveling, using social media, registering for government programs, learning, staying healthy, and simply living, people perform "biolabor" that generates data, and opportunities for profit, for capital to accumulate surplus (Morini and Fumagilli 2010).

Ursula Huws (2014, 154) understands this category of "free labor" in the context of a categorization according to two dimensions, productive/reproductive and paid/unpaid labor. Free labor includes other kinds of unpaid and productive work, sometimes called "co-creation," in which users insert their own data into algorithms for what might have otherwise been work done by a paid service worker—for example, a travel agent or taxi dispatch (Prahalad and Ramaswamy 2000).

Still, work in a digital age poses the labor-capital antagonism just as starkly as ever, as long as we know where to look. Work that is paid and directly productive for individual firms in commodity production was assumed by Karl Marx and others to be the dominant and inevitable form of labor under capitalism (Huws 2014, 154). Many workers remain in this relation to capital, but the characteristic smokescreen of the digital age is to make such work invisible—extracting minerals from distant sources, assembling devices in dispersed factories, providing back-office and customer services in offshore call centers, using armies of workers to turn online content into data on a per click basis, hiding warehouses in rural areas, and delivering products with gig-worker contractors covering the last mile. Often the workers who fulfil these roles are women, people of color, and in developing countries, making it that much easier to invisibilize their work (Di'Ignazio and Klein 2020). To make it visible once again will require particular attention to the workers of the Global South as well as the traditionally excluded groups of the Global North.

Other workers are paid and perform tasks essential to the reproduction of labor. They make possible the survival of workers, and therefore capitalism, even if they are not directly in the act of producing commodities. State workers, teachers, and providers of social programs continue their reproductive labor, and the most significant impact of digitalization is to subcontract much of this work, as private providers of data analysis insert themselves in reproductive work in part to capture the data of beneficiaries and in part because they can use digitalization to target benefits, making a more efficient, leaner, but often meaner, welfare state (Alston 2019).

Neoliberal cutbacks also shift paid reproductive work into unpaid reproductive work, forcing families and communities to undertake the work necessary to reproduce themselves. Feminist economics has long emphasized the oft ignored unpaid reproductive labor of household maintenance, childcare, and many other activities essential to worker subsistence but often relegated to excluded groups, especially women, and kept out of the market (Federici 1975; Davis 1983). Digitalization, coming as it does in the aftermath of neoliberalism, shifts many of these activities back into the market, creating a "sharing economy" for what might have previously been the affective work of driving a friend to the airport (Uber.com), offering a couch to sleep on (Airbnb.com), or courting and dating (Match.com). In the process, we once again see the increasing antagonism of capital and labor.

While the status of work under digitalization might seem blurrier, it continues to depend on social relations of coerced laborers under the control of capitalists and dependent on a wage for subsistence. This places labor in direct antagonism to capital, and it is precisely at those points in the production and distribution process where labor and capital dispute over the distribution of the surplus where labor can remove its consent and engage in struggle. Most people occupy several of these paid and unpaid, productive and reproductive forms of labor during the course of their lives, sometimes in a single day. All people live with or depend on others in each of the categories. It is by building understanding of these categories and solidarities across them that a working class in a digital age can take shape.

Global South in a Digital Age

In addition to organizing from below, popular sovereignty in a digital age will also require agency from the Global South. The Global South can be defined not solely in geographic terms, and begins with the bloc

10 | Henrique Estides Delgado and Aaron Schneider

of previously colonized, poorer, and mostly nonwhite countries of the world (Prashad 2008). They are often relegated to the most exploitative and environmentally destructive activities within globalized production, and they have been too frequently subject to intervention and imposition by stronger powers.

Further, attention to the Global South also includes the economically marginalized, especially highlighting the work of groups traditionally overlooked—the too-invisible work of women; the toil of peasants, farmworkers, and small farmers; and the hyperexploitation of those such as mineworkers, factory assemblers, app drivers, and informal sector hawkers whose precarity keeps goods and services cheap. Many of these groups are found in what is geographically the Global South, but even in what are understood to be northern, developed countries, large numbers of people find themselves economically marginalized. Yet, even in the Global North, the economically marginalized disproportionately overrepresent immigrants and those who have descended from populations drawn from the Global South, including those who were forcibly moved during the long period of slavery operating in the Americas.

Finally, any discussion of overlooked populations must also address populations minoritized on the basis of race, gender, religion, ethnicity, sexuality, immigration status, caste, and class. Their exclusion narrows citizenship, circumscribes rights, and chips away at democracy. The boundaries of those who are excluded vary by context and can change over time, often on the basis of socially constructed understandings of ascriptive difference (Ignatiev 1995). As in the case of economic marginalization, markers and attachments to the Global South, including immigration and forced migration, bear legacies of exclusion in the contemporary Global North.

These patterns of difference are central to the chapters that follow not only because of the stark inequalities they capture but also because digitalization threatens to exacerbate exclusions and divisions between Global North and Global South. In particular, because most new technologies are developed in the Global North and treat the Global South as a market, reserve of cheap labor, and source of raw data, the distribution of benefits and control of future trajectories is lopsided. While new technologies lower transaction costs and open new avenues of communication and exchange, they also close spaces by raising entry barriers and blocking innovation or competition. Digital technologies can increase the opportunities and the intensity of effective participation in the democratic sphere, but some states and corporations choose instead to use digital technology to defend authoritarian arrangements. For states in the Global North, digitalization offers the opportunity to fine-tune public policy, protect their populations, and project authority beyond their borders. Developing country states, as recipients of new technologies with little capacity to generate their own, are more likely to experience technologies as predation, surveillance, and penetration into their sovereign territory.

Digital capitalism asymmetrically concentrates power in the hands of a few firms and a few states, mostly in the Global North. While digitalization can enhance popular sovereignty, it requires transforming traditional notions of sovereignty to empower workers and improve the human condition, especially in the Global South.

Central Argument

Among the central arguments of this book is that an alternative future is more likely to the degree that popular sectors in general, and from the Global South in particular, are more organized, enjoy greater formal mechanisms of incorporation into political processes, and can force a multipolar set of international relationships to govern the digital age.

Deeply democratic governance of the digital age is impossible without the leadership of popular sectors. If elite actors believe that capital accumulation can occur more efficiently, they will operate outside democratic processes, will avoid distribution to other classes, and will concentrate wealth and power in the Big Tech powerhouses of the Global North. To achieve popular sovereignty, only mobilizations of working classes, peasants, social movements, and other traditionally excluded groups can build organizational and political power. In particular, excluded groups from the Global South have a role to play, as they are most likely to be left behind and they are the most likely to defend equitable, democratic, multipolar, and sustainable outcomes.

At least in part, expressing the power of popular sectors requires a mechanism to carry them into state institutions, and Left parties have proven to be the most effective at capturing power and channeling popular interests. Where strong Left parties mobilize popular sectors and organize their interests into the national state, popular sovereignty over the digital age is more likely. Contemporary elections in a number of Latin American countries have brought Left governments to power, providing

12 | Henrique Estides Delgado and Aaron Schneider

an opportunity to establish a project for a deeply democratic, sovereign, socially inclusive, and ecologically sustainable digital age.

Yet digitalization will also require collective international action and governance, as the power of tech companies and the scope of managing data and digital technologies now lies beyond any one set of national borders. While great powers appear willing to preserve a liberalized regime in which their companies dominate, even over the interests of wealthy country governments, collective governance among multiple poles of the international order, especially those led by lower-class, Left projects, will allow for greater popular sovereignty. To advance a (1) popular and (2) sovereign project in a digital age, critical issues of class and developing country sovereignty must be reconsidered.

Structure of the Book

This book makes the argument that entering a new phase of global capitalism defined by digitalization calls once again and more than ever for a popular and sovereign alternative. Megacorporations based in the Global North have every facility to structure productive activities in their interest, capturing the lion's share of the surplus, destroying the planet, and leaving little for working classes and the Global South. To articulate a popular, sovereign project for the digital age, this introduction highlights the concepts at the heart of "popular" and "sovereignty." "Popular" implies a concept of class, the social relation of labor to capital that is being remade and intensified by digitalization but also presents opportunities for solidarity and struggle. Considerations of "sovereignty" address the position of different countries, especially the Global South, in a hierarchical global system that denies autonomy to the developing world, especially when it comes to data and digitalization.

The second section, *Future Histories*, takes its title from the provocative work of Lizzie O'Shea, author of chapter 2. She draws on historical episodes of resistance, from the Luddites to Frantz Fanon, in which the oppressed found ways to renegotiate, and occasionally seize control, of new technologies that threatened to impose a dystopian future. Rafael Ioris, in chapter 3, considers the historical tendency of those in power to seek to limit speech and distort it in their interests, drawing conclusions for contemporary threats to democracy presented by fake news, with particular attention to Brazil. In chapter 4, Ivan Da Costa Marques considers the shifting boundaries between state, market, and science, changing over time and threatening now to elevate the market above and over the state and society it represents. Together, these chapters remind us that we have seen previous moments in history in which extreme accelerations of capitalist exploitation and extraction by great powers were masked as technological progress. While the current moment appears novel, faster, and more inevitable than ever, we can learn from prior episodes of resistance to build alternatives.

While history offers inspiration to contemporary resistance, we have not yet answered the question of what collectivities can form and advance popular interests over those of capital and great powers. The next section, *Tech, Capital, and Collectivities*, addresses some of the ways in which new collectivities are called into being, shaped, and in turn exert agency in their struggles over the terms of the digital age. Claudia Rebechi and her colleagues (chapter 5) evaluate platform work in Brazil and Latin America, creating a comparable scale by which rates of exploitation and potential avenues for organizing might be mobilized. Tássio Acosta, P. Locatelli, and Silvio Gallo (chapter 6) outline the threat to democratic politics, drawing especially on the example of Brazil, where fake news has operated consistently and effectively to undermine the Left, attack vulnerable groups, and nudge democratic institutions toward autocratic and neoliberal outcomes. Neda Atanasoski (chapter 7) offers an analysis of racial technocapitalism, documenting a conversation with leading observers of working class exploitation and class formation in platform work, focusing especially on the gendered and racialized character of allocating good and bad jobs within digitalization. Andre Leirner (chapter 8) considers the tools available to create new collectivities through coding, algorithms, and practices of data equity when incorporated into public decision-making, drawing on an example of environmental disaster and reconstruction in Brazil. Benjamin Goldfrank and Yanina Welp (chapter 9) evaluate efforts to deepen democracy using tools of participation and digitalization, reaching somewhat ambivalent conclusions about the future of participatory and inclusive democracy. Benjamin Selwyn (chapter 10) focuses attention on the system of food production and distribution to identify the ways digitalization might combine with altered social relations to create a decommodified and democratic food system, focusing especially on the United Kingdom and drawing examples from Brazil. The chapters both deepen our understanding of the nuanced and contextually specific way in which class is experienced as a result of digitalization and offer insights into the ways in which new working class identities and formations might come into being. Part of class formation is the shared experience and analysis that working classes and popular sectors experience as a result of the digitalization of work, consumption, public services, and life. And part of class formation are the institutions and organizations that bring people together and intermediate their consciousness within productive, social, and political relations.

In the final section, *Digital States, Democracy, and Development,* we consider the ways in which states and international systems shift as a result of digitalization, with implications for democracy and development. William I. Robinson (chapter 11) outlines the threat posed by capital concentrated in a few huge corporations, intertwined especially with the coercive arms of the most powerful states with reverberations across the globe, a trend only accelerated by the pandemic. Vashishtha Doshi (chapter 12) evaluates digital statecraft undertaken by two middle powers, India and Brazil, attempting with limited success to carve out room for themselves, their entrepreneurial classes, and popular sectors, in a digital order. Parminder Jeet Singh (chapter 13) considers digital industrial policies by which countries, especially developing countries, might secure benefits from the global wealth created by digitalization while also ensuring that digitalization does not facilitate authoritarianism, environmental destruction, and inequality. Alessandro Teixeira and Zhenyu Jiang (chapter 14) consider the ways China has incorporated digital technology into its development and governance tools, using close state involvement to catapult itself to the technology frontier. Marco Cepik and Pedro Txai Leal Brancher (chapter 15) turn to questions of the global digital regime, including advocacy of a multisectoral and multilateral governance of digital transformation. States are not without resources and strategies to tame digitalization. Still, the challenges to states, especially states in the Global South, are profound, and this section reminds us that action will have to be both national and global to counter the power of finance and technology from the Global North.

Before closing, it is worth reflecting on the chapters chosen for this volume. The majority come from contributors to the course "Popular Sovereignty in a Digital Age," run by the Instituto Lula in 2022. The contributors to the course were chosen from a broad range of international and social categories, including three people who present as people of color, two women, two people from India, four from Brazil, one from China, three from the United States, one from Europe, and one from Australia. For the volume, we invited additional chapters, including four chapters from students in the course. Three of the chapters include previously published material, reproduced here to bring to a new audience. By organizing the course and this volume in this way, we pursue the explicit objective of bringing popular and southern voices into the discussion of the digital age.

Notes

1. https://korbel.du.edu/news-events/all-articles/professor-aaron-schneider-receives-prestigious-appointment.

2. https://institutolula.org/instituto-lula-abre-inscricao-para-curso-sobre-soberania-popular-na-era-digital.

3. Obama called Lula the "most popular politician on Earth" (Nugent 2022).

4. There are exceptions, of course (UNCTAD, various years; Ragnedda and Gladkova 2020; Fuchs and Mosco 2016).

5. https://sourcetech411.com/engineering-laws-moores-rocks-butters-and-others/.

Future Histories

2

A Usable Past for a Democratic Future

How Looking Backward Can Help Us
Navigate the Digital Revolution

LIZZIE O'SHEA

Digital technology is in our homes, in our pockets, and under our skin. It has invaded our physical and psychological spaces, often without our consent, sometimes without our knowledge. The internet feels like a place in which we are groomed for endless consumption, we are incentivized to spend time on devices, where the parameters of public debate are set by unaccountable social media platforms. It is a place where governments spend time surveilling us, and working out ways to discipline us, where warfare is optimized and human life is cheap: digital technology is optimized for the production of billionaires, while relegating billions to insecure and underpaid work.

But the internet is also a place of community and unexpected connection. It facilitates political organizing across borders and social divides, it has served as an accountability machine, and a recorder of atrocities that would otherwise remain hidden. It's a place of beauty and fun, hope and distraction.

The digital revolution has left many of us horrified, amazed, and confounded, all at the same time. It is clear that the networked computer is the greatest innovation of the twentieth century. But we are also right to feel uncomfortable about how the digital revolution is unfolding.

Too often when we talk about technology, it is presented without context. Discussions about networks, big data, and cyber security become abstracted from everyday reality. Digital systems of engagement and social organizing are imposed upon us. Technology is treated as a natural phenomenon or a force of nature, like the weather. It's almost as though the development of technology is inevitable and unstoppable. So many of our current debates about technology are premised on treating society as an object, which digital technology does things to, rather than a community of people with agency and a collective desire to shape the future.

The public debate about such controversies gives the distinct impression that these issues are best addressed by engineers and computer scientists—that is, by people with the right technical training above all else.

But the history of technology, as the great historian Melvin Kranzberg likes to remind us, is a human history (Kranzberg 1986, 557). Technology is not just a field for programmers and developers; it's actually about systems created by humans with their own particular baggage. That requires different experience and skills if we are to make sense of technology, and make it better. The economist, historian, and great critic of capitalism, Karl Marx, observed: "All our invention and progress seem to result in endowing material forces with intellectual life, and in stultifying human life into a material force" (Marx 1856, n.p.). Marx was writing more than 150 years ago, about the Industrial Revolution, and yet it is telling how this observation is more relevant than ever for understanding our personal and political engagement with digital technology.

Siri, Alexa, and Cortana seem to possess the intellectual capabilities of humans, cars are now clever enough to drive themselves, and our phones are so smart they must be serviced by geniuses. Such advanced technologies feel a long way from the stultifying material forces of their creation, among the forgotten people working in the rare earth mines of the Democratic Republic of Congo, the factories of Shenzen, and the Amazon fulfillment centers across the US.

Technology is not some disembodied future echo of society—a possibility incarnate that drags us inevitably onward and society bends around. It is a sum of its past influences, failures, and successes. Indeed, rather than looking forward, we need to start looking backward if we want to understand the problems and potential of the digital age. History can be an illuminating guide not because it reflects a universal, natural, or inevitable march toward progress, but it can cast light on the ideas and movements that produced our present moment. History is not a story of gradual enlightenment, or inevitable progress, but a study of the struggle between social forces for power. So if we want to remember and be inspired about how things were done differently in the past, and remind ourselves that the problems of the present, however large, are not immutable, we need to look to the history books.

We Need to Make a Usable Past for the Digital Age

A usable past for the digital age helps us to understand how the problems of the present are not unfortunate accidents or functions of chance. They find their origins in human decision-making and distributions of power that we should question. And looking backwards also helps us see that we are inheritors of traditions of resistance, of struggle, of diverse ideas and new visions. A usable past helps us to learn about futures that did not come to pass. We have a duty to not let them be lost or forgotten, to not let the victors rewrite stories in ways that flatter them.

This last point is worth underscoring: those who hold power in society—those who would rather risk being forced to change than to adapt to the needs of others—have their own interest in creating a usable past that justifies their position. A good example of this is the Silicon Valley venture capitalist Ben Horowitz and his invocation of the Haitian revolutionary Toussaint L'Ouverture (Leary 2017).

L'Ouverture is a fascinating character from history. Living in Haiti, which was presided over at the time by France, he became the leader of the only successful slave rebellion in history. He saw and studied the events of the French Revolution, and picked up directly the language of freedom, equality, and brotherhood. L'Ouverture sought to extend these principles to apply regardless of race, that is, not just to the citizens of France but also to the slaves that powered the French economy.

L'Ouverture was known for his political skills and military leadership in advancing the cause of Haitian independence and the abolition of slavery. But he couldn't have achieved what he did without a movement behind him. He led a mass struggle for dignity over the commodification of the human soul that underpinned the Atlantic slave trade. The Haitian Revolution stood in opposition to the avaricious and rapacious tendencies of capitalism. It serves as an emblem of inspiration for those struggling against racial and economic injustice.

But meanwhile Horowitz, a Silicon Valley venture capitalist, has tried to label himself and his fellow tech entrepreneurs as the true inheritors of this radical history. In various presentations, writings, and speeches,

Horowitz attempts to put Mark Zuckerberg, Jeff Bezos, Elon Musk, and other CEOs of tech start-ups in the same category as L'Ouverture.

Horowitz argues that CEOs and entrepreneurs change the culture of the world, just as L'Ouverture did in Haiti. It's a neat little rhetorical flourish, but it does not survive much reflective thinking. The Silicon Valley elite are actually the people who preside over inhumane working conditions, whether it is factories or gig work economies. They have proven adept at making money from technologies of exploitation rather than empowerment. They have served the needs of elite communities via extraction of value from the least empowered sections of society, and are presiding over a yawning gap between rich and poor. It's possible to cast avaricious tech entrepreneurs as revolutionary, but not in any way that a person such as L'Ouverture would endorse or admire. To make such a comparison reflects an ideological crusade for legitimacy rather than a meaningful engagement with history.

So if we do not talk about history when we try to understand the digital revolution, those in power will write versions of it themselves, and inevitably that will be a self-aggrandizing story of individual genius setting the course of history, rather than more collective and transformative visions of freedom and equality.

In the next few pages, I want to show how a usable past can be a helpful way of understanding the digital revolution. The idea is to shine a light on moments from the past that help us understand the present, and in doing so, build a movement of thinkers, tinkerers, and activists who can make technology more democratic. This is necessarily interdisciplinary work, and the contributions of different fields help strengthen our analysis. From there we can talk about the many ways in which digital technology will either play a role in delivering a more sustainable world or stand in the way—that is, how we can reclaim our present as a cause of a different future.

When We Talk about Technology, What Do We Mean?

Ursula Le Guin was a science fiction writer who was sometimes not really thought of as being from that genre, because her stories don't always include fancy machines or devices. One of the points she made in response to these observations is that too often when we talk about technology, we imagine high-tech devices. We imagine the famous quote from Arthur C.

A Usable Past for a Democratic Future | 23

Clarke that "any sufficiently advanced technology is indistinguishable from magic." We think of spaceships, robots, and handheld devices that can talk to us, that know us better than we know ourselves. Or perhaps we think of smart bombs and surveillance drones. As Le Guin put it, human society has been explained as "originating from and elaborating upon the use of long, hard objects for sticking, bashing, and killing" (LeGuin 1986, 3).

But there is another way to look at this, she argues, which is instead to see "technology is the active human interface with the material world." Technology is how a society copes with physical reality: how people get and keep and cook food, how they clothe themselves, what their power sources are, how they build their shelter, how they find their medicine. So, on that logic, the pinnacle of humanity technological achievement is not the Blue Origin rocket sent into space with billionaire space tourists on board. Instead, it would be the carrier bag that allowed people to gather berries, nuts, and roots, which, for thousands of years, provided 85 percent of people's diets.

If we think about technology in that way, the frame of what constitutes the history of technology becomes much wider and more constructive. It measures technological advancement not in terms of our capacity as humans to dominate physical spaces militarily and culturally, but more about our capacity to support life in sustainable ways.

Australia, for example, is a land that was colonized 250 years ago, but prior to that time, sustained human life for over 60,000 years. The Aboriginal people of Australia are the oldest continuously surviving culture in the world. To be able to cope for millennia in such a hostile environment—where burning heat meets flooding rains—is a testament to the technological capacity of that culture, in Le Guin's sense of the term. Aboriginal people found a way to interface with the material world that allowed them to survive.

Too often, the story of colonization is one in which sophisticated societies encounter primitive ones. But there is much more to the story. The Brewarrina fish traps in New South Wales, Australia, are potentially the oldest human construction in the world, predating the Egyptian pyramids by possibly 36,000 years. A book called *Dark Emu* by Bruce Pascoe gathers together accounts of early settlers in Australia. One such account by a settler called Kirby is about the settler's observation of an Aboriginal man sitting by one of these weirs or fish traps. Kirby wrote an account of how the fish trap worked by the man setting a line to catch fish who were forced through a channel. Once caught, the man would reset the line.

24 | Lizzie O'Shea

Kirby the settler provides an interesting account of this activity. He describes the operation in great detail and appears to approve of its efficiency. But he concludes: "I have often heard of the indolence of the blacks and soon came to the conclusion after watching a blackfellow catch fish in such a lazy way, that what I had heard was perfectly true" (Pascoe 2018). What Kirby perceived as lazy might be considered, through a different lens, as an ingenious use of technology.

In other words, how we understand technology, whether it even is technology, is socially determined. We have a lot to learn by widening our frame, by expanding our idea of what constitutes the very human history of technology. One man's account of racialized laziness could in fact be evidence of technology of sustainability, survival, and sophistication. One man's idea of what constitutes technological sophistication may be more about his ego than a desire to direct our intellectual capabilities to the pursuit of nourishment and care.

Equally, therefore, high-tech devices that we instinctively understand as technological—like Amazon Astro, or Google Nest, or Facebooks' Oculus headset—what kind of work do these devices do? We are encouraged endlessly to bring these devices into our homes and come to rely on them for a sense of safety and convenience. But what kind of power relations and social structure are obscured when we perceive these devices as magical or divine? If such technology is treated as inherently good and useful, who stands to benefit?

Privacy Fatalism and Its Discontents

The distribution of power in society is paramount to understanding what we classify as technology and how it gets developed and used. But our language and concepts for challenging the exercise of power in the digital revolution often feel weak and inadequate. Too often, debates about power and technology are channeled through a narrow conception of privacy that can leave us feeling disenfranchised and despairing.

Privacy as a human right is conceived of as an individual behind closed doors, sealed off from view. Privacy is defined as being about consent, about a contractual negotiation of data and access in exchange for a service. We are repeatedly told that privacy is dead, or it should be dead, and we should be happy about that because it means our governments can keep us safe, or it's our own fault because we killed it by giving our information away

A Usable Past for a Democratic Future | 25

to companies in an undignified pursuit of convenience and dopamine. If we are dissatisfied with how the digital revolution is unfolding, discussions about privacy suggest it is our fault as individuals for giving in to temptation and excess, rather than any kind of systemic problem.

The reality is that companies that dominate the web have set it up as an apparatus of observational intelligence, which assesses our value through the lens of consumerism. This is what Shoshana Zuboff calls "surveillance capitalism" (Zuboff 2015, 2018).

The customers of these companies are not users like you and me, but advertisers and businesses that want to get access to users. We all know what it's like to be chased around the web by an ad for shoes we might have absent-mindedly clicked on. But these processes are not simply harmless or just mildly irritating, they are exploitative and insidious. Numerous scholars have now mapped how predatory industries, like pay-day lenders, gambling companies, and for-profit private education providers, engage in programs of extensive manipulation of web users—using algorithms to seek out those who are vulnerable and exploit that vulnerability for profit.

The problem is not just predatory companies behaving badly, it is the entire political economy for data that is created by our digital social spaces being commercialized. The more finely grained the data that companies can collect about users, the greater the capacity of these companies to segment audiences for advertising. So we know, for example, that Facebook has allowed digital redlining, by allowing advertisers to exclude people from particular ads based on race. Or Google has allowed automated ad categories that can permit companies to target those with affinities to hate speech.

These problems are symptomatic of a particular logic that infuses our online lives: users are treated as a raw material to be mined for information. The greater the engagement with these platforms, the greater their capacity to collect personal information, improving the product that they sell to advertisers—namely, eyeball time. Effective advertising, according to giant tech companies, comes from the capacity to microtarget the subject, and then engage them, both of which require endless acquisition of data. Facebook whistleblower Frances Haugan told us what many already knew: that when we allow our social spaces to be saturated with the logic of the market, we entrench discrimination and harm into the experience of online life, and undermine the foundations of a democratic society.

The concept that we somehow can consent or not consent to this fundamentally misunderstands our digital present. Companies can make inferences about the data they have not collected from data they have. If a company has sufficient intelligence about a certain class of people, it can draw conclusions about those who fit that demographic on the basis that they are part of a look-alike audience, even if that individual never shared a thing. Put differently, it is not possible to opt out of this; we all end up bound by decisions made by others to consent to invasive data collection practices.

It's not just advertisers that are interested in collecting and analyzing big data, it's also governments. The notorious Palantir, the data-mining company started by Peter Thiel, has been used in predictive policing operations for authorities in the United States and cost-reduction strategies for local councils in the UK. Palantir's products generate analytics from disparate data sets—including social media and government sources. Amazon and Microsoft are working variously with prisons, US Immigration and Customs Enforcement, and a Chinese-military-run university on facial recognition software. Other popular platforms sell information to governments directly—think of Uber selling routing and logistical data, or Toronto outsourcing its city planning to Google.

The business of surveillance capitalism is now about more than just selling advertising: it's about finding new markets for data and for products trained on that data. Increasingly, purchasers in this marketplace will include governments, who are developing their own methods for using these capacities in ways that are unaccountable.

As a result, the drive to collect and analyze data has also influenced the delivery of public services. In her book *Automating Inequality,* Virginia Eubanks argues that current models of data collection and algorithmic decision-making create what she calls a "digital poorhouse" that serves to control collective resources, police our social behavior, and criminalize noncompliance (Eubanks 2019). Governments make use of data mined from people—including data collected from social media—feeding into poor quality algorithms to make decisions about services like child-welfare monitoring and custody, the provision of food stamps, and Medicare. The result is a massive expenditure of public resources in ways that do not alleviate poverty, and instead cause cycles of human misery.

There is a huge investment by bureaucracies and the industry in these processes being neutral, scientific, and reliable—that computers make better decisions than humans about how to allocate public resources efficiently. But the reality is that rather than ameliorating inequality, these algorithms entrench and exacerbate class divides. They aim not to eradicate poverty but to manage the poor, confining them to a cycle of stigmatization and entrenched disadvantage.

This is a global phenomenon. It was explored in a report by the United Nations special rapporteur on extreme poverty, which highlighted how technology is being used by governments in various oppressive ways in the digitization of welfare services all over the world (UN 2019). In Canada, the government has automated processes associated with immigration and refugee systems. One-third of councils in the UK use algorithmic technology to help determine benefit claims, identify fraud, and manage social services. Governments in India, Kenya, and South Africa have set up national identity and welfare schemes that incorporate biometric data like fingerprints and retina scanning that are used to make decisions about all sorts of aspects of the lives of citizens.

Far from being neutral or scientific, the special rapporteur describes these transformations as "revolutionary [and] politically-driven" in which "citizens become ever more visible to their governments, but not the other way around."

So when we are told to assume the right to privacy is simply about the right to consent, it obscures a much more profound phenomenon. The right to privacy is the right to exist in a world in which data generated about you cannot be used as an indelible record of your identity. Privacy is not just a technical approach to information management delegated to individual responsibility. It is about the capacity to determine our own sense of self as part of a collective.

The context of the digital revolution encourages us to think about the right to privacy more broadly. This is not some novel reinterpretation of the idea, in fact it is possible to argue that the field of human rights lends itself to this kind of reinterpretation. The right to privacy was part of the Universal Declaration of Human Rights developed in the wake of the Second World War. Like all human rights, it was influenced and updated by the postcolonial struggles that came about in the second half of the twentieth century. These movements serve as a source of inspiration to reinterpret and update human rights, providing privacy a whole new valence.

One of the key thinkers from the postcolonial period was Frantz Fanon. He was a psychiatrist, political philosopher, and revolutionary born in the French colony of Martinique, and he is most closely associated with his support for the Algerian war of independence. Fanon wrote about how, growing up in a colonial society, his identity as a black man was curated

28 | Lizzie O'Shea

by the colonial system, and this process served those in power. His sense of self was defined by white supremacy.

For Fanon, his identity was not afforded the dignity of uniqueness or autonomy; the system of white supremacy had "woven me out of a thousand details, anecdotes, stories." There was no agency in how his identity was determined, no way to escape the judgments about him, no glimmer of autonomy. His identity was "fixed": "I am overdetermined from the exterior. I am not the slave of the 'idea' that others have of me but of my appearance" (Fanon 2009, 260). This is the theoretical basis of colonialism, and it is how the idea of race is socially constructed.

These ideas also apply to the experience of living in the digital age. How we appear online is being generated and fixed by data extractive industries. It is shunting us into filter bubbles and being used by the government to make decisions about us. Surveillance capitalism seeks to define our sense of self in ways that remind us of Fanon's account of being forced into a colonialist category. This centuries-old practice of oppression is being imported into the digital age via the political economy of big data.

Now, on one level, the surveillance capitalism of social media is not comparable to colonial oppression. But data, collected from social media, but also from all companies that have adopted data extractive business models, will only increasingly influence government policy that has real and lasting impacts on people's lives, including policing, incarceration, and social service delivery. The most vulnerable people in society are having their autonomy stripped away as their lives and identities are increasingly determined and processed by machines fed on data.

A more expansive way to think about privacy, then, is to see it as a right to digital self-determination. It is about self-governance, the right to determine our own destiny and be free to write a history of our own sense of self. Postcolonial scholars, and especially writers like Fanon, have a lot to teach us about how stereotypes and oppressive social practices uphold systems of injustice. Self-determination has a long history in legal and philosophical thinking, but it gained new meaning in the latter half of the twentieth century during the explosion of postcolonial struggles, including in the struggle for Algerian independence that Fanon was involved in. There are good reasons to see the struggle for digital self-determination as a successor of these movements.

In Algeria, Fanon witnessed firsthand how oppressed people took back technology from the control of colonizers and repurposed it to speak the first words of a new nation. Fanon wrote about how prior to the war of independence, radio had "an extremely important negative valence" for Algerians, who understood it to be "a material representation of the colonial configuration" (Fanon 1965, 73). But after the revolution broke out, Algerians began to make their own news, and radio was a critically important way of distributing it cheaply to a population with minimal literacy. Radio represented access not just to news but also "to the only means of entering into communication with the Revolution, of living with it." Radio transformed from a technology of the oppressor into something that allowed Algerians to define their own sense of self, "to become a reverberating element of the vast network of meanings born of the liberating combat" (Fanon 1965, 94).

The technology of the twenty-first century gives us a similar opportunity today. Critically for Fanon, the way that this happened was through struggle. "The same time that the colonized man braces himself to reject oppression, a radical transformation takes place within him which makes any attempt to maintain the colonial system impossible and shocking" (Fanon 1965, 95). Through struggle, we may also be able to reclaim the power and potential of digital technology.

We Should Be Luddites

In truth, technological advances are rarely, if ever, greeted with universal acclaim. Rather, there are histories of struggle, resistance, and criticism that routinely accompany such developments. But such opposition is usually cast as reactionary, rather than afforded any careful consideration. This is no accident.

The Luddites are a perfect example. When Luddites are discussed in modern life, they are dismissed as backward and anti-innovation. Luddites in the modern sense are people who want to go off grid, who are conspiracy theorists about 5G networks, who are antithetical to progress. They are portrayed as hopelessly benighted about the potential of digital technology, such that their objections are rendered infantile and meaningless.

In fact, there is a lot to learn from Luddites.

In England in the early nineteenth century, the Industrial Revolution heralded great advances in production, allowing an economic output that would scarcely have been thought possible in the agrarian society that had prevailed a few generations earlier. These breakthroughs in technology, from the loom to the steam engine to the factory, brought about a

30 | Lizzie O'Shea

new age of humanity in which dominance over nature was within reach. Humans were learning that we could transcend our frail existence and shape the world in our image. The development of technology transformed humanity's relationship with the natural world. We created a world where we could increasingly determine our own destiny.

At least, that was true for a certain few. The experience of everyday people was very different. The workday had been transformed in a rapid and unprecedented manner. From a routine of labor that was built around natural limitations, such as seasons, weather, and daylight, the Industrial Revolution brought forth the hellish possibility of ceaseless production, of an endless workday, of a twenty-four-hour economy. Industrial machinery could run continuously, meaning that the limits of the production were defined by the physical capacity of human bodies. The time that work finished was determined by exhaustion. Work was no longer a practice of care and skill, of artisanship and community, a source of self-respect—it was sweat and blood, combined with steam and coal, that powered the Industrial Revolution.

This is not to idolize what it was to be a peasant, to look back on agrarian society with rose-tinted glasses. It is rather to point out that this change in social relationships brought about by the rapid development of technology was in equal measure exciting and horrifying. It enriched a certain few and immiserated many. As Bertell Ollman put it, "some were delighted by these developments, most were appalled, and everyone was amazed" (Ollman 2005).

Of course, this was not an age of industrial peace or political calm. As machines were built to do work traditionally done by humans, humans themselves started to feel more like machines, and this stripping of agency was met with resistance.

An anonymous letter was sent to the home secretary in 1812: "Remedy for you is Shor Destruction Without Detection," it said. "Prepaire for thy Departure and Recommend the same to thy friends" (Binfield 2004, 1). It was signed by the figurative radical leader Nedd Ludd. He was perhaps better known as the emblematic leader of the Luddites.

Of course when we talk about Luddites today, they are often only glibly referenced as being antitechnology or antiprogress. The truth is that they were directly concerned with conditions of labor rather than some mindless, reactionary desire to turn back time. Their chosen tactic was industrial sabotage, in the form of frame-breaking. The frame was the stocking frame or mechanized loom to weave fabric, which stripped

A Usable Past for a Democratic Future | 31

this work of its interest and skill, and sometimes ripped the fingers and arms off those who were forced to operate it. The apocryphal Nedd Ludd, frustrated with his monotonous work, took a hammer to the frame, and in smashing it, started a movement. From then on, any time a frame was found to be broken, it was always the work of Nedd Ludd.

The Luddites sought to redefine their relationship with technology in a way that resisted dehumanization. They objected to machinery that made poor-quality products, that put workers at risk, and denied them proper pay.

There is something very modern about the Luddites. They are almost a nineteenth century version of Anonymous with their threatening letters and sabotage tactics. They serve as a reminder of how many of our current dilemmas about technology raise themes that have consistently cropped up throughout history. The digital revolution is similarly presiding over a dehumanization of labor—just ask the gig workers who deliver your food, or those who moderate your content, who prepare your packages for delivery. Never before have working people worked so hard for such a small share of the wealth produced. We often assume technology is about accelerating innovation and progress, but in the hands of a capitalist class, it has become about accelerating exploitation.

The call to arms of the Luddites holds resonance a full two centuries later, demanding that we think carefully about the relationship between technology and labor. We need to redistribute the benefits of automation. We need to stop the digital revolution optimizing the income of billionaires.

Of course, frame breaking may not the solution here. But equally it is valid to ask the question—is technological development synonymous with progress? Technology should not be treated as inherently sacrosanct but rather as something that is politically and economically motivated, and therefore must be critically scrutinized and democratically governed (Sadowski 2021).

The Luddites were in many ways an early part of a large, connected movement around the globe for shorter working hours—and this broader movement is a tradition we ought to revive. It started as a campaign to reduce the working hours of children in England. The Cotton Mills Act passed in 1819 prohibited children under the age of nine from working in cotton mills and limited the work of people under sixteen to twelve hours a day. From here, the campaign for shorter hours for all workers gained traction globally: in 1835, there was a general strike in Philadelphia that won the ten-hour day. A little over a decade later in England, the

32 | Lizzie O'Shea

Factories Act of 1847 mandated a ten-hour day for women and children. Workers in Melbourne, where I am now, went on strike in 1854 and won an eight-hour day, and that campaign increased in popularity. Eventually, May Day marked an annual international call for the legal protection of the eight-hour day from as early as 1871.

It was one of the most successful progressive social movements in history. It was internationalist in spirit, attracting support from millions across several continents. It wasn't an idea of billionaires or clever industrialists, it was a product of people organizing together based on a fundamental conviction that work should be done in conditions of dignity.

If we were to think of ourselves as inheritors of that tradition in the context of the digital revolution, what would that look like? It would involve support for organizing workers who do essential work, like working in supermarkets, transport, and delivering goods. Such work is often classified as unskilled, but it's also clear—not least from the context of the pandemic—that this work keeps many of us alive. So when Amazon workers go on strike, as they did in Germany last year, we should show our support for them; when Uber drivers demand better conditions and pay, we should back them; when Google workers form a union (not just for coders, but open to all people working in the company), we should cheer. We need to revive the spirit of the eight-hour-day movement, for a livable wage in humane working conditions, and use that movement to pressure governments to stand up to billionaires.

Rather than tech billionaires being visionaries and innovators of the digital revolution, we should see them for what they are: masters of exploitation, who are holding us back from achieving a sustainable society through their greed and decadence.

Luddites were on the side of justice. They refused to blindly accept that technology was synonymous with progress, and instead demanded (via industrial sabotage) that technology be considered in its social and historical context. If we want technology that is democratic, that is about empowerment rather than exploitation, there is a lot to be said for adopting the traditions of the Luddites.

Making the Present the Cause of a Different Future

We have a choice—we have the chance to make the present the cause of a different future. We have an obligation to engage with this task meaningfully,

A Usable Past for a Democratic Future | 33

because future generations will bear the consequences of our decisions.

The great Italian philosopher Antonio Gramsci reminded us to exercise a "pessimism of the intellect and optimism of the will" (Haider 2020). There is no call to be mindlessly utopian about the future of technology; to take any view about it inevitably serving as a force for good would be a strategic mistake. But there are reasons to be optimistic about its potential. Technology has the capacity to contribute to solutions to climate change, ameliorate poverty and wealth inequality, and address the failings of representative democracy. But this will only be true if the conditions of its development are changed.

In times where our present moment feels particularly challenging, it's important to remind ourselves of our stories from the past, to look to those who have dared to take on similar challenges and won, who have defied expectations and call to us from the past to help us contend with the future with courage. We are the inheritors of the global eight-hour-day movement, we are the inheritors of the struggles against colonialism—all of which tilted the world toward an axis of greater equality. We can restore life and autonomy to a social world destroyed by the coercive and destructive forces of technology by being Luddites, not in the colloquial sense but in the historically accurate sense. By understanding technology in its social context, we can demand that it be put under democratic control. This century will be one of uncertainty, and instability. But we are not rudderless against such bracing weather; we can shift our sails toward a world of decency, sustainability, and human flourishing.

3

Technological Innovations and Fake News

Democratic Challenges and What Is to Be Done

RAFAEL R. IORIS

Public attention to the political use of fake news has grown significantly in recent years. Key events where widespread use of new media platforms to spread misinformation with surprisingly dramatic political outcomes include the Brexit vote of June 2016, the November 2016 presidential election that brought the political outsider Donald Trump to power in the US, and Brazil's 2018 election of former military man and extreme-Right candidate Jair Bolsonaro (Allcott and Gentzkow 2017; Karp, Nai, and Norris 2018; Lazer et al. 2018; Lewandowsky, Ullrich, and Cook 2017; Nemer 2019). To make sense of these events, it is important to examine them on a longer and broader analytical perspective. In effect, though deeply disruptive in several dimensions of life, the current so-called tech revolution and its impacts on communication, economics, and politics need to be seen as a new phase of a long historical process of subsequent cycles of expansion and repression of access to public speech.

Aimed at providing some central elements for such an understanding, this chapter critically examines the evolution of technological disruptions and their impacts on the political realm. This is certainly a protracted process that presents unique challenges, which require new publicly decided legal frameworks to assure a sustained diversity of voices in the public arena. In fact, given the scale and impact of today's events, particularly in

35

36 | Rafael R. Ioris

their ability to disrupt democratic deliberation, it is ever more essential that, once again, and perhaps even more forcefully, progressive forces reassert the value of inclusion and democracy to guarantee that the initially perceived promise of internet technologies to provide connectivity and inclusion can indeed be fulfilled. This is particularly relevant in the case of societies in the Global South, where democratic institutions tend to be less resilient to attacks, particularly those coming from digital platforms based in the North. Legal frameworks to regulate these actions are still largely in the hands of private actors who have proven to be resistant to public accountability.

The Path of Technological Revolutions and Their Political Implications

The proposition of a functioning representative democracy is grounded on the notion of an informed citizenry (Madison 1787). The emerging landscape of compartmentalized publics, receiving and sharing biased, often overtly false, information from like-minded peers, and the associated erosion of a common space for debate grounded on shared accepted knowledge profoundly challenges this very proposition. We are certainly in a very different scenario, and one not very conducive to informed and inclusive public deliberation.

This is not an entirely new phenomenon, though, as over the past 200 years, newspapers have regularly published reports, the sole purpose of which seems to be to satisfy their readers' cravings for sensation (Mosco 2005). In effect, communicative innovations have historically led to profound socioeconomic, political, cultural, and identity transformations over the course of history.

These events have to be understood in light of three analytical dimensions. The first is that there is a long tradition of technological innovations, especially in communications, that have recurrently been seen as deeply disruptive, though also potentially presenting the possibility of fulfilling utopic scenarios of human emancipation from laborious work, isolation, and so forth. These events also need to be understood in the context of a protracted trajectory of attempts to expand the so-called public sphere by previously excluded political actors, a process usually followed by repressive responses from those seeking to curb the very gains of previously excluded voices (Habermas 1989). Finally, one needs to consider the actions of both private and public actors in the trajectory of expansion and curtailment of voices in the public arena so that popular sovereignty in the digital age can be guaranteed.

As indicated, political control has been sustained by limiting access to knowledge to the very few. In ancient Greece and Rome, there was significant, though still limited, enlargement of the political sphere, yet only around 10 percent of those considered to be citizens could participate in deliberations of the affairs of the polis. Further, political debate was restricted in terms of where it was expected to take place, and beyond the Roman Senate, no engagement with the "word" was seen as politically legitimate. Much in the same way, in the European Middle Ages, disputes over the control of and the accessibility to forms of knowledge and associated power ensued, and overt conflicts unfolded during the religious wars that followed the Reformation. Protestants sought to make the Bible more accessible to church members and literacy expanded into newly reformed regions of Europe. This process proved instrumental in abetting the path of nation-building on the Continent, as vernacular languages—and their utilization in "print capitalism" (Anderson 1991)—became central elements of national identity. For its part, the French Revolution significantly deepened the national experience. These tumultuous events were to a large extent grounded on the existence of a more established printing industry, which throughout the eighteenth century helped transfer some control of the "word" from states to private economic actors. Moreover, over the long nineteenth century, mainstream newspapers provided an elitist and effective control over who could provide the official narrative of events to the point that there was a clear contrast between the spoken language of the streets and the official written word of books and newspapers.

The expansion of commercial radio early in the twentieth century represented an additional change in this process, which was significantly accelerated over the course of the following decades when television became the most influential new means of communication. New mass media technologies have always presented novel opportunities for those in positions of power to influence citizens. Adolf Hitler used the intimate, one-way communication of the radio to rally German citizens behind his nationalistic agenda, and Franklin D. Roosevelt hosted radio-based fireside chats to convince Depression-weary American citizens to support New Deal reforms. Radio and TV also provided a new avenue for advertisers, who leveraged the new technology to reach massive audiences, helping to increase the role of consumerism in American culture. Similarly, these

38 | Rafael R. Ioris

new media introduced new possibilities for *persuasion* capitalized upon by politicians. Especially with the advent of cable news, news audiences began splitting into ever more entrenched ideological camps, which equally presented new opportunities for political manipulation. Moreover, with the creation of the internet, at the turn of the century, and especially with the rise of social media platforms, media coverage started becoming ever more compartmentalized. Again, political appropriation of these technologies expanded quickly, and niche narratives offered the most lucrative business model and political targeting for an ever more fragmented public (Mason, Krutka, and Stoddard 2018).

Interestingly, the perceived rising connectivity across long distances provided by internet technologies deepened the sense that the collective human experience itself was undergoing a profound transformation. To be sure, much of the self-praising narrative of the time advanced the notion that space itself was shrinking and traditional geographic constraints were on the way out. This implied an end to the limits on public deliberation based on nation-states, whose bounded national identities were to be replaced by globally oriented ones. Moreover, ideologies themselves were no longer needed, as government management could be conducted exclusively by technocratic agents (Fukuyama 1992; Ohmae 1990; Friedman 2005). These accounts echoed previous ones about the messianic, half-liberating, half-apocalyptic elements of technological transformations, which, as before, often proved to be neither. The internet was even to have "the potential to connect people in unprecedented ways, to revitalize local communities, enrich schools, reduce environmental pollution, in short, to transform the world" (Mosco 2005, 9).

While in the late 1990s the internet still seemed to many to be a liberating democratic force largely still run by academic and research institutions, the consolidation of Big Tech demonstrates that capitalism (once again) managed to cartelize not only capital but also narratives about the world. Algorithms largely act now for the sake of economic gains, operating based on providing what one "wants" to read (Kalpokas 2019). New media technologies were seen by traditional and media corporations as venues for economic gain on an unprecedented scale, and the public sphere was once again restricted to fewer voices and ever more defined by misinformation for the sake of economic and increasingly political advantage. To counter this technocratic, elitist, and triumphalist narrative, it is therefore central that we understand the political dimension of the technological innovations. As in previous cases, the current so-called internet revolution must be reclaimed in the sense of being understood as a new instrument for political deliberation to be (re)framed along democratic lines.

Fake News and the New Challenges for Democracy

What is meant by *fake news* is similarly not new, as the ability of news to distort public opinion for political or pecuniary ends has long been understood. In fact, already during Europe's Thirty Years' War, propaganda was disseminated using mass media in the form of flyers and newspapers, and the origins of modern-day propaganda are attributed to the mobilization of the peoples of Europe in the First World War by means of newspapers, posters, advertisements, and speeches (Parsons, Drünkler, and Berger 2019). Likewise, *yellow journalism* was a term used to describe exaggerated or outright fabricated stories and—like today's fake news—was connected to profit motives by news organizations, blamed even for stoking the fervor that led to the Spanish-American War and was arguably the forerunner of what became tabloid journalism (Mason, Krutka, and Stoddard 2018).

If fake news of the political use of information is not necessarily new, what is dramatically different today in terms of the role of fake news in our daily lives is the very scale and impact these developments have managed to exert in our political arenas. Information seems ever more now targeted to very niche audiences, which tend to receive news that basically reinforces their own views, biases, and positions. And the fact that distinct groups can interact collectively at ease provides a real sense that his/her worldview is corroborated by the fact that others share these very same positions, which, in turn, provides legitimacy for what is being shared regardless of its accuracy. Moreover, the more sensationalized or even entirely fabricated "news" tends to be, the more it seems to appeal to specific social groups. What is more, with the lack of regulatory enforcement, particularly one aimed at promoting the possibility of a diversity of voices and the inclusion of various social actors, media companies operating under an overt profit motive have managed to reign almost absolutely.

This same logic led to a rapid concentration such that local news coverage faded in the face of large media conglomerates producing and disseminating prepackaged news segments designed for mass dissemination among local affiliate news stations. This made political manipulation easier as the number of voices were increasingly being reduced. The administration of President George W. Bush, for one, successfully managed to create

40 | Rafael R. Ioris

a broad national consensus for its shameful incursion in Iraq largely by repeating the same version of its prowar narrative, which reverberated ad nauseam throughout all national networks. Such stories were designed to appear as *objective* news coverage and were shown on local news stations as regular segments with the aim of bolstering specific policy positions (Barstow and Stein 2005). Likewise, the administration of President Donald Trump produced short videos, where he describes a current initiative, meeting, or policy, that are made to look like he is being interviewed while the entire narrative was controlled by his media people, everything done explicitly with the goal of promoting his agenda. New media technologies thus both increase the volume of news while allowing niche marketing on an unprecedented scale, often presenting ideologically bifurcated readers and viewers with entirely different universes of discourse, further fueling political polarization (Shearer and Gottfried 2017).

Fake news sharply complicates this scenario and though such news doesn't always need to be entirely false, it certainly deepens the process of reverberating parallel narratives in self-contained echo chambers. Many times, the most *persuasive* fake news is based on some factual evidence, which is then manipulated to present a different narrative of events; and some argue that most effective fake news is rooted in a kernel of truth, similar to the supposed formula of what was used in East Germany during the Cold War: one-quarter truth and three-quarters embellishment (Parsons, Drünkler, and Berger 2019). This being so, one of the most distinguishing features of the impact of fake news in today's politics is the fact that, in a universe of conflicting information, voters tend to cling to what they know, creating self-perpetuating informational bubbles.

In what is one of its most appealing and thus damaging influences, fake news often confirms one's preestablished views and biases, making people ever less inclined to accept, or even consider, alternative narratives. This process is largely driven by emotional factors. Consequently, important political decisions tend to be driven by impulses and superficial impressions, rather than to the rational selection based on policy evaluations or economic considerations, or both (Walker 2018; Giusti and Piras 2021). What complicates matters further is the fact that social media companies are designed to induce habit-forming use with notifications and algorithms offering decontextualized fragments of information that make knowing *of* things more important than knowing *about* them, creating an environment where conspiracy theories tend to flourish (Vaidhyanathan 2018; Uscinski 2018).

This complex new scenario, in which reality, falsehood, and power interact and mix in the world of media and social networks, has been defined as the setting for "post-truth politics," to describe a new political landscape where people are inclined to accept arguments based on their consonance with their own emotions and beliefs rather than being based on facts. Truth itself thus seems ever less essential, and attempts to correct claims are less likely to penetrate deeply into public consciousness partly because of ideological segmentation where those most in need of a corrective narrative are least likely to receive it, as well as because of the sheer amount of information available (Bufacchi 2020).

Likewise, this very atrophy of expertise corresponds to the rise of emotional politics, in which facts are allowed to be replaced by what one believes or feels to be true. For democratic politics, this is deeply problematic. The structural features that have facilitated the rise and salience of fake news—the growing reliance on social media for news and information—are a global phenomenon, even if they have not been politically weaponized in every context (Loveless 2021). Moreover, the equalization of all voices does not necessarily create an open public sphere for qualified debate. Not all ideas can have equal standing and there must be an agreed upon process for distinguishing between valid and false claims and propositions. Thus, the rise of fake news as well as the growing public recognition of the phenomenon leads to epistemic uncertainty. Citizens have a harder time discriminating between facts and fiction and are increasingly alarmed and worried about what seems to be a world they less and less can make sense of, let alone influence (Chambers 2021).

In short, if the logic at work is essentially driven by economic or mutually reinforcing political gains, or both, as currently seems to be the case, it is impossible to assume that corporate actors or specific interest groups could be the ones providing new regulatory frameworks to assure that the media platforms will operate with the general public's interest in mind (Barbosa, Martins, and Valente 2022). And if it is no longer possible to distinguish between truth and lies in public discourse, the underpinnings of democratic decision-making logic are undermined. For this reason, democratic societies need to create common media standards that make deliberate manipulation more difficult, give citizens transparency about the origins of information, and, in so doing, make democratic processes such as elections possible in the first place. In fact, a democracy can only survive in the long term if its citizenry shares a similar base of information, which they can disagree about in terms of deliberation, but, at the same time, they need to agree on the factual basis and merits of the data about which they are deliberating.

But if the problems and challenges caused by the widespread use of fake news in a digital age are universal, they certainly present unique types of trials in developing countries. Indeed, as recipients, rather than creators, of Big Tech and their influence, countries in the Global South can't respond as efficiently to attacks since they don't own or create the technologies at work, nor can they necessarily exert legal pressures over private companies or platforms based elsewhere. This problem is indeed aggravated by the lack of globally defined regulations pertaining to the limits and responsibilities of those spreading fake news, which tends to occur on platforms physically and legally based in specific countries but that nonetheless exert damaging impacts across borders. At the same time, attempts by developing countries to unilaterally impose regulatory control threatens their very access to new platforms, and the innovations they allow, as Big Tech can decide simply to exit their territory.

Fake news indeed poses particular challenges to developing countries, where democracy is already weaker and the pressure to conform to the demands of international capital is greater. And the problem of a lack of regulation is further complicated by the fact of capital concentration, which leads also to an unbalanced scenario for certain voices that are more easily disseminated, while others are constrained in their reach. In fact, especially in recent cases of key political deliberations, such as elections, key players have managed much more efficiently to promote certain narratives, often with funds originating in foreign territories.

A case in point is the election of Jair Bolsonaro in 2018 in Brazil, when a real digital militia, funded by private business groups, was put in place, largely through WhatsApp groups, to reach specific audiences with different versions and narratives of what was at stake in the election. Religious voters received messages that presented the opposing candidate as a menace to the traditional values of society, while libertarian voters received messages denouncing the (false) narrative that the opposing candidate was a threat to their freedoms.

In these *personalized* messaging tactics, Bolsonaro's digital blitzkrieg provided messages that reinforced what each voter already believed, or was inclined to believe, reinforcing their inclination to vote in a certain way. Although WhatsApp eventually made changes to the way sharing of messages could be done in Brazil (henceforth limiting the numbers of people a single message can be shared with at a time), the goal, or rather the damage in terms of preventing the possibility for the functioning of a truly democratic, fair, and sound deliberative process, had been already accomplished. Moreover, akin to Trump's use of his Twitter account (at least until January 2021), Bolsonaro maintained the contacts of his earlier recipients of messages, thus cultivating a strong base of captive followers (Nemer 2019).

Needless to say, Bolsonaro's account of what was supposedly happening in Brazil at any specific moment was almost always a distorted version of what was being broadcasted in mainstream media channels. This regular provision of purposefully alternative versions of reality continuously and consistently served to reiterate to his loyal followers the very notion that regular news can't be trusted, thus sustaining the very circular logic at work. Media platforms maintain that they have created guardrails, such as what WhatsApp did in Brazil after Bolsonaro's election, but clearly there is much more to be done. Hate-speech legislation also can play some role, as well as the very fact of not allowing some main promoters of fake news to use a specific platform. But this type of piecemeal approach can only address or rather manage to ameliorate things on a case-by-case fashion, while certainly much more seems to be urgently needed.

A Challenging New Scenario and What Is to Be Done?

Liberal democracies need to guarantee not only freedom of speech and opinion but also freedom of the press and of the media in general. That is not to say though that there should be no limits on free speech and a free press. Social media is the new main realm for the functioning of the public sphere. And if increasingly facts have become either secondary or ultimately inconsequential to what one believes—or feels—to be true, public deliberation based on debating, convincing, and compromise becomes impossible.

It does indeed seem to be the case that providing more information is no longer enough to sway one's point of view, as this becomes always mired in a process of entrenching oneself in one's previous views and understandings. In this new scenario, how do we rescue the notion of public deliberation based on commonly shared information? How can democracy be sustained and renewed considering such challenges?

To assure that these much-needed answers can be provided through democratic procedures, a task very challenging in itself, given the unbalanced nature of the multiple voices and stakeholders involved, I conclude with a few notes on possible guidelines for a democratic digital public sphere. These are meant only as initial ideas and as such, as general principles, hopefully to guide further democratic deliberation, which should, by definition, be as open and inclusive as possible.

First, a democratic framework for providing the means to address at least some of the challenges provided by the new technologies of communication needs to assure open, publicly and easily gained access to the digital world. Second, public (state) actors, chosen through democratic procedures, need to be the main regulators of the internet, social media, and so forth, according to democratic forms of deliberation (beyond self-imposed industry-based norms of conduct) to assure its access, rules of operation, and limits. Third, state actors need to become more transparent and inclusive in the implementation of these regulations to assure a democratic, open, and equitable space for all.

Of course, as is always the case, these are only general principles that, one would hope, could serve as guiding goals to be buttressed by and translated into more specific applicable regulations, procedures, and so forth. As such, they are intrinsically dependent on the political will of broad sets of democratic actors, and their associated mobilization, so that actual implementation can take place.

What is clear is that it is almost past the time for these actions to occur and though this reflection does not assure their materialization, hopefully it can provide some elements for concerned democratic social actors to be able to find ways to move forward. In fact, amid the contemporary dizziness and sense of loss in the face of rising technological connectivity that has largely been understood as inexorable, it is above all important to reclaim the notion of political agency. After all, though they appear overwhelming, the tech challenges of today can only be addressed by more, not less, democracy.

4

Computing Machinery and the Modern Triumvirate

State, Market, and Science

Ivan da Costa Marques

Technology as science interacts with state relations to society and to other states, driven in part by market demands and opportunities for accumulation. Together, the state, the market, and science make up a modern triumvirate already emblematically compared to the Holy Trinity in "About Capitalist Theology" in Eduardo Viveiros de Castro's lectures. Is computing machinery throwing this time-honored arrangement out of balance? The three parts of this chapter meet by describing the gradual supremacy of private corporations over states to access, interfere, build, destroy, or obstruct (imagined or realized) communities of things and people. Are owners of computing machinery acquiring greater skill than governments in key components of modern governance by becoming better equipped than politicians and traditionally elected political parties to sell their products, their reputations, and themselves?

This chapter is divided into three parts.[1] The first part is historical. It concerns computing machinery when there were no computers.[2] Nevertheless, by the end of the 1920s, International Business Machines (IBM), which had already established itself in Brazil with its computing machinery, was able to construct an explanatory quantified framework of

45

46 | Ivan da Costa Marques

the dynamics of Brazilian foreign debt that was beyond the capacity of the Brazilian state. The framework detailed the behavior of state and municipal governments in terms of contracting and repaying foreign loans. This explanation of the crisis was adopted by Getúlio Vargas, strengthening his political hand, and earning IBM the trust of the Brazilian government.

The second part has a more sociological bias, focusing on the emergence of a "new object," a computing innovation to identify the terrorist body after the attack on the Twin Towers of the World Trade Center in New York on September 11, 2001. The political significance of this innovation is illustrated by the resulting "digital war" between Brazil and the US over requirements for biometric identification for passenger transit. Subsequently, governments and security companies have incorporated the new object into the computing machinery in ports and airports for the identification of a (terrorist? alien? criminal? vaccinated? mestizo? minority? indigent?) body, *"online"* and *"real time,"* with impacts for the perception of global space-time.

The third part is essayistic. It concerns the contemporary computing machinery, which seems to have become decisive in the formation of options regarding the fate of states. The algorithms of large companies are capable of both classifying individuals into groups and forming these same groups, facilitating or hindering individuals from accessing information that may be of interest to them and reflexively making groups a reality. Group borders gain greater or lesser clarity as a result of the ability of the algorithms to control what passes through them, making information appear or letting information be forgotten.

Computing Machinery before Computers Existed

Computing machinery landed in Brazil and, I believe, in all of Latin America at the beginning of the twentieth century, undoubtedly brought in the backwash of our coloniality. An example of the potential of computing machinery as a corporate piece of equipment, both anticipatory and characteristic, occurred in Brazil about a century ago. The case has been magnificently researched by Colette Perold, and here I rely fundamentally on her study (Perold 2020).

It was the 1920s. There was not exactly what we understand as computers today, that is, machines that store the programs and the data they process in their own memory, or, as they disciplinarily say, "stored program machines." But there were tabulators, machines that tabulated information, that is, separated, classified, formed tables, and totaled information placed through perforations in famous payroll cards.[3] A payroll card contained 960 squares distributed in 12 lines and 80 columns, each square representing a "bit" of information ("0" or "1," perforated or unpunched square).

Tabulating machines to process the large amounts of information occurred in centralized institutions, and in the case of Brazil, these institutions were, for the most part, government agencies. Gradually, throughout the 1920s, through the always vigorous performance of the IBM representative and soon its president in Brazil, Valentim Bouças, the then still newly formed company[4] became the main supplier of the tabulating machines that did the accounting of various agencies of the Brazilian government. By the late 1920s, IBM had contracts for tabulating machines installed in agencies in all ministries, with 600 employees processing payrolls, auditing budgets, and monitoring trade.

The economic crisis that hit Brazil coincided with the *crash* on the New York Stock Exchange in 1929 and caused an open battle over how the country would reorganize itself economically. With 70 percent of exports coming from coffee, the moment gave unprecedented power to São Paulo's coffee-growing elite, but the crisis provoked conflict over excessive São Paulo control and ended with the coup that swore in Getúlio Vargas. Amid the variety of groups in Brazilian politics, in addition to the excluded (workers, peasants, indigenous people, the poor), three groups stood out in the ruling elite competing for limited government resources

Figure 4.1. Payroll card. *Source*: Wikimedia Commons. Public domain.

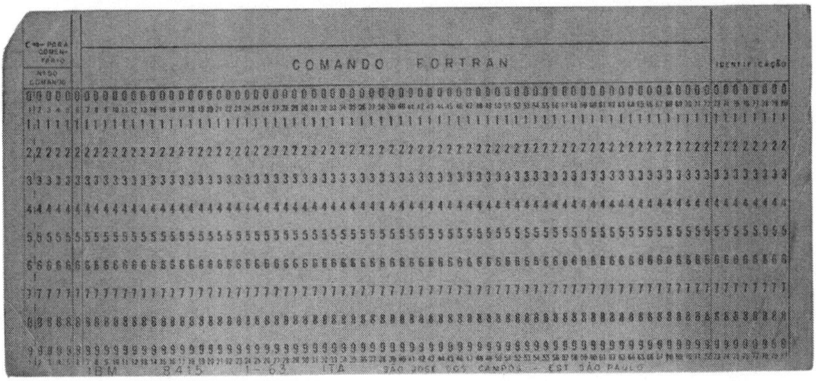

48 | Ivan da Costa Marques

in Brazil—agricultural capital (mainly coffee growers), industrial capital (mainly the textile industry), and those in favor of liberalizing policies (mainly multinational corporations).

The industrial elite wanted a restructuring that would remove the country from dependence on a single product, but this depended on subsidies and the government had committed all resources to maintaining the price of coffee. The Republican Constitution of 1891 had given significant autonomy to states, in opposition to the centralized situation during the empire, and many states had autonomously borrowed abroad. The sharp slowdown triggered a crisis in the external debt, with some states more responsible than others for the external debt.

Yet there were no mechanisms to balance these inequalities, and no measures had been taken to require state accountability. It stands out, and here is the crux of the matter that interests us, that there was no detailed material ("objective," "quantified") picture of the origins and progress of the debt crisis. Brazil had no center or government agency charged with tracking foreign loans. Precisely, there was no "data processing center" that would separate, select, classify, form tables, and totalize the information that resided in isolated government bodies that did not communicate with each other. Saddled with bad credit but unable to hold borrowers accountable, the Brazilian state was powerless in the face of the crisis.

At the same time, in December 1930, a month after Vargas took office, the Ministry of Justice began to act, cutting ties with companies that had collaborated with previous governments during the 1920s. A letter was sent to IBM determining the withdrawal of all machines installed in government agencies. As a colonial country, Brazil's development depended heavily on foreign loans; one could say that the external debt crisis stemmed from extreme regional and class inequalities. But Bouças, as president of IBM, deftly framed the issue from another angle—he defended the view that the crisis was an expression of technical weaknesses in the administration and bureaucracy of the Brazilian state. Without an information infrastructure capable of capturing and centralizing information on borrowing and repayment of loans, there was no way to analyze the crisis.

When Vargas threatened to banish the corporation from Brazil, IBM knew how to use its ability to process information to reverse the situation and consolidate its position in the country. "On January 25, 1931, Valentim Bouças published an article in *Jornal do Commércio*, from Rio de Janeiro, in which he defended the intervention of the Union in the States and Municipalities of Brazil—with the purpose of solving the problems of external public debts (DPEx) of the Union, States and Municipalities of Brazil" (Margalho 2015, 2).

By highlighting information bottlenecks, IBM translated its modern information processing methods into political power. For the first time in the history of Brazil as a republic, there was a set of tables detailing the service of external debt by state, the effects of debt repayment in each state alongside a table by item of the returns for each of the main *commodities* exported by Brazil. As Perold (2020, 43) shows, "Intentionally or not, IBM's pattern of development in the 1920s in Brazil positioned the company in 1929 to be the only agent capable of building this information infrastructure."

The tables showed, for the first time with comparable numbers, the severity of the crisis and the participation of states and municipalities in the debt. As it happens, the main "culprits" came from São Paulo, which fully served the interests of Vargas. IBM, by gathering and comparing information from the various government agencies that were its clients, was able to compose a unified panorama of the Brazilian economic situation regarding foreign trade and loans.

At the time, this quantified general view was beyond the reach of the Brazilian state. This is because—and we will save this for the rest of the chapter—it was IBM and not the Brazilian state that had the most complete set of what we would today call "databases." And it was IBM that was able to carry out what we would today call "*data mining*," making choices to gather and juxtapose some, and not other, information.

In addition to its position as a multinational corporation at the time when the strength of an exporting bloc was consolidating in the US, IBM still had a more intrinsic source of power as the holder of a certain ability to make use of the computing machinery that the Brazilian state lacked. At a time when technological developments were rapidly leading to new statistical methods, IBM could influence the directions that would eventually be taken in revising traditional administrative and bureaucratic forms sweeping much of the world and, of course, profiting from them.

A mix of business, diplomacy, and *lobbying* was the mainstay of IBM's global expansion program, and those who knew how to do it best were called "citizens of the world." Bouças was a champion in the midst of the coloniality of power in Brazil. He became indispensable to the Brazilian ambassador in Washington. He was the first to be awarded the title of "*IBM's world citizen*," dedicated to "those who know that thinking 'international' is in no way different from thinking 'only' about business or money" (Perold 2020, 39).

50 | Ivan da Costa Marques

This episode from one hundred years ago illustrates a configuration alluding to the expansion and internationalization of the computing machinery industry. This situation was prophetic because it displays the unprecedented political dominance of large corporations over states, at least over most states, including those in Latin America.

The IBM of 1930 in Brazil seems to contain the chromosomes of an adjustment between the state, the market, and technoscience, at least in the West. This adjustment is certainly provisional, that is, it serves certain demands and results from history, from the rhizome of possibilities that are configured in the constant movement of the world. These possibilities are, a priori, unpredictable, although history, as a discipline, a posteriori, can build understandings and explanations of the final course of events. It seems that, in this provisional adjustment, which may change as the clouds in the sky, the market and technoscience are finding their new positions faster than the state.

The Fingerprint War:
From Dirty Fingers to "Double-Clicking"

The construction of the modern world is associated with a parade of new objects and new subjects. Objects or "things-in-themselves"—celestial bodies, minerals, trees, CO_2, cells, biological bodies—are in a world separate from the world of "humans-among-themselves"—habits, rights, values, democracy—inhabited by subjects with identities. This is, simply put, what we learn in the modern (Western) school. Nature (things-in-themselves) is separate from society (humans-among-themselves). But a new nature, augmented by new objects, does not happen without a new society. What happens is a co-construction, a nature-society. For example, when the microbe emerged in nature, Louis Pasteur's new object acted and created a society that corresponded to it, with new identities that shuffled previously established hierarchies. "A different kind of solidarity . . . emerged when the son of a very rich man could die because the very poor servant was a carrier of the typhoid bacillus" (Latour 1989/1996). Contagious patients, healthy but dangerous people carrying microbes, immunized people, vaccinated people, and so forth, affected the hierarchies of the body as previously created by the social categories "rich" and "poor." "The enormous increase in the production and variety of goods and services [the objects of modernity]"—assert many Western historians

Computing Machinery and the Modern Triumverate | 51

in a laudatory style—"alone has changed the way of life of man [society] more than anything else since the discovery of fire" (Landes 1969, 10).

In the first decade of the twenty-first century, a new object appears in the computing machinery dedicated to the identification of human bodies, a device that we are now used to seeing at immigration counters in ports and airports around the world. Like all devices, it arises from a demand. In this case, the demand was to identify terrorist bodies after the terrorist attack of September 11, 2001. Like Pasteur's microbe, this new object displaces the nature-society frontier, shuffles hierarchies, defines new bodies and new relationships of humans-among-themselves. It co-constructs a new society that corresponds to a new nature, augmented by its existence.

What does this new device do? The new device tightly ties and joins what until recently marked the "natural" boundaries of human bodies (such as skin, facial features, fingerprints, and irises) and the "social" databases of institutions (such as name, nationality, criminal status, special rights, addresses, professions, institutional affiliations, and financial, medical, school, and police histories) to the point of composing a new entity. This junction, once disseminated throughout the world, renders obsolete the venerable human body, the ancient, fortified citadel of our identities and privacy. The new device took a further turn in the movement toward a world of, say, proper cyborgs themselves, where bodies immediately—or mediately—affect and are affected by the institutions' databases (Latour 1991; Latour 1991/1994). The data managed by police, the military, and other institutions, medical, commercial, or industrial, become an integral part of our bodies, no longer metaphorically, as we used to say, but literally.

By joining biometric data to official data on identities, criminality, access, and nationality, the new devices altered the relation between natural and social entities. More than simply accelerating the connection between these two worlds, the analysis and categorization of large amounts of biometric data fused natural and social worlds into a new entity, both natural and social, and thereby legitimated new forms of surveillance, categorization, and public treatment.

As an illustrative episode, as of January 5, 2004, the US government required photographs and fingerprints of all foreigners who required a visa to enter the United States, that is, in practice, of all foreigners except those from the twenty-seven rich countries that participate in a visa waiver agreement (*"visa waiver program"*). The Brazilian Constitution abides by the "principle of reciprocity," requiring the Brazilian government to treat foreign citizens in the same way that their respective governments treat

52 | Ivan da Costa Marques

Brazilians. Based on the constitution, following a complaint to the Brazilian federal courts regarding the new measures by the US immigration department, a federal judge, Julier Sebastião da Silva, ruled in December 2003 that, as of January 2004, photograph and fingerprints should become required of US citizens upon arrival in Brazil.

The Brazilian reaction sparked controversy. The US ambassador to Brazil, Donna Hrinak, referred to the decision as "unnecessary." Secretary of State Colin Powell complained about the slowness of the identification process. Brazilians were divided over the court decision. The mayor of Rio de Janeiro, Cesar Maia, appealed the decision, claiming that the measure would inflict huge losses on tourism in the city. The decision provoked a series of comments in the press, mainly in Brazil, but also in the US and even in other countries, with tendencies to take sides, adopting positions in favor or against the measures adopted. During January 2004, two US citizens had their visas canceled, received fines, and were sent back to the US for disrespecting the officials in charge of the identification process in Brazilian immigration. The sequence of events involved the technical, the political, the legal, the diplomatic, and the popular, and the Brazilian press referred to it as "the fingerprint war" (da Costa Marques et al. 2004; da Costa Marques 2013).

An armistice was quickly reached in the "fingerprint war," as there were general agreements previously accepted by all involved that could easily turn into specific agreements to reframe the issues and restore peace: (1) time is a precious modern commodity, therefore waiting at airports should be reduced; (2) violating the right of each state to control its borders would have an unreasonable cost in the face of the interests involved in the "fingerprint war"; (3) greater precision and effectiveness in identifying terrorist bodies was a tacitly agreed objective (da Costa Marques 2013).

The new device enacted by the North Americans fully met the demands of the situation, so much so that, after the "fingerprint war," the new device was retained. It performs certain types of interactions whose effects make possible new understandings and new ontologies for human bodies, if the notion of the body as "a provisional residence of something higher—an immortal soul, the universal or thought" is abandoned, dimming the notions until recently more stabilized in the body (Latour 2004, 206).

It is possible that we are convinced that this device, due to its effectiveness and precision, is a continuation of the ink pad and paper in a natural trajectory. But, in his provocative and detailed research, Donald MacKensie showed how, in the case of targeting nuclear missiles, increas-

Computing Machinery and the Modern Triumverate | 53

ing effectiveness and accuracy was not a natural trajectory, although it seemed to be so, but rather a "self-fulfilling prophecy." In the case of the precision of biometric identification devices, we are perhaps faced with the crucial error of the fatalism of the metaphor of the natural trajectory: "For although the obstacle to achieving greater precisions [with a given technology] cannot be overcome, it can be circumvented by adopting new forms of targeting. Those who wish to stem the increase in missile accuracy could focus their efforts on preventing these new forms from becoming a reality. But they will not do this if they believe that missile accuracies will naturally continue to increase" (MacKensie 1990, 169; and see also MacKensie and Spinardi 1996, 215–60).

With apologies for an overly schematic argument, more powerful collectives, such as Big Tech corporations and the state, have more resources to make new objects that satisfy their demands in the world. Today, that is deceptively called technoscientific progress. In the case of the "finger-print war," the rapid identification of human bodies was a priority for the powerful who aspire to build, command, and control every kind of frontier, joining the interests of the security apparatus, tech surveillance companies, and users of data, such as health insurers. Through the facial recognition device, they established a new nature-social entity in the individual as carrier of various kinds of data linked through their identifying marks, such as fingerprints and facial recognition. Once this natural-social object was stabilized in the world, the controversies and clashes that were won by the victors are erased and replaced by narratives justified by the myth of progress. The new objects appear as successors of old ones in a natural trajectory, the realization of a self-fulfilling prophecy. The technological direction from dirty fingers (an obstacle to greater precision) to double-clicking is naturalized. It's simply progress!

New Governance Directions? From State to Market?

Disputes over the direction of technoscience take place on very varied scales, can mobilize large resources, and be asymmetrical, involving groups with different powers, such as corporations, social movements, and countries. We recall above that more accurate ballistic missiles came into existence in the world from the standpoint of powerful military collectives in the US and the Soviet Union during the Cold War, collectives that were much more powerful than those that the pacifist movements could then mobilize.

54 | Ivan da Costa Marques

The forms that devices take on, be they payroll cards, ballistic missiles, human body identifiers, or algorithms that manage "social networks," result from a process in which collectives of humans and things creating different possible views of the world or, let's say, different options of devices, dispute the possibilities of what scientists and engineers can realize.

There was a phase of enchantment with the new objects brought by corporations typified by Google, Amazon, Facebook, and Apple (GAFA). These corporations were seen as fairy godmothers, bringing previously unimaginable facilities and amenities, vehicles for new ways of living everyday life. Even in Brazil, where the availability and quality of new amenities vary enormously and are not always realized so well (for whom?), they enjoyed and still enjoy great prestige. Nevertheless, as soon as it became clear that they institutionally organized themselves as private corporations and their leaders revealed their ideologies, some difficulties arose. From being admired brands, dreamed of oases for employment, they have also come to be seen as a threat to internet neutrality, people's privacy, labor and consumer rights, and the sovereignty of states. They practice tax evasion; they subject workers to inhumane conditions; they invade privacy; they sell your information; they have monopolistic practices; they influence elections; and so forth.

States can and are reacting. Working conditions imposed by tech companies can and are denounced, and from there some improvements are achieved. They will face and are facing lawsuits under antitrust laws. Of course, the sale of databases, as well as election advisory services, can be better regulated. There can be, and gradually there is, greater disclosure of intelligible explanations and increased awareness of what is progressively allowed to be done with personal data ("lawful use" may be defined in ways quite different from ethical use).

Yes, all of this is true, or at least partially true, with variations from one corporation to another due to the types of products they offer. Yet the concentration of resources controlled by these corporations only increases (Johnson 2018). Grasping the situation, however, requires one to go beyond economics framed as an academic discipline. The scale, scope, and ability to link information stored in the computing machinery databases is unprecedented. The resulting abilities to analyze/direct/induce relationships and bonds in social networks by creating groups is also unprecedented. This evidences the specific advantage that computing machinery has gradually gained for those who own it.[5]

Especially since the end of the twentieth century, the difficulties of the state in accommodating itself in the digitalized world seem to be greater than those of the market and science, which seem to already know which new positions to seek. The ideology of Thomas Watson and Valentim Bouças a hundred years ago is strictly the ideology of an entire bloc of capital that operates around the world in the name of the market: "thinking 'international' is in no way different from thinking 'only' about business or money" (Perold, 2020, 39).

The market does not act alone and is not morally against associating with the state. If the market needs help building a reliable internet, or if the state understands the value of an effective computing machinery for its own control purposes, as in the case of controlling the movement of bodies, then the state helps to develop and consolidate the computing machinery that will reside in the market, that is, that will be incorporated into the administrative structures of corporations, especially those typified by GAFA. The engineers of the corporations define and hold the knowledge of the hardware-software architectures of the computing machinery installed on the planet. Consequently, the state becomes dependent on the market to compose the frameworks in which to place its actions, past the time when the market needed the state to build the launchpad for its own computing machinery.

The hardware-software architectures of computing machinery do not only determine what can and cannot be done in terms of collecting and processing information. They also determine which behaviors can be easily monitored and policed and which behaviors require difficult and expensive research to discover and identify. Perhaps the best-known example of the difficulty of tracking is the incorporation of racist biases into Google's artificial intelligence devices, since the concern to identify and track these behaviors was not part of the architecture of the Google computing machinery that operated the product that organized photo albums (Vincent 2018; Cafezeiro et al. 2021).

The current moment has brought another important difference in relation to 1930: much of what needs to be regulated concerns cyberspace and not the space of the laws and regulations of the modern state of the twentieth century. For more than two decades, this has revealed a demand for new legal regulations: "The rise of an electronic medium that disregards geographical boundaries throws the law into disarray by creating entirely new phenomena that need to become the subject of clear legal rules but

56 | Ivan da Costa Marques

that cannot be governed, satisfactorily, by any current territorially based sovereign" (Johnson and Post 1996, as cited in Lessig 1999, 24).

When it interests them, private corporations can enter the legal system on an equal footing with states or governments, but they are not subject to the same limitations. Multinational corporations find ways to escape the constraints of being tied to single governments. The boundary between the state and large private corporations has lost its sharpness. Decisions taken in the private sphere of large corporations and their codes of ethics decisively influence political destinies. At the same time, these large corporations are becoming more skilled than governments in some of the key components of modern governance. Most of them sell their products, their reputation, the way of life they defend better than politicians or political parties. Big companies are also able to claim loyalty in a way that used to be the province of nations. Brand loyalty is not entirely new, and people can identify as "an IBM citizen." But companies are finding, through social media, new ways to deliver identity, community, and services largely unrelated to geography that make more sense for digital nomads than territorial bureaucracies.

In 2012, the acronym GAFA appeared in France to refer, usually in a critical tone, to the North American multinational corporations Google, Amazon, Facebook, and Apple, to which one could add Microsoft (Chibber 2014). Computing machinery provides these corporations with a capacity to act beyond the capacity of states, à la the capacity that the tabulators provided to IBM a century ago in Brazil. I seek to draw attention not only to what they have in common with the IBM of 1930 in Brazil but also to an additional important difference: the ability to act "back" on collectives that are arrayed in "groups" in social networks. These huge corporations extend their "technical" capacity beyond the ability of states to know the population through data mining and act further to shape the population into groups. If that is not a political action, nothing else is!

Market and science (technosciences) typified by the multinational corporations politically led by GAFA are the architects of the computing machinery. Therefore, they are the architects of cyberspace, which gives them, at least momentarily, a great advantage over the state.

Unfortunately, one can see that most activists trying to protect the diversity of ways of life against the unidimensional commodified way of life advocated by GAFA still do so cognitively imprisoned by the modern European myth of universal science and a single universal reason. The danger is increasingly clear: Left activists try to mobilize the state against the commodified one-dimensional life advocated by GAFA on the basis of abstracted crumbling pure ideas that need to be intellectually and politically readdressed. The modern triumvirate is stressed by the ideologies behind GAFA: Sergey Brin and Eric Schmidt (Google), Travis Kalanick (Uber), Peter Thiel (PayPal), and Elon Musk (Tesla/SpaceX) have "libertarian" ideological stances that resonate with Ayn Rand's "Objectivism," which directly influenced Steve Jobs, Alan Greenspan, and Donald Trump (Paraná 2020, 102–21). As Rand explained in her book *The Virtue of Selfishness*:

> The basic social principle of Objectivist ethics is that just as life is an end in itself, so every living human being is an end in itself, not a means to the ends or well-being of others—and, therefore, that man should live for his own gain, not sacrificing himself for others, nor sacrificing others for himself. . . . Objectivist ethics proudly advocates and defends rational selfishness . . . the values demanded by human life are not the values produced by desires, emotions and "aspirations." (Rand 1991, 42)

Science studies of the last decades have shown that the possible trajectories of computer machinery result from relations between collectives of people and things. Fate hesitates to eventually choose and adopt, always temporarily, paths to be followed in the development of knowledge and techniques. The choice of these paths takes place between what ends up prevailing among people's desires, emotions, aspirations, and values, and what things lend themselves to being done in interactions with scientists, engineers, and laypersons. The purpose of this chapter is not to be predictive, but perhaps just the opposite, that is, to offer a very modest warning so that what was seen here on the horizon of cyberspace does not come true as a "self-fulfilling prophecy."

Tentative Conclusions: The Chinese State

In the midst of the political project typified by GAFA, there is, outside the West, something apparently still to be deciphered, the Chinese state-market-science configuration. The BATX denomination (Baidu, Alibaba, Tencent, Xiaomi), a list that may include Huawei, has already been indicated as mirroring the Western GAFA (Chevré 2019). Despite this, dissonant

58 | Ivan da Costa Marques

Chinese corporate voices have become more audible, especially when it comes to installing 5G infrastructure, amid disputes over the construction of a planetary computing machinery.

The 5G infrastructure is not a simple generational upgrade from 4G. Not only is 5G communication faster, the latency of each transaction is much lower, which allows for online, real-time remote control of processes that require quick responses. Batteries also last much longer, and there is also a major transformation regarding the possibilities of components in computing machinery that require much longer intervals between maintenance interventions.

Furthermore, 5G infrastructure supports a dynamic decentralization of the so-called cloud. That is, transactions around a place will generate a local cloud support point. This allows for a virtually unlimited number of inexpensive sensors to be plugged into virtually everything from automobiles, bus seats, factory and office equipment, to medical and surgical devices and home appliances. Undoubtedly, the fifth generation infrastructure of cyberspace, 5G, will not only in time radically change the everyday relationship of many people with each other and with things but will also be a literally fantastic source of information about the population.

It is precisely this literally fantastic source of information about the population that has mobilized the West, led by the US, against China, currently better positioned as a supplier of 5G equipment. According to the press (for example, the BBC),

> The accusation is based on the following logic: if the whole of society is interconnected using equipment from a Chinese company—which would include transit systems, communication systems or even "smart" appliances inside our homes—we would all be vulnerable to spying by the government of China. Huawei is a private company, but a security law passed by China in 2017 theoretically allows the Beijing government to demand data from private companies if the need is classified as important for Chinese sovereignty.[6]

I don't see how Brazilians can feel more vulnerable to Chinese espionage than to that of GAFA or the US government, although coloniality in Brazil will, I believe, make them disagree with me. Especially in decisions about the implementation of 5G, computing machinery, coloniality, and lots of money are inextricably mixed in Brazil or anywhere else. To finish and complete this provocation, I reproduce a Chinese voice that questions

Computing Machinery and the Modern Triumverate | 59

the political ritual and the capacity to reform the system of government of Brazil's main metropolis, the US.

Zhang Weiwei is a former adviser to Deng Xiaopeng, the former Chinese premier. He is a professor of international relations at Fudan University, a prestigious public university in Shanghai, and a senior fellow at the Chunqiu Institute. He is the author of the influential bestseller *The China Wave: Rise of a Civilizational State*, initially published in Mandarin (Zhang 2012). Let's look at the points that Zhang calls the "genetic defects" of the Western model (of civilization):

1. The (Western) assumption that human beings are rational presumes that humans can exercise reason to make rational choices in casting their votes. So far, all relevant scientific studies have proven that humans can be both rational and irrational and even ultra-irrational. "The rise of social media has provided fertile ground for the spread of irrationality."

2. The principle that rights are absolute is also a problem, notably the inflated concept of individual rights and the decline of individual responsibilities. There are so many rights, each of which are exclusive and absolute, often leading to a conflict of rights. "The principle that rights are absolute is a problem, notably the inflated concept of individual rights and the decline of individual responsibilities."

3. Western democratic belief in procedural importance is admirable, but in practice has bogged down the government's ability to function. Worse, with attention only to procedure, it does not matter who comes into power. "Western democracy has been bogged down by procedural importance." (Zhang 2018)

In 2016, American director John Pilger interviewed Zhang for his documentary film, *The Coming War on China*: "If the BBC broadcasts something, it is happy to always mention this communist dictatorship, this autocracy. In fact, with that kind of label, you cannot understand this China as it is. If you watch the BBC or CNN or read the Economist and try to understand China, you will fail. It's impossible."[7]

He claims that no country has carried out more reforms in recent decades than China has done with one party. In the US, he provokes, there are two parties, but there are no real reforms because the economic

60 | Ivan da Costa Marques

always overlaps with the political, and this prevents reforms from the outset, which does not happen in China because the party prioritizes the political over the economic.

I tend to agree that the West still knows very little about China and Chinese ways of governance. The limits and merits of established Western rationality are increasingly problematized even in the West. Similarly, behaviors and values associated with Western individualism, for example, seem to be evaluated and lived out differently in China. Zhang suggests that China may mobilize other forces to reconfigure and shape the behavior of entities that the West calls the state, market, and science, for a dawning digital age. Such a reconfiguration might go beyond simply reordering the entities of the triumvirate; rather, China offers the possibility of alternative ways of knowing, distinct from Western philosophical and historical constructions. The West has depended on dichotomies of separate and opposing poles, such as nature and society, subject and object, mind and body, culture and science. Such dichotomies started to be more widely questioned even in the West in the last decades of the twentieth century, and China may now fuse them into new inextricable complex entities, wholly different from the Western triumvirate. But, of course, this remains to be seen.

Notes

1. I thank Marcelo Sávio, Edemilson Paraná, Gabriel Silva, and Aaron Schneider for their collaboration in the writing of this chapter. Of course, what I wrote is my sole responsibility.

2. North Americans use "computing machinery" to designate what Latin Americans call "informatics." An eloquent example is the name of the Association for Computing Machinery.

3. The use of cards to tabulate information began with Herman Hollerith in the nineteenth century, evolved into machines to tabulate pay-slip cards, and large computers (*mainframes*) continued to use punched card reader machines as the main means of data entry (*input*) into the 1970s.

4. The history of informatics is inseparable from the history of machines to support business activities, as indicated by IBM, which made its first appearance in Brazil in 1917 as the Computing Tabulating Recording Company.

5. "Trump in the Hands of Zuckerberg: Facebook Committee Maintains Veto on Trump, but Asks for Standard Punishments," *Folha de São Paulo*, May 6, 2021, A12.

6. "Huawei, Trump, Bolsonaro e China: O que o Brasil tem a ganhar e perder se ceder aos EUA no 5G?" [Huawei, Trump, Bolsonaro and China: What does Brazil have to gain and lose if it gives in to the US on 5G?], *BBC News*, October 21, 2020.

7. *The Coming War on China*, official trailer, https://www.youtube.com/watch?v=G3hbtM_NJ0s.

Tech, Capital, and Collectivities

5

Evaluating Work in the Platform Economy

The Fairwork Project in Brazil and Latin America

CLAUDIA NOCIOLINI REBECHI,
MARCOS ARAGÃO DE OLIVEIRA, TATIANA LÓPEZ AYALA,
JONAS C. L. VALENTE, RAFAEL GROHMANN, JULICE SALVAGNI,
ROSELI APARECIDA FIGARO PAULINO, RODRIGO CARELLI,
VICTÓRIA MENDONÇA DA SILVA,
ANA FLÁVIA MARQUES DA SILVA, CAMILLA VOIGT BAPTISTELLA,
JACKELINE CRISTINA GAMELEIRA CERQUEIRA DA SILVA,
HELENA RODRIGUES DE FARIAS, MARK GRAHAM,
AND KELLE HOWSON

The platform economy is gaining visibility as a topic among international organizations, academics, civil society organizations, entrepreneurs, and public institutions. Platforms mediate relations and interactions of various kinds (economic, social, cultural) between people, political organizations, companies, institutions, and other types of social actors. This topic has been the subject of a growing corpus of literature (Srnicek 2017; Evans and Schmalensee 2016; Andersson Schwartz 2017; Valente 2021). Various authors point out how digital platforms are reconfiguring social and economic relations, thereby giving rise to new economic and social constellations that are currently being discussed under the terms "platform economy" (Lehdonvirta et al. 2019), "platform capitalism" (Srnicek 2017), or "platform society" (Dijck, Poell, and De Wall 2018). According to Daugareilh, Degryse, and Pochet (2019, 22), "The platform economy can be characterized as a (virtual) technological meeting place bringing together groups of people who, in one way or another, need each other."

One of the key aspects of the platform economy is the role of digital platforms in mediating and extracting value from labor relations. Digital labor platforms provide the digital infrastructure through which businesses, workers, and consumers can connect, while at the same time extracting value from the exchange of labor power. Digital labor platforms are however not just mere mediators of labor relations. They actively coordinate the supply and demand of labor in various modalities and segments based on their own rules and establish management models that are generally automated and based on algorithms.

Some researchers (Fairwork 2021) divide digital labor platforms into two categories: "geographically tethered" labor platforms facilitate labor exchange for services that require geographical proximity, such as ride-hailing or delivery services. Cloudwork or online work platforms in turn facilitate labor services that can be carried out remotely via the internet. Cloudwork platforms hence not only "bring together workers and the objects and subjects of their work in ways that not only make proximity superfluous but also actively design against it" (Graham and Ferrari 2022, 12).

Woodcock and Graham (2019, 3) refer to this model as the "gig economy," which consists of "labor markets that are characterized by independent contracting that happens through, via, and on digital platforms." In a similar vein, Van Doorn (2017) classifies "platform labor" as service work digitally mediated by intermediaries, understood as "infrastructural agents" in the process of the reconstitution of labor relations. De Stefano and Aloisi (2019) characterize "platform work" as synonymous with the gig economy. While some authors have portrayed the global rise of the gig economy as a recent development facilitated by new digital technologies, especially scholars from Brazil have pointed out that that "gig work" has in fact been the norm in the country for a long time, with the Brazilian labor market being historically characterized by informality, precariousness, and on-demand arrangements.

Measuring platform work is a challenge for researchers (Piasna 2020). According to the International Labour Organization (ILO 2021), the number of digital platforms rose from 142 in 2010 to 777 in 2020. The revenue of these companies totaled $52 billion. The share of the population engaging in platform work varies between countries. A report by the International Labour Organization (2021) shows that the value created through platform work is unevenly distributed: of the revenue recorded in 2019, 70 percent came from just two countries: the United States (49 percent) and China (23 percent). When considering investments in these firms, 96 percent were concentrated in Asia ($56 billion), North America ($46 billion), and Europe ($12 billion), while Latin America, Africa, and the Arab states received only 4 percent of total global investments.

While platform work has hence created new streams of revenue and investment opportunities for companies and venture capital, but the labor conditions on these platforms are often precarious and entail significant risks for workers. First, digital labor platforms usually do not employ workers but instead classify their workers as independent contractors or formally self-employed "partners." As a result, platform workers are often not covered by basic rights and legal social protections defined in national labor law. Second, platform work is often characterized by what Wood (2020) calls "despotism on demand." This entails the dismantling of the workday in combination with tight control over workers through "algorithmic management" (Prassl 2018; Grohmann et al. 2022). As a result, platform workers often have to deal with high pressure to complete tasks, long hours and activities, and a significant share of unpaid labor time (Wood et al. 2019).

Against this backdrop, in 2017, researchers from the UK and South Africa founded the Fairwork project with the aim to evaluate and improve the labor practices of digital platforms. To this end, Fairwork "has put together a multi-year program of action research designed to foster more transparency about working conditions in the platform economy, and ultimately to encourage fairer working conditions" (Graham et al. 2020, 100).

In dialogue with stakeholders from various countries, including platform managers, unions, and political decision-makers, the Fairwork team developed five principles of fair platform work: (1) fair pay, (2) fair conditions, (3) fair contracts, (4) fair management, and (5) fair representation. These principles cover a range of basic labor standards and include, inter alia, guaranteed payment for completed work, remuneration of at least the local minimum wage, fair distribution of jobs by the platform, antidiscrimination policies, data protection rules, clear and accessible con-

68 | Claudia Nociolini Rebechi, et al.

tracts, a structured process for workers to appeal management decisions, and the recognition and acceptance of collective worker representation.

Based on these five principles, Fairwork produces yearly national ratings of geographically tethered platforms in different countries and a global rating of cloudwork platforms. Data are collected from desk research and through surveys and qualitative interviews with workers. In addition, Fairwork conducts interviews with the management of the evaluated platforms and invites them to provide additional evidence. This process encourages platforms to adopt effective policies and measures to ensure fair conditions according to the Fairwork principles.

Centrally coordinated by the Oxford Internet Institute and the WZB Berlin Social Science Centre, Fairwork operates through a global network of research teams currently in thirty-nine countries on all continents. In Latin America, Fairwork has teams in Argentina, Brazil, Chile, Colombia, Ecuador, Mexico, Paraguay, and Peru.

Fairwork's research in Latin America shows that the vast majority of platforms operating in the region fail to ensure basic labor standards and protections for their workers. This is the case for global platforms, such as Uber and Didi, as much as for platforms born in the region itself, such as Workana and iFood. In Brazil, high unemployment, compounded by the effects of the COVID-19 pandemic, led to a particularly strong growth of platform labor over the past two years. However, as the latest Fairwork Brazil report (2022a) shows, conditions for platform workers are highly insecure and precarious.

In the remainder of this chapter, we first introduce the Fairwork project and its principles and methodology in more detail. Thereafter, we present central findings of the Fairwork research in Brazil and give an overview of the results from platform evaluations in Latin America. We conclude the chapter by pointing out perspectives for future analysis.

The Fairwork Framework

Fairwork evaluates the working conditions on digital labor platforms based on five principles that indicate basic requirements for "decent work": fair pay, fair conditions, fair contracts, fair management, and fair representation. Digital platforms are evaluated and ranked according to their performance against these principles.

Evaluating Work in the Platform Economy | 69

The five Fairwork principles were developed in a series of multistake-holder workshops held at the seat of the International Labour Organization in Geneva as well as in Berlin, Bangalore, and Johannesburg. To ensure that these global principles were applicable in the Brazilian context, we reviewed and adjusted them in consultation with platform workers, trade unions, regulators, academics, and labor lawyers. The main criteria for each principle are summarized below:[12]

- Fair Pay: Workers, regardless of their classification, should earn a decent income in their home jurisdiction after considering work-related costs. We evaluate earnings according to the statutory minimum wage in the home jurisdiction and the ideal minimum wage.

- Fair Conditions: Platforms should have policies to protect workers from work-related risks. Moreover, platforms should take proactive steps to protect and promote workers' health and safety.

- Fair Contracts: Terms and conditions must be accessible, legible, and understandable. The party contracting with the worker must be subject to local law and identified in the contract. Regardless of the worker's employment status, the contract needs to be free of clauses that unreasonably exclude liability on the part of the platform.

- Fair Management: Platforms need to have a documented process through which workers can be heard, appeal decisions that affect them, and be informed of the reasons behind those decisions. Digital platforms should provide efficient communication channels to workers involving the ability to appeal management decisions, such as blocking of workers' accounts. The use of algorithms should be transparent and present equitable results for workers. An identifiable and documented policy should ensure fairness in how workers are managed on a platform (for example, hiring, punishing, or firing workers).

- Fair Representation: Platforms should provide a documented process for the expression of workers' voice. Regardless of

70 | Claudia Nociolini Rebechi, et al.

their classification, workers should have the right to organize in collective bodies, and platforms should be prepared to cooperate and negotiate with them.

Scoring the platforms according to the Fairwork principles relies on the triangulation of various types of data collected by the research teams in each country through three methods: desk research, semistructured interviews with workers, and meetings with platform managers.

The research process begins with desk research to verify which platforms are currently operating in the country of study. The largest and most influential platforms are selected to be part of the scoring process. The platforms included in the scoring process usually comprise both international and national/regional platforms. The desk research also considers any public information that can be used to score the performance of the platforms.

The second step consists of conducting meetings with platform managers to gain insights into the platform's operation and business model. In these meetings, managers are invited to provide additional evidence, such as internal policy documents, to prove that their labor practices comply with the Fairwork principles. Thereby, Fairwork seeks to create a dialogue with platforms to incentivize them to implement changes based on the Fairwork principles. In cases where platform managers do not agree to meetings, we limit our scoring to evidence obtained through desk research and interviews with workers.

The third method is to conduct qualitative interviews with a sample of 5–10 workers from each platform. These interviews do not aim to build a representative sample. Instead, they seek to understand the work processes and how the work is performed and managed. The interviews allow the team to confirm or refute the policies or practices that are actually in place on the platform. For the Fairwork Brazil research, due to the restrictions arising from the COVID-19 pandemic throughout 2021, almost all interviews were conducted using WhatsApp or Zoom.

Through a triangulation of the data collected from these three sources, Fairwork researchers allocate a score from 0 to 10 to each platform in a peer-review process involving members from at least two different country teams. Platforms receive a point only when they can satisfactorily demonstrate their implementation of the principles.

These scores, along with the justification for being awarded or not, are then passed on to the platforms for review. The platforms can then submit further evidence to earn points that were not initially awarded. These scores are the final annual score published in the annual country reports. More details about the Fairwork scoring system can be found in our reports (Fairwork 2020, 2022a).

To ensure the objectivity of the evaluation results, Fairwork does not receive funding or support from any platform or other company.

Fairwork Brazil 2021: Context, Scores, and Main Results

The Brazilian labor market includes a large share of workers in the informal sector, who carry out various work activities to survive and to ensure the minimum support for their families. The precariousness of work is a central structural feature of the Brazilian economy.

Platform work updates and intensifies historical informality by reorganizing different sectors and occupations, many of which already existed before the emergence of digital platforms. This work performed using applications and subordinated to the algorithmic management of platform companies is present in many countries around the world. In Brazil, platform work began to be incorporated more evidently into the Brazilian labor market in 2014, with the start of operations of the company Uber Technologies Inc. in the country.

The Brazilian platform economy comprises various work activities: delivery, passenger transport, domestic and care work, general services, freelance services, and microwork, usually performed from home.

It is difficult to determine an exact number of workers and professional occupations connected to digital platforms in Brazil based on official statistics presented by research institutes, but there are certainly millions. The Locomotiva Institute estimated that more than thirty million people in Brazil currently perform work activities through digital platforms using applications developed by companies (Cunha 2022).

Among this number, approximately 1.5 million were working in the transportation sector in the context of digital platforms by the end of 2021, as reported by the Institute for Applied Economic Research (IPEA 2022). Of this number, 61.2 percent were app drivers and taxi drivers, 20.9 percent delivered goods via motorcycle, 14.4 percent acted as motorcycle taxi drivers, and the remainder delivered goods via other means of transport.

In the passenger transportation sector, the best-known platform in Brazil is Uber, which is present in more than 500 cities. Its direct competitor is the 99 platform. In the delivery sector, the leader is the Brazilian platform iFood, founded in 2011 and declared a unicorn in 2018, with Movile among its investors. It is present in more than 900 cities and saw the number of orders rise sharply with the COVID-19 pandemic, from 30.6 million in early 2020 to 60 million in March 2021 (Fairwork 2022a). One of its competitors is the Colombian platform Rappi, operating in the country since 2017.

Academic research conducted in Brazil points out that a typical delivery driver in the city of São Paulo, for example, is a young black man. The growth of the platform economy in Brazil therefore further intensifies historical racial inequalities in Brazil (Abílio, Grohmann, and Weiss 2021).

Another important sector of platform work in Brazil is general services. The growing number of platforms in this sector reveals the potential to organize work processes across different sectors via digital platforms. The central platform for general services in Brazil is the Brazilian platform GetNinjas, founded in 2011, which offers the services of painters, masons, teachers, designers, fashion and beauty professionals, health professionals, IT engineers, and car mechanics, among others.

In the microwork scenario, over fifty platforms are active in Brazil (Braz 2021), some of them evaluated in the Fairwork Cloudwork survey (Fairwork 2021). The market involves, in the foreground, the most well-known global platforms such as Amazon Mechanical Turk, Appen, and Lionbridge. Their workers feed, annotate, and train data for artificial intelligence processes, from databases to facial recognition algorithms. There are also companies providing content moderation and transcription services to social media platforms.

In addition, so-called click farms are part of the Brazilian cloudwork sectors. These are Brazilian-based platforms whose workers are underpaid to like, comment, and click on social media profiles like Instagram, TikTok, and Youtube, with a parallel market of fake accounts and bots (Grohmann et al. 2022).

Many other digital platforms operate in Brazil, exploiting the labor of a large, heterogeneous, unemployed, and underemployed working class. In the third quarter of 2021, the country's unemployment rate was a little over 12 percent (IBGE 2021).

Along with unemployment, the Brazilian population also suffered from the pandemic of COVID-19 in 2020 and 2021, with more than 600,000 deaths and more than 22 million confirmed cases of the disease by the end of 2021. In this scenario of multiple tensions, the country faced

Evaluating Work in the Platform Economy | 73

a sanitary collapse caused by the pandemic in multifaceted economic, political, and social crises.

The drivers and delivery workers on digital platforms, for example, could not stop their work activities during the pandemic and suffered severe health and safety risks. Unprotected by labor laws, these workers have experienced a deepening of the precariousness of their work, which has caused greater tension between these workers and the platform companies, which refuse to take responsibility for ensuring decent working conditions.

Against this background, in 2020 and 2021, delivery drivers carried out temporary work stoppages to demand better working conditions from digital platform companies. The demonstrations were attended by delivery drivers in several cities in Brazil, who turned off their apps for a few hours as a form of protest. They also asked consumers not to turn on their apps but instead to rate them negatively in the app stores. Among others, workers demanded an increase in the minimum rate paid by platforms per delivery, benefits such as meal vouchers and insurance (life, accident, and theft insurance), a stop to platforms' practices of blocking workers' accounts, and the provision of protective equipment such as masks and disinfectant. This is just one example of the struggles of the heterogeneous class of Brazilian platform workers for more dignified and fair working conditions.

It is worth noting that there is no specific provision in Brazilian law regulating labor relations on digital platforms. There are bills in progress in the National Congress, some arguing for and others against the assumption of an employment relationship between workers and digital platforms. In January 2022, the Law 14,297 was passed, dealing specifically with the protection of couriers concerning the COVID-19 pandemic. However, this law was limited to the period of the Public Health Emergency of National Importance of the COVID-19 pandemic, which the federal government officially ended in May 2022.

The Consolidation of Labor Laws, in articles 2 and 3, defines the employment relationship as being characterized by the following aspects: subordination, personality, habitually, and being paid. All these characteristics can be verified in the activity of platform workers. However, platforms in Brazil continue classifying workers as independent contractors.

The first Fairwork Brazil study[3] conducted throughout 2021 presented essential results for understanding the general conditions of platform work in the country. Six digital platforms were evaluated due to their strong performance in the Brazilian market in 2021: the ride-hailing platforms Uber and 99, the delivery platforms iFood, Uber Eats,[4] and Rappi, and the general services platform GetNinjas.

The platform scores for Brazil demonstrate the general precariousness and bad conditions for workers: the highest score achieved out of ten was two by the platforms iFood and 99, while Uber scored only one point. Rappi, GetNinjas, and UberEats, in turn, did not score points on any of the principles.

Concerning the principle of fair pay, only the platform 99 was able to demonstrate—through a public statement—that all its workers earn above the local minimum wage, which in 2021 was R$5.50 per hour/R$1,212.00 per month (2021). Most platforms, however, have not reached this basic threshold, as they do not have a pay floor or charge workers high commissions or fees, or both. Rates and working hours are also highly volatile, leading to high income insecurity for workers. No platform has proven that workers earn the local living wage, calculated by the Inter-Union Department of Statistics and Socio-Economic Studies in 2021 at R$24.16 per hour/R$5,315.74 per month in 2021.

Low earnings by platform workers are produced through a range of problematic practices by platforms. First, platforms impose the cost for the acquisition and maintenance of work equipment on workers. Second, the logic of on-demand work leads to working days that often exceed forty hours a week, without the worker being paid for the waiting time between jobs. Third, platforms only pass on a portion of what the client pays for the service to workers. Without transparency about these values it is possible to observe the intensification of the workday with reduced remuneration.

As for the principle of fair conditions, only the platforms Uber and 99 could evidence actions to protect workers from task-specific risks. The good practices of these platforms involved the adequate provision of personal protective equipment and clear accident and health insurance policies. While some other platforms offered personal protective equipment, workers found it difficult to access the material, which had to be picked up by workers in often geographically distant offices of the platform company. Therefore, no other platform scored on this principle. Hence, it is important to highlight the multiple risks to which workers are exposed without the platforms insuring them in case of accidents, theft, or illness.

For the principle of fair contracts, only the platform iFood managed to evidence the implementation of basic standards. As a result of the dialogue with Fairwork researchers, iFood created accessible terms and conditions for workers with illustrations. However, most platforms still do not provide a contract communicated in clear, understandable, and accessible language to workers. Contracts often state terms and conditions in small print, which most workers accept without even reading the contract. Moreover, changes in the terms and conditions are usually not notified to workers within a reasonable time frame. No platform could prove that their contracts were free of unfair terms.

No platform was able to score on the fair management principle. Platforms failed to evidence effective communication channels, transparent appeal processes, and antidiscrimination policies. There are no clear policies regarding deactivation or blocking processes on platforms, resulting in workers being blocked unfairly and unable to satisfactorily appeal platform decisions. Workers have reported, "I only talk to robots, not human beings." Algorithmic management accentuates opacities in the relationship with workers regarding rating systems and data collection. Moreover, algorithms often produce unequal outcomes for workers from disadvantaged groups, thereby deepening social inequalities along lines of gender, race, and other dimensions.

Finally, for the principle of fair representation, only the platform iFood received a point for implementing measures to promote the voice of workers. From its involvement with the Fairwork project, iFood created the "Delivery Riders Forum" as a communication channel with leaders. Most platforms, however, do not have a documented policy that recognizes worker voice and collective worker organizing. The principle of fair representation highlights that platforms should ensure freedom of collective organizing and worker voice. In other words, the expression of dissatisfaction about working conditions shall not be inhibited or penalized. However, many workers have stated that they have been blocked for participating in demonstrations and protests.

Platforms can choose to reduce inequality and unemployment. However, the annual Fairwork Brazil rating report provided evidence that Brazilian platform workers—as in many countries worldwide—face unfair working conditions and lack basic protections. More details can be found in the report *Fairwork Brazil Ratings 2021: Labor Standards in the Platform Economy* (Fairwork 2022a).

Fairwork in Latin America

As an international action research project, Fairwork increases the possibilities for dialogue and the collective construction of knowledge and awareness about working conditions worldwide. By the first half of 2024, thirty-four countries from Africa, Latin America, Asia, and Europe had released annual rating reports. Our global network of researchers not only enables us to portray and compare the situation of platform workers in different countries around the world, it also creates the opportunity for country teams to dialogue, share experiences, and revisit the appropriateness of Fairwork's principles and methodology in different contexts.

Considering the integrated nature of the research, using the same methodology and principles, Fairwork's global research activities hold unique potential for comparative analyses of the differences of platform work between the Global South and the Global North. Any study of decent work and the expansion of digital labor platforms must look at the effects of platformization on different realities. The results of the Latin American reports seem to paint a telling picture.

Among the four continents where Fairwork has evaluated the working conditions on digital labor platforms, Latin American countries have the worst results. By May 2022, the highest platform score on the continent was in Argentina, with the company Didi scoring four points (Fairwork 2022b). However, all other platforms in Argentina did not score on any of the principles. In Ecuador, the highest score achieved by a platform was three, in Chile the highest platform score was two. Both countries had several platforms with a minimum score of only one point. As already mentioned, in Brazil, the maximum score achieved by a platform was two points, with half of the evaluated platforms scoring zero. With one point, the only country with a lower maximum score was Bangladesh.

With this in mind, we must consider how labor conditions in Latin America reflect the effects of coloniality on the capitalist constitution in the Global South and how this relates to exploitation through digital labor platforms. Aníbal Quijano, a key author of decolonial theories, has critiqued modernity as a process coined by capitalism and racism. According to Quijano, the expropriation of labor and natural resources through coloniality was necessary to sustain the bourgeois industrial, economic, and political revolutions in Europe (Quijana 2005).

Moreover, Quijano argues that coloniality functioned on three levels: that of "power," that of "knowledge," and that of "being." While "power" refers to economic and institutional domination, "knowledge" refers to the knowledge forms and social organization that have been destroyed or stolen by the dominators. Finally, in the sphere of "being," there is the negation of the subjectivity of the dominated, while the dominator also creates his identity through this relationship: to create the notion of the "white" it was necessary to create the "other" in people of color; while labor rights emerged in Europe, in the Americas and Africa there was still formal slavery.

In this way, we must question the mere introduction of institutions derived from modernity, also verifying how the forms of capitalism instituted in Latin America carry specific issues of coloniality. This does not mean refusing comparisons with realities on other continents, much less ignoring concepts or norms with origins in the Global North, but recognizing how coloniality runs through our experiences in Latin America, including the conditions and regulation of labor (Oliveira 2022).

This notion is central to labor in peripheral living in Latin America (Abílio 2020). While the term "gig economy" is used to represent a shift from "secure and continuous work" to "unsafe odd jobs" in the Global North, the construction of capitalism in the Global South has been done through unsafe work and informality. Thus, the exploitation of labor by digital platforms is not necessarily new. Through algorithmic management and increasing attacks on labor protection, digital labor platforms are now also introducing characteristics of peripheral living associated with the Global South into the Global North by replacing formal employment relations as well as preexisting forms of labor contracting. The resulting precarization of labor relations primarily affects vulnerable population groups such as immigrants, people of color, and women.

This brings us to the most recent Fairwork report in Latin America on labor conditions in the platform economy in Colombia, released in early June 2022. The report portrayed the first company evaluated in our continent that managed to satisfy all basic criteria of the five Fairwork principles, reaching a total of seven points (Fairwork 2022c). The company Hogarú operates in the field of domestic work and ensures that workers are hired under the Colombian domestic work law.

By respecting the rights and guarantees provided by the law, the working conditions on this platform were significantly better than the average situation revealed by Fairwork in Latin America. Hogarú could achieve such a comparatively high score because the company respects the specific and general Colombian labor laws. The case of Hogarú thereby

78 | Claudia Nociolini Rebechi, et al.

shows that respecting national labor and social legislation can contribute to ensuring decent work. While Fairwork reports in Latin America indicate that most platforms choose to ignore and break labor laws, the case of Hogarú in Colombia indicates that alternative, better practices by platforms are also possible.

On the other hand, the large share of companies that do not comply with labor laws in our continent demonstrates that worker exploitation through platforms is still the norm. Global companies such as Uber had equivalently low scores in Latin America to the rest of the world. Regional companies such as iFood, Rappi, and 99/Didi showed slight variations in different countries, but overall none of them was able to demonstrate that they meet the minimum criteria of the Fairwork principles.

In conclusion, the expansion of precarious living through the "gig work" model currently represents the norm in Latin America, with platforms largely evading national labor and social legislation. However, the growing worker movements across the continent instill hope that this reality can change. Pressure from labor, civil society, and political movements can put pressure on platforms to improve their labor practices, including by respecting and ensuring workers' rights as defined in national labor and social legislation.

Conclusion

The Fairwork project was created to shed light on the situation of platform workers and to evaluate the labor practices of digital platforms against five principles of fair work. The project's organization, with teams in almost thirty countries, combines the analysis of platform work in specific national contexts with a methodology that allows it to detect global trends as well as specific dynamics in each country or region.

However, the aim of the project goes beyond of the mere production of academic knowledge. Its action-research frame involves a permanent dialogue with workers to gather their demands and with platforms to present identified problems and incentivize changes to promote fairer labor practices, from payment to representation. In several countries, the platform evaluations conducted by Fairwork have helped platforms to improve their internal policies and practices and to offer workers better conditions.

However, Fairwork's research in Brazil and Latin America shows that most platforms in the region fail to ensure basic labor standards and rights for their workers. Against this background, the publication of the first Fairwork Rating Report for Brazil in 2022 represents a first important step toward a fairer platform economy. Platform work is one of the central issues on the agenda for the country in the present and the future. Fairwork principles—involving fair pay, working conditions, contracts, management, and representation—can help analyze and transform the world of work in the country.

During the research period, the team engaged with workers, platforms, social movements, political parties, cooperatives, unions, and policymakers in a dialogue based on transparency and respect. All are central agents for ensuring decent work and continuous updating of the Fairwork principles.

Fairwork has continued to analyze the main digital platforms in Brazil, adding ten more platforms during 2022 and 2023. Based on the dissemination and discussion of our research results, we hope to build collective efforts in the fight for decent work on digital platforms, involving all institutions interested in the topic.

The Fairwork project also understands that consumers are essential agents in changing the platform economy in favor of decent work. With enough information, many consumers will make informed choices about the platforms they interact with. Our annual ratings give consumers the ability to choose the highest scoring platform operating in an industry, thus helping to put pressure on platforms to improve their working conditions and scores. We enable consumers to be allied with workers to fight for a fairer platform economy.

We have also introduced the Fairwork Pledge as part of this change process, a public commitment to fairer platform work and to the Fairwork principles. The Fairwork Pledge harnesses the power of organizations' investment and partnership policies to support fairer platform work. Organizations such as universities, schools, businesses, and civil society institutions that use platform work can make a difference by committing to only using the platforms with the best labor practices, guided by our five Fairwork principles.

In April 2022, Fairwork hired the Locomotiva Institute to survey data on the perception of inhabitants of the city of São Paulo regarding decent work in the platform economy. The main results, released to the general public by the Brazilian press (Brigatti 2022), show that 93 percent

80 | Claudia Nociolini Rebechi, et al.

of respondents think that digital platforms should offer fairer working conditions to workers; more than half of the respondents agree that workers currently do not receive fair pay (64 percent); 84 percent consider it unfair to punish workers with blockades and cancellations without mentioning the reasons; 53 percent think digital platforms do not respect labor laws; 87 percent think apps should be regulated by the government to provide basic protections for deliverers and drivers; 82 percent think strikes by app workers are fair; and 87 percent think digital platforms should be forced to listen to and negotiate with groups representing workers.

In summary, the reality in Brazil and other Latin American countries shows that there is still much to be done. As an action-research project, Fairwork will continue to work on increasing the number of countries involved, conducting new studies, and provoking debates about measures for improving the conditions of platform workers. The dialogue with platforms can contribute to incentivize platforms to adopt new policies to ensure fairer parameters and working conditions.

At the same time, Fairwork seeks to expand the network of organizations committed to fairer platform work through the Fairwork Pledge. By joining the Fairwork Pledge, universities, public institutions, civil society organizations, and companies contracting platform services can contribute to the demand for fair conditions for platform work. The Fairwork Pledge has provoked debates about adequate public policies for the regulation of platform work, a debate that is growing not only in Brazil but throughout Latin America.

Actors concerned with promoting fair platform work, which is becoming an alternative for more and more workers worldwide, especially in the Global South, face significant challenges in preventing the platform economy from becoming a driver for the precarization of labor relations. Therefore, initiatives to improve working conditions in the platform economy must be embraced and supported by more and more segments of society.

Notes

1. For more details, we recommend consulting our reports (e.g., Fairwork 2020, 2022a) and the project website: https://fair.work.

2. To learn more about our principles and research methdodology for the evaluation and rating of cloudwork platforms, see our Fairwork Cloudwork report (2021).

Evaluating Work in the Platform Economy | 81

3. There are many Brazilian universities engaged with the project—currently Unisinos University, the University of São Paulo (USP), the Federal University of Rio de Janeiro (UFRJ), the Federal University of Rio Grande do Sul (UFRGS), and the Federal University of Technology—Parana (UTFPR).

4. We kept Uber Eats in the results report because the survey was conducted throughout 2021, before the platform announced its exit from Brazil in January 2022.

6

The Role of Fake News in the Erosion of Brazilian Democracy

Tássio Acosta, P. Locatelli, and Sílvio Gallo

A Theoretical Approach

More and more in the present time, the problem of fake news has generated ruptures, both regarding interpersonal relationships—whether in person or virtual—and in terms of institutional crises of democracy. The present chapter analyzes how the problem of disinformation is consolidated in institutional crises to specifically oppose the democratic order and produce more reactionary, conservative forms of governance.

According to Michel Foucault (2008), modern states have been "governmentalized," transforming power machineries into ways to govern populations, which implicates a new concept: governmentality. To the philosopher, the exercise of power by the state is very different in modernity: it is not a practice of domination but a system of shaping behavior. In his own words, "governing people in the large sense of the word is not to force them to do what the governor wants; we have always an unstable equilibrium with complements and conflicts between the coercive techniques and the processes by which the self is constructed and changed by itself" (Foucault 2013, 39). On the other hand, Foucault (2012) affirms that his research leads him to the idea that people are governed by truth. The subjectivation processes are guided by the adhesion to a truth regime. According to him, we have concurrently many truth regimes disputing people's beliefs, and each one of us is seduced by one or the other. In

84 | Tássio Acosta, P. Locatelli, and Sílvio Gallo

other words, lives are governed by a truth regime, and we live always inside a truth regime defining what is truth.

Following the works of Foucault to analyze the Brazilian situation, we defend the hypothesis that with the process of redemocratization of the country, since the mid-1980s, a "democratic governmentality" was constituted, based on the construction of the citizen to be governed democratically, explained in the intense biopolitical production of public policies in the various areas, including education, calling individuals to participatory action in a democratic society (Acosta and Gallo 2020). Some keywords become evident: collective decision, participation, inclusion, universal education, and so on. It was about including as many as possible to govern as much as possible, since those excluded from the democratic system would also be excluded from the order of government. If we want to define a maxim, it could well be "include in order to govern."

Democratic governmentality in Brazil was not an invention of one party, and the various parties that governed the country in the last decades committed to it. However, during the Partido dos Trabalhadores (PT)'s period of government (2003–2016), democratic governmentality was expanded, drawing public participation into the production of public policies. Subsequently, there has been a backlash, with a transformation in Brazilian governmentality to leave behind the democratic approach. The hegemony of the truth regime based on citizenship loses space, and fake news has played an important role in constructing a different kind of governmentality and subjectivation.

New Ways of Governing Lives

The discrediting of institutions aims to create truths and control narratives, and in that way make possible a populist or fascist form of governance. Such control of truth is essential for totalitarian regimes; as Arendt (1973) shows, they need loyal followers who do not distinguish between true and false information.

Once the institutions of power take over the production of subjectivity in a society, they establish discourses of truth for social control. Foucault (1979, 12) reminds us that "the truth does not exist outside of power or without power," just as "there is no exercise of power without a certain economy of the discourses of truth that function in that power, from and through it" (Foucault 2010, 22).

When analyzing the specificity of Brazilian totalitarianism, historian Lilia Schwarcz (2019, 220) indicates that "any democratic process, by definition, is incomplete, unfinished, and always asks for improvement." In opposition to this democratic improvement project, fake news seeks to contaminate institutions, impose fear, and persecute difference.

By feeding back through daily life practices, truth and power co-constitute each other, producing new truths and new regimes of governance. This manifests in the individual and collective subjects of society, which then further validates new narratives. It will then be, from this "conversion of the spectacle into surveillance" (Foucault 2015, 22), that the truth begins to manifest itself in bodies producing new regimes of truth and governance in a given society.

To create room for new discourses and narratives, fascism and populism must first vilify existing institutions of power, such as science, as they are linked to existing patterns of knowledge production. Jason Stanley, when analyzing the functioning of fascism, highlights that "fascist ideology seeks to naturalize group difference, thus giving the appearance of scientific and natural support to a hierarchy of human value" (Stanley 2018, 8), naturalizing not just false discourses, but imposing them as "new truths." Similarly, "populist leaders have been at the same time destroying the historical record in a literal sense and manipulating memory and experiences . . . , which confuses lies with truths" (Finchelstein 2020, 129–30). In sum, fascist self-consciousness leads to the "equation of power, truth and violence" (Finchelstein 2020, 127).

The importance of social networks for the propagation of fascist ideology is due to the individualities cultivated there. Individuals experience a new subjectivity when they gain relevance in virtual spaces, collecting likes and shares. "Inseparable from the emergence of this new form of collective constitution, a possible new form of individuality can be seen emerging" that is present in these new places of sociability (Santos and Cypriano 2014, 73).

State practices operationalize subjectivities not only in the individual, but as collectives within society, as in the case of state racism (Foucault 2010). State racism designates certain bodies that deserve to be developed and purified, and those who will not have the same merit and, consequently, may be placed on the margins, silenced, and made invisible.

At the limit, state racism designates some bodies to be exterminated, sustaining a necropolitics, in which the state decides who is not a valid subject, and therefore can die. "The State can, by itself, transform itself

86 | Tássio Acosta, P. Locatelli, and Sílvio Gallo

into a war machine. It can also appropriate a war machine or help to create one" (Mbembe 2018, 55), generating tensions in order to increase institutional fragility and social weakness. State racism, in this discussion of necropolitics, refers to the infusion of race into the collective subjectivities established through the operation of social networks.

Margareth Rago (2019, 258) explains that this policy of erasing subjects is of great importance for "totalitarian regimes, which appropriate the past for utilitarian purposes, producing a unique system of historical interpretation and construction of 'truth.'"

Fake News

This section will discuss how fake news contributed to the consolidation of institutional crises through the sedimentation of fraudulent news and disinformation in the social imaginary, making use of viral propagation present in social networks.

Narrative disputes have always been present in the form of fake news. During the Cold War, one can recollect the manufactured controversy around whether man stepped on the moon, and both the Iraq War and the current invasion of Ukraine by Russia were justified in real time by fake news. What is unique about contemporary fake news is its power to go viral, circulating through communication networks and permeating the social imaginary.

Online social networks are the new space for sociability (Santos and Cypriano 2014; Carvalho 2016), making the impact of fake news even stronger and more prevalent. Such news disseminates in social network forum posts or in sending and sharing messages in communication applications, such as WhatsApp and Telegram.

Himma-Kadadas (2017) highlights that in order for fake news to propagate more intensely in the social imagination, it needs to be anchored in journalistic narratives. By highlighting a journalistic narrative, adding or deleting other underlying information, and relating them, fake news has greater possibility of going viral. That is, when making use of some scientific research or journalistic report, the author of the false post brings certain contrary "data" or opposite "experience," precisely to discredit the original. Fake news entrepreneurs elevate their perspectives and understandings to the same value as the scientific study or journalistic news used as a basis or reference.

The Role of Fake News in the Erosion of Brazilian Democracy | 87

Interested in giving greater intelligibility to the expression of fake news, the editorial director of *Folha de São Paulo*, the print newspaper with the largest national circulation in Brazil, states that fake news should be understood as "all information that, being demonstrably false, is capable of harming third parties and has been forged and/or put into circulation through negligence or bad faith, in this case, with a view to easy profit or political manipulation" (Frias Filho 2018, 43).

However, for fake news to have a high probability of going viral, it is necessary to have its audience targeted to those already predisposed to accept its arguments, above all because it echoes "prejudices and worldviews of social actors (the so-called 'confirmation bias')" (Recuero and Gruzd 2019, 33). The reader's identification with the news is of great importance for its viralization, and precisely for this reason virtual environments offer a fruitful place for dissemination of fake news. In virtual environments, algorithms can delimit social networks by recording user clicks, categorizing users as likely targets for different kinds of fake news. To increase clicks and thereby expand their target audience, fake news applies a particular aesthetic to increase engagement—or what is called clickbait. The more a news item manages to generate clicks, the more it will be indicated to other readers of that same algorithmic profile and, as a result, the greater its viral power for propagation.

To be successful, fake news must (1) carry a significant emotional charge capable of capturing the reader's attention and (2) produce a larger reaction emanating from the reader to the wider network identified by algorithmic targeting. These two characteristics produce a strong enough link for fake news to consolidate itself as viral content.

According to Jenkins, Ford, and Green (2013), clickbait is understood to be a specific aesthetic of writing capable of generating attention, interest, and engagement in a given subject and of producing sharing with other possible readers. This power of propagation is embedded within the ecosystem of social networks, above all because the user is able to send a certain story directly to a person, through their messaging app, or to an indistinct number of readers publicly within a designated network. Humor and satire are ideal tactics to generate clicks and encourage sharing on social networks, which explains, therefore, the amount of memes created for greater engagement and "attention" by the algorithms (Jenkins, Ford, and Green 2013). Another widely used expedient for propagation is the use of communicational micronetworks. For example, a given user produces content, sends it to his WhatsApp group with users interested in that content, and they share it through their other communication networks with other users interested in the same content, producing a snowball growing over time.

As an example of the potentially rapid spread of fake news 54 percent of all Brazilians use WhatsApp groups. Each group can have up to 256 people, and if all groups were full, a single meme produced and sent to the parent group would be able to be shared to the next twelve groups, totaling 3,328 users. For content to be able to go viral, it must first find a space in which to propagate enough for an algorithm to identify it. Fittingly, the already-existing community of like-minded virtual users accomplishes an initial degree of propagation. Since much of fake news is apocryphal, its authorship is not recognized and, consequently, it is difficult to identify and hold its creators accountable.

Another feature for the viral spread of content on social networks is in the kinds of individual subjectivity forged over decades of neoliberalism. Neoliberalism has highlighted the role of individuals as users and content producers, often with a priority on immediacy and virtual social contact. At the same time, neoliberalism has undermined those collective subjectivities (unions, interest associations, communities) that might play a role in checking facts and slowing the pace of viral propagation. It "tends to prioritize quick, simple and direct responses, putting in check institutions and professionals whose specialized work follows rules for checking facts and evidence" (Miskolci 2021, 40).

Due to the huge impact that fraudulent news can have on society and the resulting challenges to the democratic process of elections, the Superior Electoral Court, through Ordinance-TSE no. 510, of August 4, 2021, instituted the Electoral Justice Permanent Program on Combatting Disinformation "in order to face the disinformation related to the Electoral Justice and its members, the electronic voting system, the electoral process in its different phases and the actors involved in it."[1] In particular, companies used for propagating fake news are on the radar of Brazilian superior courts during election periods.

One area of concern was the contribution of fake news to the consolidation of hate machines targeting specific victims. In the virtual environments of social networks, people victimized by fake news campaigns usually have their lives exposed to public opinion, often without possibility of defense, since the disproportionality of attacks is multiplied by engagements through algorithms.

The Role of Fake News in the Erosion of Brazilian Democracy | 89

Pariser (2012) alerts us to the fact that these virtual groups are understood as filter bubbles, that is, meetings of people in virtual spaces who have similarities in political-ideological thinking and, consequently, yearn to consume certain and similar content, increasing the resonance and extending the power of fake news on "arrival" in society.

Fake News in Brazil

Within the complex ramifications of fake news, we will highlight two aspects that seem central to contemporary Brazilian politics: (1) suspicions about the electronic voting system and (2) the moral agenda in education. Although they may seem different, they are indeed connected.

The turning point in the Brazilian institutional crisis occurred with the end of the 2014 election, when the then-defeated candidate Aécio Neves of the Brazilian Party of Social Democracy (PSDB) cast doubt on the national electoral system, hinting at the possibility of fraud in electronic voting machines[2] and, consequently, requesting a recount of votes by the Superior Electoral Court. After a year of intensive analysis of the Brazilian electoral system, no possibility of fraud that could jeopardize the outcome of the Brazilian elections was identified.[3]

Even with internationally recognized and highly secure electronic voting machines (Brasil 2016), as well as the participation of various entities accompanying the Brazilian electoral process (Brasil 2014), the defeated candidate continued to shroud his electoral defeat in suspicion. This suspicion was aggravated by the fact that the vote was very tight, with a small percentage difference between the winner and the loser in the second round. By creating such insecurity and disseminating it to the popular imagination, institutions that had appeared solidly constructed were effectively undermined. In this context, we will highlight some episodes that led to conjunctural shakes and fissures.

The June Journeys in 2013 are understood here as an important turning point in the political-national scenario. The June protests began as a complaint against rising bus fares but took on diverse social demands. Protests were putatively apolitical, but they evolved into a clear target in President Dilma Rousseff and the PT. One indicator of distortion was turning transportation protests into dissatisfaction with the Olympics and World Cup protests. When the 2014 election ended in a narrow PT win, the same public that had supported the Olympic and World Cup protests now mobilized against the legitimacy of the elections. It is important to emphasize that the audience was mostly made up of young people aged around twenty years old, that is, young people who grew up in a country already connected and socialized to social networks.

While new ideas were associated with the protests (Pomar 2013), an apolitical stance gained notoriety, since protesters carrying flags of political parties or social movements heard universal shouts of "no flag" or "no party." Armed with their smartphones, young people posted videos and made live streams at the demonstrations, calling for the participation of their contemporaries to increase the movement. New agendas were added to each demonstration and what started as a protest against the increase in bus fares saw a proliferation of social demands.[4] "Since then, political lines of force inseparable from its technological-communicational character marked the inflection for a new grammar of disputes, more conflictive and moralistic" (Machado and Miskolci 2019).

The second aspect, the moral agenda, refers to a weakening of norms of science and rationality and decreasing support for education. Although Dilma Rousseff was reelected president in 2014, the election produced the most conservative Congress since the redemocratization of the country in 1984.[5] From Congress, conservatives gave fake news new form, advancing especially a conservative social agenda. Obstacles were imposed, for example, on studies of gender and sexuality in Brazilian schools (Acosta and Gallo 2020). In the same period, discussions of the Ten-Year State Education Plans and the National Education Plan made the aforementioned theme an electoral wedge issue, both for defenders and for detractors. Once their debate entered the virtual sphere, it became attractive as clickbait and gained even more media coverage.

In the wake of such debates, the movement known as Escola Sem Partido (School without Party) (Frigotto 2017) organized with a clear interest in curtailing the freedom of faculty by inviting students to record their teachers and denounce any discussion of sensitive topics in the classrooms.

The conflict posed scientific knowledge against a system of knowledge rooted in hierarchies of gender and sexuality. To reduce gender- and sexuality-based violence, scientific knowledge valued debates on gender and sexuality in teaching-learning spaces. In opposition, fascist discourses of truth opposed scientific knowledge with the ultimate aim of weakening institutions and exacerbating social tension. The old power game through which science built its social legitimacy was reactivated, now in an inverted way, with scientific truth being questioned by fascist frames of knowledge.

The Role of Fake News in the Erosion of Brazilian Democracy | 91

The attacks on educational institutions consolidated fascist practices of persecution of everything other than heteronormativity. Veiga-Neto (2019) points out that "the curriculum ended up functioning as a condition of possibility for the disciplinary logic to make the school this broad and efficient machinery for manufacturing the modern subject and the disciplinary society itself" (Veiga-Neto 2019, 17).

The denial of institutions as agents of social mediation, distrust in teachers, education, and schooling, systematic attacks on scientific discourses, and harassment of the press and reduced circulation of ideas are pillars that sustain the practices of the fascist machinery that occupied the Brazilian state in contemporary times. In addition to this movement restricting educational and scientific activities, there was purposive action to create a national network of civic-military schools, with a project of disciplining children and young people, especially from poorer areas. The fascist subjectivation inherent in this educational model attempts to transform the public, republican, and pluralist school into a space of military discipline, in which hierarchical order and blind obedience prevail.

Armed with their smartphones, visitors to museums and exhibitions on gender and sexualities began to be recorded and exposed on social networks, especially on YouTube channels that "denounced" the people who patronized the art on display. When there were children, even accompanied by their guardians, the complaints echoed with greater magnitude. In an extreme case, an investigation was opened at the Federal Public Ministry due to the recording and dissemination on social media of a girl "under 12 years old, accompanied by her mother, touching the artist's ankles and legs (naked), during the performance 'La Bête,' inspired by the work of Lygia Clark, in September 2017, at the Museum of Modern Art in São Paulo." Other cases of persecution and attacks against democratic norms of equity and tolerance occurred. An example is the persecution that the philosopher Judith Butler suffered when giving a lecture in Brazil, including being attacked in the airport lounge, in 2017, when she returned to the United States.

The 2018 electoral campaign was replete with such episodes of intolerance. President Lula was a political prisoner in Curitiba, forcing the PT to nominate the former mayor of São Paulo, Fernando Haddad, to the top of the presidential ticket and former federal deputy Manuela D'Ávila as candidate for vice-president.

Fake news played a pivotal role, associating Haddad's name with various inaccuracies. In one, he was associated with the made-up distribution of a bottle with a nipple in the shape of a penis to children in day care centers in São Paulo. Also, a T-shirt he wore with the word "rebel" and a picture of Jesus was altered to say "Jesus was a transvestite." The vice-presidential candidate, Manuela D'Ávila, had her photos edited, also.

The tight timeline for Haddad to replace Lula heightened the damage of such fake news attacks.[6] Haddad was unable to inherit Lula's votes and, in the second round, lost the election with 44.87 percent. Although the vote for the 2018 National Congress produced the highest turnover since the country's redemocratization, the result of the election even surpassed the record conservatism of the 2014 Congress in terms of right-wing party representation.[7] The theme of gender and sexualities brought to the Brazilian public scenario in the previous four years returned to the political agenda in the 2018 electoral period and asserted itself as a significant electoral platform. As a candidate, Jair Bolsonaro shouted on television shows and in his live stream feed that the PT wanted to return to power to impose a "Gay Kit," an imagined set of tools and instructions for homosexuality that would destroy the traditional Brazilian family and spread communism in the country.

At the end of Bolsonaro's first year in office, the new coronavirus emerged, known as COVID-19. Borders started to be closed, yet in Brazil, government agencies participated in fake news campaigns to systematically deny the pandemic. Bolsonaro built a media communication team to deny the existence of the pandemic (Morel 2021; Calil 2021) or to affirm China's responsibility for the creation of what they termed the "Chinese virus" (Azzi et al. 2020; Silva 2020).

With the pandemic, a new line of government action appears: denying science. Like the political use of gender and sexuality issues, vaccine immunization acted as a political wedge issue throughout 2020. Political rivals disseminated images defending or attacking the immunization of Brazilian society (Falcão and Souza 2021). Deniers claimed that the vaccine liquid would include microchips capable of manipulating the DNA of immunized people. Vaccine believers emphasized the importance of immunization for saving lives, whether of adults or children, and the relevance of science in the debate on public health.

In the midst of a discussion "in defense of science," it is worth noting that, according to the Technical Note to the Brazilian Parliament on Budget Cuts produced by the National Forum of Deans of Research and Graduate Studies, "in the last six years there has been a vertiginous decrease in investments in Brazilian science, decreasing from R$ 13.97

billion in 2015 to R$ 4.40 billion in 2020," significantly impacting existing research and making it impossible to initiate new projects.[8]

The difficulty of doing science in the country has been highlighted by professionals from different areas of knowledge (Goés 2021) and, on July 26, 2021, professors and scientists were surprised when the Lattes Platform system, an integrated database of science and technology research maintained by the Brazilian government, failed for technical reasons.[9] According to a report by the National Council for Scientific and Technological Development (CNPq report number 10[10]), linked to the Ministry of Science, Technology, Innovation and Communications, access to the Lattes Platform was only restored on August 7, 2021.

In a note published by the Brazilian Society for the Progress of Science analyzing the seventieth anniversary of CNPq, the body "has never known such a deep crisis. . . . The blackout of the CNPq may be followed by the blackout of Brazilian science, and of a country's project. There is no sovereignty and social welfare without science, technology and innovation. Let's defend the CNPq!"[11]

This section has provided some examples of episodes of fake news, demonstrating how inaccuracies penetrate public discourse and knowledge. Further, these episodes are consistent in their orientation—each period targeted the political left, scientific reason, and traditionally excluded groups. In short, fake news was propagated with a particular objective, and its impact was to undermine trust in political institutions.

Mistrust in Institutions and Democratic Erosion

Repeated episodes of fake news gradually eroded trust in political institutions and the democratic process and increased polarization and violence. In an interview with the newspaper *Folha de São Paulo*, the United Nations special rapporteur on freedom of assembly and association, Clément Nyaletsossi Voule, highlights that the country's democracy is in crisis and the political debate is contaminated by successive incidents of violence. He cites, as an example, the lack of conclusion of the investigation into the execution of councilwoman Marielle Franco, in Rio de Janeiro, and how her case contributes to an environment of fear and impunity.[12]

Nobel Peace Prize winner Maria Ressa, recognizing the risk to Brazilian democracy, highlights that attacks on journalists have systematically

94 | Tássio Acosta, P. Locatelli, and Sílvio Gallo

reduced their credibility with society, allowing new narratives to be produced by dominant groups. The annual report produced by the Brazilian Association of Radio and TV Broadcasters (2022) on violations of freedom of expression highlights "145 cases of non-lethal violence, which involved at least 230 professionals and media outlets, a number 21.69% higher than in 2020" (2022, 12). This amounts to an average of 2.7 cases per week throughout the year.

Also, according to the Abert report, "for the first time in 20 years, Brazil passed, in 2021, to the so-called 'red zone' of the World Ranking of Press Freedom of the international organization Reporters without Borders," ranking 111th among the 180 countries evaluated (Brazilian Association of Radio and TV Broadcasters 2022, 11).

At a time when institutions are being systematically denigrated and attacks on direct elections and electronic voting machines are publicized by sectors of civil society and political elites, civil society sectors in journalism, communications, and human rights advocacy, published a document[13] on May 3, 2022 calling for guarantees for press freedom in the elections, highlighting various types of attacks that these professionals have suffered in recent years, especially in the 2018 and 2022 elections.

After a series of questions about the Brazilian electoral process, the Superior Electoral Court published a document,[14] sent to the Cyber Defense Center of the Brazilian Army Cyber Defense Command, stating that "not even the equipment manufacturer itself has the power to defraud hardware or run any software that compromises voting" (Tribunal Supremo Eleitoral 2022, 69). The Superior Electoral Court attached approximately 700 pages to this document that endorsed its statements of the security and inviolability of electronic voting machines.

In this sense, the numerous speeches made by President Bolsonaro, attacking and discrediting electronic voting machines in Brazil, and how these fake news reports encourage distrust in the electoral system, stand out. Such attacks have occurred since the beginning of his term and tend to increase when negative news about his government is revealed by reports or research institutes referenced as hyperinflation, police violence, and misuse of public money, among other problems experienced by society in Brazil.

As an example, we cite the most recent survey published by the Datafolha institute to analyze trust in the Brazilian electoral system, carried out between May 25 and 26, 2022. In this research, the trust rate dropped from 82 percent to 73 percent, of which "42% trust a lot and 31% trust a little. Almost a quarter (24%) do not trust electronic voting machines and

The Role of Fake News in the Erosion of Brazilian Democracy | 95

2% has no opinion" (Datafolha 2022, 4). The aforementioned survey also identified that "compared to the last survey, in March, the rate of those who trust electronic voting machines fell by eight percentage points—this is the first time that the index has declined—while the rate of those who do not trust it grew by seven percentage points: on that date, 82% trusted electronic voting machines (47% a lot and 35% a little) and 17% did not trust them. In the first survey of the historical series, in December 2020, 69% trusted electronic voting machines and 29% did not" (Datafolha 2022, 4).

Another important piece of data identified by the survey was that "the trust index in electronic voting machines is predominant in all sociodemographic variables and reaches higher rates among the most educated (79%), among Lula voters (82%) and those who disapprove of the Bolsonaro government (83%). Already, the distrust rate is higher among businessmen (38%), among evangelicals (31%), among Bolsonaro voters (40%) and among those who approve of the Bolsonaro government (43%)" (Datafolha 2022, 4). The survey also asked about trust in the election:

> The largest portion (55%) is concerned about the possibility of Bolsonaro trying to invalidate the elections before or after the vote. For 40%, there is no need to worry and 5% has no opinion. The concern rate is highest among those aged between 16 and 24 (66%), among Lula voters (70%), among those who disapprove of the Bolsonaro government (73%), among those who believe that there is no chance of fraud in the elections (63%) and among those who believe that the president's statements, questioning the security of the electoral system, greatly hinder the elections (78%). (Datafolha 2022, 5)

Faced with such tensions and institutional crises, former president Lula, eventually elected president in 2022, both in an interview in *Time* magazine,[15] on May 4, 2022, and in his speech at the launch of his presidential candidacy,[16] on May 7, affirmed the importance of valuing democracy, strengthening institutions, and respecting differences in Brazilian society for the consolidation of a country that is equally democratic for all.

Conclusion

In order to better fight fascism, it is of great importance to value several fronts: "at the molecular level, against the fascist in each of us, at the micropolitical ethical level and, at the macro level, against the 'great fascism,' against fascist rulers" (Gallo 2019, 368). Therefore, the importance of combating fascism lies precisely in improving the confrontation with the racist state that seeks to erase other subjects and all expressions of difference.

The ecosystem of social networks, especially WhatsApp and Telegram, resonated with the neoliberal individual subjectivity and collective identity of dominant groups. Fake news preyed on issues such as gender and sexuality to accelerate propagation in these contexts, contributing to institutional distrust and provoking a moral panic powerful enough to inflate polarized and antagonistic opinions. In this way, fake news weakened institutions, eroded democracy, and generated a new form of governance and subjectivity—the production of fascist lives, based on intolerance, hatred, and posing a significant risk to the democratic state in Brazil.

This process evidences a radical change in the governance of lives taking place in Brazilian society. With the movement analyzed here, in which fake news and the production of new regimes of truth were of central importance, new forms of governing lives were developed. Institutional public space and republican institutions such as education were replaced by action on social networks. As Arendt (2013) showed, totalitarianisms use isolation, which fractures the social field, to erect a government that acts through terror. The type of social networks that have been put into practice by conservative political actors produce political isolation, in which subjects act, communicate, and think through social networks, without building social ties.

This implies another order of governance of lives, crossed by segregation and state racism, allowing for distinctions between the groups that must live and the groups that must die, affirming the lives of some to the detriment of others. We have witnessed how public machines are being equipped to produce this isolation, at the same time that the civic-military schools project advances, from the interior of the country to the periphery of large centers, producing and reinforcing moral panic. From a democratic governmentality, we seem to be transitioning to a fascist governmentality, which subjects individuals through isolation and terror.

The urgency of the struggle is imperative for those who do not want to see a young and fragile democracy, built with great difficulty, collapse in the face of this authoritarian, antidemocratic, and deceptive project.

Notes

1. https://international.tse.jus.br/en/misinformation-and-fake-news/brazil-electoral-justice-permanent-program-on-countering-disinformation.

2. https://g1.globo.com/politica/noticia/2014/10/psdb-pede-ao-tse-auditoria-para-verificar-lisura-da-eleicao.html.

3. https://www.conjur.com.br/2015-nov-06/tse-analisa-dados-auditoria-feita-psdb-pleito-2014.

4. https://www.youtube.com/watch?v=v5iSn76I2xsandlist=PLFLY9ksMkKQ3CIiaBa3E3TrNRK2bOSZCgandindex=2.

5. https://agenciabrasil.ebc.com.br/politica/noticia/2014-10/mais-conservador-congresso-eleito-pode-limitar-avancos-em-direitos-humanos#.

6. The campaign even made available a website to combat fake news but was unable to keep up with the large volume of viral content. https://lula.com.br/tag/fakenews/.

7. https://www.diap.org.br/index.php/noticias/agencia-diap/88896-novo-congresso-veio-pior-que-a-encomenda (accessed May 2, 2022).

8. http://www.foprop.org.br/uploads/downloads/2021_10_11/Nota-Tecnica-ao-Parlamento-Brasileiro-Cortes-Orcamentarios_retificado.pdf (accessed May 5, 2022).

9. https://www.andes.org.br/conteudos/noticia/apagao-no-servidor-do-cNPq-compromete-dados-de-pesquisas-e-expoe-desmonte-do-orgao1 (accessed May 5, 2022).

10. https://www.gov.br/cnpq/pt-br/assuntos/noticias/cnpq-em-acao/informe-sobre-o-restabelecimento-da-plataforma-lattes (accessed May 5, 2022).

11. http://portal.sbpcnet.org.br/noticias/os-70-anos-do-cnpq-aniversario-em-crise/ (accessed May 6, 2022).

12. https://www1.folha.uol.com.br/poder/2022/05/violencia-politica-no-brasil-esta-matando-a-democracia-diz-relator-da-onu.shtml (accessed May 6, 2022).

13. https://www.portaldosjornalistas.com.br/organizacoes-pedem-garantias-para-a-liberdade-de-imprensa-nas-eleicoes-2022/ (accessed May 7, 2022).

14. https://www.tse.jus.br/imprensa/noticias-tse/arquivos/respostas-as-forcas-armadas-em-relacao-ao-processo-eleitoral-16-02-2022/rybena_pdf?file= https://www.tse.jus.br/imprensa/noticias-tse/arquivos/respostas-as-forcas-armadas-em-relacao-ao-processo-eleitoral-16-02-2022/at_download/file (accessed May 7, 2022).

15. https://time.com/6173104/lula-da-silva-trancricao/ (accessed May 7, 2022).

16. https://www.youtube.com/watch?v=USMQ9Nb3Ers (accessed May 8, 2022).

7

A Conversation with
Julietta Hua and Kasturi Ray

Feminism, AI, and Racial Technocapitalism in the Uber and Lyft Economy

NEDA ATANASOSKI

Julietta Hua and Kasturi Ray's *Spent Behind the Wheel: Drivers' Labor in the Uber Economy* (University of Minnesota Press, 2022) is a groundbreaking study demystifying the rhetoric that upholds app-based on-demand driving services like Uber and Lyft as convenient innovations for both drivers and riders. In the last decade, numerous media and political outlets have touted the technological disruptions to the global economy. This includes the spread of the so-called sharing economy exemplified by corporations such as Airbnb that market peer exchange. Although companies like Airbnb have undoubtedly changed real estate and rental markets, and Uber and Lyft have transformed the traditional landscape of hired driving, the novel argument that Hua and Ray develop in *Spent Behind the Wheel* is that the racialized and gendered scaffolding of devalued service work (in which they notably include driving) endures across capitalist modes and modalities of managing driving for hire.

While most of the chapters in this book focus on digital capitalism and sovereignty in the Global South, this chapter focuses on the impact of digitalization on working classes in the US, demonstrating many related and

100 | Neda Atanasoski

interrelated forms of digital precarity and power relations experienced by working classes in the Global South. The racial and gendered dimensions of augmented labor exploitation under digital capitalism described in Hua and Ray's book, especially as they pertain to immigrants from formerly colonized nations working in the United States, further exemplify the interconnectedness of exploitation under technocapitalism across the Global South and Global North. The point of these observations is to emphasize the need for solidarity across North and South. This is an increasingly important task as think tanks like the Brookings Institute argue that the growing gig economy in the US, where workers are choosing "flexibility," can be a model for the Global South.

One report, for instance, argues that in Africa, "gig platforms have the potential to provide a source of consistent work, and, with centralized governance and support, a pathway to reduce informality and boost productivity by leapfrogging informal economies. . . . The potential for gig platforms to provide a source of consistent work and centralized governance and support is even more exciting in Africa where platforms can leapfrog informal economies" (Grunewad 2019). In this context, it is critical to understand how the US model of labor precaritazation, or what Hua and Ray call "gigging," is being transposed onto Global South contexts that will further already entrenched global inequalities. After all, "Digital labour platforms do not have an equal presence across the world. While platform revenue is channeled to the Global North, labour is concentrated in the Global South. This is especially the case for web-based online platforms. [For instance], as of March 2022, India supplied 25 per cent of online web-based labour, yet in 2019–2020 represented only around 3 per cent of the global revenue from digital labour platforms" (Tony Blair Institute 2022). Paying attention to the entanglement of precaritization of labor across the US and Global South (included in the migration patterns that facilitate a "gigged" workforce) is critical to our understanding of popular sovereignty in the age of digital capitalism.

Contextualizing US Racial Technocapitalism as a Part of Global Racial Capitalism

Spent Behind the Wheel adds to the growing scholarly and political conversations of the last decade that develop feminist and critical race approaches to artificial intelligence (AI) under racial technocapitalism.

A Conversation with Julietta Hua and Kasturi Ray | 101

Activist and scholar Erin McElroy uses the term *racial technocapitalism* to name the accelerating conditions of racial dispossession under the technological updates to capitalist relations established over the last two decades (McElroy 2019).

Building on Cedric Robinson's original formulation of racial capitalism in the book *Black Marxism*, Jodi Melamed has argued:

> The term "racial capitalism" requires its users to recognize that capitalism is racial capitalism. Capital can only be capital when it is accumulating, and it can only accumulate by producing and moving through relations of severe inequality among human groups—capitalists with the means of production/workers without the means of subsistence, creditors/debtors, conquerors of land made property/the dispossessed and removed. These antinomies of accumulation require loss, disposability, and the unequal differentiation of human value, and racism enshrines the inequalities that capitalism requires. Most obviously, it does this by displacing the uneven life chances that are inescapably part of capitalist social relations onto fictions of differing human capacities, historically race. We often associate racial capitalism with the central features of white supremacist capitalist development, including slavery, colonialism, genocide, incarceration regimes, migrant exploitation, and contemporary racial warfare. Yet we also increasingly recognize that contemporary racial capitalism deploys liberal and multicultural terms of inclusion to value and devalue forms of humanity differentially to fit the needs of reigning state capital orders. (Melamed 2015, 77)

Following this definition, what is clear is that it is *not* the case that racism is an ideological supplement to capitalism. Rather, capitalism depends on diversification of exploitable populations (in the Global North as well as in the Global South). And if all capitalism is racial capitalism, it is important to consider and to dwell on the technological updates to racial capitalism that have occurred under the conditions of what some have called the fourth industrial revolution, the second machine age, digital capitalism, surveillance capitalism, platform capitalism—and what Hua and Ray term the Uber and Lyft economy. These various terms have all been introduced over the last decade to describe the social, economic, and cultural changes stemming from advancements in artificial intelligence, robotics, the internet of things, 3D printing, genetic engineering, and other technologies. We can think about GPS systems, Apple's Siri or Amazon's Alexa, algorithmic recommendations on platforms like Facebook or Netflix, or facial recognition systems as a part of these updates. We might put these terms under the umbrella of "technocapitalism"—or how scholars have been attempting to theorize what recent technological developments have meant for the operations of capital and labor. They are also terms that grapple with the rise of the so-called sharing economy and how it has shifted what we think of as labor, free time, and commodities.

One key shift to the future of work that the internet has introduced lies in the "what" and "how" of accumulation. While initial forays into internet capitalism were about mirroring the physical storefront in the internet landscape, the possibilities presented by the architecture of the internet leveraged the management and facilitation of user-participation as itself an activity that would accumulate for the manager (i.e., Google). As Gavin Mueller explains, "activity would produce data. . . . The data could be used to rationalize online behavior, extending the duration of activity within a platform and rendering it ever more productive and valuable. This was not democracy, but the transformation of the web into a distributed machine for the capitalist production of value" (Mueller 2021, 109). This logic of accumulation shifted value into the management, ownership, and analysis of (user) behavior: "With Google, all user behavior—every word in an email, every search, every mapped commute—becomes information that further improves the system, which is ultimately focused on selling advertising. This data is the property of Google, hoarded by the higher-ups in a company and used to extract value, with nothing delivered to those who produced the data but Google's services" (Mueller 2021, 110).

In a sense, though a platform company like Amazon.com looks like a traditional trader of commodities, what Mueller and others describe is a shift in where the value accrues; the "what" that enables accumulation is no longer the commodity being traded, or even the labor of the worker, it is the interaction of the user with the platform—and this is what platform providers then own. In other words, companies like Amazon, Google, and Uber accumulate precisely because they monopolize *how* users interact online. Managing and controlling the experience of being online, or the exchange of so-called peer services, itself becomes the locus of capital accumulation. The commodity or service is rendered secondary in this way; Amazon does not care about what is being sold on its platform by and to whom, just as Uber and Lyft do not care about drivers who provide rides (though for good measure, Amazon also still participates as a seller on its platform). Instead, the potential for accumulation lies in the control over facilitating the exchange itself. Manipulating and owning "user behavior" online is where the potential for accumulation sits, and this is nowhere clearer than in Uber's various tactics to manipulate the market for rides (Calo and Rosenblat 2018). In this way, the person's very being—how they interact and relate with others through the platform—becomes something to be owned and capitalized.

One of the main interventions that feminist scholars have made into analyses of technocapitalist relations is to foreground how emergent technologies and digital platforms have exacerbated and further invisibilized racialized and gendered labor. These approaches to technology, as Lauren Klein and Catherine D'Ignazio discuss in their book *Data Feminism*, come from a long history of feminist critiques of labor that goes unseen—service and domestic work, care work, and affective and emotional labor (D'Ignazio and Klein 2020). Racial technocapitalism thus continues the obscuring of and dependence on racialized labor that has long been a part of capitalist operations. In the context of platform capitalism, feminist criticisms can apply to the "ghost work" that still must sit at the heart of artificial and algorithmic intelligence that enables automating labor. In this case, the automation of labor, just as feminist scholars of domestic and household work contend, simply relies on the invisibilizing of the gendered human worker (Mueller 2021, chapter 3). Much of this invizibilizing happens to immigrant workers and workers in the Global South.

Technological shifts to the capitalist economy and the exacerbation of the racialized and gendered inequalities they have produced have only intensified during the COVID-19 pandemic. We might consider how the laboratory for technological futurity based in Silicon Valley startups paved the way for the technologized aspects of the COVID-19 pandemic. But, rather than technology freeing the privileged and the wealthy for creative tasks that accounts of the techno-revolution promised before the pandemic, in the present moment we see that these technologies deliver a reprieve from risk for those same privileged subjects. The freedom of the fully human subject became the freedom from risk.

Put otherwise, in 2019, technological platforms came to serve as risk management tools. At the level of platform capitalism, service workers like Uber and Lyft drivers shouldered the brunt of loss of income and care at the start of the pandemic as demand for services plummeted. Demand for other services, like food and grocery delivery, expanded, relying on growing precarious pools of gig workers. Staying home and not exposing oneself to risk by needing to work outside the home is now a luxury good. Meanwhile, the fantasy that the technological future is enchanted and doesn't need human workers has been further exposed. Take for instance the US grocery store chain Whole Foods (owned by Amazon), where at some locations during the pandemic Amazon shoppers would line up at a separate entrance before the store opened in preparation for surrogate shopping and fully contactless delivery to paying customers. The need for workers has, if anything, increased.

Naomi Klein, in writing about what she calls the pandemic shock doctrine, or the current incarnation of disaster capitalism, has argued that the pandemic is paving the way for

> a future in which, for the privileged, almost everything is home delivered, either virtually via streaming and cloud technology, or physically via driverless vehicle or drone, then screen "shared" on a mediated platform. . . . It's a future that claims to be run on "artificial intelligence" but is actually held together by tens of millions of anonymous workers tucked away in warehouses, data centers, content moderation mills, electronic sweatshops, lithium mines, industrial farms, meat-processing plants, and prisons, where they are left unprotected from disease and hyper-exploitation. It's a future in which our every move, our every word, our every relationship is trackable, traceable, and data-mineable by unprecedented collaborations between government and tech giants. (Klein 2020)

Focusing on surveillance capitalism and loss of privacy, Klein is suggesting that what she calls a permanent and highly profitable no touch future consolidated during this high-tech pandemic is a fascist one, and one that builds on a prior, more liberal-democratic selling of tech that led people to be fooled into accepting the fascist present. As Klein writes, "pre-Covid, this precise app-driven, gig-fueled future was being sold to us in the name of convenience, frictionlessness, and personalization." Yet concerns about loss of privacy and data extraction expressed by those who have always experienced themselves as fully human, fully free, or self-possessed individuals express the fear of becoming property that is a foundational threat within racial capitalism—not a new threat.

A Conversation with Julietta Hua and Kasturi Ray | 105

Alessandro Delfanti has argued that Amazon warehouses have long been sites where we see the imbrication of technology and the authoritarian tendencies in capitalism (Delfanti 2019, 39–55). Moreover, since the inception of the US settler state in genocide and chattel slavery, the consolidation of political liberalism and capitalism has relied on brute violence to secure its primacy. Rather than a reordering of things, we might apprehend the pandemic moment as an amplification of the everyday violence produced through the imbrications of liberalism and fascism within racial capitalism. Discussing the slipperiness of the category *essential worker* at the start of the pandemic, one reporter stated: "The pandemic's . . . immediate effect may be to illuminate the routine cruelties of more normal times. The [*New York*] *Times* . . . reported that immigrant farmworkers have begun carrying a copy of the DHS order identifying them as critical infrastructure workers, in case ICE or local police stop them. It won't protect them from deportation. They have long been essential, even as the cruelest elements of state power deem them illegal and disposable" (Leary 2020).

As Hua and Ray, as well as other feminist science and technology studies scholars, have argued, even as things seem to be changing at an exceptionally high rate, many of the racialized and gendered structures of exploitation have remained in place or have even been exacerbated.

Racialized and Gendered Exploitation of Gigged Workers

Of the many significant contributions of *Spent Behind the Wheel*, perhaps the most original and insightful one is that driver labor can best be understood as "gendered intimate service labor congruent with other, more traditionally legible forms of intimate service labor like household work" (5). While feminist scholars of reproductive and feminized labor have long theorized the kind of work that is purely meant to uphold and protect the value of certain kinds of lives (male, white, wealthy), Hua and Ray deftly show that assessing driving, a masculinized and racialized profession, as reproductive labor can extend the scope of feminist approaches to how feminized labor is devalued, and how this devaluing is essential to capitalist accumulation. By reframing driving passengers as attending to passengers, *Spent Behind the Wheel* showcases how driver lives are literally expended, their vitality extracted, even to the point of debility

106 | Neda Atanasoski

and disability due to their laboring conditions. Thus, in contrast to Uber and Lyft promotional materials that advertise freedom and flexibility for drivers, the book demonstrates that these apps are able to be lucrative ventures because they depend on devalued reproductive labor that enables the flourishing of consumer lives (who have the "convenience" of a ride at their fingertips).

Rather than replicate more commonplace assumptions that the interests of taxi drivers and Uber and Lyft drivers are diametrically opposed, Ray and Hua follow the lead of the New York Taxi Worker Alliance union and emphasize the shared experiences of taxi and gig drivers, as well as the relationship of these drivers to passengers, police and regulatory agencies, health and safety, and urban space. For instance, in the first chapter, Hua and Ray argue that social invisibility links the fate of the app gig driver to the taxi driver. In the case of apps like Uber and Lyft, the driver is rendered invisible by being cast as incidental to the technological innovation and improvement offered by the app itself, while in the case of taxi drivers, the unskilled (racialized) worker is cast as a threat necessitating regulatory measures. The chapter historicizes the medallion system and the mechanisms regulating the taxi industry and connects this history to an astute analysis of how Uber and Lyft have attempted to recast their business being not about driving, but about technology. Meanwhile, in both instances, the promise of self-ownership (of one's time, mode of transportation, and working conditions) belies the structures of debt, dependency, and exploitation that dispossess both gig and taxi drivers in equal measure.

One of the most insightful aspects of the book is its ability to track the centrality of property (as both the promise and condition of dispossession) to the work of driving. A particularly striking example of this is the second chapter, which moves from the account of the driving industry's assurance that drivers can have ownership over the conditions of labor (including vehicles and time) to the conditions for owning a whole person and their future potential. The chapter does so by turning to an analysis of insurance and risk. Connecting driving to broader conditions of racial capitalism, including the central premise of slavery as the inaugural condition of possibility for the flourishing of US capitalism, this chapter connects how insuring slaves (and their potential to work) preceded and informed the rise of industrial insurance. Industrial insurance, meanwhile, "transformed the value of work into the value of life" (57). In the context of driving, the chapter showcases how for both taxi drivers (recognized as workers) and gig drivers (who may not be), workplace injury and harm take a life toll that may manifest later in life and cannot be captured as a work-related injury that can be compensated through insurance.

The Conversation

NEDA: I'm very excited to have this chance to be in conversation with you, and by way of opening things up, I was wondering if you could tell me a little bit about what brought you together to write this brilliant and timely book, *Spent behind the Wheel*?

JULIE: Thank you for inviting us to be in conversation. Professor Ray and I are longtime colleagues. Some of our collaborative research emerged organically from our time together in San Francisco State University's Women and Gender Studies Department where we have both been faculty since 2006. This book brings together Professor Ray's prior work with labor organizing and domestic work and my own prior research on human trafficking and human rights. So generally, you could say that our interest is in informal economies and the politics of labor.

NEDA: Your first chapter is titled "It's Not the App." I know when you originally wrote this book, you were making a distinction between gig driving and taxi driving. In the book, you argue that it is important not to make these kinds of distinctions. How did you change your line of thinking on this?

JULIE: Yes, initially this started as a project about the surprising successes, gained through traditional labor organizing, by a taxi drivers union, the New York Taxi Workers Alliance, in New York City. For example, we write about the 2010 struggles of the taxi drivers around having health insurance access [in the US access to health care is facilitated through insurance tied to one's job]. That, according to one union activist, was an unlikely win for the drivers. Drivers did win the ability to create and control a health insurance plan tied to their employment, which had never before existed. Another recent win for the New York taxi union is in implementing a new citywide regulation in 2018 that would provide Uber, Lyft, and other gig drivers a basic minimum wage. In no other city (yet) have gig drivers been able to have a minimum wage. Now the union is working toward raising the minimum wage for all drivers, taxi and gig.[1] Once we started researching what was happening in New York City, we found that their

108 | Neda Atanasoski

work was speaking to the gigging of the industry; as their work shows, the union is just as interested in extending and protecting the rights of gig drivers as it is taxi drivers.

KASTURI: It's important to define what a gigged worker is. Gigged Workers Rising, a union based in California, understands gigged workers as those who work for corporations, but by way of apps—which means they are cut off from traditional employee recognitions and protections. You can go to https://gigworkersrising.org/ to learn more about the group. When work gets "gigged," we mean that workers get classified as independent contractors rather than employees so that infrastructural and other supports (like insurance) can be offloaded onto them. The Uber economy is the drive to gig all work.

JULIE: Right. So, the entry of Uber, Lyft, and other ride-hailing app companies into the New York City passenger ride industry all of a sudden created ride services not part of the traditional taxi industry. Initially, we had thought of them as sort of two related but separate [and potentially antagonistic] phenomena—taxi driver unionizing and ride-hailing apps disrupting traditional taxi services. But what we found very quickly was that many of the people who were entering the gigged driving economy were actually also taxi workers. And what we also further found were that many of the conditions of the work were shared. So whether you worked for a traditional taxi company or a ride hail gig company like Uber or Lyft, the way the work was structured and the toll it took on the worker was actually not that different. This is in contradistinction to all of the advertising from Uber and Lyft that presented these companies as somehow very, very different from taxis. So that's the origin of the project.

KASTURI: We really thought we would be writing just about taxis, and then we found, because of the actual work experiences on the ground, that we were talking about folks who drive for long durations. So, we saw how their experiences cut across the two sectors of the professional passenger driving industry—the formal taxi industry and the app based services.

NEDA: That brings me to my second question, which is if you can describe this moment that we're in in digital capitalism. I'd like to ask you about your choice of the term *Uber economy*. Why do you think Uber and Lyft emblematize the changes to capitalism and labor in the digital age? I'm

A Conversation with Julietta Hua and Kasturi Ray | 109

thinking specifically about what you term the "gigging of relations" that is emblematized by the ride app industry as well as your discussion in the introduction of the innovation of the digital economy as abstracting value from life processes themselves.

KASTURI: I think what we saw in the San Francisco Bay Area after the 2008 recession were a lot of folks who could no longer make ends meet. So this idea of the casualization of labor appealed to folks who also wanted to think of the downturn in their finances as temporary. However, those temporary, short-time drivers are a very small sector of folks who ended up driving for Lyft and Uber in the Bay Area. For these short-term workers, Uber allowed you to pretend you still had leisure when many other folks were severely underemployed; while others were being massively displaced, you still had capital investments like mortgages and car loans which, without gig driving, you could not pay off otherwise. But in the disruptions following the recession, there were whole swaths of people who were not just vulnerable but were ruined by the recession, who also became drivers, but long duration drivers. So the Uber economy took off during the recession, or took advantage of the recession, and what they were able to do was marshal a mass of employees that they didn't have to call employees.

So I think that was what I understood as the origins of the Uber economy: being able to capture this restless labor, and being able to put a spin on it as casualization. And in fact, the Uber economy has been seen by some as a corrective to what was happening in the larger market. But that rescue narrative is a part of Silicon Valley's cyber optimism, claiming tech innovations are cutting edge when, of course, we've had lots of companies swoop in and capture disenfranchised workers in different ways in the past.

JULIE: As Professor Ray pointed out, most of the drivers, especially in the early years with the gig companies, were actually full-time drivers, not just people who were working part-time. And when we did interview some part-time drivers, even they actually spoke to some of what that driving labor is, which is very much a kind of service labor. That is, the toll of attending to other people's needs, even in a part-time capacity, feels like full-time work. And so that's the feminist perspective that we took to it.

I feel like I didn't really answer your question about the gigging of relations. I suppose maybe it sort of looks like what a number of feminist

110 | Neda Atanasoski

scholars of domestic work have pointed out, which is that really it's about the work we do in an economy that is not just about commodities [but also about relations and services]. This is an economy that is actually about the human body, and the kind of efforts and energies (I think Professor Ray calls it exertions) of human life—where human life is itself both a productive source of capital accumulation and commodity.

KASTURI: There is something interesting happening with the way that labor is gigged, in the ways that the reproduction of the conditions of work is offloaded onto the driver, as we discussed a few minutes ago. So maintaining a clean car or cab becomes the task of the driver and entails expense. Comportment, too, is extracted from the driver as a form of unpaid labor that directly affects their job (in terms of earning tips and not getting a bad rating). Gig work makes these extractions okay because Uber and Lyft sell a key mystification of their drivers' labor—that it occurs during their leisure or "off" time while "real" waged labor occurs elsewhere. And the drivers who are helping out their peers by providing convenient rides are simply monetizing their leisure time. Besides the premise of this leisure time, Uber and Lyft also sell the idea that their drivers' cars are just commodities sitting idly in the garage when they could be used to make a buck. Their message is: that car that you're not using, why not do something with it on your Saturday, and make a little bit of money?

But this is a mystification because it actually is not leisure time that is being spent behind the wheel. And the cars may well be rented through Lyft or Uber themselves, through predatory loan schemes.

NEDA: That context is so helpful. Building on your answer, I'd like to ask you about your use and redirection of feminist analyses of care and reproductive labor in the book. Your choice of that analytic is really striking because you're talking about a population of drivers who are primarily not women. In fact, you argue in your book that perhaps it is a mistake to understand care and reproductive labor as *only* feminized labor. I'm hoping you could speak a little bit about why it's so important to understand gig driving work as reproductive labor, and also to ask whether the digital economy does allow us to see care and reproductive labor as not feminized or not only feminized in a way that we weren't able necessarily to see before.

KASTURI: For some political economists, reproductive labor has become synonymous with women's unpaid work in the household. But as feminist scholars of labor and law, we are concerned about how these terms—reproductive labor, women, unpaid work, the household—have become collapsed into each other. These terms often can only be defined through each other in a closed iterative discourse that does not consider how labor itself genders workers; for example, how the ideology of the patriarchal household demands different forms of labor from the subjects gendered within it (transactional or bartered labor from subjects socially constructed as girls and women; waged work from those constructed as boys and men). Further, this discourse does not easily admit sexual and gender differences, and thus enables the marking, for example, of trans identity as a threat to the family structure. When we argue that taxi drivers, who are workers mostly drawn from a population identified as male, are engaging in reproductive labor, we are not talking about the masculinization of reproductive labor. We are arguing that some work has always been done that required workers to expend their vitalities in the service of consumers of that labor; and while this extraction has resonances in the private home (and, indeed, passenger driving was a household labor), an intersectional analysis which foregrounds race places a great swath of reproductive labor outside the realm of women/household.

In this understanding of the power of labor to gender, we borrow from feminist thinkers like Chandra Mohanty, who asks us to not think about subjects of capital as preformed subjects, but rather as people who enter into different institutions through work, where their gender/racial intersectional identities then get translated into differential values. So, for example, in different markets, people become legible and differentiated as women when they do particular tasks. For example, take domestic work. If you are understood as a Filipina maid [in the US], you will automatically earn more than an African American maid. Because that labeling is very, very important in the nanny trade. We see that particular nannies get paid more depending on their perceived ethnic background, because ethnicity is supposed to correlate to gender values. If workers are understood as caring or selfless—that is, they care little about the wage—their wage actually increases. Filipina maids are said to be caring and childlike, and African American maids are said to be scheming (these values of course resonate with US colonialism and slavery, respectively). Their market value is a strange way that capital obscures and translates value. For domestic workers of course this value is institutionalized through different payment schemes by their employment agencies, who are invested in these labelings. Foregrounding intersectional understandings of gender, it was really important to us to not think of reproductive labor as always already done by subjects that were identifiable as women before they even entered these institutions that formed and created and marketed them.

We also understand that gender is fluid, right? Male, female, transgender are all intersectional identities that shift in context. It's really not that useful to use gender terms before we understand how they gain meaning in different sites of capital. So that's why we just didn't want to talk about "women's work." It just seemed, you know, more useful to avoid that mystifying shorthand and instead show the power of capital to translate gender and race into exchange value.

JULIE: I will just add that I think the "feminization of labor" as a phrase is important and useful to describe the uneven access to the labor markets that was primarily impacting women. Yet, conceptually, the "feminization of labor" can be limiting when feminization is taken to mean identitarian gender, for example, when the conversation just becomes about the gendered wage gap. Closing the gap, or creating parity for women and men workers, doesn't necessarily mean that labor exploitation goes away. So what we wanted to do is to think about gender power at work in shaping capitalism—the way it constructs value and distributes value to different kinds of exertions unevenly.

NEDA: So gender as an analytic versus identity, right?

JULIE: Absolutely.

KASTURI: Yes. I also think what we wanted to try and understand about the Uber economy, or the gigging of labor relations, is that it is part of a larger racial history. And this is really Professor Hua's argument: the moment of slavery was the inaugural moment in the US nation when lives, in the aggregate, got collapsed into work: when a particular population's value was based on the work that they could do for others and when ownership of such people was synonymous with ownership of their labor. The entirety of the overarching structures that designated and exerted complete control over this aggregate surplus population (slaves) provided a key engine for the US national economy. This was a revolution in labor identity and extraction, made possible through gendered, colonial, and racial logic. This logic was carried through the end of legal slavery, into the period of US Reconstruction [after emancipation in 1863], through the mechanism of life and worker compensation insurance. As Professor

A Conversation with Julietta Hua and Kasturi Ray | 113

Hua writes in chapter 2: "Slavery's logic of owning a person . . . also facilitated a concurrent logic [through insuring slaves] of owning future work potential and mitigating against the risk of losing this work potential. This logic . . . transforms the value of work into the value of life . . . [and is a] calculus that financializes life" (57–58). Drawing on the work of Dan Bouk, Professor Hua sees a repetition of the racial project of insurance in contemporary life insurance schemes:

> the direct use of eugenic records and phrenology to determine policy benefits . . . [take] as matter-of-fact the higher mortality rates and shorter life spans of Black Americans. . . . A Black life would require higher pay-ins by individuals seeking insurance, while garnering smaller pay-outs, benefitting the industry investors. . . . As [Michael] Ralph points out, what initially began as slave insurance in the postbellum period becomes Black life insurance now sold to the very person whose life is being insured. In this way, the industry extracts from Black lives both in the premiums now owed by Black insurance buyers and the financialized values generated almost exclusively for white owners of insurance-related investment products. (61)

Throughout our book we talk about how our understanding of reproductive labor in the US extends from the history of racial power consolidated through slavery and postemancipation. This racial power distributes differential value to differently racialized bodies, and extracts capital from this difference—especially from Black workers. Value comes from the extraction of their livelihood in the service of others. So to go back to Uber and Lyft, we heard a report from a driver about a passenger requesting a ride to the airport on the Lyft app, but once the passenger had entered her car, they asked her, the driver, to swing by Fisherman's Wharf first. In this scenario, because it's supposedly peer-to-peer driving, the app user feels free to ask for a special stop, but then the driver has to figure out if she can afford the time, the added resources (gas), and headache of pulling on/off the freeway to enter a busy tourist destination. And, of course, the ride has only been recorded and charged for the airport trip, not the extra stop. Anything that may happen to the driver while straying from the booked ride will be the driver's responsibility and may even violate the terms of the ride. The passenger may be treating the driver like their personal driver but the reality is that the driver works for Lyft. To smooth over these awkward expectations, the driver may have to perform extra emotional labor—absorb and deflect passengers' disappointment if you, the driver, decline; and comport yourself with eagerness if you accept. This is the mystification of gigging—supposedly, drivers' work is done at their leisure, drivers and passengers are simply out for a ride at the convenience of both—that hides the reality that all infrastructure is offloaded onto the worker, and reinforces the logic that you the worker is only worth what service you can provide.

Neda: To round out our conversation I'd like to ask you about some recent developments. In the United States 2021 was dubbed the year of the great resignation. On March 24, 2022, the *New York Times* ran an article about how New Yorkers ordering Uber would soon be able to choose a yellow cab through the app, and that this change was happening because of the labor shortage. So, in contrast to the context that led to your book, which was essentially people out of work making ends meet (as you stated at the outset of our conversation), right now there is a labor shortage. I'm curious what your thoughts are on this development.

Kasturi: Uber and Lyft have by now driven many local taxi companies out of business. It's as if they're hoping that if they completely crush the taxi industry, they can appropriate the labor of taxi drivers. And I think it's really damaging because we have to ask what does it mean to have taxi drivers on that app. Although it's not just the app, as we argue in the book, the app *does* collect surveillance on the driver, including how much time will a particular driver take to pick up a ride so we might toss more work at them. What are the habits of these drivers; what paths do they take that location services don't already know about? Taxi drivers have long challenged the installation of app-based driving aids. For example, taxi drivers have challenged the installation of Fast Trak (an electronic toll tag) in their cabs, not just for the added surveillance they bring to the driver, but for the ways it may cheat passengers who might feel obliged to pay the full price of a tunnel/bridge crossing, not knowing that taxis might receive a discount. But these services are nothing compared to the apps installed by Uber and Lyft. Their software programs, including location, are notorious. For example, their apps keep running and collecting data even when the user has closed the app (signaling that they want the services to end). Another concern comes in the wake of Proposition 22.

Proposition 22 is a California November 2022 ballot initiative sponsored by Uber and Postmates. This proposition sought to overturn a California state bill, AB5, that had protected gig workers by proclaiming that all workers were employees, not independent contractors, unless proven otherwise by their employers. AB5 was historic because it put the burden of proof for worker classification on the employer, not the employee. Prop 22, however, overturned that ruling, and created, in effect, a third class of laborer, the gig worker, who is neither an employee nor an independent contractor, but one who lies outside the recognitions and protections of either. Instead, gig workers will receive only what gig companies want to give them. Further, to ensure this aggregate designation, Prop 22 overturned the democratic process both by prescribing that any change to the proposition would require an impossible and unprecedented seven-eighths vote in the California state Assembly, and that the state of California itself would have to hire counsel to protect Prop 22 from any future legal challenges.

Prop 22 has met workers' calls for health insurance by building a scheme whereby workers' earnings can be pooled in a fund from which health costs could eventually be taken. If you work a certain amount of engaged hours, you might be eligible for some health credits. But some drivers are saying that once they get close to making that eligible amount, they stop getting rides or opportunities to earn further credits. So I wonder if adding taxi drivers to the pool of workers might dilute some of the benefits that these app drivers are supposed to get, if Prop 22 were to spread to New York. On the other hand, I think some union organizers are extremely excited to swell their numbers with Uber and Lyft drivers, presenting Uber and Lyft with a nightmare they have not yet imagined. And that's what we hope happens. Uber and Lyft, are you sure you want your drivers in such intimate contact with powerful taxi labor organizers? Good luck to you. It will be exciting for sure.

NEDA: I really can't thank you both enough for taking the time to have this conversation with me. I encourage everyone interested in the future of work in relation to technology to read and engage with your brilliant and important book!

Note

1. See https://www.nytwa.org/home/2022/2/11/weve-secured-a-53-pay-raise-for-all-nyc-uber-lyft-via-drivers-drivers-on-average-will-earn-3800-more-this-year.

8

On Coding Democracy, Popular Data-Equity, and Algorithmic Action

Notes from Brazil

ANDRE ISAI LEIRNER

This chapter draws the possibility of creating participative legacy structures. It argues that participative legacy building can be used to create community cohesion and generate *popular equity*. In turn, it positions citizen participation at the ontological core of public policies, including those based on artificial intelligence and being implemented for the management of smart cities.

It starts from the assumption, and seeks to demonstrate, that the collective will is something capable of formal structuring. It goes without saying that this is a wicked problem, which is why this text is in the form of an essay and not an academic paper. And, as is well known, wicked problems challenge disciplinary discretion (Head and Alford 2015).

This essay is structured, roughly speaking, in five parts. The first, "Notes on Smart Cities from the Perspective of the Global South," mentions the range of forms that the urban environment (aka cities) can acquire. The second, "Smart Cities as Social Communication and Control Ecosystems," is about the current centrality of technological systems in the production and management of the public realm. The third part comments on recent deployments of these control frameworks, that is, on "The Use of Artificial Intelligence in Electronic Government" in Brazil.

117

118 | Andre Isai Leirner

The fourth part offers remarks about such governance arrangements as being subject to the *control–performance* dilemma and the need to overcome it by granting power to the street level.

The fifth part states that the answer to the conditions presented above is essentially *techno-political* and reports the development of a *techné* whose effect is political and emancipatory. Finally, it argues that the deployment of a *servo-oriented teleonomic instrument* may bring to form an interactive, adaptive, and complex social environment, that is, the emergence of an embryonic form of postcapitalist economy.[1]

Notes on Global South Perspectives on Smart Cities

Urban space has undergone major transformations in recent decades. This concept, normally associated with the perimeter of a city, as opposed to a rural or forested area, today often comprises a constructed network that can take different forms. When established in order to connect contiguous cities, this network can constitute a built environment bringing together distinct urban centralities, which is called a metropolis. This denomination, however, is not necessarily applicable since cities often bring together different centralities and reach dimensions comparable to those of metropolitan arrangements. In turn, noncontiguous built arrangements can present a systemic behavior due to links of an economic, political, or cultural nature, and operate in an integrated way, constituting an urban environment of a broad, discontinuous, and dispersed nature, to a greater or lesser extent (Zuboff 2019).

This apparent paradox arises from the relationship between the aggregate population distribution in the built territory and its governance systems, used to manage common services offered to them. These systems, in turn, can be more or less centralized and territorially coordinated, and depending on their historical constitution, can establish different relationships within the federative scope—city, network of cities, metropolis, macro-metropolis, region, macro-region, and so forth.

Currently, the provision of urban services in these territories occurs through the incidence of socio-technical arrangements (Law 1992; Ekbia 2009), including those understood within paradigms such as smart cities, examined below (Chourabi et al. 2012; Picon 2015; Goodspeed et al. 2023).

In the Brazilian context, two additional conditions must be considered, and also the effects felt from their combination. The *first* concerns the unequal impact of extreme events in Brazilian cities. Extreme events have become increasingly frequent as a consequence of climate change. Floods and landslides in large urban centers have threatened urban infrastructure and city inhabitants. Risk scenarios and urban fatalities have been associated with irregular occupation of land, marked by urban illegality resulting from unequal access to public investments by vulnerable and lower-income segments of the population. The population residing in these precarious human settlements are more exposed to socio-environmental risks than those settled in more structured wealthy areas. These "announced disasters," therefore, cannot be seen as accidental, natural, or unpreventable, since in most cases they can be predicted and avoided (Jacobi and Sulaiman 2016).

The *second* condition concerns the inadequacy of current paradigms of smart cities to achieve the imperative of promoting human and social development in Global South economies. The absence of normative-technological alternatives of "smart" goods and services suitable for urban precariousness contexts is latent and well known, not to mention the inadequacy of such technological arrangements in promoting the *right to the city* in the face of social inequality (Verhulst 2018; Verhulst, Sandor and Stamm, 2023; Alizadeh and Prasad, 2023).

The interrelationship of these two factors allows us to affirm that, in the Global South, the effectiveness of "smart" urban management is related not only to the technological capacity of urban service delivery systems but also to the social distribution of risks arising from urban precariousness. Considering that there is a strong social dimension in what is understood as risk, aggravated by the vulnerability of populations and the physical context in which they are located, the question that arises is *how can these risks be managed while taking these populations into account? In other words, how can these populations be incorporated into the socio-technical and governance arrangements involved in offering smart urban services?*

Smart Cities as Social Communication and Control Ecosystems

Smart cities are urban agglomerations that use technology to collect environmental and social data to improve the quality of life for their citizens. Management systems in these cities aim to support planning processes, strengthen communities, and present mutual benefits by the sharing of common resources, subsidizing the implementation of agreements and shared goals, without relieving each citizen from their responsibilities. The International Organization for Standardization (ISO) 37105 standard goes even further and says that "cities and communities are systems composed of physical and social systems, and their interactions, and as such, guide and are guided by human behavior."

In practice, this entails a condition of mutual constitution between supply and demand for services. That is, in this process we witness not only the capture of people's reactions through technological devices and their treatment and processing by data models, but also the response offered by these systems in the form of service provision promoting in a continuous cycle the formation of patterns of variable supply of services deployed to the territory (Sunstein 2014).

The pattern resulting from this interaction framework allows both the emergence and induction of collective behaviors of a systemic-adaptive nature. The relationship between the social body and technological systems becomes, therefore, mutually constitutive, contextual, and dependent not only on the business models of which urban services are a part but also on the mediation processes designed for their operation and provision (Picon 2015; Zuboff 2019). In turn, the service supply may affect the territory in more or less centralized and territorially coordinated arrangements.

A wide variety of creative, expressive, and individualized forms of participation and engagement, activated digitally, can now be classified as everyday instruments of citizenship, activism, and political participation (Theocharis and Van Deth 2018).

Studies show that the use of these communicative instruments is crucial to reinforce values and symbologies associated with the identity of populations and communities. They also demonstrate that they have an instrumental role, as opposed to a structural function, in the processes of social transformation (Sartoretto 2015).

This means that they can mitigate, or worsen, information, engagement, and participation asymmetries without, however, significantly transforming the political or governance structures to which they are related. They operate between the cognitive-symbolic and socio-institutional dimensions (Lavalle et al. 2019) or, more broadly, between *life* and *system* (Baxter 1987).

To understand the functioning of a smart city, therefore, is to make contact with the infrastructural dimensions of urban services, communication resources, and data transmission that mediate relationships between beneficiaries and system components, measuring performance and impact. It is also, therefore, to make contact with the means and modes of production and purposes of the information involved in the management, maintenance, and support of these infrastructural systems (Zuboff 2015).

Getting in touch with these dimensions implies exploring design specification mechanisms, including decision-making rights regimes and accountability frameworks incorporated in these systems. Ideally, by doing so, it becomes possible to construct explanations understood and accepted by the parties involved, making the collective action processes that formulated them legitimate, instilling trust in these communities. In the extreme, we are talking about democratic governance (March 1995) and algorithmic accountability (C4AI 2022); in this regard, what mechanisms of representation can be used for the social control of these mathematical models?

The Use of Artificial Intelligence in Electronic Government

THE NARROWING OF PARTICIPATORY CHANNELS: EXCERPTS FROM
THE BRAZILIAN CASE

The way in which the use of artificial intelligence in electronic government is being implemented in Brazil has narrowed participatory channels. Examples show a notorious absence of mechanisms of collegiate governance and civil representation. This absence is striking in the regulatory and institutional framework that has been developed, a worrying omen of an equivalent future for other "developing" countries, and a premonition of colonization.

Law 14.129,[2] published just over a year ago, regulates electronic government in Brazil. This rule has within its competence "managing public policies based on data and evidence through the application of a data intelligence digital platform" (VII). Paragraph 2 states, "Scientific, technological and innovation institutions will be assured to access knowledge networks and the establishment of a permanent communication channel with whomever it fits within the federal agency responsible for coordinating the activities provided for in this article." It should be noted here that the term "whomever it fits" designates the indeterminacy of an accountability mechanism and the absence of a council, or collegiate representative body.

122 | Andre Isai Leirner

The Brazilian government recently published a *Guide to Public Governance Policy*.[3] The guide recommends that the social control of public policies be transferred to an ombudsperson (51), discarding any mention of public policy councils as they traditionally exist in Brazil. Nor does it recommend the implementation of a collegiate representative body as a means of external social control. In 2022, the Organization for Economic Cooperationn and Development published a white paper called *The Strategic and Responsible Use of Artificial Intelligence in the Public Sector of Latin America and the Caribbean* (OECD 2022). Here, again, there is no mention of or recommendation for implementing any social accountability mechanism or collegiate representative bodies.

Finally, Law 13.460,[4] which provides for the participation, protection, and defense of the rights of the user of public services of the public administration, leaves at the discretion of the ombudsperson and the public body the possibility and faculty of eventual constitution of any external social control mechanism, whether collegiate or not, and whose composition is also at the discretion of the ombudsperson in charge.

The legal-normative frameworks being implemented, mentioned above, position the ombudsperson (state bureaucracy) as the only mediation authority between society and public services with regard to digital public services, giving that entity absolute moral authority. It goes without saying that such a framework characterizes a narrowing of channels of participation and demonstrates an advance of an illiberal democratic practice in the governance criteria being adopted in the use of electronic government in Brazil.

Public policy councils have been important in the history of Brazilian and international democracy. Together with collegiate bodies, they have constructed narratives of historical and social representation, and consequently of moral and critical substance (Mezzaroba 2020).

MORAL ANOMIE OF MACHINES, THE IMPERATIVE OF HUMAN ACTION, AND OLD DILEMMAS OF REPRESENTATION

The critical and moral anomie of artificial intelligence (AI) and the need for human interference in the epistemic and cognitive modeling of these computational systems is something more than known. Even so, this theme is often absent in debates involving e-government and smart cities, whose underlying agenda is the intensive use of machines as resources for large-scale social mediation.

AI is not aware of what it does not know and, as a result, is unable to make judgments and moral hazard assessments, unless "instructed" to do so. AI is also not capable of dealing with socially complex situations, since AI operates from regularities and does not know how to interpret, or even value, exceptionalities (Trentesaux and Karnouskos 2022). In other words, a person facing the unknown is cautious, whereas in the same situation a machine simply ignores any danger because, for it, the unknown does not exist.

The debate around the mechanisms of representation and social control of these mathematical models, therefore, involves, in addition to a discussion about the potentials and limits of the use of AI, the debate about the elaboration of criteria and institutional mechanisms to regulate the production of data analytics.[5]

Various pathologies of representation in the regulation of AI can be overcome by the extensive and permanent renewal of members in their collegiate bodies. The path to be traced, therefore, is one that reconciles representative renewal and identity representation. The model offered by liquid democracy meets these requirements. In this delegative model an elected representative's seat may receive delegated agents in its place, allowing representative variation within a defined political, epistemic, and identity pattern (Blum and Zuber 2016). The model we present below, the *popular panel*, offers the same, but in broader terms.

This debate becomes even more complex when we focus on factors such as scale of participation and technology. Here is a rhetorical question whose answer would point to the utopian overcoming of the economic logic of exploitation and control: *Is it feasible to think of a networked state, connected to society? If so, how would it be possible to create a shared legacy of public and social action that would allow for the optimal and efficient allocation of social production resources in the territory, instilling community cohesion?*

Social Legacies as a Problem of Public Administration

The Need to Overcome the Control–Performance Dilemma

In capitalism, the allocation of resources aims to sustain strategies of material and human exploitation and systematically concentrate wealth. Central to this strategy is the promotion of alienation from work and territory and, consequently, from its productive legacy (Hochuli 2021). Moving forward in the formulation of an alternative model implies the consideration of specific aspects of the administrative rationality of the public sector. It is not just a matter of overcoming the alienation of work, but of creating an alternative rationality to the one existing in the private sector, a specific rationality aimed at optimizing the allocation of goods and services of common social interest.

Effectiveness often implies trans- and interdisciplinarity, incurring low fiscal performance. According to Rezende (2008), the core of this dilemma is the contradiction between fiscal control and the (economical) recognition of the conditions of execution—also called the *control–performance* dilemma, a problem of public administration carrying all the political and ideological burden that these terms may convey.

Considering that this debate currently involves information management policies, measures proposed by Singh (2020), such as asserting collective ownership rights over data and providing data and digital intelligence as public goods, constitute an essential path in solving such contradictions.

Truly overcoming the control–performance contradiction involves in addition, we argue, overcoming the alienation of work and its productive legacy at both the management and operational level. In possible consonance with Singh's perspective, one way to achieve this objective is to grant rights of societal participation to the popular realm (business control level). The following section present some examples of the application of models of societal participation rights (equity) that show that this may in fact be possible.

Another way, complementary with the latter, is to develop large-scale participatory processes (*operational level*) and, from that, databases (*legacy level*) that consolidate community cohesion around popular capital (*popular equity*). The Rio Doce case, presented below, offers an example of the successful implementation of these practices at an operational level and demonstrates the feasibility of constituting a properly structured shared social memory and legacy.

A Practical Application of Cumulative Preferential Participation: The Case of Rio Doce

Climate change is expected to provoke extreme events, affecting vast parts of the territory and their populations. The effects of these events will extend beyond administrative and economic boundaries, impacting in a multidimensional way on the well-being of populations. They configure

On Coding Democracy | 125

postnormal phenomena, emergent in nature and in constant transformation, events that challenge normality and prediction scenarios (Jacobi and Giatti 2014). In this sense, the study of the governance system implemented to mitigate the effects of the Rio Doce disaster is a rare opportunity for empirical observation of the application of *collective intelligence* resources applied in a highly complex context. We depart from a typical assumption arising from approaches centered on society and state interactions, that institutional changes in the state and public policies, on the one hand, and in civil society, on the other, are reciprocally determined, configuring governance patterns and conditioning the solution of problems that affect society in general (Skocpol 1992).

The case reported below shows an example of institutional design in which broad modes of participation were applied, allowing for incremental learning by means of collective intelligence (Wolpert and Turner 1999; Landemore 2017a). In the case we present, the collective intelligence mechanism used was the *popular panel* methodology, an interpersonal comparison and cumulative voting process (Bhagat and Brickley 1984) that was combined with collective action.

This scientific experiment puts to the test a techno-political resource employed by the means of action research (Santos, Galdeando, and Cardoso 2019). In turn, this involved the development of a *techné* whose effect was both political and emancipatory. In other words, this required the improvement of a servo-oriented (Simon 1990) teleonomic instrument (Resse 1994),[6] deployed as an adaptive complexity model (Holland 1992; Dooley 1997; Namatame and Iwanaga 2004; Leirner and Alves 2009) to self-organize collective discourses arising from rules of reciprocal relationships of participatory equality. Its deployment, as will be seen later, allowed the construction of a collective, dynamic, and complex sense of participatory claiming, from which a *data-oriented social accountability legacy*, arising from the participation on a large scale.

The collapse of a dam retaining Samarco's mining waste in 2015 had devastating effects on the Rio Doce surrounding communities. It is in this context that the research, Com Rio Com Mar Opinião Popular (With River With Sea—Public Opinion), was deployed, which sought to experiment and transfer social technologies to the inhabitants of the mouth of the river, by the sea, and thus favor policies for the recovery of that territory (Lavalle et al. 2021; Lavalle et al. 2019).

To implement the participatory process, contact was established with local communities and their leaders. The training workshops were the starting point for this process. In these workshops, the panel methodology was presented and the consultation cycle began. After a debating session, participants were invited to exchange impressions about their life conditions and expose their main concerns. They were, then, asked to write the raised concerns in small leaflets and to deposit them in a ballot box. This information was then processed, listed, and returned to the participants. This list was also distributed in a broader territory, expanding the reach of information circulation, allowing the participants, old and new, to further engage in debate either by submitting new proposals or by voting on existing ones.

Proposals were identified but anonymous. The number of votes per day on each proposal was also limited, framing a practice of interpersonal comparison. The realization of successive voting and proposal cycles, in turn, allowed participants to critically position themselves with respect to the results. In a continuous cycle, this process of stimulus (voting) and response (result) created a systemic-responsive dynamic of collective action sensitive to the environmental context. This was manifested in the list of collective priorities, whether they were interpreted literally, as proposals, or, more broadly, as specific themes or subjects. In this experiment, this effect was observed in a multiscale and multithematic scope, expressing an autopoietic nature, that is, of a collective self-organized body responsive to environmental conditions (Maturana and Varela 2012; Hernes and Baker 2003).

Figure 8.1. Newspaper for circulating results and registering rights. *Source*: Adrian Gurza Lavalle and Euzeneia Carlos, eds., *Desastre e desgovernança no Rio Doce: Atingidos, instituições e ação coletiva* (Rio de Janeiro: Garamond, 2022), 338.

On Coding Democracy | 127

The maturity of this process is reached when (1) debate and discussion reach sufficient specificity to address a collective vision for the future and inform shared implementation strategies and tactics, and (2) a

Table 8.1. Top Two Priorities Voted by Muncipality, Espirito Santo State

Place	Most Voted	Percent	Second Most Voted	Percent
Colatina	Participation in the collection, analysis, and dissemination of studies of the water table	17.92	Guarantee the right to potable water	10.23
Serra	Recognize unrecognized impacted areas in the sea, lakes, mangroves, rivers, and springs, especially in the Serra region, including all productive activities	27.97	Participation in the collection, analysis, and dissemination of studies of the water table	17.68
Vitoria	Generation of work, employment, and income programs in other areas such as tourism, surfing, crafts, culture, and so forth	16.98	Generate work and income alternatives for fishmen, such as fish farms, and support fishermen's organizations oriented toward productive fishing arrangements	15.34
Linhares	Basic health clinic with complete equipment, ambulance, and basic pharmacy	17.32	Generation of work, employment, and income programs in other areas such as tourism, surfing, crafts, culture, and so forth	9.40
São Mateo	Basic health clinic with complete equipment, ambulance, and basic pharmacy	18.98	Guarantee the right to potable water	10.11

symbolic identification of users to the panel medium/mechanism occurs. This becomes an organic process of communication between spheres of deliberation or arenas of collective action and the collective body of contributors (social accountability), or both.

The process in Rio Doce received 6 months of preparation and was conducted for 18 months, during which it brought together 3,483 individual participants from 5 municipalities, who made 507 proposals prioritized by 23,990 votes. Results made it possible to assess both proposals and preferred themes, over time, by theme and scale of location (figs. 8.2 and 8.3). The circulation of newspapers containing excerpts from the shared database, in turn, promoted the identification of populations with the fight for rights and created social cohesion in the region (fig. 8.1). In turn, this allowed the formation of working groups composed of those affected, the Federal Public Ministry, the Public Defender's Office, municipal departments, and universities, which worked on data processing and the formulation of specific reports based on the gathered data.[7] This process was led by the Rio Doce Academic Consortium research group (www.comriocommar.com.br).

Similar work was developed for the Environmental Education Plan of the Paraíba do Sul River. In this case, the dynamic brought together

Figure 8.2. Preferred theme by municipality. *Source*: Gurza Lavalle and Carlos 2022, 34.

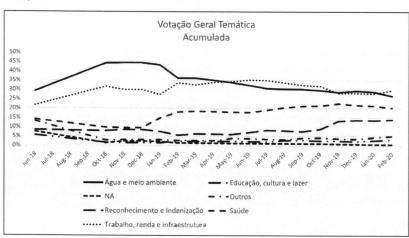

Figure 8.3. ES: Collective vote/theme. N = 23.990. *Source*: Gurza Lavalle and Carlos 2022, 76.

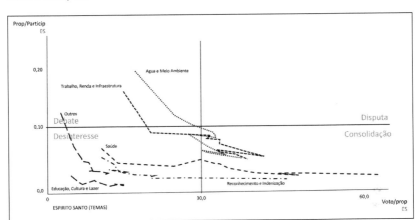

201 participants from 160 entities and 34 municipalities. The H. H. Fauser Institute organized and facilitated the process, receiving 137 proposals prioritized by 1,308 votes.[8]

The case of Rio Doce, in particular, portrays an example of collective intelligence operationalized through interpersonal comparison and cumulative voting. The periodic collection of beneficiary perceptions gave rise to assessments of the environmental conditions of the territory. In turn, demand aggregation oriented the making of programs.

The communication and information system deployed was one of the cohesive elements of these process. The permanent circulation of information and the possibility of different communities being able to see their agenda of demands, and that of the others, in evolution, allowed, in both cases, a collective prefiguration of the territory, that is, a broad visualization of the collective voice and the conditions of the territory, giving rise to a broad process of debate about its possible future.[9]

This example demonstrates the possibility of capturing collective preferences and constituting a topology of social demands—a topology that makes it possible to compare thematic or general demands, at a local or global scale, and at different time scales. This makes it possible to monitor and evaluate priorities and the performance of resource allocation in an integrated manner. This methodology of social reading triggers debates

130 | Andre Isai Leirner

with new modes of economic and financial accounting for social and environmental governance (Bebbington, Brown, and Frame 2007; Camargo 2022) and, with debates about the rationality of public administration, in overcoming the control–performance dilemma (Rezende 2008).

This is a concrete example of overcoming the alienation of information production and creating a common data legacy for social cohesion. The participatory process, therefore, operated as a political-pedagogical instrument and gave rise to the construction of a collective vision of that territory, including an institutional registering of local battles for human rights.

Preferential and Cumulative Participation and Social Data Accountability as a Community Cohesion Technology

ON MORAL CHOICE AND DILEMMAS OF COLLECTIVE ACTION

In the cases above, the *collective will* was expressed by the aggregate vote. This expedient allows scenarios in which majorities can impose themselves on minorities, even in the face of the vote being accumulated over time. This scenario, of majority imposition, can be avoided by applying a criterion of data collection and interpretation, which, in turn, constitutes an action of moral judgment.

In the work of Rio Doce, portrayed above, the interpretation of the database and the aggregation of demands were carried out by a collegiate of representatives from the affected population and other stakeholders, such as the Federal Public Ministry, the Public Defender's Office, universities, and municipal secretariats.

This path points to future applications where collective arrangements may either be composed from random choice expedients (mini-publics) or constituted by specific or contextual collegiates, making use of different criteria of representation and allocative prioritization. Although certain collective identities are easier to form and identify, others are more complex and subtle and will require more intense or elaborate processes of representative construction.

In practice, despite applying popular choice, the deployment of collective action expedients reproduces representation dilemmas characteristic of democratic governance that are still unresolved today. The mitigating factor, in this case, is that the basis for collective action is a popular demand,

On Coding Democracy | 131

expressed in voting, and not only the representatives' perception of their own reality. Considering that in societies with a high degree of inequality, this nondifferentiation results in influence from the most powerful and rich over the representative process, making their interest "the common interest" (Young 2002), this type of expedient already presents progress toward a more equitable and egalitarian expression of the social field.

Are there other paths to democratic legitimacy? We present below a soon to be empirically tested alternative to the path outlined above. This latest example makes use of algorithmic resources but preserves the prerogative of moral choice in the hands of citizens. In this scenario, the moral choice also happens at the moment of proposals and voting, and not only at the moment of analysis and judging of the vote counting. The example of Rio Doce addresses issues of bounded rationality (Simon 1990), the possibility that deliberation can influence citizen views and make them more likely to engage in future deliberations (Burkhalter, Gastil, and Kelshaw 2002, 416–18), producing higher quality knowledge and decisions, and more legitimate outcomes.

Hence, we start from the assumption that the free possibility of proposal, choice (vote), and association is enough to guarantee identity self-determination to diverse and plural interests. Further, the account-able algorithmic computation of choices can configure a collective moral choice and, by doing so, may mitigate agency dilemmas (Emirbayer and Mische 1998) that arise from the information asymmetry existing in representation systems.

As a result, there are limits to the likely oppression of minorities by majoritarian interests: one specific mechanism for controlling major-itarian tendencies is the *accumulation of votes on propositions over time*, as mentioned above, another is the accounting of this computation by the *accumulation of votes per person* over time. In turn, this opens the democratic landscape to interesting possibilities.

Proposing and voting anonymity create conditions for free affiliation between subjects and agendas. In turn, this allows the voting agglutination around narratives whose content motivates the participants' engagement. The dissolution of collective action does not affect the data's representative validity, either qualitatively or quantitatively, since the participants' choices are reflected in the voting on existing propositions.

Multiple preferences can emerge, coexist, dilute, and transform as a vote accumulates over time, and collective preferences change. These convergences can also occur in conditions of *disinterest, dispute, debate,*

132 | Andre Isai Leirner

or *consolidation* of the agenda (fig. 8.4 above).[10] Also, the tally of votes accumulated by proposal and per person can be calculated for daily averages, which allows the measuring of the probability of consensus on a proposal, or theme, a continuous ratio with a maximum value of one for consensus and zero for dissent.

Different combinations of vote per day ratio can, however, produce the same resulting number, indicating the same level of support for a proposal. With such metrics, it is possible to map and compare consent (distribution of choice) and purpose (strength of choice) both in general and specific terms and observe the perception of emergent social feeling arising from territories and parts of society.

In an unequal country a policy of linear incidence, such as a fixed ratio per person, can offer different results. If it is a tax, it has a smaller impact on high-income strata, while if it is a place in school, it implies a redistributive action of education resources. This shows how sense is context dependent to meaning in a data architecture and illustrates the moral nature underlying these informational processes. Hence, the need for collective action and social control for governing these systems.

Thus, we do not propose either the overcoming or the elimination of collective action, or any deliberative *loci*, by technology. We do advocate, however, that agenda making happen with contributions from within the popular realm, nurturing the deliberative arena, new and traditional ones, in constant and mutual constitution. It's a scenario where the popular realm changes and is changed by the political deliberative sphere and where permanent information feedback loops powered by technology and algorithms, parameterized by moral evaluation criteria arising from the political democratic realm, may shape efficient allocative action responsive to popular voice.[11]

The constituting of a quasi-autonomous popular-agenda space brings representation and collective will dilemmas to the foreground and creates a counterpoint to institutionalized political power struggles. Thus, this proposal adopts the perception that deliberation is capable of organizing the procedural body of political communication (Gastil and Black 2007) and, by doing so, gives centrality to the political and pedagogical nature of participation, essential resources for the construction of moral judgment in the democratic process.

Thus, this proposal is not about overcoming democracy, but about unfolding it, turning it more accessible and transparent so that it can fulfill its social and emerging working nature in the context of mass society and distributed communication.

On Coding Democracy | 133

Technology as Means of Scaling Up
toward a Postcapitalist Market Economy

The Rio Doce experiment collected demands and votes from ballot boxes and votes. The voting had, nevertheless, to be fed into a system. That led to the possibility of transcription errors and other human mistakes. Extremely simple voting rules minimized error: each user would be anonymous but would have an identification. He or she could make as many proposals as they wanted, but vote only for nine different proposals a day, every day. In this case, the votes would be entirely cumulative, and not cumulative per a limited amount of time.

The algorithm deployed was a guarantee of egalitarian opportunity and information transparency, fostering democratic coherence. These rules, and their easy understanding, helped sustain the feeling of popular trust in the process. The rules were simple (equal number of opportunities for proposals, access to information and voting, for all participants), and immediately understood and accepted by the most vulnerable people. In other words, even without programming, a "code of conduct prescribing participation rights" was written, that is, a "democratic algorithm" was used.

In practice, the case of Rio Doce constituted a stock of popular demands: the population had the opportunity to create, choose, and vote on future options, made by each participant, creating a common data legacy and a feeling of trust and social cohesion. This common vision of the future, in turn, informed the reports that were prepared and forwarded to the authorities.[12]

We believe that for small-scale communities this expedient can be done manually, as happened in Rio Doce. However, in the case of larger, more complex, and eventually more dispersed populations, the use of technology is a natural step. Thus, in future cases, a specific technical body (bureaucracy) can teach, disseminate, and lead the process, including formal procedures for external control, coherent with that proposed by Singh (2020) and Page (1996, 6).[13]

Considering that the interpersonal comparison technique here deployed is used for price formation, there is a possibility of establishing a real market system around popular demand. To confer solid normative substance to popular participation, a financial value can be assigned to each vote/support, whether this value comes from one's pocket or from tax incentives. We are talking about the possibility of creating public-private-popular partnerships. In these partnerships, the major portion of the nonstate contribution would come from popular contributions, which in combination with private or state contributions would constitute the societal design of the enterprise. The social control (social accountability) of the investment, in turn, would be carried out by the population or community involved, or by both.

Citizens can invest portions of their tax in a project close to their home and oversee the investment they have made with their neighbors. They can choose from many public-private-popular partnerships, creating an investment portfolio, and earn remuneration from the output. The state acts as guarantor, as in a public-private partnership, and the jurisprudence of public and private operations guarantee execution.

This proposal expands citizen rights through the banking of social participation, a measure whose inevitable consequence is the radical expansion of the economic base and a change in planning paradigms. It's a meeting between participatory social technology—where social investment is collectively arbitrated—and capital agglutination architecture, such as that of a *no-loss lottery*,[14] where depositors cluster future options with satisfactory return and minimized risk. In this case, it's a system of popular capital (*popular equity*) in which transparent and open results are part of the logic of collective aggregation, as in stock exchanges, and only employ inclusive and democratic equity rules, aimed at social and environmental development.

The attentive reader, however, would ask in whose custody is the data in this context? It is well known that in the information economy data custody is the most valuable strategic asset. Singh (2020) proposes that these assets be collectively owned, which leads to the creation of enterprises like the exploitation of public goods, only in this case the resource exploited would be social behavior. This solution overcomes the dilemma of unilateral exploitation for private purposes, but not necessarily for corporate purposes. Thus, additional layers of data guardianship need to be established. We are talking about user-owned wallets capable of intermediating citizens and technology providers, whether private or state-owned.

Considering that the centralization of a user data repository would offer the intermediary entity (*broker*) the same surveillance and exploitation privileges currently granted to governments and large corporations in the surveillance economy, the data should be under the custody of the user. That technology already exists. DeFi (decentralized finance)[15] markets already operate this way, and in open source, in the intermediation of cryptocurrency. Similar solutions are also being developed for wider use,

On Coding Democracy | 135

in proprietary code,[16] and will soon constitute a new market paradigm of an equity participation economy.

Far from being utopian, this proposal points to a pragmatic path. Far from being a revolutionary one, it is an antirevolutionary one, as it does not break, but hacks and appropriates for social purposes instruments already in use. Likewise, it does not propose a break with profit-making, but points to the possibility of a radically distributive association endowed with strict social control.

This work offers arguments that the use of adaptive-complex models applied to democratic participation algorithms allows the emergence of collaborative economies and the construction of *social accountability data legacies* on a large scale, giving rise to the possibility of formation of postcapitalist forms of economic organization.

This hybrid model of participation and public funding can be written in the form of process and programmed in computer language.[17] This is not democracy written in code but a scalable solution that incorporates democratic principles in its design framework. It is, thus, an outline for environmental, social, and governance policies for cities and their data systems (smart cities) and also a design proposition aligned with the *humane tech agenda* proposed by Harris (2019). It places citizen choice at the center of public policy governance, fulfilling rights to expression, free association, and the inalienability of human moral choice.[18] Thus, it seeks to outline alternatives to e-government policies instrumentalized by artificial intelligence and behavioral economics (Sunstein 2013), not necessarily by replacing them, but by repositioning them within a paradigm of democratic production of social data.

This proposal is an attempt to show the power of utopias to frame new technologies of collective intelligence as opportunities to expand social participation, protect the environment, and realize the collective potential of our society. Thus, coding democracy is not about transforming democracy into a code, but designing social services and common social legacies taking into account democratic relationships, and by using code. We hope many more will come.

Notes

1. Harvey's critique of postcapitalism notes the collective provision of goods and services and a collective change of mind, allowing alternative capital mobilization and new perspectives of economic and sociopolitical configuration (2020).

2. http://www.planalto.gov.br/ccivil_03/_ato2019-2022/2021/lei/l14129.htm.

3. https://www.gov.br/casacivil/pt-br/centrais-de-conteudo/downloads/guia-da-politica-de-governanca-publica.

4. https://www.in.gov.br/materia/-/asset_publisher/Kujrw0TZC2Mb/content/id/19141395/do1-2017-06-27-lei-no-13-460-de-26-de-junho-de-2017-19141216.

5. Challenges to effective representation through collegiate bodies include the independence and autonomy of the regulatory body (Lima 2022; Newton 2022), legitimate representation of societal interests through mini-publics (Fung 2007; Romão Netto and Cervelini 2021), mini-publics' difficulty in embodying historical patterns of social struggle or in the gestation of emancipatory epistemologies of political collectives (De Faria 2020), cognitive exhaustion (Hong and Page 2009; Landemore 2017b), and self-limitation (Cohen and Arato 2000, 134–35).

6. Teleonomy is applicable because it designates a quality of the system of relationships being deployed (algorithm), and not the behavior arising from the interaction by its use (Resse 1994).

7. www.comriocommar.com.br.

8. https://ihhf.org.br/.

9. The work addresses nonelectoral modes of democratic control, and dialogues with new conceptions of collectivity (De Faria 2020) and with methodological paths of militant research (Bringel and Varella 2016).

10. See the Vocalization and Convergence quadrant in Lavalle et al. 2021 and Lavalle et al. 2019.

11. According to Chambers (2021), mediated communication of the broad democratic public sphere can be understood through the lens of deliberative democracy only if we adopt a systems approach to deliberation, though often dividing labor between ordinary citizens and experts (knowledgeable elites). In response, one may turn to Jürgen Habermas and his idea of a feedback loop.

12. The work carried out in Rio Doce (Lavalle et al. 2021; Lavalle et al. 2019) provides empirical evidence that participation can increase citizens' deliberative communication skills and identification of populations with their community (Burkhalter, Gastil, and Kelshaw 2002, 413–15, 419).

13. Page (1996, 6) argues that in mass society the complexity of the public space requires a "division of labor" between the "mass audience" and "professional communicators."

14. See https://decrypt.co/resources/what-is-pooltogether-the-no-loss-crypto-lottery-explained.

15. See, for example, https://www.pods.finance/.

16. See https://dwave.ai/dwallet-personal/.

17. For open code, see www.priorize.net.

18. This work is also inscribed in the debate about the inclusion of publics in algorithm-assisted deliberation (Shen et al. 2022).

9

Participatory Institutions, Digital Technologies, and Democratic Crises

BENJAMIN GOLDFRANK AND YANINA WELP

Revolutionizing democracy by including citizens in decision-making processes and making government more transparent and accessible in new ways was one of the great hopes of the 1990s. Thirty years later, the focus in much of the Americas and Europe is concentrated on impeding democratic backsliding. Even before the COVID-19 pandemic, the level of satisfaction with democracy in 2019 reached its lowest point ever across the globe, and the Latin American region scored worst (Segovia, Pontarollo, and Orellana 2021, 418). While in the 1990s the literature on citizen participation centered on understanding its democratizing potential, today we might ask the opposite question: Did the participatory wave and the rise of digital communications technology contribute to the erosion of democracy? With citizens growing increasingly apathetic and detached (with variations and exceptions, of course), many scholars, activists, and political entrepreneurs identified the introduction of new technologies in political processes and the incorporation of new participation mechanisms as two key—and sometimes overlapping—ways of increasing transparency, legitimacy, and citizen engagement. At the time, some viewed the expansion of participatory institutions and digital technology with either unfounded optimism—imagining a global interconnected direct democracy—or unrelenting gloom, predicting a cybernetic nightmare or unmanageable mob rule. In 2023, what assessment can we make?

138 | Benjamin Goldfrank and Yanina Welp

While it is obvious that the world remains far from the utopian vision of digitally connected participatory democracies, assessing where we are and the prevailing direction of change is not clear, as technological change proceeds rapidly and with multiple and often unpredictable effects. Take, for example, Pippa Norris's influential article "Preaching to the Converted" (2003) about the effects of websites for political parties. Norris demonstrated that, rather than amplifying political participation by incorporating the previously excluded, digitalization was increasing the distance between those who were already politically active (and already counted on digital tools like blogs and email to make their voices heard) and those who were now even more disconnected from politics. Just a few years later the panorama changed radically with the rise of social media, which have had a powerful double effect, changing the prior trend. On one hand, right-wing extremists pushing disinformation and "fake news" have found fertile ground for fomenting their views. Social media have turned out to be ideal platforms for authoritarians to spread extreme views and false narratives in order to attract followers, as the examples of Donald Trump using Facebook and Twitter or Jair Bolsonaro using WhatsApp groups and Telegraph show. On the other hand, social movements focused on addressing climate change and advancing racial and gender equality have also been able to amplify their voices and engage new activists through social media, as the experiences of Fridays for Future, Black Lives Matter, and Ni Una Menos (Not One Less) demonstrate.

If new digital technologies and social media have allowed so-called influencers and political leaders to spread (dis)information to their followers faster, often bypassing political parties, while simultaneously facilitating collective action by social movements, what happened to institutional participation? Our chapter tries to answer this question by drawing on our own work and that of others in the past couple of decades, with a focus on Latin America. While we pay some attention to strictly digital mechanisms of participation, we focus especially on the analysis of whether and how digitalization has affected other participatory institutions and the overall effects, if any, on democracy. Here we will argue that rising experimentation with participatory institutions is not responsible for the erosion of democracy in the digital age. There was, however, a too optimistic view of what participation could produce, while the constraints under which participatory institutions were developed were underestimated. This explains why they were not able to minimize democratic erosion; thus, we will argue in favor of better designed and implemented institutions

Participatory Institutions, Digital Technologies, and Democratic Crises | 139

of participation. Notice that we say better participatory institutions, not simply more, because we would argue that just "more" can serve to weaken, distract, or diffuse social movements.

We propose here that, first, the institutions of participation activated have been mostly limited in their effects on democracy and frequently controlled by political incumbents in ways that reduce the impact or autonomy of participants. However, second, even if limited, these institutions can and sometimes do have positive, democracy-enhancing effects, and could be expanded to enhance popular sovereignty in the Global South. Such effects are more likely under certain formal conditions, mostly related to their institutional design, and informal conditions, such as political actors' behavior and acceptance of rules, among others. Digital participation shows a similar path but with an even more reduced impact and more weaknesses in their institutional designs and implementation.

The rest of the chapter is structured in three sections. The first briefly reviews the literature on the emergence and main characteristics of the key participatory institutions and the rise of digital initiatives; the second analyzes a selection of the most widely used and touted forms of participatory institutions and their interaction with digitalization; and the third offers our final reflections.

Debating Participatory and Digital Innovations

Since the 1980s, the Latin American region has pioneered the expansion of institutions intended to increase public participation beyond regular elections. Whether labeled "democratic innovations" or "participatory democracy," the initial (and, for some actors, ongoing) goals of these institutions included the revitalization of democracy by providing an answer to increasing citizen distrust in formal, elite-driven politics and representative institutions. The focus on participatory institutions aims to engage citizens in decision-making processes centered on specific communities or city districts (e.g., participatory budgeting), on nonbinding deliberation (e.g., many forms of citizen audits and assemblies), and on binding decisions (e.g., referendums) (Abers 2000; Cameron, Hershberg, and Sharpe 2012; Font, Wojcieszak, and Navarro 2015; Pateman 2012; Ruth-Lovell, Whitehead, and Yelp 2017).

The diversity of mechanisms and practices has led to many studies with sometimes contradictory assessments identifying participatory institutions as a driving force promoting authoritarian populism (Rhodes-Purdy 2015; García Guadilla 2008); as a means of citizen empowerment, democratic deepening, and improving well-being (Dagnino, Olvera, and Panfich 2006; Goldfrank 2011; Wampler, Sugiyama, and Touchton 2020); as symbolic exercises of scarce value or as smokescreens (Welp and Soto 2021); or even as tools for polarization and manipulation (Balderacchi 2015). Something similar has happened regarding new technologies, where studies are divided between those that highlight an instrumental use (i.e., manipulation) and those that emphasize the capacity to boost direct democratic participation (Weyland 2012; Morozov 2009; Castells 2009). These contradictory conclusions are due to both some scholars' perpetuation of myths related to citizen participation and to the fact that different participatory institutions operate in different contexts, using different rules, and with differentially motivated political actors driving implementation (Zaremberg and Welp 2020; Goldfrank 2021).

Participatory institutions include different mechanisms that can be classified according to who can participate (e.g., individuals or civil society associations) and how they participate (e.g., by defining the agenda, or through deliberation, consultation, elaboration of proposals and decision-making, as well as implementation and oversight). There are mechanisms whose goal is to complement electoral representation by engaging the public in the regular process of policymaking, for example with agenda-initiatives (Ruth-Lovell, Whitehead, and Yelp 2017). Others could have a more disruptive effect on the political system, for instance when an abrogative or a recall referendum can be addressed to veto a law approved by the parliament or to remove an authority before the end of his or her term (Lissidini 2012; Ruth-Lovell, Whitehead, and Yelp 2017). There is even more diversity of forms, as shown by the deployment of communal councils with the capacity to directly manage budgets, as seen in Venezuela (Garcia Guadilla 2008); the implementation of public policy conferences and councils, as seen in Brazil (Romão, Lavalle, and Zaremberg 2017); the activation of participatory budgeting, as seen globally in thousands of cities across more than forty countries (Dias, Enríquez, and Júlio 2019); as well as the development of new technologies to promote citizen participation (Breuer and Welp 2014).

The diffusion of information and communications technologies (ICTs) was initially expected to promote the growth of democracies, increase individual democratic participation, and improve democratic governance. In practice, however, such expectations about the digital age have proven to be overly optimistic. Authoritarian regimes have mostly succeeded in blocking ICTs they deem dangerous to their own persistence. And positive

Participatory Institutions, Digital Technologies, and Democratic Crises | 141

correlations between ICTs and democracy may be best understood in the opposite direction; that is, democratic contexts are more prone to develop the democratizing possibilities of ICTs (Groshek 2009).

The effects on individual behavior are mixed. Anduiza, Jensen, and Jorba (2012) discuss the implications of digital media for political engagement along three main dimensions: *political participation*, defined as actions taken by citizens to influence political outcomes; *consumption of political information*, which is particularly relevant in contexts where trust in the reliability of mainstream media reporting is lacking or where mainstream media are subject to heavy state censorship; and *political attitudes*. According to these authors, while the increase in digital media use appears to have little effect on political attitudes, it results in increasing the prior gaps in participation and information consumption between those who are already politicized and those who are not. In a review of sixty studies of the effects of the internet and social networking websites on political participation, Casteltrione (2015) finds mixed results as well, with scholars divided between those who find that digital platforms have a positive effect on participation, a negative, demobilizing, effect, and a "normalizing" effect that reinforces already existing patterns of participation; several studies reviewed find differing effects that depend on the type of technology or the type of participation.

The use of ICTs by Latin American governments is widespread, but with varying effects on the quality of democratic governance and often serving to reinforce previous differences and trends. All national governments in the region and many subnational governments have developed government portals and have strategic or action plans, or both, to further expand their online activities. Although with many particularities, while e-government (the use of ICT to improve the efficiency and quality of the public administration) is well established on government agendas, e-democracy (understood as the use of ICT to increase citizens' access to information and open new channels for participation) has an uncertain place given the limited data available (Breuer and Welp 2014). While ICTs were viewed as potentially most valuable for increasing government transparency, in fact the rise of ICT usage by governments has occurred simultaneously with continuous revelations of high-profile national and transnational corruption scandals in the region, which have likely decreased citizen trust. Increasing information transparency when not accompanied by the fair and impartial application of measures to control and penalize corruption may do more harm than help to the legitimacy of governing institutions in the eyes of citizens.

The great diversity in the usage of participatory institutions and ICTs complicates any evaluation of their impacts on democracy. Our review of this field suggests that neither a utopian nor a dystopian perspective is warranted. Rather, as our analysis of several of the most prominent participatory institutions and their connections to ICTs suggests, their impact on democracy varies substantially, and, with a few exceptions, is most often quite limited.

Analysis of Selected Participatory Institutions

To illustrate our arguments about the diversity and mostly limited impact of participatory institutions (PIs) and especially of digitalization, we focus on a wide spectrum of PIs, allowing a panoramic view of the region that enables comparisons of specific institutions both across and within countries. The institutions examined vary in terms of levels of government (national and local); format (consultation, deliberation, decision-making, and various combinations); and goals (constitution-making, decision-making on laws or constitutional reforms, recall referendums, budget-making, and more). The section is structured in ascending order of the importance of ICTs in the participatory institutions analyzed: (1) deliberation in constitution-making; (2) mechanisms of direct democracy; (3) local development and public policy councils; (4) participatory budgeting; and (5) digital participation initiatives.

Participation in Constitutional Reform Processes

In Latin America, the "new constitutionalism" has emphasized the participatory nature of the processes observed in the Andean region, especially in the analysis of Venezuela (1999), Ecuador (2007–2008), and Bolivia (2006–2009) (Viciano Pastor and Martínez Dalmau 2011). However, the role of citizen participation has been overrated, with not enough attention paid to the intrinsic characteristics of these processes and in particular to their (lack of) autonomy from the ruling governments, inclusiveness, and the transparency of the processing of their content. Other research has analyzed the extent to which pluralism conditions the results of the constituent processes (Bejarano and Segura 2013). Most studies have focused on case analysis without paying enough attention to the requirements that deliberative participation in constitution-making should meet in order to represent advances toward popular sovereignty.

Participatory Institutions, Digital Technologies, and Democratic Crises | 143

With this aim, we propose two groups of basic requirements regarding *the mechanism of deliberation* (access to information, time given for it, actors included, and the openness of the agenda) and the *method of processing the content generated* (if it exists, has been disseminated in advance, is traceable, and if it is controlled by the government) (Welp 2021). The eleven cases analyzed for Latin America (see table 9.1) share certain elements and differ on others. The mechanisms of participation show that,

Table 9.1. Classification of Citizen Deliberation in Constituent Processes (1970–2018)

Conditions of Deliberation	Procedure for Content Aggregation	Type	Cases
Meets conditions of temporality and inclusiveness, but not pluralism or access to information (biased information)	Participatory stage planned but no previously informed processing method; government controls the process	Biased and controlled	Cuba 1976, 2018
Meets conditions of temporality, access to information, inclusiveness, and relative pluralism	Little or no planning of the process; no traceability or requirement of consideration	Participatory overflow	Venezuela 1999 Ecuador 2008 Bolivia 2006–2009
Meets conditions of temporality, inclusiveness, pluralism, and access to information	Clear method of aggregation and final synthesis document, but no formal requirement of consideration	Constituent opening	Colombia 1991 Nicaragua 1986 Guatemala 1994–1999 Dominican Republic 2007 Chile 2017
Meets conditions of temporality, inclusiveness, pluralism, and access to information	Clear method of aggregation, traceability, and requirement of consideration	Constituent participation	Brazil 1988

Source: Welp (2021).

with the exception of Cuba, the processes were open and plural. Only in Cuba was there political persecution and restrictions placed on what could be discussed. However, despite the emphasis on the participatory nature of the new regimes in Venezuela, Ecuador, and Bolivia, there was no real planning of a civic stage or of citizen deliberation, or both. The Chilean experience in 2017 stands out as the best-organized process but, interestingly, it did not end in constitutional replacement (though a series of protests in 2019 forced a referendum on drafting a new constitution). In contrast to the openness, planning, and pluralism that characterized most of the countries in the first dimension, the procedure for systematizing the contents generated was only clearly fixed in three cases (Brazil, Chile, and the Dominican Republic), and only Brazil really worked in terms of connecting the citizens' demands to the constitution-making process. In Cuba in 1976 and 2018, the final decision was in the hands of the government. The same applies to Venezuela, Ecuador, and Bolivia, but in these cases, there was no report summarizing citizens' proposals and, accordingly, no evidence to suggest a connection between citizens' requests and final decisions.

Interestingly, this research confirms that deliberative processes implemented in nondemocratic contexts tend not to meet the minimum requirements to be considered open and plural, but it also shows that deficiencies exist as well in the processes implemented in democratic contexts (e.g., Ecuador). The conclusions suggest that it is essential to define standards for fair deliberative processes and invite readers to discuss the most appropriate mechanisms (two possible examples are citizen assemblies through sortition combined with referendums or deliberation processes, or both, that allow initiatives to be generated when backed by signatures). At the level of policy design, these findings invite promoters of deliberative participation, in general, to take into account the minimum criteria that a process of these characteristics requires.

Digitalization played little role in Latin American constitution-making, with the very partial exceptions of Cuba in 2018 and Chile in 2017. In Cuba the role played by digital media was strictly that of providing information. While control from above was tight, more information was available than on previous occasions as a result of the use of new communication technologies, which enabled a greater systematization and publication of results (Welp 2021). In Chile, however, digital platforms were used alongside traditional face-to-face forums during the citizen dialogues launched in 2017 to debate a constitutional replacement, ultimately

Participatory Institutions, Digital Technologies, and Democratic Crises | 145

yielding mixed results (Welp and Soto 2021). Although digital platforms contributed to increasing the number of participants, they neither resulted in more inclusiveness (men and residents of bigger cities were the most active participants, and the middle class was also overrepresented) nor did they grant legitimacy to the process. The reasons are not only related to technology; part of the legitimacy problem derived from the suspension of the constitutional reform after the debate (a separate constitutional reform relaunched in 2020).

Mechanisms of Direct Democracy

Another form of citizen participation that has grown in use in the past thirty years in Latin America are mechanisms of direct democracy (MDD), which allow citizens to make decisions (e.g., ratify a constitutional reform, abrogate a law approved by parliament, promote a constitutional change, remove a representative) directly through their votes rather than through representatives. One can distinguish between MDDs based on the process by which they are activated. Some MDDs are initiated "from above" by the president or the congress, some "from below" by citizens or civil society organizations through gathering signatures, and some by law, such as when the constitution requires a referendum in predefined situations, most commonly to ratify constitutional reforms. After the third wave of democracy in Latin America, a trend of constitutional reforms and replacements, starting with Colombia in 1991, led to, among other changes, the adoption of some form of MDD in every country in the region by 2012, when Mexico passed a law of popular consultation.

Uruguay was the pioneer, given that its first law regulating referendums was in 1912 and they were carried out regularly in the twentieth century (see Lissidini 1998; Ruth-Lovell, Whitehead, and Yelp 2017). Nearly all Latin American countries now permit the president or the congress, or both, to activate popular consultations; a large number allow activation of MDDs through signature gathering (Bolivia, Colombia, Costa Rica, Ecuador, Honduras, Mexico, Peru, Uruguay, and Venezuela, among others) or by legal mandate (such as Bolivia, Ecuador, Panama, Uruguay, and Venezuela), or both. Nonetheless, in practice, while presidents are regularly successful in activating consultations, citizen-initiated referendums through signature gathering remain rare. Besides Uruguay's numerous citizen-initiated referendums, the only countries to host even one are Venezuela (2004, the failed recall against President Chávez), Peru (2010, about public savings

146 | Benjamin Goldfrank and Yanina Welp

expropriated by former president Alberto Fujimori), and Colombia (2018, to promote anticorruption measures). Constitutionally mandated referendums are also relatively rare: Brazil (1993), Venezuela (2007 and 2009), Bolivia (2016), and Panama and Uruguay on several occasions.

Effective, democratic application of MDDs is rare for several reasons that can be grouped in three clusters pertaining to both actors and institutions: (1) the lack of political responsibility of official representatives; (2) defective institutional designs; and (3) the weakness (or co-optation) of the bodies that control and supervise the procedures, especially the electoral institutes and constitutional courts (Tuesta and Welp 2020). With regard to the lack of political responsibility, most of the attempted popular consultations in the region vary along a spectrum that moves from flagrant disregard for the rules of the game by political leaders (blocking recall referendums against President Nicolás Maduro in Venezuela in 2016 and 2022, for example) to subtle or blatant manipulation of the rules by leaders to influence the results in their favor. A key example of subtle manipulation occurred in Costa Rica in 2007, when the social organizations that started a signature-gathering process for a referendum on the Central America Free Trade Agreement, or CAFTA—with the intention of rejecting it—were first stymied by the legislature and then outmaneuvered by the president and the Constitutional Court. The initial obstacle was that the constitutional reform allowing referendums in 2002 had still not been regulated by 2006. The Constitutional Court finally obligated the legislature to approve the corresponding regulations. However, shortly after the Supreme Elections Tribunal authorized the gathering of signatures, President Óscar Arias—who had opposed the citizen-initiated consultation—decreed a popular consultation of his own, with the approval of the legislature. The Supreme Elections Tribunal then approved the president's decree, obviating the need for signature collection. While the rules were not violated, this clearly took the initiative away from the citizenry, after which the campaign was highly unequal, with political elites drawing on considerably more resources and media to promote votes in favor of CAFTA (Raventós 2018).

A second example of elite manipulation involves changing the rules with ad hoc criteria in order to favor the incumbent government. This occurred in Colombia, where for the peace plebiscite promoted by the president in 2016, a participation floor of 13 percent was established, while for the citizen-initiated anticorruption consultation two years later, the participation minimum was set at 33 percent. A few countries do not establish a participation threshold (notably, Switzerland), while most do. There are reasonable arguments for both positions. What is problematic—though not illegal—is manipulating the rules that are supposed to provide legitimacy and stability to the process.

With regard to institutional design, the principal deficiencies involve the many obstacles impeding or hindering the implementation of citizen-initiated referendums. The limitations on topics make such referendums difficult or almost useless (when no relevant topic can be submitted to a vote) or impossible (when procedures prevent activations) in many countries. Specific rules include, for example, limiting citizens' ability to promote and vote on more than one initiative at a time (Costa Rica); unclear procedures (Ecuador); and unrealistic time limits for voting (Mexico). As important as the rules of the game is that the official organizations in charge of ensuring the mechanisms are implemented properly actually do so. The obstacles in this regard stand out in Costa Rica, where the courts have ruled several citizen initiatives unconstitutional, and in Ecuador.

One of the main problems for MDDs in Ecuador derives from how to determine the constitutionality of each attempted use, which has generated contradictions and conflicts when the courts fail to issue rulings, as in the last consultation in February 2018. Another dilemma is the product of the lacunae in the law that has caused disputes between the Constitutional Court and the National Elections Council over the process. Specifically, which comes first, the constitutional ruling or the signature collection? Dozens of initiatives were handed back and forth between institutions without a resolution and then forgotten before this was finally clarified in 2019.

Overall, new technologies like ICTs have played virtually no formal role in MDDs in Latin America. Of course, informally, politicians, political parties, and social movements have used digital media for disseminating information during campaigns surrounding MDDs. However, except in one pilot process at the subnational level in Mexico, digital media have not been introduced for voting or collecting signatures in MDDs. They could have considerable effects on citizen-initiated referendums, making signature collection much easier for example, but that topic has not been on the agenda in Latin America thus far.

Local Development Councils and Public Policy Councils

While the first two sets of participatory institutions examined above take place at the national level, in fact local-level PIs are even more widespread, institutionalized, and implemented in practice in Latin America. Two of the most common local-level PIs are territorially based development and planning councils and sectorally based policy councils. Depending on the country and the type of council, they may be voluntarily created by individual mayors or mandated from above by national laws (though mandates do not always lead to implementation). Given the diversity of how these councils are organized and implemented and under what conditions across and within countries, the experiences vary dramatically. Recent evaluations of such councils emphasize their uneven spread across municipalities, their frequently limited importance and impact (McNulty 2019; Mayka 2019), and the tendency of incumbents in several countries to use them for partisan purposes, especially but not only in Venezuela (Rhodes-Purdy 2015). One country that stands out against this pattern is Brazil, where tens of thousands of municipal policy councils have gradually and incrementally helped make democracy work to improve the well-being of local residents (Wampler, Sugiyama, and Touchton 2020). This section briefly compares Brazil's municipal policy councils with Venezuela's communal councils (a specific form of development councils)—the two countries where, respectively, sectoral and territorial councils are most prevalent—to help understand the differences between them that lead to such diverging outcomes.

As of 2013, there were about 47,000 policy councils across Brazil's roughly 5,500 municipalities covering seventeen specific types of policy ranging from health and education to women's rights and the environment and involving hundreds of thousands of citizens (Wampler, Sugiyama, and Touchton 2020). The policy councils range in size from ten to thirty members and are typically composed of half government officials and half civil society representatives (from unions, community organizations, or NGOs), who cogovern by jointly deliberating over policies and budgets in their respective areas. In their careful, comprehensive study of Brazilian municipal democracy from 2000 to 2013, Wampler, Sugiyama, and Touchton (2020) find that the presence of policy councils, especially when combined with inclusive local state capacity and rights-based social policies, leads to tangible improvements in health, poverty reduction, and women's empowerment. Venezuela's communal councils can be formed—voluntarily—by between 150 and 400 families in cities or by smaller groups of families in rural areas, and their main purposes are proposing, planning, and implementing community projects. As the national government provided several billion dollars for these projects, the number of communal councils grew from 33,000 in the late 2000s to over 45,000 across the country's 335 municipalities by 2015; roughly 8 million Venezuelans have participated in at least one communal council meeting (Goldfrank 2020; 2021). Recently, communal councils became increasingly involved in the Local Committees for Supply and Production (Comités Locales de Abastecimiento y Producción, or CLAPs), which distribute subsidized food baskets. Evaluations of the communal councils—even prior to the economic crisis and the creation of the blatantly clientelistic CLAPs, which make nutrition dependent on party membership in a context of severe scarcity—have become increasingly and even overwhelmingly negative over time. Observers nearly uniformly acknowledge that the communal councils face problems ranging from corruption and lack of transparency to co-optation and subordination of social movements, exclusion, and electoral manipulation (García-Guadilla 2008; Briceño 2014; Rhodes-Purdy 2015; Silva 2017).

What are the key differences between Brazil's policy councils and Venezuela's communal councils that make the former a prime example of participatory democracy at work and the latter a paragon of what one should avoid? The sectoral versus territorial basis is connected to who participates—the issue of representatives of civil society organizations versus individuals may play some role, but the crucial differences are in other aspects of the institutional design. Particularly important here are the clarity and impartiality of the rules governing policy councils, rules that give them important roles within city governments, compared to the opacity of the rules for the communal councils, rules that simultaneously make them dependent on the national government. While government officials fund the communal councils in a partisan manner and utilize them for partisan gain in Venezuela, the policy councils in Brazil are institutionally intermeshed with city governments through their propositive and oversight functions. For example, for the municipal departments like health and education, with pertinent policy councils, mayors need that policy council's approval for the department's annual budget. According to Wampler, Sugiyama, and Touchton (2020, 76), the policy councils "are now an integral part of the policy formulation and approval process." This is a far cry from the communal councils.

As far as we know, ICTs have not played a major role in Brazil's municipal policy councils. With the communal councils, however, and especially with the newer CLAPs, which often function through group chats, digital technology may be facilitating clientelism. Certain government benefits in Venezuela—extra pension payments, vaccines, "bonuses"—require official party membership or extra steps like applying for the Carnet de la Patria (Patriot Card) via online registration, which offers members direct payments through mobile apps.[1] Most recently, on May 1, 2022, President Maduro announced the creation of a digital bank for the working class, where government benefits to workers will be paid in the national cryptocurrency known as the petro.[2]

Participatory Budgeting

One of the most highly touted participatory institutions of the past thirty years, to the point that it has become a prominent Latin American institutional export alongside conditional cash transfer programs, is participatory budgeting (Peck and Theodore 2015). Participatory budgeting (PB) is a process by which citizens, either individually or via civic associations, can voluntarily and regularly contribute to decision-making over at least part of a public budget through repeated interactions with government authorities, and which is most commonly practiced at the subnational level. Experiments with this kind of participation increased in the 1980s, especially in Brazil, where the city of Porto Alegre dubbed its process *orçamento participativo* and eventually both the name and much of the design of Porto Alegre's process spread across the larger Brazilian municipalities (those with a population over 50,000). From 12 Brazilian cities at the start of the 1990s, the practice of PB reached its peak of 138 cities in the 2001–2004 municipal term before declining to 43 cities by 2020 (Wampler and Goldfrank 2022). While PB lost prominence in Brazil, thousands of cities spanning the globe began adopting some version of PB in the 2000s, with over 3,000 cities in Latin America alone (Dias, Enríquez, and Júlio 2019). Like the other participatory institutions analyzed here, the design of PB, the conditions under which it is implemented, and the motivations of its implementers vary substantially across cases, as do the results in terms of advancing democracy toward something resembling popular sovereignty (Goldfrank 2021).

Within this variety, two correlated patterns can be found. First, early adopters of PB, mostly in Brazil, tended to follow the Porto Alegre model, which had an open design that allowed and facilitated broad participation, especially of the popular sectors; offered participants the opportunity to deliberate over and decide on tangible projects (mostly but not only infrastructure) as well as PB rules themselves; brought city district delegates together in a citywide council as well as in oversight committees;

and allocated resources in a way that favored poorly served low-income communities. Later adopters, by contrast, frequently adopted a much less open model. Especially outside of Brazil, PB design often included one or more of the following: participation restricted to specific neighborhoods, demographic groups, or civic associations; addition of government or party officials as budget councilors; a focus on predetermined or small infrastructure projects; lack of a social justice resource allocation formula; no citywide council or oversight mechanisms; and deliberation among active participants replaced by a simple electoral process sometimes accompanied by competition between civil society organizations to promote their own proposed projects. The second pattern is that the mostly positive, though incremental, results of PB for democracy, accountability, civil society, public service provision, and well-being that have frequently been found in Brazil are much less apparent for cases of PB outside of Brazil (Wampler and Goldfrank 2022, cf. Wampler McNulty, and Touchton 2021). In short, the design of PB matters.

The original Porto Alegre or Brazilian model of PB was more meaningful (and not just window dressing) but proved hard to sustain over time as nationally imposed fiscal rules changed, other forms of institutional participation proliferated, politicians found voters unmoved by PB, and cities using PB found it difficult to keep up with citizen demands for new investment projects while completing and maintaining prior projects (Wampler and Goldfrank 2022, chap. 6). The newer designs of PB are easier to adopt and maintain but tend to be less substantive, a pattern that continued as electronic PB became increasingly popular in the digital age. In the past dozen years or so, more and more cities have either added voting in PB via the internet or have adopted or switched to completely online forms of PB. This trend accelerated during the COVID-19 pandemic. There are at least two main drawbacks with online participation in PB. One is that online platforms tend to attract disproportionately wealthier and more highly educated participants (Sampaio 2011). The other is that the digitalization of PB further dilutes if not eliminates its deliberative and solidaristic aspects, turning it into a competitive electoral process. This can occur whether PB is strictly online (Goldfrank and Pineda 2022) or an online channel is added (Goldfrank and Legard 2021).

Varieties of Digital Participation

Despite the ongoing digital divide in Latin America, the region has seen a remarkable uptick in the number of experiments in strictly digital forms of citizen participation. According to the LATINNO database of "democratic innovations" in 18 Latin American countries from 1990 to 2020, of the 2,564 led by a national or subnational government (as opposed to international organizations, private stakeholders, or civil society), 509 involved electronic participation.[3] The cases are fairly evenly divided between the national (251) and subnational (311) levels, with some operating at more than one level. These sound like potentially large numbers, yet if one explores the cases of electronic participation, one finds that the focus is on digital tools for providing information to citizens, citizen reporting of problems or information (including COVID-19 status), and surveys or consultations. Roughly half of the 509 cases are apps or hackathons, the latter of which typically last a day. Only fifteen of the total cases involved voting on an outcome, and all but one of these were in single cities (and only four were ongoing, regular processes); the last was in multiple municipalities throughout Uruguay and lasted for three iterations from 2011 to 2013. The often-overlapping policy issues addressed vary widely, but "institutional performance" and "transparency and monitoring" feature prominently.

Though digital tools and platforms for citizen participation continue to multiply, as of yet they do not appear to provide many meaningful venues for collective deliberation and decision-making in Latin America.[4] Experimentation, however, is fairly recent: of the 509 cases, only 34 predate 2010. One potentially promising avenue of digital participation is that which links citizens to their elected representatives.

Online features that allow for citizen communication and intervention in the process of lawmaking are infrequent although growing to some extent. Some of these features appear to follow a strategy whereby ICTs are employed merely to create a symbolic impression of citizen participation. Such was the case of a pioneering experience, the Senador Virtual in Chile. Here, a team of lawyers, journalists, and a secretary of each Senate commission selected certain law projects for debate by the general public and provided information about the proposed law on a citizen-friendly digital platform. Users of the platform may then vote on the proposed law and eventually compare the results of their votes to the vote in the Senate. More recent initiatives followed a similar pattern in which results of the vote by the platform's users are nonbinding and appear to serve public relation purposes rather than to increase meaningful citizen participation. In Brazil, Ecuador, and Peru, parliamentary websites feature different forms of online discussion forums. The website of the Brazilian Chamber of Deputies, for example, offers links to the institution's presence

Participatory Institutions, Digital Technologies, and Democratic Crises | 153

on different social networks (e.g., Orkut, Twitter). It also enables citizens to interact with MPs, to provide their opinions on laws, to propose bills, and to discuss with MPs.

The website of the Peruvian Congress, too, offers different types of discussion forums. One type of forum invites citizens to generally debate on politics. Participation in this type of forum is high but given that they lack moderation by a forum administrator, posts are often unrelated to politics and often contain vulgar comments and abusive language. The contribution that these forums can make to the parliamentary process therefore remains questionable. The other type of forum requires user registration and invites discussion on specific law proposals. Here, user participation is relatively low and, similar to the Chilean project Senador Virtual, it remains unclear how far citizen participation in these forums will impact the formal process of political decision-making (Welp and Marzuca 2016). Lastly, and fortunately, we have not seen key dangers of digitalization—government surveillance, leaked or sold private information—appear with any frequency in the e-participation initiatives. Nonetheless, as experiments in digital participation continue to proliferate, governments should consider regulations to ensure that data gathered through e-participation is not abused.

Final Remarks

In this chapter we review a variety of participatory institutions and the conditions they require to work as effective democratic tools, noting the weak development of PIs overall. We argue that the constraints under which participatory institutions were developed were underestimated, which helps explain why they were not only unable to fulfill the optimistic dreams of their most fervent proponents but failed to minimize the democratic backsliding seen in much of the region. When it comes to ICTs, these findings are even clearer, given that participatory institutions based on ICTs are less developed and played only a minor role in policymaking at best.

After examining multiple examples of government-led initiatives—deliberation in constitution-making, referendums and initiatives (MDDs), local development and public policy councils, participatory budgeting, and e-participation—we observed that, regardless of the degree of digitalization, their effects on democracy have been quite limited. Presidential referendums are an exception, as they can be highly disruptive when it comes to the promotion of institutional changes. However, far from feeding an argument against participation, what this calls for is better institutional designs, designs that promote autonomous citizen participation. In other words, PIs should follow transparent rules and not be controlled and manipulated by political incumbents. Besides this negative example, other institutions (such as the policy councils and participatory budgeting) sometimes do have positive, democracy-enhancing effects even when they may be incremental. Other mechanisms, such as deliberation in constitution-making, tend to have a more symbolic than practical impact, but they could contribute to enhancing popular sovereignty when basic rules—access to information, inclusion, transparency—are fulfilled. Finally, institutional design is crucial but is not enough; political actors' behavior and acceptance of rules is critical, which holds true for both participatory institutions and representative institutions, and not only for deepening democracy but for preventing dictatorship.

Notes

1. See https://www.patria.org.ve/ (accessed May 2, 2022).

2. https://noticias.patria.org.ve/presidente-maduro-anuncio-creacion-banco-digital-trabajadores/ (accessed May 2, 2022).

3. Authors' calculations from https://www.latinno.net (Pogrebinschi 2021). Accessed May 5, 2022.

4. See Freitas, Cardoso, and Andrade (2019) for a more detailed examination of e-participation initiatives in the region that yields similar conclusions.

10

Britain's Food Crisis

Capital, Class, Technology, and Alternatives

BENJAMIN SELWYN

Even before the coronavirus (COVID-19) pandemic, the Inter-Academy Partnership characterized the world's food system as broken. Over 800 million people were hungry, 600 million suffered from obesity, and another two billion people were overweight, while one-third of food produced globally (about one billion tons) is wasted every year (Carrington 2018). This is not just a problem for poor countries. The UK's food system is also regularly described as "broken" (Wilson 2021).

The UK's food system is highly globalized, dynamic, and concentrated—characterized by one of the highest degrees of retail and land concentration in the world. It is environmentally destructive. It is also a vector through which food poverty and inequality are reproduced in the UK.

Mega retailers such as Tesco enjoy an almost 30 percent market share of food sales in the UK while high street grocers have become increasingly marginal (statista 2022). Land ownership and use in the UK is highly concentrated, specialized, and wasteful, oriented around the dominant corporate-driven food system. In-work poverty (entailing low wages and "flexible" working hours), including within the food industry, means that an increasing number of people and their families across the UK cannot exercise a genuine choice over how and what to eat.

155

156 | Benjamin Selwyn

In the UK, the birthplace of free wage-labor-based capitalist agriculture, the COVID pandemic has exacerbated existing food inequities. Five million people were food insecure in mid-2020, with people of color disproportionately at risk (Butler 2022).

Digital technology is rapidly being deployed in the food system. It is immensely profitable (often for financial investors), and it is based upon a "gig economy" model of work, where workers are self-employed and do not enjoy any of the benefits of secure employment (from regular pay to limits to working hours to pension contributions). This illuminates how employment patterns long associated with the Global South are increasingly common in the Global North.

Are there alternatives to the current corporate food system in the UK? This chapter argues for a democratic socialist alternative—entailing decommodification and democratization of the food system. It draws on Belo Horizonte's experiment in establishing an alternative food system to combat racialized and gendered patterns of hunger and on some of the research and policy suggestions of the recently established Right to Food Campaign, to suggest ways for every person in the UK to enjoy a plentiful and healthy diet. In doing so it hopes to stimulate solidaristic links between progressive campaigns in the Global North and Global South for the popular control of food. It suggests that digital technologies could be deployed to ameliorate the UK's food crisis, but only if they are subject to democratic objectives. It also aims to contribute to the campaign by providing a systematic analysis of the UK's food crisis and by considering additional transformative measures.

The root problems of the contemporary UK food system are threefold: (1) it is rooted in, and depends upon the commodification of labor, food, and natural resources (including land); (2) these commodities are subordinate to capitalism's endless drive of exploitation-based accumulation; and (3) the food system itself incorporates, and contributes to reproducing, these dynamics throughout the wider capitalist system. An alternative democratic socialist food system must be constructed through combating exploitation, decommodification, and democratization.

What might an emergent alternative food system look like? How could it decommodify food in order to reduce laboring class market dependence while enhancing workers' health? How could it increase workers' democratic control over its production, distribution, and consumption? How could it reduce race and gender inequalities? How could the construction of such an alternative system facilitate political alliance-building among oppressed and exploited groups? How could it enable workers' organizations to encroach upon the power of capital? This contribution suggests that new digital technologies, and new social relations in the spheres of food production and consumption, could contribute to a socialist strategy to solve some of the afore-mentioned problems.

Gøsta Esping Andersen refers to decommodification as "the degree to which individuals, or families, can uphold a socially acceptable standard of living independently of market participation." While decommodification exists in various settings (some more amenable to the reproduction of capitalism than others), "when work approaches free choice rather than necessity, de-commodification may amount to de-proletarianization" (1990, 37). To consider how alternative food systems may facilitate a shift from decommodification to de-proletarianization means thinking about how individuals are transformed from market-dependent worker-consumers to what Jennifer Wilkins (2005, 269) calls food citizens. These citizens engage in "food-related behaviors that support, rather than threaten, the development of a democratic, socially and economically just, and environmentally sustainable food system."

The remainder of this chapter is organized as follows. The second section provides an overview of how capitalist food systems are based upon generalized commodification and labor exploitation. The third section documents the extent of food inequality and labor exploitation in the UK. The fourth section outlines the Right to Food's campaign for a socially just food system, followed by a conclusion.

Capitalist Food Systems: Commodification and Exploitation

World food production has undergone long-term commodification, where food is produced increasingly as an exchange value for sale in markets. Far from entailing the establishment of free markets in food, as in liberal ideology, these production and exchange relations have required the continual presence of leading capitalist states. As Karl Polanyi noted, "The road to the free market was opened and kept open by an enormous increase in continuous, centrally organized and controlled interventionism. . . . the introduction of free markets, far from doing away with the need for control, regulation, and intervention, enormously increased their range" (2001, 146–47).

The rise of an increasingly globalized capitalist agriculture was achieved through long-term, state-facilitated/directed social restructuring across four key world historical moments. First, from the sixteenth cen-

158 | Benjamin Selwyn

tury, enclosures in England gave rise to the first form of wage-labor-based agricultural capitalism, in the emergent United States "unproductive" land was seized and cleared of indigenous populations, while both states promoted transatlantic plantation slavery and the triangular trade. In a second period, from the nineteenth century, Britain organized the first world market for food through free-trade imperialism, the US granted land rights to railroad companies to expand the North American frontier, imposed tariffs and protection, and encouraged the mass production of grains and livestock in the Midwest based on family agriculture. In the third moment, around the mid-twentieth century, the US and EU regulated trade and subsidized systematic overproduction. The US rolled out the Green Revolution across parts of the "third world," used buffer stocks to protect farmers' income, and implemented a grain disposal system (PL480) designed to establish relative food dependence in emergent postcolonial states. Finally, from the late twentieth century, structural adjustment programs encouraged so-called nontraditional agricultural exports from the Global South to the Global North, boosting the power of giant retail capital (Wood 2002; Williams 2014; Weis 2007; McMichael 2009).

Capitalist food systems rest upon the simultaneous commodification and externalization of nature—where its use and destruction are either not incorporated as a cost into production or it is done very cheaply. The word's agricultural system, generating between 20 percent and 35 percent of anthropogenic greenhouse gases, is a major contributor to the sixth mass extinction of wildlife (Clapp, Newell, and Brent 2018).

The commodification of food serves to reproduce laboring class market dependence under capitalism. Accessing food via the market necessitates money, wages, employment, and subordination to capital inside and outside the workplace—the former where surplus value is generated, the latter where subsistence goods are purchased and surplus value realized. Much food preparation is predicated upon unpaid, gendered, domestic care work. Given that food is arguably the most essential wage good, its availability and affordability for laboring classes is an important determinant of wage rates. Cheap food can enable low wages (cheap workers) while expensive food can lead to upward wage pressures and, potentially, to political instability.

While sufficiently available food is necessary to feed capitalism's laboring classes, high-energy food is required to facilitate capitalism's intense labor process. For example, as Sydney Mintz (1986) argued in his *Sweetness and Power*, sugar from the colonies represented an essential source of cheap energy for Britain's industrial labor force. For these reasons the cost and content of energy in food has been a concern for capitalists and their states since (at least) the Industrial Revolution.

Since capitalism's early days food has been increasingly commodified—produced as an exchange value for sale in markets using inputs purchased on markets—rather than as a use value for self-consumption. Commodity fetishism, the ideological expression of commodification, hides ways in which food becomes available for purchase through the market, such as exploitative labor and environmentally destructive practices. This generates "food from nowhere"—the mass production, distribution, and sale of cheap, undifferentiated, and often highly processed foodstuffs (McMichael 2009).

Far from being financially self-sustaining, as in liberal mythology, industrial food production relies upon extensive state support. Approximately $530 billion of an annual $700 billion of global public funds to agriculture is paid to farmers engaged in high-input, chemically intensive, monocrop-based farming (Selwyn 2021).

Often brutal labor exploitation is central to the reproduction of global agriculture:

> Of the 1.3 billion people employed in agriculture . . . there are some 450 million waged workers, over half of whom are women. Seventy per cent of child labor globally takes place in agriculture . . . and agriculture produces over 170,000 work-related deaths annually. Agricultural workers are twice as likely to die at work than in any other sector. Between three to four million pesticide poisonings occur each year, some 40,000 of them fatal . . . chronically high rates of malnutrition occur among agricultural workers. (Rossman 2012, 61)

Rather than a system oriented to meet human needs through environmentally sustainable and socially equitable practices, the global agro-industrial system is one where "people, animals, plants and the environment [are] controlled in order to maintain order, authority and predictability" (Lang and Heasman 2015, 279). Nowhere is this more evident than in the United Kingdom.

160 | Benjamin Selwyn

Food Inequality and Labor Exploitation in the UK

Even prior to the COVID-19 crisis, around four million children in the UK lived in households that struggled to afford to buy enough healthy food to meet official nutritional guidelines. Food poverty in the UK takes the form of the paradoxical affliction affecting ever-larger sections of the population—an inability to consume sufficient calories *and* an inability to consume sufficiently healthy foods.

Buying cheap, highly processed but unhealthy food often represents a survival strategy for these households. These combined pressures have accelerated problems of child and adulthood obesity derived from the consumption of empty calories contained in high-energy, low-nutrient foods. As Jane Dixon (2009, 326) puts it, working classes in the Global North "may now be portrayed as . . . over-consumers, but their overweight bodies are the result of insufficient incomes to consume fewer, less energy dense foods."

The UK has the worst diet, and the highest prevalence of obesity, in Europe. Over half of all food bought by families in the UK is "ultra-processed"—foods that are produced in factories, using industrial ingre-dients (including additives) designed by food technology corporations to enhance flavor. Ultra-processed foods include sugar-sweetened drinks, packaged breads, cakes, biscuits, and other baked products, and recon-stituted meat products (Monteiro et al. 2018).

Patterns of domestic food preparation reproduce gender norms and inequality. Most of this care work is done by women, contributing to their double burden of paid work and unpaid domestic work. In the UK prior to COVID-19 approximately 9.1 million people (mostly women) under-took unpaid care work for relatives. Since the onset of the pandemic an additional 4.5 million people have become unpaid carers of which the vast majority are women (Hill 2020). The pandemic has also knocked out a large swath of independent local restaurants.

Food Poverty

In the UK the Trussel Trust is the largest single provider of emergency food packages to poor people, distributed through its network of food banks. In 2015–2016 it distributed just over one million food bank par-cels, rising to approximately 2.5 million food bank parcels in 2020–2021 of which 980,000 went to children (Trussel Trust 2022).

Popular media and political commentary reproduce Victorian-era stereotypes about the "underserving poor." Poor people are portrayed as out of work, benefit-dependent, and incapable or uninterested in working their way out of poverty (Garthwaite 2016). This is untrue. However, it is part of a ruling ideology that diminishes the suffering of the UK's poor and attempts to portray them as responsible for their own poverty.

A recent survey by the Bakers Food and Allied Workers Union (BFAWU 2021) shows how even its own members, who work in the food sector itself and are crucial for the provision of food to the UK's population, are often too poor to afford to purchase sufficient (still less sufficiently good) food. During the crisis, 40 percent of its respondents reported that they had not eaten enough food due to lack of money; 20 percent lived in a household that had run out of food due to insufficient income; 35 percent of respondents ate less to ensure that others in their household had enough to eat; 20 percent relied on friends and relatives to put enough food on the table; and over 7 percent of respondents relied at least once on a food bank to feed their household.

The principal cause of food poverty among these workers is low wages. A female worker in the retail sector said a pay raise would mean that "we could eat properly and pay the bills." A male worker in food processing described how "I'm currently minimum wage, zero hours. A pay rise would mean I could start to get some more independence and perhaps escape what is a very difficult and unhealthy situation at home."

Consuming insufficient calories is only one side of the face of food poverty in the UK. The other side is the rise of obesity. In 1980 the prevalence of obesity among men and women over sixteen was 6 percent and 9 percent, respectively, rising to 13 percent and 16 percent in 1993, to 27 percent and 29 percent by 2019 (UK Health Security Agency 2021). The incidence of obesity in poor areas is higher than in rich areas of the UK. The production, availability, and sale of highly processed foods has boomed over the last four decades worldwide. Buying and consuming cheap, processed, and unhealthy food is often a survival strategy for people who cannot afford more healthy foods.

These trends have been exacerbated during the COVID pandemic. Around one in seven children are obese at the start of primary school in England. By the time they are ten or eleven years old these numbers have quadrupled. Between 2019–2020 and 2020–2021 the rate of obesity among ten or eleven year olds increased from 21 percent to over 25 percent. Children in poor neighborhoods are twice as likely to be obese

162 | Benjamin Selwyn

as those from wealthier areas. Among reception-aged children (4–5 year olds) 20.3 percent are obese in the most deprived areas compared to 7.8 percent in the least deprived areas. Among year six pupils (11–12 year olds) in these areas the figures range from 33.8 percent to 14.3 percent, respectively (Gregory 2021).

Food Inequality

The inability of large segments of the UK's population to feed themselves satisfactorily is rooted in poverty wages and increasingly generalized economic insecurity (including, for example, the proliferation of zero hours contracts that do not provide workers with guaranteed incomes). Such insecurity is a product of institutionalized capitalist social relations, including the exclusion of the mass of the population from the means of production.

Private land ownership in the UK enables a small number of big farmers, landowners, and investors to decide upon what is produced, to whom it is sold, and how, subsequently, it is consumed. In England, around half of all land is owned by less than 1 percent of the population—approximately 25,000 corporate entities and individuals. The public sector possesses 8 percent of land in England. By contrast, oligarchs and city bankers own 17 percent, corporations own 18 percent, members of the gentry and aristocracy (including the royal family) own about 30 percent (Shrubsole 2019), and 432 landlords own half of private land in Scotland (Crichton 2013).

Private land use in the UK is both environmentally harmful and fails to provide adequately for the public good. UK farming, particularly livestock, accounts for approximately 9 percent of national CO_2 emissions (Financial Times 2019). The sector is also grossly inefficient. For example, sheep occupy about four million hectares of land in the UK, about as much as all cropland. However, they provide just 1 percent of calories in the UK diet (Monbiot 2017).

Digital technology—which could be used to lighten workers' loads— has been used by segments of capital to generate new forms of labor exploitation. Many workers are immigrants who are particularly easy for firms to exploit. Platforms like UberEats and Deliveroo offer multirestaurant food-delivery services. These "match and coordinate interactions between workers, restaurants and consumers via their digital eco-systems while retaining flat organizational structures" (Veen et al. 2019; Woodcock

2020). These platforms classify their workers as independent contractors rather than employees, thereby avoiding employer responsibilities such as health and safety provision, health insurance, and pension contributions. Workers must purchase, and are responsible for, their own equipment (smartphones with data, bicycles/motorbikes/cars, delivery bags). As the eminent food expert Tim Lang (2020, 390) writes, "British employers are free-riding on the back of countries who have paid and trained staff only to see them migrate and take their skills elsewhere, filling gaps in the labor force the indigenous population resists."

Workers are paid predominantly by piece rate. Some platforms have "core" workforces who are guaranteed a minimum number of jobs per shift, while noncore workers hustle for work from the platform by accepting jobs as quickly as possible. Workers are not paid as they wait for jobs or wait at restaurants to collect meals. A Deliveroo driver describes how this works:

> You log in to work at about 6pm or 6.30pm for the evening rush, and you find that there are already 20 other people at the branch waiting for work. You often sit around waiting for an order. By 7.30pm there might be 50 people logged in. All you end up getting is about £20 to £25 a day. I only work for Deliveroo. I used to do work for Uber Eats but they blocked me after a customer complained that I hadn't delivered something, when I had. (Collinson 2018)

The Right to Food: Alternatives to the Food Crisis

What kinds of institutions, technologies, organizations, and policies could be implemented in the UK to begin to overcome the unsustainability of the current food system—land concentration and land degradation, poverty wages in production, widespread mal- and undernutrition, social inequalities of class, race, and gender, very high levels of unpaid care work, and the disappearance of many local eateries? This section draws upon and aims to contribute to discussions by the Right to Food campaign, to discuss new social arrangements and technologies for food production and provision that could radically alter the UK's existing food system.

The Right to Food campaign portrays access to and consumption of food as a class issue, rooted in the unequal socioeconomic relations

164 | Benjamin Selwyn

in the UK. It draws upon Article 25 of the United Nation's Universal Declaration of Human Rights: "Everyone has the right to a standard of living adequate for the health and well-being of himself and of his family, including food, clothing, housing and medical care and necessary social services, and the right to security in the event of unemployment, sickness, disability, widowhood, old age or other lack of livelihood in circumstances beyond his control" (United Nations 2022).

The UK was one of the fifty-eight signatories to the declaration. That food poverty is so prevalent in the contemporary UK reveals the government to be in serious breach of one of the core principles of the declaration. The Right to Food campaign argues for the reenshrinement and enforcement in UK law of the right to food.

Given that successive UK governments have failed to realize the right to food, it will require a considerable democratization of the economy, society, and politics for class-based movements to be able to guide government policy. A more democratically representative and environmentally oriented government could undertake many progressive policies that would contribute to realizing the right to food. State funding, and direct production, of alternatives to meat could represent an important starting point. Currently the UK state subsidizes the fossil fuel industry by over £10 billion a year (Carrington 2019), considerably greater than other EU countries. Under a more democratically representative and environmentally oriented government these subsidies could be redirected—toward alternative energy and food sources. Restructuring the UK's food system around principles of public good rather than private profit could be achieved in a number of ways.

Subsidizing New Technologies and Their Diffusion

Agricultural technologies have long been part of the story of farming land concentration. The expansion of capitalist agriculture has historically been associated and driven forward by ever-increasing on-farm simplification— the trend toward monocropping. Monocropping, in turn, generates new demands—for regular and deeper ploughing of land with increasingly large tractors, for greater control of the natural environment through increasing fertilizer, pesticide, and herbicide use, and for the elimination of plant formations (such as hedgerows in the UK) that complicate land topography. These dynamics generate "get big or get out" tendencies in farming, as increased scales in technologies and land use raise entry barriers, effectively making farming ever less viable for smaller producers (Weis 2007). The pressures upon small producers are exacerbated further by the concentration of capital upstream and down (by input providers and by retailers).

A political agenda aiming to democratize and decommodify the food system can propose several alternatives to the contemporary setup. On the one hand, it could advocate and promote the expansion of a small farmer sector (such as those promoted/facilitated by the country farm scheme, see below). On the other hand, large-scale farms could be maintained but their ownership structures transformed into farming cooperatives. In both cases, however, increasing biodiversity as part of democratization/decommodification of the food system should be an essential part of transforming the food system into one that is socially and ecologically sustainable.

A relatively successful attempt to partially decommodify food is the Brazilian city of Belo Horizonte's experiment in establishing an alternative food system (Lesa and Rocha 2009; Gerster-Bentaya, Rocha, and Barth, 2011). The experiment was established in 1993 by the local municipality led by the Workers' Party in response to racialized and gendered patterns of hunger. The program has represented an early and radical attack on hunger (significantly before the Workers' Party's national Zero Fome program). Its core elements include the following:

1. The use of popular restaurants, school meals, and food assistance to supply working class communities with food.

2. The establishment and subsidy of fruit and vegetable markets and fairs and the institutional procurement of food from family farms to provide cheap food to local communities directly from organic farms.

3. The establishment of an agroecological system to fortify small-scale family rural and urban agriculture—the latter through community gardens.

4. Education and training in food preparation. (Lesa and Rocha 2009; Gerster-Bentaya et al. 2011)

Increasing on-farm biodiversity can be facilitated by the application of agroecological principles. These include the reliance upon biodiversity to regulate and reproduce ecosystems; multifunctional (diverse) agricultural

166 | Benjamin Selwyn

systems such as polycultures to safeguard the human-natural metabolic interaction and provide diverse food sources; and use of traditional knowledge (including farmer innovations and technologies) (Portes, Reed, and Percy 2017). Aspects of agroecology include conservation agriculture and forestry practices, crop and forest species diversity, appropriate crop and forest rotations, organic farming, integrated pest management, the conservation of pollinators, rainwater harvesting, range and pasture management, and precision agriculture systems (IPCC 2019).

New advances in digital technology—precision farming—could be combined with agroecological principles to contribute to a democratizing/ decommodifying political economic agenda. Precision farming could be used to support the transformation of social relations on the land and throughout the food system (see Harris 2018). Small robots will soon be capable of contributing to most stages in the agricultural cycle—land mapping, seed planting, crop maintenance, weeding, and harvesting. For example, robots are now capable of "laser weeding" whereby software enables them to identify up to 800 different types of weeds and use precision targeting to destroy them. Such technologies eliminate the need for chemical herbicides, facilitating a technologically advanced transition to greater agroecological-based farming.

In 2020, Singapore passed legislation approving cultured meat production (also commonly referred to as lab-grown meat) (BBC 2020). Such moves could be emulated by the UK government, and investments could be channeled away from fossil fuels toward sustainable food sources. Such investments would help generate economies of scale, driving down production costs and enabling a generalized provision of healthy plant-based food to the public. A new subsidy regime that prioritizes human food over animal feed crops would shift market signals, pushing up the price of meat while reducing the price of plant-based food, further encouraging a healthy dietary shift.

COMMUNITY RESTAURANTS

Community restaurants, financed by progressive taxation, sourcing local produce, serving healthy plant-based dishes, and providing a combination of free and cheap meals should represent a core socialist demand, as part of the quest for the democratization of social life. School kitchens, which provide nutritious meals to children during weekdays, could be transformed into community restaurants and community social hubs—providing meals to neighborhoods morning, noon, and night, and providing cooking lessons, dining clubs, and meals on wheels.

The legitimacy of such a political demand could flow from Article 25 of the UN's Universal Declaration of Human Rights that everyone has the right to a standard of living adequate for the health and well-being of themselves and their families, including food. As a socialist demand, the idea of decommodifying food through community restaurants could build upon, and then extrapolate from, prior and already existing moves in this direction.

During the Second World War, community feeding enters, later renamed "British Restaurants" at Prime Minister Winston Churchill's behest (because he deemed the word *community* as socialistic), were established by the Ministry of Food. They helped people who had been bombed out of their houses, had run out of ration coupons, or were too poor to afford to buy food. By 1943 over 2,000 such restaurants were serving around 600,000 meals a day for today's equivalent of £1. They were disbanded in 1947.

Much more recently, the Sheffield Food Hall project was established in 2015, "for the community, by the community," in response to rising food bank use under Tory-government-imposed austerity. It intercepts and uses food waste from local traders to produce food on a "pay what you can" basis. The project also contributed to establishing the National Food Service in 2018, which by early 2020 had thirteen branches across the UK. The National Food Service is rooted in solidaristic conceptions of food equity:

Imagine a social eating space in every street and high rise created in common by people from all backgrounds. Places free at the point of entry, use, and delivery. Social equality integrated into the very fabric of urban life and with people able to live happily in their city and community. Around the dinner table barriers are broken down and real change is made; these spaces should be at the heart of every city (National Food Service 2022).

The ability of National Food Service restaurants to generate food equity through decommodification in the UK is strictly limited, however, as they are run by unpaid volunteers and rely on food provided by local traders, such as supermarkets off-loading surplus food.

More promisingly, the idea of the National Food Service was adopted by Jeremy Corbyn's Labour Party, as part of its Green New Deal agenda prior to the 2019 general election campaign. Although Labour lost that election, and has since shifted away from explicit socialist rhetoric and policies under Kier Starmer, the issue of food equity has not disappeared. In fact, the COVID crisis, and now the cost-of-living crisis, is keeping food poverty and equity in the public eye.

A campaign for community restaurants providing decommodified food would combine demands for centralized funding with decentralized management. Local councils could be funded by the central government to buy up closed restaurants, pubs, and other vacant retail properties for conversion into community restaurants.

The funds for such a venture could be raised through progressive taxation. If the UK treasury were to tax UK-based wealth at the same rate as income, it could raise up to £174 billion a year. One study, based on assumptions of a 48 percent participation rate for seven meals a weak averaged across the population, estimates that "this option would have a total [annual] cost of around £21.2bn, with values to households ranging from £45/week in the lowest deciles to £1.63/week in the highest deciles. Our cursory distributional analysis assumes lower take up rates in higher deciles, with 5% of those in the highest decile only using the service for 0.5 meals/week, while those in the lowest deciles would use 14 meals/week" (Portes et al. 2017, 45).

Such restaurants could represent regenerative hubs for communities battered by austerity, poverty, and rampant individualism. They could start by providing a set number of free meals to community members, to be increased over time. Electronic meal coupons would be allocated to families and individuals on a use-it-or-lose-it basis, to avoid creating parallel coupon markets.

Diners could preorder electronically to facilitate preparation, and once established, demand could be predicted in order to prepare sufficient food and minimize waste. Subsidies would ensure that, in addition to free meals, such restaurants could produce and sell cheaper food than local junk food outlets, contributing further to a healthy dietary shift. Like other state provisions, such as the National Health Service, there would be no obligation to dine at these restaurants, and people who want to eat at fast-food chains could do so. What would change would be that the economic pressure to eat cheap, health-damaging food would be reduced.

Community restaurants could be locally run, with neighborhood-wide elected management teams coordinating supply with regional farms and alternatives-to-meat producers. Staff would be employed by local councils. Communities' different dietary preferences (vegan, vegetarian, diverse world cuisines) could be catered to through participatory planning.

For decommodified food to be readily available to working class communities, delivery networks would have to be established. While already-existing networks such as Deliveroo and UberEats are profit-oriented, part of the demand for community restaurants would be their regulation, or the establishment of parallel community-oriented delivery networks. As Callum Cant (2019, 153), a former Deliveroo rider, argues, "a platform-based worker-run 'meals on wheels' service could begin to provide the needs of an ageing population and expand the support available to those with additional temporary or permanent care needs."

State funds could enable the establishment of large-scale production units of alternatives to meat to supply community restaurants with cheap, high-quality ingredients. The government should legislate that wages in agriculture should be living wages. Agrarian reform and the establishment of increasingly publicly owned and run agriculture must be part of the project of decommodifying food. Community owned and run farms, supported by research and development extension services, could coordinate production and provision with community restaurants.

A shift by the UK's population to a plant-based diet would liberate approximately fifteen million hectares of land that are currently used for livestock and feed crops (Fairlie 2009). This land could be rewilded and contribute to the expansion of the UK's carbon sink by diversifying habitats and reintroducing native animal and plant species. It could also be made accessible for the public, for leisure and education (including about farming and the environment).

In the past in the UK, county farm schemes enabled budding farmers to enter the sector. These farms were owned by local authorities and leased cheaply to farmers. From the late 1970s onwards, as a consequence of land privatization and state funding cuts, the acreage of such farms declined from 426,695 acres in 1977 to 215,155 acres in 2017 (Shrubsole 2018) If such schemes were revived, they could support the entry of potential farmers into the food system, supported by a research and extension program to disseminate agricultural techniques and technologies designed to facilitate relatively high food output with minimal chemical input (Monbiot et al. 2019).

In the UK agricultural workers' wages are currently about two-thirds of those in the rest of the economy (Clutterbuck 2017). A more socially just food system would increase these to, at least, a living wage. In her first speech as prime minister, Theresa May promised to address the "burning injustices" of the UK's economy. She even suggested placing workers on company boards (Baker 2016). This suggestion was quickly dropped, but

170 | Benjamin Selwyn

it could be part and parcel of a recentering of power relations within the food economy, away from private capital and toward unionized labor. Ending in-work poverty through a decent living wage (of £15 an hour) and eliminating zero-hours contracts are essential components of increasing the economic security of the UK's workforce.

Conclusions

The UK's food system is often described as "broken" because of its apparent dysfunctionality—highly concentrated land and retail markets, the highest degree of adult and child obesity in Europe, and a proliferation of the population that cannot afford sufficient food. Viewed from the perspective of labor, the UK's food system does appear to be broken. However, viewed from the perspective of capitalist profitability it is finely tuned and functioning well. Capital's reproduction within and through the food system is based upon a historically unprecedented degree of commodification, working class market dependence, and proliferating poverty wages, all of which simultaneously generate the above-noted maladies for labor and profits for capital.

This chapter draws upon the Brazilian city of Belo Horizonte's experience of combating hunger through establishing an alternative food system, and the emerging movement in the UK's Right to Food campaign to discuss, and hopefully to contribute to, ideas about how to transform the food system. The great strengths of the Right to Food campaign is that it views the food crisis in class-relational terms—as resulting from the reproduction of class inequalities (including poverty wages). Its proposals seek to transform the food system through broader shifts in class relations. This chapter hopes to contribute to these discussions by proposing further measures, from land reform (including dissemination of new technologies) to social reform through decommodified community restaurants.

Digital States, Democracy, and Development

11

Global Capitalism after the Pandemic

WILLIAM I. ROBINSON

Karl Marx and Frederick Engels famously declared in *The Communist Manifesto* that "all that is solid melts into air" under the dizzying pace of change wrought by capitalism. Not since the Industrial Revolution of the eighteenth century has the world experienced such rapid and profound changes as those ushered in by globalization. But now it appears that the system is at the brink of another round of restructuring and transformation based on a much more advanced digitalization of the entire global economy and society. This restructuring had already become evident in the wake of the 2008 Great Recession. But the changing social and economic conditions brought about by the coronavirus pandemic are accelerating the process. These conditions have helped a new bloc of transnational capital, led by the giant tech companies, to amass ever greater power during the pandemic and to consolidate its control over the commanding heights of the global economy. As restructuring proceeds, it will heighten the concentration of capital worldwide, worsen social inequality, and aggravate international tensions. Enabled by digital applications, the ruling groups, unless they are pushed to change course by mass pressure from below, will turn to ratcheting up the global police state to contain social upheavals.

The emerging postpandemic capitalist paradigm is based on a digitalization and application of so-called fourth industrial revolution technologies. This new wave of technological development is made possible by a more advanced information technology. Led by artificial intelligence

(AI) and the collection, processing, and analysis of immense amount of data ("big data"), the emerging technologies include machine learning, automation and robotics, nano- and bio-technology, the internet of things, quantum and cloud computing, 3D printing, virtual reality, new forms of energy storage, and autonomous vehicles, among others. Computer and information technology (CIT), first introduced in the 1980s, provided the original basis for globalization. It allowed the transnational capitalist class to coordinate and synchronize global production and therefore to put into place a globally integrated production and financial system into which every country has become incorporated. Just as the original introduction of CIT and the internet in the late twentieth century profoundly transformed world capitalism, this second generation of digital-based technologies is now leading to a new round of worldwide restructuring that promises to have another transformative impact on the structures of the global economy, society, and polity.

The first generation of capitalist globalization from the 1980s and onwards was based on simple digitalization—the so-called third industrial revolution. What distinguishes the fourth from the third revolution is a fusion of the new technologies and the blurring of lines between the physical, digital, and biological worlds (see, for example, Schwab 2016). If the first generation of capitalist globalization from the 1980s on involved the creation of a globally integrated production and financial system, the new wave of digitalization and the rise of platforms have facilitated since 2008 a very rapid transnationalization of digital-based services. By 2017, services accounted for some 70 percent of the total gross world product (Marois 2017) and included communications, informatics, digital and platform technology, e-commerce, financial services, professional and technical work, and a host of other nontangible products such as film and music.

It is hard to overestimate just how rapid and extensive is the current digital restructuring of the global economy and society. According to United Nations data (UNCTAD 2019), the "sharing economy" will surge from $14 billion in 2014 to $335 billion by 2025. Worldwide shipments of 3D printers more than doubled in 2016, to over 450,000, and were expected to reach 6.7 million by the end of 2020. The global value of e-commerce is estimated to have reached $29 trillion in 2017, which is equivalent to 36 percent of global GDP. Digitally deliverable service exports amounted in 2019 to $2.9 trillion, or 50 percent of global services exports. By 2019, global internet traffic was sixty-six times the volume of the entire global internet traffic in 2005, whereas global Internet Protocol traffic, a proxy for data flows, grew from about 100 gigabytes (GB) *per day* in 1992 to more than 45,000 GB *per second* in 2017. And yet the world is only in the early days of the data-driven economy; by 2022, global Internet Protocol traffic reached 153,000 GB per second, fueled by more and more people coming online for the first time and by the expansion of the internet of things.

The coronavirus pandemic has spotlighted how central digital services have become to the global economy. But more than shine this spotlight, the pandemic and its aftermath, to the extent that it accelerates digital restructuring, can be expected to result in a vast expansion of reduced-labor or laborless digital services, including all sorts of new telework arrangements, drone delivery, cash-free commerce, fintech (digitalized finance), tracking and other forms of surveillance, automated medical and legal services, and remote teaching involving prerecorded instruction. The pandemic has boosted the efforts of the giant tech companies and their political agents to convert more and more areas of the economy into these new digital realms. The giant tech companies have flourished during the contagion, their digital services becoming essential to the pandemic economy, as hundreds of millions of workers worldwide moved to remote work at home or through enhanced platforms, or became engaged in digitally driven service work, and as in-person services were replaced by remote digital services. The postpandemic global economy will involve now a more rapid and expansive application of digitalization to every aspect of global society, including war and repression.

New Capital Bloc Led by Tech, Finance, and the Military-Industrial Complex

Technological change is generally associated with cycles of capitalist crisis and social and political turmoil. Indeed, digitalization has been spurred on by capitalist crisis. The coronavirus was but the spark that ignited the combustible of a global economy that had never fully recovered from the 2008 financial collapse and has been teetering on the brink of renewed crisis ever since. But the underlying structural causes of the 2008 debacle, far from being resolved, have been steadily aggravated. Frenzied financial speculation, unsustainable debt, the plunder of public finance, overinflated tech stock, and state-organized militarized accumulation have kept the global economy sputtering along in recent years in the face of chronic stagnation, and concealed its instability (Robinson 2020a).

There are three types of capitalist crises: (1) cyclical, (2) structural, and (3) systemic (Robinson 2014). The first type is *cyclical*, or the business cycle, involving economic downturns or recessions approximately once a decade. There were recessions in the early 1980s, the early 1990s, and at the turn of the century. The second type is *structural* and appears about once every forty to fifty years. These are called structural, or restructuring crises, because their resolution involves restructuring the capitalist system. The restructuring crisis of the late 1870s into the early 1890s was resolved through a new round of colonialism and imperialism. The 1930s Great Depression was resolved through the rise of a new type of capitalism based on redistribution and state intervention to regulate the market, known technically as Fordism-Keynesianism, and led to the social welfare systems of the twentieth century. The next structural crisis hit in the 1970s and led to globalization and the rise of a transnational capitalist class from the 1980s and on. As A. Sivanandan famously noted in the late twentieth century, "the handmill gives you a society with the feudal lord and the steam-mill gives you society with the industrial capitalist, the microchip gives you society with the global capitalist" (Sivanandan 1998, 11).

A new restructuring crisis began with the 2008 financial collapse (Robinson 2014). Leading the way in this restructuring, the giant tech companies, among them Microsoft, Apple, Amazon, Tencent, Alibaba, Facebook, and Google, and to which are now added Zoom and other companies boosted by the pandemic, have experienced astonishing growth over the past decade. Apple and Microsoft registered an astounding market capitalization of $1.4 trillion each in 2020, followed by Amazon with $1.04 trillion, Alphabet (Google's parent company) with $1.03 trillion, Samsung with $983 billion, Facebook with $604 billion, and Alibaba and Tencent with some $500 billion each (Rashotee 2020). To give an idea of just how rapidly these tech behemoths have grown, Google's market capitalization went from under $200 billion in 2008 to over $1 trillion in 2020, or a 500 percent increase (Macrotrends 2018.). Meanwhile, in just two years, from 2015 to 2017, the combined value of the platform companies with a market capitalization of more than $100 million jumped by 67 percent, to more than $7 trillion (UNCTAD 2019).

A handful of largely US-based tech firms that generate, extract, and process data have absorbed enormous amounts of cash from transnational investors from around the world who, desperate for new investment opportunities, have poured billions of dollars into the tech and platform giants as an outlet for their surplus accumulated capital. Annual investment in

CIT jumped from $17 billion in 1970 to $65 billion in 1980, then to $175 billion in 1990, $496 billion in 2000, and $654 billion in 2016, and then topped $800 billion in 2019 (Federal Reserve Bank 2020). As capitalists invest these billions, the global banking and investment houses become interwoven with tech capital, as do businesses across the globe that are moving to cloud computing and artificial intelligence. By the second decade of the century, the global economy came to be characterized above all by the twin processes of digitalization and financialization.

Data shows that, from the 1980s onwards, those corporations that transitioned to CIT were dramatically more productive than their competitors, managing to resolve the so-called productivity paradox, whereby the growth in productivity notably slowed starting in 1973, the date of the onset of a structural crisis and subsequent globalization (Brynjolfsson and McAfee 2014, 100–101). As a result, the center of gravity in the circuits of accumulation began to shift toward those corporations developing and producing CIT. Digitalization is a "general purpose technology," meaning that, like electricity, it spreads throughout all branches of the economy and society and becomes built into everything. Those who control the development and application of digital technologies acquire newfound social power and political influence. As this process deepens, those transnational capitalist class groups that control general digitalization develop new modalities for organizing the extraction of relative surplus value and increasing productivity at an exponential rate. Hence the new technologies disrupt existing value chains and generate a reorganization among sectors of capital and fractions of the capitalist class. They allow the tech giants and digitalized finance capital to appropriate ever-greater shares of the value generated by global circuits of accumulation.

In this process there emerge new configurations and blocs of capital. The rise of the digital economy involves a fusion of Silicon Valley with transnational finance capital—US bank investment in tech, for instance, increased by 180 per cent from 2017 to 2019[1]—and the military-industrial-security complex, giving rise to a new bloc of capital that appears to be at the very core of the emerging postpandemic paradigm. This new bloc will emerge even more powerful than it was going into the health emergency, spurring a vast new centralization and concentration of capital on a global scale. At the head of this bloc, the tech behemoths are larger financial entities than most countries in the world and are able to wield enormous influence over capitalist states. New York governor Mario Cuomo showcased this emerging capital-state relation when, in

May 2020, he appointed three tech billionaires, Eric Schmidt of Google, Apple, and Facebook, former Microsoft chief executive officer Bill Gates, and Michael Bloomberg, media mogul and former New York City mayor, to head up a blue ribbon commission to come up with plans to outsource public schools, hospitals, policing, and other public services to private tech companies (Klein 2020). Such "public-private partnerships" privatize to capital traditional state functions, while converting public funds into corporate subsidies.

The third leg in this triangulated bloc of capital is the military-industrial-security complex. As the tech industry emerged in the 1990s it was conjoined at birth to the military-industrial-security complex and the global police state, which created much of its technology, for example, the internet (see Robinson 2020b). Over the years, for instance, Google has supplied mapping technology used by the US Army in Iraq, hosted data for the Central Intelligence Agency, indexed the National Security Agency's vast intelligence databases, built military robots, colaunched a spy satellite with the Pentagon, and leased its cloud computing platform to help police departments predict crime. Amazon, Facebook, Microsoft, and the other tech giants are thoroughly intertwined with the military-industrial and security complex (Levine 2018). The rise of the digital economy blurs the boundaries between military and civilian sectors of the economy, and brings together finance, military-industrial, and tech companies around a combined process of financial speculation and militarized accumulation.

Worldwide, total defense outlays grew by 50 percent from 2006 to 2015, from $1.4 trillion to $2.03 trillion, although this figure does not take into account secret budgets, contingency operations, and "homeland security" spending. By 2018, private military companies employed some fifteen million people around the world, while another twenty million people worked in private security. The new systems of warfare, social control, and repression are driven by digital technology. The market for new social control systems made possible by digital technology runs into the hundreds of billions. The global biometrics market, for instance, was expected to jump from its $15 billion value in 2015 to $35 billion by 2020 (Robinson 2020b, chapter 3). The concept of *militarized accumulation* helps us identify how transnational capital has become more and more dependent on a global war economy that, in turn, relies on perpetual state-organized war-making, social control, and repression, and is driven by the new digital technologies.

Laborless Production and Surplus Humanity

Crises provide transnational capital with the opportunity to restore profit levels by forcing greater productivity out of fewer workers. The first wave of CIT in the latter decades of the twentieth century triggered explosive growth in productivity and productive capacities, while the new digital technologies promise to multiply such capacities many times over. Specifically, digitalization vastly increases what radical political economists, following Marx, refer to as the organic composition of capital, meaning that the portion of fixed capital in the form of machinery and technology tends to increase relative to variable capital in the form of labor.

In laymen's terms, digitalization greatly accelerates the process whereby machinery and technology replace human labor, thus expanding the ranks of those who are made surplus and marginalized. One US National Bureau of Economic Research report found that each new robot introduced in a locale results in a loss of three to 5.6 jobs (Acemoglu and Restrepo 2017). In 1990, the top three carmakers in Detroit had a market capitalization of $36 billion and 1.2 million employees. In 2014, the top three firms in Silicon Valley, with a market capitalization of over $1 trillion, had only 137,000 employees.[2]

This increase in the organic composition of capital aggravates over-accumulation and social polarization, which has reached unprecedented levels worldwide. As is now well known, just 1 percent of humanity owns over half of the world's wealth and the top 20 percent own 94.5 per cent of that wealth, while the remaining 80 percent have to make do with just 4.5 percent (Oxfam 2015). As savage as these inequalities already were, the wealth gap widened rapidly during the pandemic, as many governments turned to massive new bailouts of capital with only modest relief, if at all, for the working classes. The US and EU governments provided an astonishing $8 trillion handout to private corporations in the first two months of the pandemic alone, an amount roughly equivalent to their profits over the preceding two years.[3] In the United States, the richest 600 billionaires increased their wealth by $700 billion from March to July 2020, even as fifty million workers lost their jobs, and as poverty, hunger, and homelessness spread. Not surprisingly, top among the earners were tech tycoons.

Such inequalities, however, end up undermining the stability of the system as the gap grows between what is (or could be) produced and

180 | William J. Robinson

what the market can absorb. The extreme concentration of the planet's wealth in the hands of the few and the accelerated impoverishment and dispossession of the majority have meant that transnational capital has had increasing difficulty in finding productive outlets to unload the enormous amounts of surplus it accumulated.[4] The total cash held in reserves of the world's 2,000 biggest nonfinancial corporations increased from $6.6 trillion in 2010 to $14.2 trillion in 2020 as the global economy stagnated.[5] But capital cannot remain idle indefinitely without ceasing to be capital. Can the current wave of restructuring open up enough new opportunities for the transnational capitalist class to invest this overaccumulated capital in the new technologies and circuits of accumulation?

The apologists of global capitalism claim that the digital economy will bring high-skilled, high-paid jobs and resolve problems of social polarization and stagnation. It is true that the first wave of digitalization in the late twentieth century resulted in a bifurcation of work, generating high-paid, high-skilled jobs on one side of the pole, giving rise to new armies of tech and finance workers, engineers, software programmers, and so on. On the other side of the pole, digitalization produced a much more numerous mass of deskilled, low-wage workers and an expansion of the ranks of surplus labor. But the new wave of digitalization threatens now to make redundant much so-called knowledge work and to deskill and downgrade a significant portion of those knowledge-based jobs that remain. Increasingly, cognitive labor and gig workers face low wages, dull repetitive tasks, and precariousness. As big data captures data on knowledge-based occupations at the workplace and in the market, and then converts it into algorithms, this labor itself is threatened with replacement by artificial intelligence, autonomous vehicles, and the other fourth industrial revolution technologies. Digital-driven production ultimately seeks to achieve what the Nike Corporation refers to as "engineering the labor out of the product" (Ford 2015, 198). The end game in this process, although still far away, is laborless production.

A 2017 United Nations report estimated that tens, if not hundreds, of millions of jobs would disappear in the coming years as a result of digitalization. As an example, the report estimated that more than 85 percent of retail workers in Indonesia and the Philippines were at risk. The report also said that the spread of online labor platforms would accelerate a "race to the bottom of working conditions with an increasing precarity" (UNCTAD 2017). A series of International Labour Organization (ILO) reports documented these conditions. A 1998 study found already in the late twentieth century some one-third of the global labor force was under- or unemployed. The ILO then reported in 2011 that 1.53 billion workers around the world were in "vulnerable" employment arrangements, representing more than 50 percent of the global workforce. Eight years later, in 2019, it concluded that a majority of the 3.5 billion workers in the world "experienced a lack of material well-being, economic security, equality opportunities or scope for human development."[6]

Even before the pandemic hit, automation was spreading from industry and finance to all branches of services, even to fast food and agriculture. It is expected to eventually replace much professional work such as lawyers, financial analysts, doctors, journalists, accountants, insurance underwriters, and librarians. AI-driven technologies are at this time becoming more widely adopted worldwide as a result of the conditions brought about by the contagion. The pandemic allows the transnational capitalist class to massively push forward capitalist restructuring that it could not previously accomplish because of resistance to the digital takeover. Those economic sectors bolstered by accelerated restructuring during the pandemic are where precarious forms of employment prevail, that is, the self-employed, contract, temporary, platform, and other such workers (ILO 2020, 4). There appears to be a new bifurcation of work spurred on by the pandemic, between those who will shift to remote work (more than half of all employees in the United States were working at home in May 2020, whereas worldwide, according to the ILO, some 20 percent of employment may become permanently remote),[7] and from their homes face new forms of control and surveillance, and those locked into high-risk "essential" in-person work, such as health care providers, cleaners, transport, and delivery workers.

Yet with heightened digitalization brought about by the pandemic there will be tens, even hundreds, of millions, who lost their jobs but will not be reabsorbed into the labor force as technology takes over their former tasks. One University of Chicago study estimated that 42 percent of pandemic layoffs in the United States would result in permanent job loss.[8] As well, large corporations will snatch up millions of small businesses forced into bankruptcy (the ILO estimates that some 436 million such businesses worldwide are at risk) (ILO 2020, 2). Capitalists will use this mass unemployment along with more widespread remote and precarious work arrangements as a lever to intensify exploitation of those with a job, to heighten discipline over the global working class, and to push surplus labor into greater marginality.

Conclusion: The Fire This Time

The pandemic lockdowns served as dry runs for how digitalization may allow the dominant groups to restructure space and to exercise greater control over the movement of labor. Governments around the world, from India to South Africa to El Salvador, decreed states of emergency and violently repressed those who violated stay-at-home orders (Robinson 2020a). The lockdowns may have been necessary from the perspective of the health emergency. Yet they showcased how the transnational capitalist class and capitalist states may more tightly control the distribution of labor power, especially surplus labor, by controlling movement and by locking labor into cyberspace and therefore making it disaggregated and isolated. As new digital technologies expand the cognitive proletariat and the ranks of workers in the gig economy, they also allow for a stringent surveillance and control of this proletariat through cyberspace.

Capitalist states face spiraling crises of legitimacy after decades of hardship and social decay wrought by neoliberalism, aggravated by these states' inability to manage the health emergency and the economic collapse. In the aftermath of the pandemic, there will be more inequality, conflict, militarism, and authoritarianism as social upheaval and civil strife escalate. The ruling groups will turn to expanding the global police state to contain mass discontent from below. Well before the contagion, the agents of this emerging global police state had been developing new modalities of policing and repression made possible by applications of digitalization and fourth industrial revolution technologies (Robinson 2018). These include artificial-intelligence-powered autonomous weaponry, such as unmanned attack and transportation vehicles, robot soldiers, a new generation of superdrones and flybots, hypersonic weapons, microwave guns that immobilize, cyber-attack and info-warfare, biometric identification, state data mining, and global electronic surveillance that allows for the tracking and control of every movement.

The sustained uprising in the United States (and worldwide) sparked by the May 25, 2020, police murder in the US state of Minnesota of an unarmed black man, George Floyd, brought these technologies of the global police state out in full force against hundreds of thousands of antiracist protesters across the country. State data mining and global electronic surveillance have allowed the agents of the global police state to expand theaters of conflict from active war zones to militarized cities and rural localities around the world. These combine with a restructuring of space that allows for new forms of spatial containment and control of the marginalized. We are moving toward permanent low-intensity warfare against communities in rebellion, especially racially oppressed, ethnically persecuted, and other vulnerable communities. All of this was displayed in the state repression against antiracist protesters. Yet this low-intensity warfare is defensive, meant to disarticulate popular insurgency from below. The antiracist uprising was the first full-scale pushback against the global police state in the richest and most powerful country in the world. It hit at the jugular vein of the machinery of war and repression, giving us a glimpse of how states and ruling groups will try to ratchet up the global police state, but also how the popular majority of humanity is prepared to fight back.

There has been a rapid political polarization in global society since 2008 between an insurgent far right and an insurgent left. The ongoing crisis animates far-right and neofascist forces that have surged in many countries around the world and that have sought to capitalize politically on the health calamity. But it also roused popular struggles from below as workers and the poor engaged in a wave of strikes and protests around the world. We have entered into a period of mounting chaos in the world capitalist system. Capitalist crises, let us recall, are times of intense social and class conflict. Depending on how these struggles play out, structural crises may expand into the third type of crisis, a *systemic* one, meaning that the crisis must be resolved by moving beyond the existing socioeconomic system, in this case capitalism.

Whether a structural crisis becomes a systemic one depends on a host of political and subjective factors that cannot be predicted beforehand. What is clear is that mass popular struggles against the depredations of global capitalism are now conjoined with those around the fallout from the health emergency. While the ruling groups deploy the new technologies to enhance their control and profit-making, this same technical infrastructure of the fourth industrial revolution is producing the resources in which a political and economic system very different from the global capitalism in which we live could be achieved. If we are to free ourselves through these new technologies, however, we would first need to overthrow the oppressive and archaic social relations of global capitalism.

Notes

1. Research Brief, "Where Top US Banks Are Betting on Fintech," *CBinsights*, August 20, 2019, accessed July 18, 2020, https://www.cbinsights.com/research/fintech-investments-top-us-banks/.

184 | William J. Robinson

2. "The Superstar Company: A Giant Problem," *Economist*, September 17, 2016, accessed July 20, 2020, https://www.economist.com/leaders/2016/09/17/a-giant-problem.

3. "Corporate Bail-Outs: Bottomless Pit, Inc.," *Economist*, April 4, 2020, 8.

4. Over the past few years there has been a rise in underutilized capacity and a slowdown in industrial production around the world (Toussaint 2020).

5. "Hanging Together," *Economist*, May 16, 2020, 60.

6. For this data, see the following three ILO reports: "World Employment Report 1996–97"; "Global Employment Trend 2011"; "The Challenge of Job Recovery; World Employment and Social Outlook: Trends 2019," all published in Geneva by the United Nations.

7. For the US data, see Barrero, Bloom, and Davis (2020, 3). For the worldwide data, see ILO, "COVID-19 and the World of Work: Concept Note," 4.

8. For a summary of the report, see Rapoza (2020).

12

Building Digital Sovereignty in Middle Powers

The Role of Intended and Spillover Effects

VASHISHTHA DOSHI

Developing countries face challenges with respect to the technology sector, which offers advantages but also risks sovereignty over the domestic market. Key points advanced in this chapter are as follows: (1) even in a world where interdependence can be weaponized, middle powers like Brazil and India have certain policy space to affect their domestic sphere and defend sovereignty and development, (2) there is a hierarchy of concerns that range in frequency of occurrence and economic pain, and (3) concerns addressed have spillover effects that sometimes advance the country's digital sovereignty. Utilizing Julia Pohle and Thorsten Thiel's framework, the chapter defines the concept of "digital sovereignty" as the "idea that a nation or region should be able to take autonomous actions and decisions regarding its digital infrastructures and technology deployment" (2020, 8).

The first section introduces the theoretical setup of the major concerns that developing countries face with respect to moderating the side effects of globalization of the technology sector. Developing countries are caught between attracting Big Tech companies to their shores and the problems emanating from Big Tech monopolizing the technology landscape. The chapter identifies four key concerns in the "Hierarchy of Concern": consumer protection, industrialization, market volatility, and hegemonic action. Consumer protection concerns occur the most but have the least economic opportunity costs, whereas concerns about hegemonic action occur most sparingly but have the most economic impact. The second section explains the role middle powers play in the global economy and the policy space that is available to them. The third section expands upon why only the United States, as of now, has hegemony in technology and finance, and thus actions taken by developing countries are essentially moderating the role of US hegemony. The fourth section describes an example of actions that countries have taken to address a particular level of concern, but those actions end up having spillover effects of insulating the country from hegemonic action. It focuses upon the spillover effects of policy actions undertaken by middle powers.

Throughout the chapter the focus is on two industries—finance and technology. These two industries are chosen because of the prevalence of their importance in literature on hegemonic action (Farrell and Newman 2019), the transmission of market volatility[1] (Higgott 1988; Cardenas, Graf, and O'Dogherty 2003), and issues of consumer protection[2] (Miklós and Simons 2021). Further, finance and tech are increasingly intertwined. The examples below of India's United Payments Interface (UPI) and Brazil's instant payment ecosystem, Pix, will show that financial sector policy is effectively technology sector policy and vice versa, because of the hydra-like nature of Big Tech's activities. In fact, the next big arena for Big Tech is financial services.[3] Apart from explicit entry into financial services, Big Tech firms form the backbone of data services of the entire financial sector. For example, the Bank of England, in a 2020 survey, estimated that more than 70 percent of banks and 80 percent of insurers rely on just two cloud providers for infrastructure as a service.[4] "Ultimately, failure of even one of these firms, or failure of a service could create a significant event in financial services, with a negative impact on markets, consumers, and financial stability."[5] The connection between technology and financial firm vulnerability takes multiple forms.

> The Financial Stability Board, in its reports on the potential financial stability implications of Big Tech,[6] discussed that Big Tech could potentially affect financial stability in three ways: (1) even if their isolated financial activities might not be systemic, they could but cumulatively generate significant financial risk, especially because these could be scaled-up very rapidly, (2) risks could be magnified by their interlinkages with regulated financial entities, such as partnerships to originate and distribute

financial products, and (3) they could generate risks as they carry out a systemically important activity ancillary to financial services, such as cloud services.[7]

Thus, as finance and technology sector policy lines blur, it is best to compare these two industries in tandem, as is done in this chapter.

Hierarchy of Concern

Democratic polities in the era of liberalization and globalization are confronted with multiple concerns when setting the technology policy agenda. Their main concerns are consumer protection,[8] industrialization,[9] external sources of market volatility,[10] and, finally, insulating their countries from hegemonic action by superpowers.[11]

CONSUMER PROTECTION

In her seminal paper analyzing how Amazon's business model hurts competition, Khan (2017) argues that Amazon's structural dominance stems from, inter alia, expansion into multiple business lines (754), its logistics dominance and leveraging of that to disadvantage rivals (774),[12] and premature acquisition of rival firms (768). Regulators have found that once Amazon moves into a particular business line it disadvantages sellers on its platform and centralizes consumer behavior toward its own product by gleaning off consumer data on their rivals' products, eventually leading to rivals leaving that business.[13] This entire hydra-like business strategy is cemented by accumulation and targeting of data that centralizes consumer behavior in ever more sectors on Amazon's platform, further entrenching the irreplaceability of Amazon. This is not an issue particular to just Amazon; other Big Tech companies like Google,[14] Facebook,[15] Apple,[16] and Microsoft have such market power that they can run other businesses out of the market,[17] limit consumer choice,[18] charge monopoly rents,[19] and in some cases even raise prices in the economy.[20]

Thus, the first level of concern—consumer protection—is shared by all countries, from developed to developing as it affects the basic functioning of the market economy. While these concerns are the most frequent, since they evolve and change as domestic markets change, they are also the most addressable with less of an economic impact.

188 | Vashishtha Doshi

INDUSTRIALIZATION

The second level of concern is less frequent than the daily needs of consumer protection, but it is still important for developing countries. This concern is labeled as industrialization. Developing countries largely face three subconcerns in this regard: (1) the need to move up in global value chains (GVCs), (2) increasing the tax base for benefits of welfare and development, and (3) making sure key intellectual property is with domestic companies. An advanced technology sector allows countries to integrate into high quality, high-value GVCs, allows for a larger share of the value chain's profits to be booked at home, and aids the creation of an intellectual property repository to expand into more cutting edge and newer GVCs.

After the failures of neoliberalism, developing countries pursued the strategy of neodevelopmentalism—"a set of political economic ideas for revitalizing industry without repeating the errors of import-substitution industrialization" (Treacy 2022, 224–25). They pursued a strategy of upgrading from being primary product exporters to entering global value chains, and progressively making products and providing services with more value addition. Neodevelopmentalist policies for the tech sector allows a country to entrench itself in technology GVCs, leading to (1) job creation; (2) technology transfer (typically from multinational enterprises to local partners); (3) capital inflow; (4) backward linkage establishment; and (5) spillover effects in the local economy (Homma 2022, 400–401).

Neodevelopmentalism is characterized by the "pursuit of economic growth with social equity through the inclusion of popular interests and demands" (Treacy 2022, 224). In order to pursue policies to benefit popular sectors, governments need more fiscal capacity, which means an ever increasing tax base. Developing countries face an environment in which technology companies shift profits and value generated from the host country into offshore, difficult-to-tax locales.[21] This is the catch-22—governments need technology companies for the benefits highlighted in the previous paragraph, but tech tax strategies hurt the social development goals of neodevelopmentalism.

Finally, the third important subconcern in "industrialization" is access to intellectual property (IP). Technology companies house immense amounts of IP.[22] As countries move up the ladder in the technology sector from business process outsourcing toward, say, semiconductor manufacturing and autonomous vehicles, execution of more complex tasks requires more intellectual property licensing from Big Tech firms, which domestic companies must pay for in foreign currency and which tend to be price inelastic, especially if the IP input is a standard across the industry.[23] Further, even if products are produced in-house within Big Tech firms, they execute intrafirm IP agreements where the domestic subsidiary is licensed to use the parent company's global IP at artificially high rates, in effect creating a pseudo-transfer pricing strategy to avoid paying taxes in the developing country (Schwartz 2019a).

In order to ameliorate these three subconcerns, countries have pursued neodevelopmentalist policies to promote domestic enterprises becoming critical players in GVCs or supplanting foreign tech companies. Countries have used measures such as data localization, state-directed below-market credit through nationalized banks or state investment funds (DiPippo, Mazzocco, and Kennedy 2022, 11), mandatory tech transfers,[24] skewing of government procurement toward domestic firms (DiPippo, Mazzocco, and Kennedy 2022, 20), and explicit market access restrictions.[25] Countries have utilized these and other measures to build domestic competitors to international platforms, which allows them to still be part of high value and keep profit and IP "at home" by supporting domestic companies.

MARKET VOLATILITY

Developing countries are also concerned about protecting domestic market stability in the face of unpredictable volatility emanating from beyond their shores. Latin American debt crises of the 1980s and the global financial crisis of 2008 showed that exogenous factors emanating from market dynamics in the West can unravel domestic stability in developing countries (Crivelenti e Castro 2022, 43–44). Open capital accounts along with interconnected financial markets allowed what was a North American housing crisis to engulf developing countries in a global financial crisis. In 2022, in the wake of the COVID-19 epidemic, developing countries are gripped by another perfect storm created beyond their borders led by rising food and fuel prices coupled with the most aggressive interest rate hikes in a generation from the US Federal Reserve.[26]

External market volatility affects developing countries through two channels: the financial economy and the real economy. The impacts in the financial channel are capital flight, domestic bank problems, devaluation (still having to pay debt in foreign currency), a fall in aid, a fall in foreign direct investment, and a fall in remittances (Green, King, and

190 | Vashishtha Doshi

Miller-Dawkins 2010, 9). The impact faced through the real economy channel are reduced exports, decreased GDP, decreased domestic demand and consumption, and lower government social expenditures (Green, King, and Miller-Dawkins 2010, 9).

Market volatility concerns have the second highest level of economic pain but only occur during times of distress in Western financial and technical markets. In order to minimize these infrequently occurring but economically painful effects, developing countries have pursued a multitude of strategies.

HEGEMONIC ACTION

Power, in international relations, comprises autonomy and influence. Influence is the ability to affect others, while autonomy is the ability to prevent others' actions from affecting oneself. As argued by Cohen, "power must begin with autonomy, which generates a potential for leverage. Influence—the deliberate activation of leverage—should then be thought of as functionally derivative" (2019, 23). In this logic, states must possess autonomy before they can influence those outside their borders. Autonomy then becomes a necessary, but not sufficient, condition for influence (Cohen 2019, 23). Great powers, like the US, possess both autonomy and influence.

Farrell and Newman (2019) describe weaponized interdependence as an influence on the entire network of interdependence—arguing that it works through two mechanisms: the "panopticon effect" and the "chokepoint effect." They classify the panopticon effect as "states that have physical access to or jurisdiction over hub nodes can use this influence to obtain information passing through the hub," while the chokepoint effect involves "states' capacity to limit or penalize use of hubs by third parties" (56). They argue that as of now only the US has this power to do both.[27]

In the world of weaponized interdependence, the US exhibits structural power[28] (akin to influence) in the technology industry via nodes (such as jurisdictional authority over the world's internet traffic) that are also chokepoints (Strange 1987; Farrell and Newman 2019). By combining insights from Farrell and Newman (2019) and Cartwright (2020), it can be safely concluded that the US can weaponize interdependence by exercising jurisdictional authority over its market-dominant firms.

Weaponization of interdependence exposes developing countries to risks emanating from hegemonic action because US firms form the core of technology services utilized by them. However much this level of concern,

Building Digital Sovereignty in Middle Powers | 191

Figure 12.1. Hierarchy of Concern. *Source:* Created by the author.

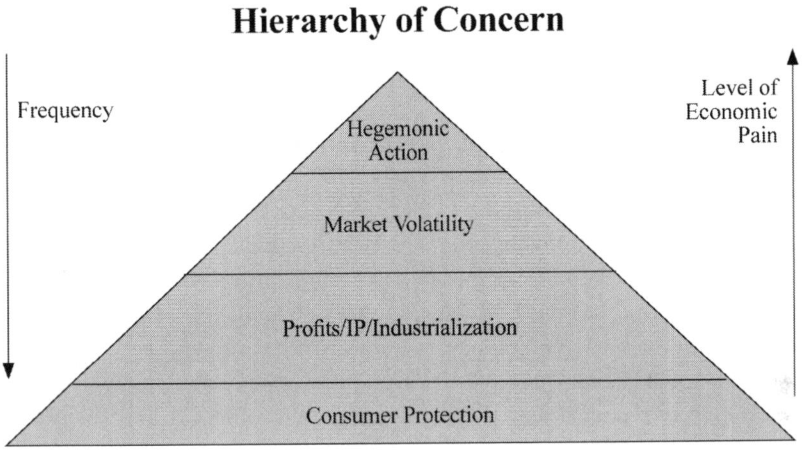

Hierarchy of Concern

hegemonic action from the US has the lowest frequency of occurrence. Still, as countries from Iran to Russia to Venezuela are finding out, it can cause the highest level of economic pain.

Role of Middle Powers

Power hierarchies pervade the international system (Lake 2011), in which a set of countries are engaged in subordinate relationships with the hegemon (Lake 2007). International hierarchies exist in various facets of the international economic system as well (Cohen 2000). If hierarchy was a pyramid with the US at its apex, the countries that occupy space between the apex and bottom would be classified as middle powers. This chapter's understanding of middle powers is not that dissimilar to how semiperipheries are described in world systems theory (Wallerstein 1976). Middle powers are still engaged in a subordinate relationship with the hegemon but have significant market dominance in their home countries and presence in the countries surrounding them (Wallerstein 1976, 464). The difference is that instead of deterministic outcomes—derived from an "antipossibilist" policy orientation as once criticized by Hirschman (1980)—the emphasis is on the possibility of agency and statecraft as being able to create apertures and innovation in the system.

192 | Vashishtha Doshi

Middle powers are defined according to Jordaan's (2003) definition as "states that are neither great nor small in terms of international power, capacity and influence, and demonstrate a propensity to promote cohesion and stability in the world system." According to the framework of Cooper, Nossal, and Higgott (1993) and Holbraad (1986), middle powers' policy behavior is a product of their contextually located deliberate action emanating from their position in the world order.

Considering the dual nature of power—autonomy and influence—these countries certainly cannot exercise influence in the fields of finance and technology like the hegemon. However, due to their large internal markets, relevant levels of human capital, and financial capacity, they are not completely subordinated either. They still retain a modicum of agency (Narlikar 2021). This means that middle powers can ward off potentially adverse effects emanating from the panopticon and chokepoint effects exercised by the hegemon on the network. However, they are not able to influence the entire network—as the hegemon does. Their power is thus limited to autonomy only and not to influence. That is, middle powers can carve out policy spaces in a world of weaponized interdependence, should they want to bear the costs. In essence, they have the potential to safeguard their sovereignty but do not have the ability to undermine the sovereignty of others by influencing the network.

Thus, middle powers have the potential "policy space" to address different levels of the Hierarchy of Concern at different times. They have the ability to limit effects from happening to them, such as providing protection to their consumers, preventing the effects of market volatility, and so forth.

US Hegemony in Tech

The theoretical argument begins with an emphasis on the role of United States hegemony. This hegemony is manifested here as extraterritorial exercise of digital sovereignty at global scale. This section argues that the US—and as of now only it[29]—exercises hegemony in the fields of finance and technology that are analogous and important for comparison. We discuss the variables through which power resides in the technology industry and the centrality of US firms within it. Finally, the section concludes with a discussion on how the US externalizes its power through the centrality of US technology firms.

US firms are central to the technology sector (Starrs 2013, 822). Out of the top one hundred technology companies in the world, thirty are US firms.[30] Out of the top one hundred websites visited in the world sixty of them are US firms' websites.[31] Further, "More than half of all network traffic in 2021 (57 percent) was attributable to Google, Netflix, Facebook, Apple, Amazon, and Microsoft."[32] More importantly, a significant chunk of this traffic passes through a single geographical location—Loudon County, Virginia.[33] Similarly, Google dominates worldwide search engine market share (over 85 percent market share).[34] Facebook and other US firms dominate social media market share.[35] Google's Android is the dominant mobile operating system in India (with a 95 percent market share)[36] and Brazil (with over 85 percent market share).[37] And most Indians and Brazilians connect to the internet via their mobile device. Thus, any cessation of Android services would collapse the digital economy. Similarly, in India, Amazon's AWS, Google Cloud, and Microsoft's Azure account for over 60 percent of the market share,[38] with similar market shares in Brazil.[39] Further, as these firms grow bigger, they will funnel more global data within their ambit. The majority of these firms' business model is dependent on the extraction of value from personal data processing (Zuboff 2019; Birch, Cochrane, and Ward 2021). This requires the immense collection and storage of personal data, and then the ability to monetize it for profits (Birch, Cochrane, and Ward 2021, 9).

The global dependence on US technology firms, their need to accumulate data, coupled with the US legal framework—which includes the lack of a general data protection law matched with legislation allowing both international surveillance and access to data treated or stored domestically and abroad by US firms—allows the US government to create a panopticon effect on global information flows.[40] As stated by General Michael Hayden, former CIA director, "because of the nature of global communications, we are playing with a tremendous home field advantage, and we need to exploit this edge. We also need to protect this edge and those who provide it."[41] For example, this level of centrality of the internet's key services in the hands of corporations from a single country—the US—exposes developing countries to acute extraterritoriality risks. These factors combined gives the host state of these market-dominant US firms an immense ability to weaponize the network.

The Edward Snowden leaks revealed how the US utilizes the dominant position of its internet firms to conduct mass surveillance in the world (Greenwald and MacAskill 2013). Cartwright (2020, 5) lists more examples of how the US government has utilized the dominant position of its technology companies to create a panopticon effect. For some analysts, unless there is a decline in the usage of US digital technology companies for most of the global internet traffic and personal data, it seems highly unlikely that the US's panopticon effect can be curtailed in any meaningful way (Osborne 2019). As Farrell and Newman (2019) describe—for reasons of US industrial policy goals together with specificities of history and context—the US government has not yet turned this advantage from the panopticon effect into more than a small-scale chokepoint effect. However, it is not an inconceivable scenario where one day the US could order its firms to exercise a chokepoint effect on the data of extraterritorial entities (whether it be public or private).[42] As discussed above, the requisite recipe—concentration of data on US soil, US firms' market dominance, and the legal framework—is in place to exercise this option at a large scale with the potential of a major disruption to others' national security, as well as economic and human rights.

Before ending the discussion on US centrality in the technology industry, it is important to clarify that the section is not arguing that data in the possession of or passing through US technology firms is the sole basis of the US ability to weaponize interdependence. Positioning its technology firms at the core of the data economy—some providing services presented as "free" but in reality paid with data—is one of the ways in which the US maintains the upper hand in the digital age. Moreover, data concentration follows from such centrality and makes it impossible for other firms to compete.[43] Through a combination of the centrality of US firms, provisions (and practice) for US government agencies to access data that flows within the ambit of these firms,[44] and the willingness of the US to utilize this privilege to achieve state goals,[45] the US enjoys extraterritorial projection of its digital hegemony while other countries face constraints on their digital sovereignty. Moreover, the levels of data concentration in a few US tech giants are unsurmountable barriers to entry that make it impossible for other firms to compete, even in their home markets.

There are several other ways through which the US can weaponize interdependence. For example, most of the world's location-based devices are connected to the US GPS system. It is not inconceivable that the US could block a country's access to the GPS system.[46] Another variable is undersea cables. A significant amount of data that passes through US firms' servers in the US goes through undersea cables. It is not inconceivable that the US could utilize this privileged position to block access to these cables for certain entities. Protection of undersea cable is a significant part of American geopolitical strategy,[47] and the country even forced a joint Facebook-Google undersea cable to avoid landing sites in Hong Kong. The US State Department's Clean Network, an initiative publicly delineated in 2020, provides an insight into the technology industry variables that the US considers geopolitically relevant.[48] In short, there exists the *potentiality* for the US to weaponize interdependence along with other variables of the technology industry.

The above discussion delineates how the US exercises both forms of power—autonomy and influence—in the fields of finance and technology. In this section, we focused on the role of US firms as conduits through which the US state can exercise power. Combining the concepts of Farrell and Newman (2019) and Cartwright (2020), the high international market dominance of US firms in finance and technology, combined with US jurisdictional authority over them, allows the US to weaponize interdependence (both the panopticon and the chokepoint effect) over the entire network.

Intended and Spillover Effects of Policy Space Utilization by Middle Powers

Middle powers have utilized the policy space discussed in section two to address various levels of concerns at different times. The central argument here is that measures used to address different levels of the Hierarchy of Concern can end up having spillover effects. For example, actions undertaken to create policy space for consumer protection may end up insulating countries from hegemonic action. Conversely, those actions taken for explicitly geopolitical reasons may end up enhancing consumer and human rights protection at home. This section looks at variables in tech and finance where available space was utilized by middle powers to address a particular level in the Hierarchy of Concern pyramid (intended effect) but also ended up having a spillover effect addressing another level of the pyramid.

Intended and Spillover Effects: Finance

Middle powers have utilized defensive financial statecraft to shield the domestic economy from external financial pressure (market volatility)

(Armijo and Katada 2014, 8). Countries have used the strategies of capital controls, local currency debt issuance, and foreign currency reserve accumulation "to shield their country not against a particular foreign state but rather against systemic influences, whether coming from global markets or from the rules and institutions of global financial governance" (Armijo and Katada 2014, 169). The authors label this as defensive but systemic financial statecraft. Thus, even if the actions were undertaken to mitigate risk from market volatility they amounted to carving out policy space that addressed other levels of the Hierarchy of Concern pyramid.

For example, the accumulation of foreign exchange allows countries to weather market volatility without severely impacting residents' purchasing power and ensures a store of value of domestic currency for them. Thus, a measure intended to address market volatility ends up being useful for consumer protection. After the Latin American debt crisis, developing countries predominantly started issuing debt in local currency. This measure was used to make sure that market volatility in Western markets did not to a large extent undermine government funding; it also meant that the domestic central bank would have more levers to help maintain monetary stability in times of stress. However, even though local currency debt issuance was mainly enacted as a policy to address concerns related to market volatility, it ended up addressing the consumer benefit level. Local currency debt issuance allowed for countries to continue with social policies without severe cuts that would otherwise be required if only foreign currency debt was issued. It prevented a run on the financial account, which would rapidly destabilize exchange rates of local currency, thus diminishing the purchasing power of residents. Finally, capital controls form another measure where countries enacted a policy to address concerns of market volatility but the spillover effect was to ensure the safety of the store of value for residents—a consumer benefit.

In order to propel the vision of Digital India,[49] the government of India enacted the JAM policy[50]—Jan Dhan (roughly translated as mass financial inclusion), Aadhaar (unique identity provision to every Indian to avail themselves of government services), and Mobile. To provide infrastructural support for the J and A aspect of the JAM trinity, the government decided to step in with the provision of digital public infrastructure (DPI).[51] This is also colloquially referred to as the India Stack.[52]

The India Stack is a three-layered infrastructural setup with Aadhaar—which means "foundation" in Hindi—forming the base layer. "In just 5 years, more than one billion Indians had received an Aadhaar card. . . . this makes it one of the most successful rollouts of any tech product anywhere in the world . . . , covering more than 94% of the country's entire population" (Vir and Sanghi 2021). Aadhaar forms the basis of India's e-authorization system.[53]

Most Indians had remained unbanked for so long because they couldn't physically show papers authenticating themselves to open a bank account. Aadhaar's e-KYC function allowed previously unbanked Indians to prove their identities digitally and instantaneously to open a basic, free of charge bank account (Jan Dhan). Between 2011 and 2018, the total number of adults with bank accounts went from 20 percent to 80 percent.

On top of the Aadhaar layer is the payments layer. Newly banked Indians would not be able to do anything with their banking access if it was not connected seamlessly to commerce and services in the real world. This leads to the DPI of payments. Further, the concern was that if the DPI of payments was not built, a fragmented marketplace in payments would result. Individual internet platforms would create their own systems with walled moats and the whole purpose of seamlessly interoperability available to all Indians would be lost. Thus, comes the United Payments Interface (UPI) and RuPay (similar to Visa and Mastercard), a nonprofit entity.[54] UPI provides the public rails that handle the routing of payment messages. All regulated banks are plugged into the UPI system, so any third-party apps or consumers that are connected to one bank can access instant transfers to all bank accounts. UPI is currently "the world's 5th largest payment network by volume, behind only Visa, Alipay, WeChat Pay, and MasterCard" (Vir and Sanghi 2021).

The intended purpose of creating UPI was to boost financial inclusion, provide efficient and leakage-free delivery of government services (which was a major problem before), and induct small and medium enterprises into the formal economy. However, the spillover effect of UPI's success has been to limit potential hegemonic action, such as preventing what happened when the United States government ordered Visa and Mastercard to halt payments in Russia overnight.[55] Thus, "the link between plastic and politics has acquired a more serious dimension: circumventing potential denial of service."[56] In the eventuality of hegemonic action, India already has a homegrown and operated domesticated payments network that functions at scale, thus blunting the effect of potential weaponization of the two big American payment networks.

Brazil, similarly, has, at scale, a domesticated payments network in the form of Pix and the Elo card. Elo, a wholly Brazilian credit card brand, was launched in 2011 as a partnership between three of Brazil's largest banks, Banco do Brasil, Bradesco, and CAIXA. Together, these three banks represent nearly three-quarters of total banking accounts in the country.[57] Thus, Elo's domestic market share grew quickly and it became very popular. While the decision to set up Elo may have been a corporate strategy by Brazil's top three banks (CAIXA and Banco do Brasil are government owned) to capitalize on the network effects and capture more of the value from each transaction, the spillover effect of having Elo is that Brazil now has a domesticated payments network that is scalable and thus preempts pain from any potential hegemonic action that may occur from the weaponization of Visa and Mastercard.

Similar to India, Brazil created an instant payments system called Pix. The goals of Pix, as envisioned by the Brazilian Central Bank, were similar to the ones set forth by India. Brazil wanted to further financial inclusion in the country and also kick-start a digital, formalized economy. However, initially the Brazilian authorities gave a go-ahead to WhatsApp to conduct financial transactions. While WhatsApp's largest user base is in India, the second largest is in Brazil. The authorities quickly realized that this would give WhatsApp a first-mover advantage and allow the company to build financial moats around its business that would be detrimental to competition. WhatsApp was blocked from conducting transactions for almost a year. In the meantime, the Brazilian Central Bank launched Pix. By launching Pix first, and then reauthorizing WhatsApp to conduct financial transaction (but only on the Pix network), the Brazilian Central Bank helped to promote broader competition in this area.

Thus, similar to India, while the goals of having a fully domesticated digital and plastic payments network was financial inclusion and promotion of the local digital economy, the spillover effects of both these country's actions is to insulate themselves from weaponization of payments network (should it ever materialize).

INTENDED AND SPILLOVER EFFECTS: TECHNOLOGY

In the technology industry, countries have concerns at all levels of the pyramid, and try to address them in a manner in which they see fit. This subsection explores two such variables that countries have tried to address, their intended and spillover effects.

One of the prime concerns for developing countries is to ensure that their vast small and medium enterprises, which provide livelihoods to millions, are not submerged under an oligopolistic foreign-owned corporate architecture.[58] Another is to ensure that vast profits from lucrative technology businesses are booked at home to add to tax buoyancy and thus governments are able to expand social services budgets. To address both—consumer benefit and industrialization—Brazil and India have adopted different strategies.

India has primarily adopted a two-pronged approach. First, India explicitly attacked the digital moats of the e-commerce firms of Amazon and Walmart through techno-legal regulations.[59] One such solution is India's Open Network for Digital Commerce (ONDC).[60] On December 31, 2021, ONDC was incorporated as a private sector, nonprofit (Section-8) company to democratize e-commerce in India and offer alternatives to proprietary e-commerce sites. "ONDC was incubated by the Department for Promotion of Industry and Internal Trade (DPIIT) at the Quality Council of India. The initiative has been touted as necessary to end the dominance of behemoth platforms like Flipkart and Amazon that have been accused by the government of exercising monopoly, contrary to the law."[61]

The big idea behind ONDC is to unbundle the current model of e-commerce marketplaces. Today, big e-commerce firms (Amazon and Walmart control 80 percent of the e-commerce market share in India) own both the "seller ecosystem" and the "buyer ecosystem." This is how mobile wallets operated before UPI. Just like how UPI enables users to send money from app A to a merchant who is using app B, ONDC does this for e-commerce. Put simply, ONDC is to e-commerce what UPI is to payments.[62] "Buyers and sellers can transact on ONDC irrespective of whether they are attached to any specific e-commerce portal. For instance, even if a seller X is registered on platform A, while the consumer is registered on platform B, the consumer can directly purchase products of seller X without d registering on platform A from the ONDC network."[63] With an open network, ONDC will enable all the buyers in the network to be discoverable to all the sellers. With ONDC, all e-commerce companies in India have to operate using the same processes.[64]

India's second approach tries to make sure domestic markets remain competitive spaces and that profits are booked at home by promoting national champions. India has tacitly supported two private conglomerates—TATA and Reliance—to enter the e-commerce field and take on the foreign giants of Walmart and Amazon.[65] When Amazon entered India, there were regulations in place prohibiting multibrand retail under the same firm for foreign companies.[66] Further, "Foreign Direct Investment

Policy 2017 ("FDI Policy") prohibited foreign-funded marketplace players from engaging in inventory-based model of e-commerce, though there was no such bar on domestic-funded marketplace players."[67] This was a tacit way for the government to promote domestic industry to tie up with foreign retailers and then expand within the country. Out of this policy was born Amazon's joint venture with the company of one of India's most respected businessmen, Narayana Murthy of Infosys. This firm, Cloudtail, quickly became the largest seller on Amazon's platform. However, as e-commerce took off and it started seriously hurting India's small and medium retailers, the lifeblood of its employment, the traders' association "requested" that Murthy end his association with Amazon.[68] They wrote letters to the government. After two years of interaction between Murthy, the government, and the traders association, Cloudtail ceased its joint venture with Amazon India.[69] "Interestingly, the decision came soon after the Supreme Court of India allowed the Competition Commission of India to investigate Amazon and rival Flipkart for unfair trade practices."[70] This would prove to be step one, ensuring that Indian conglomerates were on the side of the government.

India's step two was to ensure that it supported its domestic conglomerates launch of e-commerce firms. In this regard, the government gave tacit support to Reliance and TATA to kick-start their ventures. Reliance was engaged in a full-throated battle with Amazon for a retailer with a big domestic presence, Future Group. In this battle, Amazon even won the arbitration case in Singapore in its favor, but eventually Reliance won the war and was able to acquire the assets of that company.[71] This allowed Reliance to consolidate its offline presence in the country through physical big box stores, thus giving it more touch points and access to ubiquitous last-mile logistics, which is key to fast deliveries, a major competitive factor in e-commerce firm success.

In the case of Brazil, no techno-legal solutions like ONDC were employed to maintain competitive markets, but Brazil has explicitly and tacitly supported its domestic enterprises in the e-commerce space to ensure that concerns about "industrialization" are addressed. Whereas in the supermarket/groceries side of retail, the biggest players are controlled by French capital—Carrefour and Casino—both online retail as well as on the ground logistics to deliver the products are dominated by Brazilian players. Firms such as Magazine Luiza, Via (through brands such as Casas Bahia), B2W (through brands such as Americanas and Submarino), plus the Argentine Mercado Libre are dominant in the local market. Amazon is just one player and not the best positioned one, even though it arrives with a capitalization that only the world's largest retailer has available.

While the intended effects of actions such as these address the bottom two layers of the pyramid—consumer benefit and industrialization—the spillover effect of this is to mitigate any potential hegemonic action that could result from weaponization of the services provided by these e-commerce firms. For example, in the recent rounds of sanctions on Russia, American firms such as Coca-Cola, Pepsi, Starbucks, and McDonald's immediately suspended operations.[72] It is not inconceivable to imagine that American e-commerce firms with dominant market share give the US government power to suspend operations and inflict pain on the domestic economy of another country. However, if the domestic market is competitive with a healthy mix of foreign and domestic corporations, all functioning at scale, then a potential weaponization action by the US government would cause much less pain and economic adjustment, blunting its effects. Thus, measures undertaken by developing countries to address the bottom two levels of the Hierarchy of Concern pyramid end up having the spillover effect of addressing a concern at the very top—insulation from hegemonic action.

On the next page is the list of other variables depicting actions undertaken by Brazil and India to address concerns at one level of the Hierarchy of Concern pyramid with spillover effects on another level of the pyramid.

Conclusion

The central argument of this chapter is that developing countries have different levels of concern. These concerns range from protecting consumer benefits to preventing being negatively affected by hegemonic action. However, these concerns are not equal. The frequency of concern increases as you move down the pyramid but the level of economic pain increases in the inverse direction (as you move up the pyramid).

Middle powers occupy the proverbial middle space between great powers and small countries where they have the "policy space" to enact measures to affect their domestic economy but not much beyond their borders. This policy space allows them to affect concerns on the pyramid to safeguard their autonomy.

Table 12.1. Actions and Spillovers in Brazil and India

	Measure	Brazil	India	Intended	Unintended
FINANCE	Reserve Accumulation	X	X	Market Stability	Preserve Store of Value for Consumers
	Nationalized Banks	X	X	Industrialization/Consumer Credit	Market Volatility
	Domestic Payment System	X	X	Financial Inclusion	Hegemonic Action
	Capital Controls		X	Market Stability	Profits/Industrialization
	Local Currency Debt Issuance	X	X	Market Stability	Hegemonic Action/ Consumer Benefit
TECH	Nationalized Cloud	X		Hegemonic Action	Profits/Industrialization/ Consumer Benefit
	GPS Alternative		X	Hegemonic Action	Profits/Industrialization
	Data Localization		X	Profits/Industrialization/ Consumer Protection	Hegemonic Action
	Domestic Carriers		X	Profits/Industrialization	Consumer Protection/ Hegemonic Action
	Removing Platform Moats		X	Consumer Benefit/Profits/ Industrialization	Hegemonic Action

Countries take different measures to address different levels of the Hierarchy of Concern pyramid. However, these measures, along with the intended effects, end up having spillover consequences that sometimes enhance a country's autonomy. Measures affecting the bottom two levels have spillover consequences of addressing the top two levels of concern, and vice versa.

Brazil and India are two such middle power countries that have utilized their policy space to address different levels of concern at different stages. In the financial sector, both Brazil and India have undertaken similar policy measures addressing a particular level of the pyramid and having similar spillover effects. The example discussed in detail in this chapter concerns the domestic payments network. Both Brazil and India came to develop a domestic payments network from different intentions but ended up with similar intended and spillover effects. Both RuPay/UPI and Pix/Elo have the same spillover effect of protecting the domestic economy from the potential weaponization of payments networks.

In the technology sector, both Brazil and India wanted to execute similar intended effects—protecting consumer benefits and addressing the needs of industrialization—but took different approaches. Brazil, at the outset, took its existing, large physical retail sector and promoted it to transition and dominate the e-commerce sector. India was slow to realize the potential of e-commerce. As domestic interest groups rose, the Indian government took a two-pronged approach using techno-legal solutions to ensure consumer and small traders' benefit, all the while promoting domestic conglomerates in the e-commerce sector. Despite both countries trying to address concerns at the bottom two levels of the pyramid, the spillover effect is to insulate the domestic retail sector from potential weaponization.

Normatively, this chapter argues that middle powers have policy choices available to them to address their various levels of concern. The best approach for middle powers, like Brazil and India, would be to utilize their available policy space and take measures to address whatever level of concern they can. Sometimes addressing one variable at one level of the pyramid may end up seeing spillover consequences at another level. States can also take a more deliberative approach whereby they strictly address concerns at the bottom two levels of the pyramid but do so in such a way that it ends up having the spillover benefit of addressing one of the top two levels. This chapter does not argue for autarky, but rather for a deliberative strategy to affect different variables at different levels of concern.

Notes

1. https://indianexpress.com/article/explained/amazon-google-financial-services-rbi-concerns-7498521/; https://www.business-standard.com/article/finance/why-rbi-is-concerned-about-equitas-sfb-s-new-scheme-for-google-pay-users-121090700025_1.html.

2. https://www.npr.org/2022/04/23/1094485542/eu-law-big-tech-hate-speech-disinformation.

3. https://www.wired.co.uk/article/big-tech-versus-big-banks.

4. https://www.bankofengland.co.uk/bank-overground/2020/how-reliant-are-banks-and-insurers-on-cloud-outsourcing.

5. https://www.imf.org/en/News/Articles/2021/06/16/sp061721-bigtech-in-financial-services#_ftn2.

6. https://www.fsb.org/2019/12/bigtech-in-finance-market-developments-and-potential-financial-stability-implications/.

7. https://www.imf.org/en/News/Articles/2021/06/16/sp061721-bigtech-in-financial-services#_ftn4.

8. https://www.marketplace.org/2022/04/01/another-cure-for-inflation-making-markets-more-competitive/; https://www.npr.org/2022/04/23/1094485542/eu-law-big-tech-hate-speech-disinformation; https://www.politico.eu/article/eu-strikes-deal-on-law-to-fight-illegal-content-online-digital-services-act/.

9. https://www.csis.org/analysis/red-ink-estimating-chinese-industrial-policy-spending-comparative-perspective; https://www.imf.org/Publications/fandd/issues/2019/09/tackling-global-tax-havens-shaxon.

10. https://www.bis.org/publ/work709.htm; https://www.bis.org/publ/bisbull05.htm; https://www.voanews.com/a/as-us-federal-reserve-raises-rates-emerging-markets-brace-for-impact/6560242.html.

11. https://www.washingtonpost.com/opinions/2022/05/12/biden-sanctions-russia-could-erode-dollar-power-financial-economic/; https://www.opindia.com/2022/03/mos-meity-rajeev-chandrasekhar-aatmanirbhar-internet-to-prevent-weaponization-big-tech-russia-ukraine-war-india/; https://www.politico.com/news/2019/12/20/policymakers-worry-china-drug-exports-088126.

12. The EU and Italian regulators have judged this practice as anticompetitive and have hit Amazon with massive fines for this precise reason. https://fortune.com/2021/12/09/amazon-antitrust-fine-italy-billion-steering-vendors-shipping-service/.

13. https://www.wsj.com/articles/amazon-scooped-up-data-from-its-own-sellers-to-launch-competing-products-11587650015.

14. https://www.justice.gov/atr/case/us-and-plaintiff-states-v-google-llc.

15. https://www.ftc.gov/news-events/news/press-releases/2020/12/ftc-sues-facebook-illegal-monopolization; https://www.cnbc.com/2019/02/07/german-antitrust-watchdog-cracks-down-on-facebook.html.

Building Digital Sovereignty in Middle Powers | 205

16. https://www.wsj.com/articles/apple-abused-dominance-in-mobile-wallets-markets-according-to-preliminary-eu-view-11651487879.

17. https://www.wsj.com/articles/amazon-scooped-up-data-from-its-own-sellers-to-launch-competing-products-11587650015.

18. https://www.cbsnews.com/news/washington-dc-amazon-antitrust-lawsuit-higher-prices/.

19. https://blog.adif.in/p/apple-google-app-store-policies-actions?s=r.

20. https://www.epi.org/blog/corporate-profits-have-contributed-disproportionately-to-inflation-how-should-policymakers-respond/.

21. https://www.imf.org/Publications/fandd/issues/2019/09/tackling-global-tax-havens-shaxon; https://www.pbs.org/newshour/economy/business-jan-june09-taxhavens_04-15; https://actionaid.org/sites/default/files/how_tax_havens_plunder_the_poor.pdf; https://www.cfr.org/blog/tax-games-big-pharma-versus-big-tech.

22. https://www.wired.com/story/big-tech-patent-intellectual-property/.

23. https://papers.ssrn.com/sol3/papers.cfm?abstract_id=949599.

24. https://theweek.com/articles/831859/chinas-forced-technology-transfer-actually-pretty-good-idea.

25. https://www.nytimes.com/2018/08/06/technology/china-generation-blocked-internet.html.

26. https://www.bloomberg.com/news/newsletters/2022-04-21/the-big-take-how-inflation-fed-rate-hikes-impact-emerging-markets; https://www.voanews.com/a/as-us-federal-reserve-raises-rates-emerging-markets-brace-for-impact/6560242.html; https://www.nytimes.com/2022/05/17/business/inflation-developing-economies.html.

27. https://www.nytimes.com/2022/03/16/opinion/us-russia-sanctions-power-economy.html.

28. Strange (1987) defines structural power as the power "to decide how things shall be done, the power to shape frameworks within which states relate to each other, relate to people, or relate to corporate enterprises" (25).

29. Even the EU is concerned that European states are "gradually losing control over their data, over their capacity for innovation, and over their ability to shape and enforce legislation in the digital environment" (European Parliament 2020, 1).

30. https://www.forbes.com/top-digital-companies/list/.

31. https://www.visualcapitalist.com/ranking-the-top-100-websites-in-the-world/.

32. https://techmonitor.ai/technology/networks/big-tech-accounts-for-over-half-of-global-internet-traffic.

33. https://www.voanews.com/a/usa_all-about-america_heres-where-internet-actually-lives/6184090.html.

34. https://www.proceedinnovative.com/blog/google-dominates-search-engine-market/.

35. https://gs.statcounter.com/social-media-stats.

36. https://gs.statcounter.com/os-market-share/mobile/india.

37. https://gs.statcounter.com/os-market-share/mobile/brazil.

38. https://www.thehindubusinessline.com/info-tech/amazon-microsoft-google-accounted-for-61-of-the-total-cloud-infra-services-spend-in-q2-2021-report/article35713733.ece.

39. https://www.bnamericas.com/en/features/spotlight-who-leads-brazils-cloud-market-and-in-which-verticals.

40. See "18 USC Ch. 121: Stored Wire and Electronic Communications and Transactional Records Access," U.S. House of Representatives, 18 U.S.C. §§ 2701 § (1986); https://uscode.house.gov/view.xhtml?path=/prelim@title18/part1/chapter121andedition=prelim. See "H.R.5949—FISA Amendments Act Reauthorization Act of 2012," https://www.congress.gov/bill/112th-congress/house-bill/5949/all-info.

41. https://fas.org/irp/congress/2006_hr/072606hayden.html.

42. This scenario is actually not very far from what happened when Android was prohibited from supplying software to Huawei in 2019. https://www.france24.com/en/20190520-business-huawei-google-android-ban-saudis-iran-opec-oil-china-african-swine-fever-pork.

43. See the reasoning behind EU efforts to "open" access to US tech giants' databases via the Digital Service Act and Digital Markets Act.

44. https://timesofindia.indiatimes.com/world/us/Google-Facebook-and-others-got-money-from-US-govt-to-spy-on-users/articleshow/22012312.cms.

45. https://techcrunch.com/2021/03/29/united-states-myanmar-sanctions-internet/.

46. In order to minimize the potentiality of weaponization of interdependence by the US, countries such as Russia (GLOSNASS) and China (BeiDou) have deployed their own global navigation satellite system analogous to the US (GPS) system and mandate that mobile phones sold in the country either have to run on domestic systems or both domestic and GPS.

Russia: https://www.gpsworld.com/glonass-to-be-required-for-phones-sold-in-russia/.

China: https://www.globaltimes.cn/content/1196983.shtml.

47. https://www.csis.org/analysis/securing-asias-subsea-network-us-interests-and-strategic-options.

48. https://2017-2021.state.gov/the-clean-network/index.html.

49. https://www.digitalindia.gov.in/.

50. https://www.brookings.edu/research/is-india-ready-to-jam/.

51. https://www.deccanherald.com/international/india-using-public-digital-infrastructure-to-achieve-economic-goals-at-home-connect-globally-jawed-ashraf-843135.html.

52. https://www.indiastack.org/.

53. Aadhaar continues to face serious cybersecurity issues, https://jsis. washington.edu/news/the-aadhaar-card-cybersecurity-issues-with-indias-biometric-experiment/. Also, *Puttaswamy v. Govt. of India* guaranteed every Indian the right to privacy, kick-starting India's discussion of a comprehensive data protection law, https://globalfreedomofexpression.columbia.edu/cases/puttaswamy-v-india/.

54. UPI is one of the payment systems within the National Payments Corporation of India umbrella, setting standards and protocols by which all the banks, the third-party apps, and senders connect, https://www.npci.org.in/who-we-are/about-us.

55. https://www.bbc.com/news/business-60637429.

56. https://www.bloomberg.com/opinion/articles/2022-03-13/india-wants-to-overthrow-visa-and-mastercard-s-dominance-it-has-several-options.

57. https://www.ipass.com/wp-content/uploads/2017/11/iPass-Customer-Success-Story-Elo.pdf.

58. https://inc42.com/buzz/retailers-vs-amazon-cbi-probe-demand-over-search-results-rigging/; https://economictimes.indiatimes.com/small-biz/sme-sector/cait-fully-geared-up-to-fight-amazon-flipkart/articleshow/83501204.cms?from=mdr.

59. https://exmachina.substack.com/p/smart-regulation.

60. https://www.aljazeera.com/economy/2022/4/28/this-indian-billionaire-is-working-to-curb-the-powers-of-amazon.

61. https://www.india-briefing.com/news/what-is-the-open-network-for-digital-commerce-ondc-and-how-will-it-impact-ecommerce-in-india-23463.html/.

62. https://swarajyamag.com/technology/explained-how-the-ondc-is-all-set-to-democratise-e-commerce-in-india.

63. https://www.india-briefing.com/news/what-is-the-open-network-for-digital-commerce-ondc-and-how-will-it-impact-ecommerce-in-india-23463.html/.

64. https://economictimes.indiatimes.com/tech/technology/flipkart-ril-amazon-may-join-ondc/articleshow/91500926.cms.

65. https://on.ft.com/3PP06Zy.

66. https://law.asia/retail-fdi-india-restrictions-solutions/.

67. https://corporate.cyrilamarchandblogs.com/2020/02/indias-foreign-investment-policy-on-e-commerce-retail/.

68. https://www.thehindubusinessline.com/companies/sellers-body-urges-narayana-murthy-to-end-partnership-with-amazon/article35413164.ece.

69. https://timesofindia.indiatimes.com/business/india-business/amazon-to-end-jv-with-murthy-firm/articleshow/85197875.cms.

70. https://www.moneycontrol.com/news/business/startup/amazon-ends-partnership-with-nr-narayan-murthy-catamaran-ventures-from-may-2022-7298651.html.

71. https://www.livemint.com/companies/news/how-reliance-stunned-amazon-in-battle-for-india-s-future-retail-read-here-11646553177687.html; https://

www.reuters.com/world/india/amazons-battle-with-reliance-india-retail-supremacy-2022-03-08/; https://www.thehindubusinessline.com/news/reliance-to-walk-away-with-947-stores-despite-future-deal-being-called-off/article65351323.ece.

72. https://www.cnbc.com/2022/03/08/coca-cola-follows-mcdonalds-starbucks-in-suspending-business-in-russia.html.

13

Digital Economy Policies for Developing Countries

PARMINDER JEET SINGH

Toward a Digital Industrial Policy

Digital must be considered as distinct from the information technology/ software and internet sectors or phases, even as it builds over them. Digitalization is about the actual economy, and not just the technology, or information and communication, parts of it.[1] Digitalization concerns very considerable changes in all aspects of all economic sectors—from transportation, hotels and tourism, to finance and logistics, to health, education, agriculture, and manufacturing. Digitalization is a wholesale change in the operation of the global economy, requiring new forms of industrial policy if developing countries are to compete (Singh 2020).

Economic value chains once used to be centered on manufacturing capabilities, and in the last decades intellectual property ownership has risen to the top of these value chains. Digital economy is the next stage, as economic value chains become centered on digital intelligence services in each sector. Core digital intelligence services extending across a sector have a natural monopoly characteristic. The current digital economy model is for a sector's core intelligence to be privately owned, by one or two monopolistic corporations, based on exclusive control of core sectoral data, even if the data is collected mostly from "commons" sources. Alternatively, core sectoral data and digital intelligence could be in the form

210 | Parminder Jeet Singh

of public infrastructures. Employing it, a set of digital businesses could develop further private data and digital intelligence and provide digital intelligence services in an open and competitive manner.

Even e-commerce companies like Amazon and Alibaba have gone much beyond selling goods to reengineering the entire consumer goods economy and controlling it digitally. Online marketplaces transcend traditional definitions of open markets by manipulating access for sellers to different buyers, prices dynamically among buyers, and prices across buyers and sellers. Further, they penetrate the entire value chain from manufacturing to inventory management to logistics to delivery and payments. They are therefore far from just neutral platforms for buying and selling. The area that needs focus as their main business asset is sector-wide digital intelligence across the consumer goods value chain. They may more appropriately be treated as monopolistic digital intelligence service businesses rather than e-commerce. This makes an Amazon quite like an Uber, or a Monsanto setting up a digital agriculture services platform. It is not necessary for a digital intelligence business to be monopolistic, and public or "commons" data infrastructures in a sector can enable a competitive environment for digital businesses.

Strategy for Developing Countries

Like with earlier phases of industrialization, developing countries must first focus on digital industrialization, where they are severely lagging behind, before entering into commitments on global digital trade. A digital industrial policy begins with developing enabling legal and regulatory frameworks to support easy and legally recognized digital interactions, and protecting the interests of all actors in this regard. The importance of this is well recognized by most countries, and necessary frameworks are either already in place or being developed.

One aspect of any digital industrial policy would be to build a supportive environment around tech and digital start-ups that have begun to emerge in most developing countries. This new sector must be recognized in its peculiarities and unique needs, and its great national importance. Meeting its capital requirements, including through venture funds, is vital. As important is to undertake ease-of-doing-business measures, especially quick and easy entry as well as exit for these businesses. Developing and supporting incubators and accelerators, in association with industry groups, will have a significant impact on shaping a local start-up ecosystem.

Effective start-up supporting policies depend on policymakers' understanding of the tech and digital start-up sector, and the various kinds of start-ups involved. For example, with the cloud-based software as a service industry, a further consolidation has happened in the software space with even fewer viable industry centers globally than existed for the on-premise software (coding) model. A proper assessment should therefore be made whether any particular location has comparative advantages to globally compete in this area, in a market that is highly integrated and whose structure is most suited to a single, global market. In the current conditions, it may not be easy to create locational advantages for most developing countries; for example, only a few centers in India have achieved the feat. But there does exist space for cloud-based companies catering to niche domestic and regional software needs and markets, especially if these markets are given some protection. This space will expand as the digital phenomenon seeps deeper into all parts of the economy and society.

Meanwhile, even as cloud-based solutions are becoming the mainstay, considerable local IT/software related work, outsourced from abroad and aimed at the domestic economy, is still required. There continues to be business opportunity in this area for many relatively established, as well as emerging, software center across the developing world, and for smaller companies and new entrepreneurship.

The other kind of start-up, typified as digital start-ups, need special attention and new policy orientations. This is because they have a unique characteristic of localness of their key resource, that is, data. But they still need to compete with global businesses, with huge financial muscle, that are entering every country's digital space. They also need to be protected from being sucked into monopolistic platform/ecosystem owning businesses, on unfair terms—for them and for the larger economy. Public management of some digital/data infrastructures can provide significant support to domestic digital industry. Some such possibilities will be mentioned presently.

Digital transformation has come at a good time for many developing countries experiencing a big surge in the number of educated and aspiring youth, seeking to break away from the shackles of underdevelopment, for themselves and their societies. The current digital ferment can trigger new entrepreneurial energies and cultures, helping shape a new phase in economic and social development. Entrepreneurship is as much cultural, a matter of a certain kind of individual and collective spirit and behavior, as its conditions are institutional. Both these aspects need to be promoted simultaneously by appropriate strategies and policies. Much digital innovation is currently being tried out in almost all sectors in India (among other countries), and the landscape here is useful to study and learn from for other developing countries.

But the innovation and start-up discourse needs to be carefully moderated. While innovation is important, much late industrialization in most countries has always involved just copying successful business models and technologies from outside and applying them to the local contexts. This holds true for digital industrialization as well. Not every start-up needs to set out to become the next global unicorn. It is important both to manage expectations and keep the focus considerably domestic (or to regional markets). It may be noted that even with relatively favorable conditions, there is hardly any traditional-sectors-oriented digital start-up in India that has made a prominent global mark.

Digitalization in Traditional Sectors

As traditional sectors go digital, much of the early innovation in technology and digital business models has already taken place in the US and elsewhere. A major part of the digital challenge is to adapt these to local conditions. In this regard, some established domestic traditional businesses can take a lead on digital efforts in their respective areas. In India, for example, Ashok Leyland is building a digital platform for the end-to-end needs of the goods transport sector (Maru 2017). For its part, the European Union (EU) is focusing on an "insider model," which may also be attractive to developing countries. It aims at existing European industrial champions in different sectors building the digital platforms that will dominate the concerned sector. "Industry in Europe should take the lead and become a major contributor to the next generation of digital platforms that will replace today's Web search engines, operating systems and social networks," observed Günther Oettinger, European commissioner for the digital economy and society (Oettinger 2015). This "insider model" is contrasted with the US "outsider model" where outsiders—digital start-ups and larger digital companies—are "disrupting established industries from without." And it is distinct from "the Chinese version of the same

Digital Economy Policies for Developing Countries | 213

'outsider' model, in which Beijing bars American digital companies from operating and replaces them with Chinese equivalents: Alibaba for Amazon, Baidu for Google" (Fidler 2015).

Within the "insider model," traditional businesses have the advantage of sectoral expertise. They can also come up with the needed funds (beyond venture capital), willing to take some amount of risk within the sectors that they understand and where they have a foothold. Such alternative sources of finance need to be explored because venture capital is scarce in developing countries. There is the problem, however, that digital seeks to disrupt and transform existing business models, which is not easy to do from within. To meet the requirements of innovation and "disruption," it may be useful to get start-ups to partner with traditional businesses, especially involving young leaders from the latter. Banks and health companies in India have been developing partnerships respectively with fin-tech and health-tech start-ups. Special strategies and initiatives need to be devised in this regard.

Governments can provide incentives to people and businesses to undertake a digital makeover and nudge them in other ways. The Indian government has taken a lot of very useful, and far-reaching, steps in this direction. However, individual and social behavior, as well as every social/economic system, has considerable inertia. Any large-scale change carries a cost, especially if done quickly. As with any other economic and social change, the interests of different people, groups, and businesses may be affected differently in any digital makeover. Digitalization tends to favor the formal sector over the informal sector, and where there exist competitive overlaps between the two it can be of considerable detriment to the latter. It is therefore advisable not to take any blunt social-engineering approach in this respect and carefully chart out the way forward.

Pilots and phased rollouts are useful methods, although the appropriate means of implementation would depend on the context. All the involved trade-offs should be carefully evaluated, especially the impact on weaker sections of society. As industrial development centrally required public investments in infrastructure, a digital industrialization policy must also focus on building public digital and data infrastructures. This is the single most important, and yet neglected, area for governments to urgently address. It goes beyond connectivity/access, and the IT/software layers, that are often discussed. These predigital infrastructures remain important; digital cannot exist without them. But whichever stage a country may be in terms of these predigital infrastructures, it needs to concurrently

214 | Parminder Jeet Singh

begin developing digital and data infrastructures as well. Taking a relaxed sequential approach could result in a debilitating exclusion from key digital economy/society developments.

Being successful in developing digital/data infrastructure may be less difficult for governments than generally thought. The barriers are more of conceptual understanding and political will than physical- and resource-related. Unlike connectivity/access infrastructure, which is a physical layer, and thus takes considerable resources and time to universalize, digital is a soft layer and can be developed much more quickly, and at relatively less cost. And unlike the IT/software layer, where the offerings of global digital corporations may be difficult to beat or replace, data infrastructures have a very strong local character, and governments have traditional competence and advantage in large-scale data systems. While national efforts to develop search engines were not very successful in Europe and national efforts at operating software were not very successful in India, there have been some pathbreaking steps by the Indian government in terms of data infrastructures.

Public Data Infrastructures

The public sector must explore its role in three kinds of data infrastructures; (1) horizontal—digital transaction enabling; (2) personal data architectures that are safe while providing the best social and economic value for the individual and the society; and (3) core sectoral data for different sectors (here may also be included important society-wide datasets).

Appropriate public digital and data infrastructures can ensure a robust, competitive, and inclusive digital economy that supports new and diverse digital business models. It also enables easy access to the social and economic data required to meet various public interest objectives, like policymaking and governance. It can also provide leverage for governments to effectively regulate digital businesses. Apart from India, some initiatives and policy frameworks in the EU provide good lessons in this regard.

For example, promising new thinking is emerging in the EU regarding appropriate regulation for data, digital, and platform businesses. Data regulation is one of the most important regulatory issues right now. Developing countries need to understand both privacy rights and the economic value/ownership aspects of data, and their interplay. Digital platforms that dominate and shape complete sectors urgently require

Digital Economy Policies for Developing Countries | 215

new regulatory approaches. They increasingly constitute the all-powerful intelligence infrastructure of every sector. From economic, social, and security/strategic/political points of view, digital sector platforms represent extremely critical infrastructures. All these standpoints should inform their regulation.

An important way to support domestic digital industry is through government procurement. Alibaba's e-commerce platform relied considerably in the initial stages on government purchases (Carsten and Ruwitch 2015). Where needed, governments may themselves have to get into developing some digital services, possibly in partnership with domestic industry. For example, the Indian government set up the rather successful e-agriculture marketing platform. It is planning to set up a cloud service called "Farmer-Zone" that would be "a shared resource framework . . . where(by) [the] right kind of agridata will be collated, analyzed, and then distributed to take care of day-to-day needs of farmers. . . . Data related to weather prediction, disease and pest surveillance and control, soil nutrition, irrigation needs, seed selection, credit linkages and market access will be used for developing the cloud-based platform" (Mohani 2017).

In another example, an electronic agriculture trading model was pioneered by the state of Karnataka, whose capital is Bangalore. A total of 105 markets spread over twenty-seven districts of the state were brought under the Unified Market Platform by 2016. Private traders including large companies are also allowed to register on this platform. This model became so successful that it was emulated by many other states, and the central government has now launched an electronic trading platform called the National Agriculture Market (e-NAM).

Beginning with twenty-one agricultural markets from eight states, the initiative has been taken to 585 markets across the country. Twenty-five crops, including wheat, maize, pulses, oilseeds, potatoes, onions, and spices, were included for trading on the platform (Chand 2016). This is an important public initiative for developing the digital marketplace of a key sector.

Institutional Change

Different from the IT/software industry, technical skills by themselves are not sufficient or very useful in the digital phase. Basic technical skills, in large quantities, first established India in the global software market, but technical, business, and other educational processes need to focus on understanding the digital phenomenon, and the development of appropriate digital business, social, and policy skills. Chinese governments and academic institutions have made a quick and extremely remarkable transition to centrally promoting digital knowledge and skills. Some of the world's cutting-edge work in the digital area today comes from China. Much of this effort involves public sector partnerships with Chinese digital corporations (Gershgorn 2017). This area requires urgent public investments in all developing countries. It is important to see business, social, and policy skills in the digital area as quite different from the relevant technical skills, and all should be promoted.

Digital policy and programmatic requirements are so new, intense, and cross-sectoral that considerable institutional change will be required within governments. It is not adequate for IT ministries to keep dealing with this sector in a technology-centric manner. On the other hand, commerce and industry ministries remain too focused on industrial age thinking, and normally do not possess enough digital knowledge and orientation. There is a need to create a new ministry or department for the "digital economy"—preferably for the "digital society," with the "digital economy" as a specialization. It is possible for IT ministries to evolve in this direction, but the thinking, orientation, and expertise must undergo considerable change. As the digital economy represents the application of digital to all sectors and industries, including manufacturing (the phenomenon of "Industry 4.0" and "Internet plus"), commerce and industry promotion ministries too must make a conscious transition to a new skill set. IT and industry ministries need to work together on developing digital industrial policies.

As an urgent starting point, developing country policymakers need to begin obtaining appropriate knowledge and policy perspectives in this area. They cannot remain dependent on global venues where knowledge seems to be determined by northern interests. This is even more so in crucial emerging areas like the digital economy where economic models and global comparative advantages are still being formed and entrenched.

Unfortunately, a singular narrative on the digital economy has been established, and depending on whether one subscribes to it or not, one is taken to be either for a digital economy or not. The digital economy is a given, as much as industrialization was inevitable on the invention of a means of incorporating steam and later fossil fuel and electric power into manufacturing. Industrialization was about disembodiment of physical power from humans and animals to machines; the digital revolution is about the disembodiment of intelligence from humans and human systems to machines. It is not a matter of being for or against it. It is about what kind of digital economy we should have. And it is about exploring the different possible pathways, along with mapping the differential interests that are involved. "Development agendas" in trade and intellectual property areas were about differential contexts and interests of developing countries vis-à-vis those of developed ones. A development agenda for the digital economy needs similarly to be articulated, based on an alternative narrative that takes proper account of developing country interests.

It is not easy for individual developing countries to build and maintain the required knowledge competence in this complex and fast-moving area. Institutions of South-South cooperation in economic areas, like UNCTAD (United Nations Conference on Trade and Development) and the South Center, should therefore step in to meet their knowledge and policy needs.

The Global Digital Economy and the Developing World

Developing countries are facing great pressure at global trade forums to opt into the dominant US-led global digital economy model (USTR 2016), which still goes under the name of "ecommerce" at these forums. The 1998 e-commerce work program at the World Trade Organization (WTO), developed at a very different time, is currently sought to be revived for new purposes by the OECD. A problematic example of the way this has biased global discussions can be found in the draft Trans-Pacific Partnership chapter on e-commerce, which posed threats from liberal civil rights and "openness" perspectives (Malcolm and Sutton 2015), as well as economic and social rights standpoints (Kelsey 2017).

The strong transformative winds of the digital economy, however, cannot be denied. Resistance to the dominant US model can only be effective if it moves from a reactive phase—finding problems with its proposed trade rules—to a proactive one—where developing countries present their own vision and model of a digital economy. This should be based on new thinking at domestic levels toward an appropriate digital industrial policy.

Very different kinds of goods and services get traded electronically. The first kind are electronically traded physical goods—such as manufactured or agricultural goods. These goods still travel across borders. The normal wisdom should be that irrespective of the means by which the deal is made, they remain subject to the trade rules and tariffs applying to the concerned category of goods. However, e-commerce greatly changes global transaction costs in a manner that locally made goods can lose existing cost advantages that they may have enjoyed. Because of their likely impact on importing countries, great caution therefore needs to be exercised in any discussion even on the "facilitation" of electronic exchanges, which account for most of the proposals at the WTO.

Domestic markets for cheap goods manufactured and consumed locally may earlier have remained protected, as the transactional and logistics costs for importing them were too high relative to the cost of manufacturing. Such goods constitute a very large proportion of goods in small local markets, especially in poorer economies, and their production supports much of the small- and medium-enterprise sector. With giant global e-commerce companies reorganizing the global trading ecosystem, altered transactional costs disproportionately threaten such local markets. For example, a Chinese e-commerce company, KiKUU, operates in six African countries, focusing on selling Chinese goods (KiKUU 2016). It also organizes complementary services like logistics, payment, and delivery. Similarly, Alibaba is discussing and setting up special border arrangements with the Malaysian government for speedy custom clearance of its goods entering Malaysia (Cher 2017). One can very well envision a KiKUU-like platform doing the same in Africa and other places. It will aggregate local demand in a locality, and every few days big containers will land from China with all the individual small deliveries, quickly cleared by customs. The efficiency of the whole supply/logistics chain will be so high that the platform will be able to sell more cheaply than locally manufactured goods, serving even small, dispersed markets. Additionally, as Alibaba has now begun to do in China, a KiKUU kind of platform can potentially also take up supply chain and logistics management for small shops. Since the digital context allows the effortless and inexpensive combining of mass manufacturing with customization, these supply chains can easily adapt to such small and dispersed markets.

Promotors of the dominant e-commerce narrative concerning physical goods like to cite examples of small and medium enterprises producing niche goods, often with cultural-artisanal value. But a very large proportion of any economy, especially in its poorer parts and small- and medium-enterprise sector production, consists of mundane goods of regular use. Mass manufacturing of such goods in a few specialized centers will easily

Digital Economy Policies for Developing Countries | 219

flood open-market systems with very low transaction costs, as provided by e-commerce. Developing countries need to carefully weigh their options. The huge efficiencies of digitalization must first be utilized to strengthen the domestic economy, which requires a sound digital industrial policy, before opening it up globally.

Very different from physical goods, even if traded electronically, are goods and services that can exist fully in a digital form. These are of five kinds; (1) cultural goods; (2) traditional services that are provided physically on premise, but can also be delivered digitally from afar, like back-office services, transcription, tuitions, medical, or other professional consultations; (3) core technology services—software and applications over the cloud (or through downloads); (4) services involving data flows within a business system, with full clarity on data ownership (this category could include some services from categories 2 and 3 above); and (5) global digital services, centered on data and digital intelligence.

UNESCO's Convention on Protection and Promotion of the Diversity of Cultural Expressions declares that "cultural activities, goods and services have both an economic and cultural value . . . and must therefore not be treated as solely having commercial value" (Voon 2006). An observer notes this treaty as granting "nations the sovereign right to protect and promote the diversity of cultural expressions within their territory against the sweeping tide of globalization (Articles 5 and 6)" (Pauwelyn 2005). Perspectives from this convention, and other similar ones, should be brought to digital cultural flows, which are more intense cross-culturally than ever before (UNESCO 2016). Cultural goods have their specific regulatory context and cannot be treated as normal commodities of global trade.

The second category above is of IT enabled services involving the electronic transmission of traditional services that can exist physically on premise—like back-office services, transcription, tuitions, medical or other professional consultations, and so forth. These need centrally to be looked from the lens of the WTO's General Agreement on Trade in Services and other services agreements, as applicable.

Core technology services—software and technology applications over the cloud (or through downloads)—currently constitute a well-functioning global market without any specific trade deals. Issues of monopolies and excessive profits, and denial of user rights, exist in many cases, which require regulatory solutions like interoperability rules. In general, however, it serves developing countries' interest to retain relatively free global technology flows, insofar as they involve core technology services. These should be subject to necessary domestic regulation, especially in the area of critical technologies, and governments should be able to favor domestic industry in its procurements and partnerships. High-quality software and applications are crucial to the functioning of all sectors today, and while it is not easy for most countries to develop them, such efforts should be made.

Software/internet services mostly follow global templates, with little attempt or need for local customization. For this reason, once they are established in the North it does not cost much to extend these services to developing country markets, while earning huge additional profits. There is no danger therefore that northern suppliers of such technologies will withdraw them if they do not get further liberalization commitments or other sacrifices from developing countries. Developing countries can continue to benefit from the global technology market without negotiating any new trade agreements, which will only take away important domestic policy options. And for countries like India that see a great opportunity to export in these global technology markets, there is not much to gain either from exploring new trade deals.[2]

The remaining two categories involve considerable data flows, but of very different kinds. The fourth category of services, from the above list, involves global data flows where there is full clarity about who owns the data and various values arising from it. Data largely stays within a specific business system, and its ownership is clear and uncontested between the business parties interacting across borders.[3] For example, companies send out data to other companies for back-end processing, including possibly to help analyze it and obtain insights, or multinational companies moving data globally across operations. This includes data flows involved in global cloud computing service interactions, a model that is increasingly becoming mainstream.[4]

The element of public interest in such data flows is mainly about legal and regulatory remits, and the corresponding need for unhindered access by the concerned authorities. Adequate privacy protections are required as per the domestic law of the place where the data originates. Access to data may be required for criminal investigations, or simply because the concerned business activity is of critical importance, and subject to special regulatory oversight. What is needed for these purposes are global or intercountry data protection and access agreements. The matter does not directly concern digital trade regimes. Agreements may need to be reached on issues like standard minimum data protection and security regimes, categories of critical industries requiring special data protection

Digital Economy Policies for Developing Countries | 221

and regulation, conditions and means for cross-border regulatory or law enforcement access, and so on.[5]

The fifth category is global digital services, defined as those whose business model centers on data and digital intelligence as the key economic resources. These services work on data that is collected mostly from sources outside the concerned business's strict ownership realms. Such data also gets transported across borders. These are extremely large collections of very detailed data about a sector—data about people (including personal data), social processes and conditions, machines and other artifacts, and nature and the environment. Employing this "outside" data, from all possible sources, digital businesses develop deep and granular digital intelligence about the complete ecology of a particular service, or a whole sector. This business model tends toward sector-wide operations, and monopoly formation, in the shape of sector-platforms; these are the centerpiece of digital economy. Such monopolistic digital intelligence services are increasingly oriented to all sectors. It is with regard to these globally operating businesses that the global "free flow of data," and related issues like data localization, become key. These are currently the main bones of contention in global digital trade forums.

The real cross-border data issue that directly concerns global trade is when data is collected, and retained, by global corporations from outside their business systems, and for time periods, much beyond what may strictly be required for specific narrow business interactions, with unclear data ownership and data use-rights. "Global free flow of data" is really a euphemism for global digital corporations asserting the right of unhindered global collection, privatization, and economic appropriation of such general social or "commons" data. It is not a trade facilitating concept, as projected. It is about expropriation of the most valuable resource in the digital economy, without clear legal rights to do so. Global data flows must first be discussed in a political economy framework before talking about their trade facilitating role.

Unlike the category of business data flows,[6] the national interest in this case is not so much legal and regulatory access to data (which concern may concurrently exist), but the ambiguity around ownership rights over data collected from "outside" or nonproprietary sources, and the nature of its possible further use. The source of such data may be "personal"—related to dispersed individuals—or "social/public." This possibly renders such data as a collective national resource—directly if the sources were "public," and in trusteeship for the dispersed individuals if "personal."[7] In the latter case, the concerned individuals have no way to leverage their ownership of such data other than through a collective agency like the state. The central problem with the current digital economy model is the economic (as well as social and political/strategic) appropriation of a key resource, without clear rights to do so, and its subsequent transfer outside the country. Such extraction of valuable national data by foreign corporations will result in various kinds of economic/social/political control and exploitation, and corresponding dependencies of the target countries. Once collected, data retains very long-term value, and therefore these controls and exploitations are not just for now but for decades to come.

It is this kind of general data, with unclear ownership rights, which is important to protect from cross-border "free flows of data" regimes. It is the most significant economic and social resource in the digital economy. Oddly enough, this aspect of data flows has not even been identified properly in global e-commerce or digital economy discourses. Concerns about data flows that are usually cited, including by developing countries, almost entirely relate to regulatory and law enforcement issues. It is up to developing countries to anchor a new discourse centered on the relationship of the "global free flow of data" to "economic value" and "national ownership" of data.

Such general data can be considered a national resource. Corresponding frameworks regarding its ownership, use, and economic value appropriation need to be developed and enforced nationally. Before any negotiations of trade rules around data can begin, much less a commitment for unhindered flow of such data across borders made, discussions must be held at national and international levels on (1) developing appropriate frameworks for individual and collective ownership of such general data (including, but not limited to, personal data); (2) understanding and conceptualizing the nature of economic flows that are implicated when such general data is (a) privatized, (b) transferred outside a country, and (3) recognizing the nature and importance of digital intelligence built from such data, as the key economic resource that is globally used to control whole sectors and entrench rent-seeking positions.

Work needs to be done at international and national levels to identify, separate, and describe different categories of electronic transmissions that are, very problematically, clubbed under one term, *e-commerce*. This should be followed by exploring different corresponding treatments that they require in terms of business development, regulation, trade, and so forth.

Digital Economy Policies for Developing Countries | 223

UNCTAD and other such global organizations that have a development-friendly mandate are appropriate to take up such work.

The term *e-commerce* employed at global trade venues needs to be replaced with *digital trade* as better representing this vast field. Digital economy's key valuable resources and business models must be examined and understood first, along with the contexts and interests of different countries in this regard. Cross-cutting issues of a general enabling nature can only be taken up after that. The same can be said for the new terminology of "facilitating e-commerce" that is now being proposed at the WTO by some countries. It is difficult to facilitate something without knowing sufficiency well its basic nature and substance. Commitments sought like rules or e-commerce facilitation frameworks will render it very difficult, if not impossible, to develop the necessary public digital/data infrastructures and various digital regulatory powers. Both are key to successful digital industrialization by developing countries.

China is the only country that has been able to stand up to the global digital dominance of the US, which was the first mover in this area. It did so by following very protectionist policies, whether disguised as security interests or not. This holds an important lesson for every late starter on how difficult it is for a domestic digital industry to develop unless some amount of protection, and appropriate government support, is provided. This is true for most industries, but it is even truer for the digital industry because of its special structural features. Even with its formidable technical skills and business muscle, the weak position of the EU in the global digital economy provides good evidence of this. Protection for the domestic digital industry does not have any necessary trade-off with freedom of expression, an ideological cover that the "free flow of data" narrative often hides behind.

The EU is discussing ways to check Chinese takeovers of its digital and tech companies that are considered strategic for security or economic reasons. This makes it evident that digital is no ordinary sector, in terms of its structure as well as its strategic significance. Developing countries need to make a careful assessment in this regard, and accordingly shape digital policies.

The digital sector requires a critical mass of a large enough market to be successful. This can present a problem for countries, especially small- to medium-sized ones, in developing a strong domestic digital industry. Europe is creating a digital single market, with a single policy

224 | Parminder Jeet Singh

and regulatory space, and some emerging common public digital infrastructures. Developing countries should also explore regional digital single markets as an important part of their digital industrial strategy. African countries are in talks to develop a free trade zone for Africa (Juma 2017), and its digital aspects should be seriously, and perhaps separately, examined. Such sufficiently large, but somewhat protected, spaces are vital for development of a healthy digital economy in the South. Within these, a set of countries with similar or complementary digital positioning and advantages can promote their digital businesses.

This does not mean disengaging from global digital value chains. Digital technologies are fast evolving, complex, and require continued smooth global flow and exchange. These technologies work on data to give rise to digital businesses, and, as discussed, the data end of this amalgamation is more locally oriented. This data side or aspect is what needs better management for the common good as well as greater protection, at least initially. Developing countries must work with global value chains but simultaneously protect enough local market space and degrees of freedom for their domestic industry. What this means, at the very least, is that the current global technology and digital markets are working well without any new binding trade commitments by countries. Any premature agreements in this area will simply compromise the technology and data regulation powers of governments. In these times of great ferment, the latter are very important to retain to appropriately shape the domestic and global digital economy.

Notes

1. Digitalization encompasses e-commerce and other applications of data.

2. The issue about business process outsourcing and software as a service companies processing foreign data is a data flow issue and not about technology flow. It will be discussed presently.

3. This holds for back-office processing, an area with global stakes for India, but other data services require different trade rules.

4. When a business uses the cloud computing facility of another business, it rents only the technology facility, and there should be no confusion or doubt about who owns the involved business processes and data.

5. Business process outsourcing, and now cloud computing, in India shape desires for free flows of data, generating conflicts with high privacy requirements, such as those with the EU. What India needs is a data-secure status.

Digital Economy Policies for Developing Countries | 225

6. It is important to distinguish business data flows (internal to a business, and its partnerships ecology) from the flow of personal and social data, which does not belong to the business involved in its collection.

7. Interestingly, India has used the term *data sovereignty* both in terms of a citizen's right over her data and in the sense of a country having full rights over data originating from the country (Press Trust of India 2017).

14

The Chinese Digital Revolution

How Digital Transformation Is Shaping a New China

ALESSANDRO TEIXEIRA GOLOMBIEWSKI
AND ZHENYU JIANG

The internet has profoundly affected the world economy since Tim Berners-Lee created the World Wide Web in the 1980s. At almost the same time, China began its reform and opening up under the leadership of Deng Xiaoping. China was lucky to catch the ride, experiencing both the industrial and digital revolutions.

In the 1980s, the market economy system was yet to be fully established in China and the government was playing a leading role. At that time, reform policies like China's household contract responsibility system in rural areas and special economic zones were implemented. China became a country of strengthened profit and, along with modern management reforms in the 1990s, gradually privatized the state economic system. In particular, Deng Xiaoping inspected southern China and delivered an important speech. Then the 14th Chinese Communist Party National Congress was held, so the industrial policies were established during the period of the initial establishment of the market economy system. After entering the twenty-first century, China has adopted a series of industrial policies such as urban job growth, rural tax reforms, export growth strategy, engagement with the World Trade Organization, and so on. However, with the intensified pollution at the same time, greater attention was paid to social and environmental concerns. China's industrial structure and development have reached a higher level, and its industrialization marched toward the "world's manufacturing powerhouse."

Due to fantastic timing, China has been focusing on digital transformation for a long time. In 2000, Xi Jinping, then governor of Fujian Province, was the first in China to propose a construction plan for a digital transformation, Digital Fujian, which became the origin of the idea and practical starting point of Digital China. In 2017, Digital China was part of the report of the 19th National Congress of the Communist Party of China.

Nowadays, international market demand has shrunk, global currency has deflated, and trade volume has declined. China has proposed a "Made in China 2025" strategy to combat the impact of the economic crisis and COVID-19. Made in China 2025 is a ten-year government initiative, and the first stage of a larger three-part strategy, aimed at transforming China by 2049 into one of the world's most advanced and competitive economies (Zenglein and Holzmann 2019). China aims to utilize innovative manufacturing technologies, also called smart manufacturing, to continue to move up the manufacturing value chain. In this process, the digital economy plays an important role, and it provides the possibility for China's economic take-off.

Figure 14.1. China's digital economy market size and proportion in GDP from 2005 to 2020. *Source*: Created by the author using data from Wind Database.

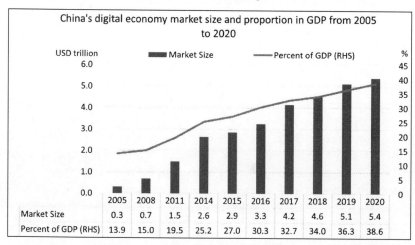

The Chinese Digital Revolution | 229

In 2002, the size of China's digital economy reached $5.4 trillion (fig. 14.1), ranking second only to the United States. The number of internet users has increased every year and was almost one billion individuals in 2020, and the number of 5G base stations in China exceeds 1.5 million. The conditions provide opportunities for the rapid development of China's digital economy. To meet the wave of the digital economy, in recent years, local governments at all levels have introduced digital-economy-related policies to promote the development of local digital transformation. Beijing proposed to build a "global digital economy benchmark city." Shanghai proposed to accelerate the creation of an "international digital capital" with world influence. Guizhou Province released the first provincial digital economy development plan. And all industries are undergoing a dramatic digital transformation.

Communication operators in the 1990s experienced a period of great development of mobile communications, dedicated lines, broadband, installed fixed-line, and market competition, all of which decreased bottlenecks for enterprise development. In recent years, the telecommunications market has encountered development difficulties, voice and SMS industry and other traditional business scenery no longer dominate, data traffic growth and operators have increased revenue disproportionately, the proportion of investment in technology has been climbing, communications operators have begun to look for new market growth points, and enterprises have been forced to respond and embrace digital economy business opportunities.

The industrial internet is the deep integration of the industrial system and the internet system under digitalization, supporting a new round of the industrial revolution and a key to promoting China's structural reform on the supply side. From a global perspective, the industrial internet has become a transformation trend for enterprises in various countries. According to the latest available data from the Internet Data Collection, countries spent $154 billion on industrial internet software in 2019. The United States and China spent the most, followed by Japan, Germany, South Korea, France, and the United Kingdom. Over the past fifteen years, cases of China's industrial internet fueling the digital transformation of manufacturing abound.

China has also launched a national digital currency, Digital Currency Electronic Payment, or DCEP, and initiated blockchain-related programs. According to the China Academy of Information and Communications Technology, there are more than 1,400 blockchain enterprises

Figure 14.2. Most AI patent filings are made in the US and China. *Source*: Created by the author using data from WIPO 2018.

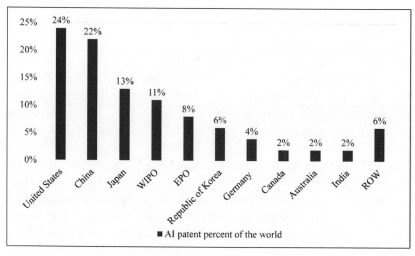

in more than forty industrial parks in China, facilitating the growth of other emerging technologies, such as artificial intelligence. The Chinese government has elevated the development of blockchain technology to a national strategic level, which will further support China's global technological rise, its digitalization process and fintech development, and bring many positive impacts to China's macro economy and leading industries.

The digital revolution began in the 1980s when Tim Berners-Lee created the World Wide Web, and in less than thirty years, the internet has had a profound impact on the world economy. Whereas it took nearly 300 years for the West to realize all the changes brought about by the Industrial Revolution, it took less than thirty years for China to leap from an underdeveloped country to one of the world's largest economies. China's digital revolution is proceeding even faster. China is becoming a leader in digital transformation around the world, bringing a new impetus to its economic growth.

The Importance of the Digital Economy for Modern China

The digital economy injects "fresh blood" into China's manufacturing industry. The manufacturing industry has always been the pillar of China's economic development. As the core of China's system, industrial production efficiency and capacity level are directly related to the speed and quality of

China's total economic growth. Since the reform and opening up, China's manufacturing industry has maintained a high growth trend for a long time. Moreover, in 2010, China's manufacturing industry accounted for 19.8 percent of the global manufacturing industry, surpassing the United States to become the world's largest infrastructure power and industrialized country. By 2021, China had further consolidated its position as a major manufacturing country, ranking first in the world for eleven years and accounting for nearly 30 percent of the global total (National Bureau of Statistics of China 2022). However, at present, China's industrial development is facing headwinds.

First, as China's population growth rate in 2021 was only 0.34 percent (fig. 14.3), the lowest since 1960, and the proportion of the elderly over sixty-five years old has reached 14.2 percent, China has officially entered the "aged society" from the "aging society." The disappearance of demographic dividends and the decline of labor advantage have become an irreversible fact. Second, China is a manufacturing power, but it faces limitations. China has long been at the low end of the global value chain, mostly engaged in low-value-added, low-demand-elasticity, labor-intensive or resource-intensive products, and China has become the "factory of the world," which has also resulted in a crude growth model that not only consumes more energy but also pollutes the environment. At the same time, China is also facing criticism as a "pollution sanctuary." Again, now the world economic situation is turbulent, international financial uncertainty makes countries nervous, political, economic, diplomatic, security, and many other factors are intertwined, China-Ukraine trade friction and the Russia-Ukraine conflict and other factors make the prices of commodities

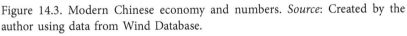

Figure 14.3. Modern Chinese economy and numbers. *Source*: Created by the author using data from Wind Database.

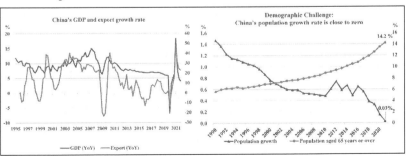

and other factors of production rise sharply, and there has been a new round of inflation. For China's manufacturing industry, it is even more "snowy." Finally, the sudden outbreak of COVID-19 has disrupted the world's original production and development plans, and China needs to find a new direction and breakthrough. The digital economy is a breakthrough.

Currently, more than 22 percent of global GDP is closely tied to the digital economy. By 2025, the digital economy is expected to drive about half of global output growth (UNCTAD 2021). The digital economy has enabled the creation of new industries and business models, allowing companies and people to connect across borders, linking producers to consumers and workers to jobs. Digitalization has already had a transformative impact on a variety of industries. The globalization of the internet provides the prerequisites for the flow of the digital economy around the world. With the widespread adoption and penetration of the next generation of digital technologies, China has officially entered the digital economy. Relying on innovative technologies such as artificial intelligence, robotics, blockchain, and algorithms, China's digital economy has grown rapidly over the past five to ten years. Digital industrialization and industrial digitization are driving a high degree of integration between the digital economy and the real economy. They are also contributing to multiple changes in the

Figure 14.4. E-commerce sales in China are still growing fast. *Source*: Created by the author using data from the China Academy for Information and Communications Technology (2021).

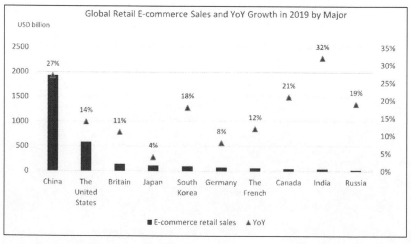

structure of the economy and society. With the rapid global rise of digital technologies, the global manufacturing industry is to some extent facing an unprecedented "digital" revolution. China's overall positioning of digital technologies has now risen from the previous level of emerging industries to the level of national strategy. The digital economy has enabled "Made in China" to grow into "Smart Made in China." To achieve this goal, China must vigorously develop high-tech technologies such as big data, blockchain, and cloud computing.

The digital economy has become an important driver of global economic and social development. It has gained even more momentum due to the prominent role of digital technology in the prevention and control of new coronaviruses and the resumption of economic activity during a pandemic. According to a report by the China Academy of Information and Communications Technology, China's digital economy was worth $5.4 trillion in 2020, second only to the United States globally, accounting for 38.6 percent of China's GDP and contributing 67.7 percent to GDP growth (China Academy of Information and Communications Technology 2022). The report also notes that the digital economy accounted for 51.3 percent of GDP in developed countries in 2019, while this figure was only 26.8 percent in developing countries. This suggests that China's digital economy boom is different from that of developed countries because it embraced digitalization before completing industrialization, urbanization, and agricultural modernization.

China's digital economy boom is largely attributed to a number of forward-looking government policies in building digital infrastructure. According to official figures, by the end of 2020, China will have 980 million internet users, the internet penetration rate will be 70 percent, with 749 million online shoppers and 805 million online payment users.[1] Fast and affordable internet access has transformed China's demographic dividend and huge market into a data dividend, which has led to a boon for the digital economy. China may have the world's richest data resources, which provides a solid foundation for the country's booming digital economy. Currently, most of the world's AI patent applications are in the US (24 percent) and China (22 percent), and the top three highest funded AI startups are from China: ByteDaily, Sensetime, and UBTECH. China ranks first in the world in terms of government spending on AI (about $22 billion).

The digital economy is a valuable opportunity for China's economy to change lanes and overtake other economies in the fourth industrial revolution. It is of great strategic significance to achieve high-quality development and the rejuvenation of the Chinese nation. Accelerating the digital transformation of industry can help China's digital economy catch up with the world's advanced level in terms of GDP share, and the real economy with manufacturing as the core will also achieve quality and efficiency development.

The automotive industry as an example is a standard catch-up industry, but the combination of automotive with digital technologies such as driverless cars and the expansion of the industry into the service sector provides opportunities for China's automotive industry to catch up. For example, for the leading household appliance industry, digitalization can be used to enhance the value chain and continue to maintain a leading edge. Through the development and growth of the digital industry, the direct effect of the digital economy on economic development will be increased. Through the digital economy empowering various industries, data and digital technology will be used to accelerate the catch-up of lagging industries and maintain the advantages of leading industries, providing momentum to achieve China's high-quality development in the new era and new journey.

The development of China's digital economy has three advantages. In terms of new technologies and industries represented by big data, artificial intelligence, and internet applications, China not only stands on the same starting line as developed countries but also has certain comparative advantages in terms of data resources, human capital, and market scale. First, the data advantage—big data is a new factor of production, known as the "oil of the twenty-first century." China has more than one billion Internet users, generating a large amount of data resources. China has the highest coverage of communication base stations in the world, which generates a massive information flow; it has the most widely used electronic payment system in the world, which generates a huge data flow. Second, talent advantage—China is a large human resource country with a large absolute number of innovative talents, which gives it an advantage in R&D. Third, market advantage—China has the most complete industrial support. It is not only a data and population powerhouse but also a market and application scenario powerhouse. China has the fastest transportation infrastructure in the world. Logistics, information flow, and data flow are all the most valuable foundations for developing a digital economy, generating a huge market volume. These advantages combine to offer broad prospects for the development of China's digital economy.

The Chinese Digital Revolution | 235

Over the past decade, driven by its vast market and supportive policies, China has taken a leading position in the digital industry. China's digital economy has become the second largest in the world. China has the world's largest e-commerce market, accounting for 40 percent of the global total. It is also one of the leading markets for virtual reality, self-driving cars, drones, and artificial intelligence (Zhang and Chen 2019). Mobile payments, in particular, are in full swing in China, with total annual transactions more than ten times those of the United States. Network effects, combined with access to data and economies of scale and scope, have led to a monopolistic trend and increased market power for the world's largest digital platforms, located primarily in the US and China. China is actively leveraging the urban network effect to promote digital technology development.

For example, in 2020, China's digital economy grew by 9.50 percent year-on-year to a total of 39.20 trillion yuan, placing it firmly in second place in the world.[2] The Guangdong–Hong Kong–Macao Greater Bay Area is an important region to drive the development of China's digital economy in the smart era by achieving coordinated development of software R&D, hardware production, and services within a limited area. In 2020, Guangdong Province led the country in the size and growth rate of its digital economy, which will reach 5.2 trillion yuan, ranking first in the country for the fourth consecutive year.[3] The digital economy accounts for more than 46.8 percent of Guangdong's GDP, with an annual growth rate of 13.3 percent, about 7 percentage points higher than the GDP growth rate in the same period. The Hong Kong government is committed to economic transformation and smart city development. In December 2017, the Hong Kong government released the Hong Kong Smart City Blueprint, which includes nearly twenty plans to implement relevant policies and measures in six areas: smart mobility, smart living, smart environment, smart citizenship, smart government, and smart economy. From 2013 to 2017, the number of internet users in Macau increased by more than 50 percent and the number of cell phone users increased by more than 30 percent. In August 2017, the Macau Special Administrative Region government and Alibaba Group signed the Framework Agreement on Strategic Cooperation in Building a Smart City. The agreement places emphasis on cloud computing, big data, and other internet technologies. Alibaba will assist Macau in improving the efficiency of urban governance and decision-making through cloud computing technology, professional training, and other areas to promote Macau's new smart city and the digital transformation of its economy.[4]

The development of the digital economy is an important way to promote China's high-quality development. First, it is conducive to promoting the optimization and upgrading of the industrial structure. Many industries in China have excess capacity at the low end and an insufficient effective supply of high-end products. Promoting the deep integration of digital technology and the real economy is conducive to driving the intelligent upgrading of production and service systems, promoting the extension and expansion of the industrial chain and value chain, and driving the industry to the middle and high end. Second, it is conducive to accelerating the transformation of old and new economic dynamics. The accelerated breakthroughs and applications of information technology have triggered the rapid rise of a large number of new products, new models, and new industries; the digital economy has become an important engine of economic growth (Sun et al. 2020). Third, it is conducive to promoting the transformation of the mode of development. The development of the digital economy, giving full play to the important role of data and information as new factors of production, can significantly reduce the cost of economic operation, so that economic development relies more on scientific and technological progress and improving labor skills, thereby improving total factor productivity.

However, promoting high-quality development of the digital economy does not mean allowing disorderly and unfair competition. Didi's initial public offering and a series of regulatory incidents reflect the chaos of data security vulnerabilities and data abuse on Chinese internet platforms in recent years. Digital technology promotes the diversification of data application scenarios and participants, the extension of data security is constantly expanding, and data security governance is faced with multiple dilemmas. The Chinese government has increased the regulation of digital platforms with such measures as "Amend the Antimonopoly Law and improve the supporting rules of the Data Security Law and the Personal Information Protection Law," "Formulate and promulgate regulations prohibiting unfair competition on the Internet," and "Establish and improve the platform economy fair competition supervision system." These measures all reflect China's determination and confidence in safeguarding the security of the digital economy.[5] The government should monitor the market more strictly and create a level playing field for all enterprises, while allowing the market to play a decisive role in resource allocation. Compared with the industrial economy, the digital economy has lower operating costs and a more convenient transaction process. However, given the unfair and even destructive competition that may be triggered by digital enterprises, the government should strengthen regulation and supervision. The rapid development of the digital economy also brings new challenges. For example, a significant "digital divide" still exists within and between countries due to inequalities in access to infrastructure and digital knowledge. This divide can prevent societies from taking full advantage of the benefits that digital technologies can bring.

The development of the digital economy is a major trend in the new technological revolution and industrial transformation. The digital economy is an important support for unblocking economic circulation, stimulating growth momentum, and enhancing economic resilience. Data has become a key factor of production and productivity, and penetrates deeply into all aspects of production, circulation, exchange, and consumption, leading to the networked sharing and intensive development of labor, capital, land, technology, management, and other factors, and the efficient use of integrated, collaborative, and open flow of blocked resource elements, greatly improving the efficiency of resource allocation in all areas of the economy and society (Zhang and Chen 2019). At present, digital technology innovation and iteration speed has significantly accelerated and has helped create most innovations, the most promising applications, and the strongest diffusion-driven technology innovation areas. The rapid development of a new generation of information technology, represented by artificial intelligence, big data, the internet of things, cloud computing, blockchain, virtual reality, mobile internet, and so forth, has continuously given rise to new products, new business models, and new industries. In recent years, the world's major economies have introduced medium- and long-term digital development strategies in an attempt to build a digital-driven economic system and create new competitive advantages by relying on their respective advantages in information, technology, manufacturing, and other fields. The ability to accelerate the development of the digital economy is related to whether we can seize the opportunity of the new round of technological revolution and industrial change, and win the initiative in future development and international competition.

At present, change is accelerating, and the international power contrast is undergoing a profound adjustment. China's economic development is facing the triple pressure of shrinking demand, supply shocks, and weakening expectations. New and higher requirements have been put forward to accelerate the development of the digital economy. We should take the strategic support of achieving a high level of self-reliance and self-improvement, take the deep integration of digital technology and the real economy as the main line, let more people enjoy digital dividends as the fundamental goal, improve the digital economy governance system, build a firm digital security barrier, build a digital cooperation framework, and continuously grow, improve, and expand China's digital economy. The development of the digital economy is of great significance.

Digital Transformation and Social Change

The internet has changed Chinese people's lifestyles and the digital economy has made life even more convenient. We see great roles that smart technology plays in various sectors whether it is AI, education, health, climate change, agriculture, and so forth, especially in the past two years when the world has been under COVID-19. New modes for various online activities, like remote offices, online education, online shopping, remote medical services, and unmanned commerce and services, have also emerged. Digital technology has changed Chinese lifestyles, and as of the third quarter of 2021, Chinese internet users spent on average of five hours and fifteen minutes per day using the internet (fig. 14.5).

Figure 14.5. Average daily time consuming and interacting with media by internet users in China. *Source*: Created by the author using data from Statista 2022.

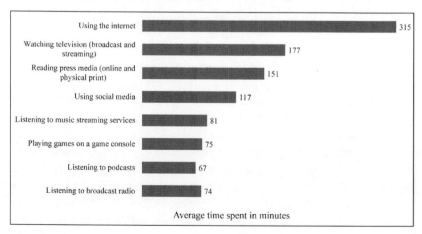

Mobile payments have been on the rise for many years with various platforms such as Apple Pay and Google Play dominating the market. But in various parts of the world, apps and platforms such as Alipay in China are leading the way in rolling out mobile payments. Mobile payments will accelerate the move toward a world without cash, creating efficiency gains for governments, businesses, and households. For Chinese employees, especially white-collar workers, telecommuting tools such as video conferences and online office software make working from home more feasible. According to *China Daily*, Alibaba's all-in-one mobile workplace Ding Talk has served more than ten million enterprises and over 200 million people. Tencent Meeting can provide free use for over 300 participants per audio or video conference.[6] Meanwhile, like Ding Talk, many apps have been used by students and their teachers for online classes. Private classes and tutoring is a US$120 billion industry in China. As technology has improved and with the shift to online learning during the COVID-19 pandemic, the online education market grew to almost US$40 billion in 2020. "More than 75% of 6–18 year olds attended after-school tutoring classes in 2016, and it isn't cheap." Those parents spend an average of "US$17,400 a year on tutoring for six hours a week—with some parents spending US$43,500 a year."[7] Besides, "cloud platforms" have also been provided by the Ministry of Education as an approach to continuing education among students across the country. Internet companies, such as NetEase, recently opened a full chain of contactless recruitment through online resume submission and online interviews. The candidates can also sign contracts, attend training workshops, and even begin work over the internet. During COVID lockdowns, many museums and galleries in China were also closed to visitors, but they have launched various online exhibitions to provide a creative touring experience for the country's vast number of stay-at-home visitors.

At the same time, China's internet courts improve the efficiency of the judicial process. This new mode of online trial has brought about judicial openness and public participation. Internet courts aim to use big data analysis technology in cases involving network data modules, combing regularity, and characteristics of the formation of structured, standardized internet rules of judicial judgment, to create a safer, more efficient, and more humanized cyberspace legal process.

The ongoing process is seeing major internet players striving to reshape people's livelihoods. They are revamping the physical consumption experience and innovating the manufacturing sector using novel

Figure 14.6. China technology internet company revenue. *Source*: Created by the author using data from CITIC Securities.

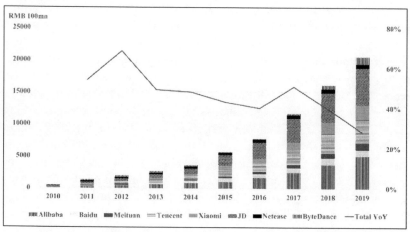

technologies. For instance, Meituan-Dianping, China's largest provider of on-demand online services spanning food delivery, hotel bookings, travel, and entertainment ticketing, is integrating big data, artificial intelligence, and cloud computing. This integrated platform offers people all-in-one life experiences. People can find nearby restaurants, reserve hotels, order take-out, or book a film ticket, all with a tap on a smartphone screen. The company also entered the ride-hailing sector recently to link dining with transportation, enabling users to directly book a taxi to where they have reserved a restaurant table for lunch or dinner. With 320 million active users (fig. 14.7) of its platforms and more than four million merchants listed on it, the Meituan-Dianping company began trial operations of its driverless delivery vehicles and plans to promote the service on a large scale to make the dream of 24-hour delivery a reality.

Intelligent, digital, and networked transformation also upgrades China's transportation. IBM took the lead in introducing the idea of a smart city at the end of 2008 in China with many seminars hosted within the Chinese market. Smart transportation, as a major pillar of a smart city, was embraced warmly as a Western advanced governance style in the post-Olympic era. As the years went by, Didi became one of the world's largest ride-hailing apps. Years ago, Didi and Uber competed in China. In 2016, after a two-year price war, Didi bought Uber's China operations. In the 12 months ended March 31, 2021, Didi had 493 million annual

Figure 14.7. China online food delivery app users. *Source*: Created by the author using data from Wind Database.

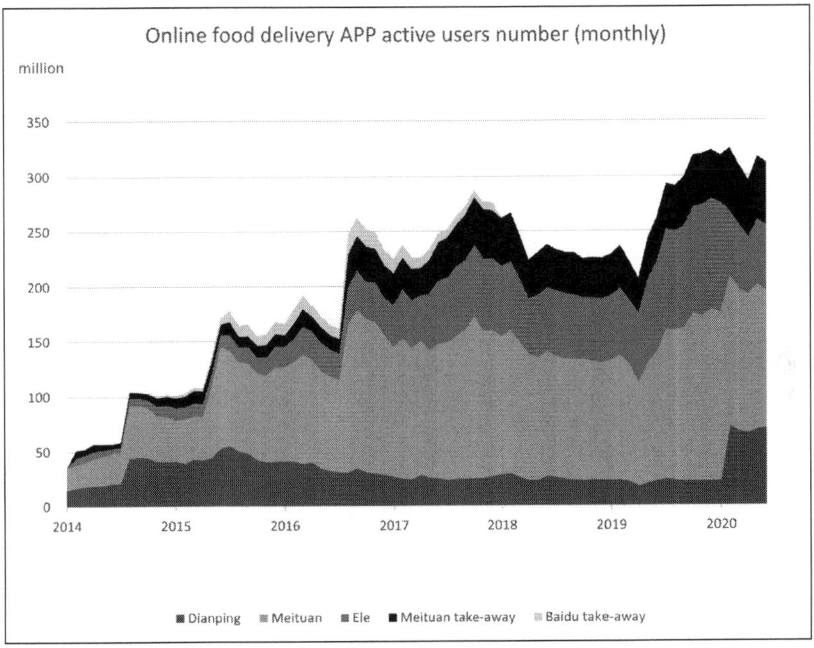

Online food delivery APP active users number (monthly)

Legend: Dianping, Meituan, Ele, Meituan take-away, Baidu take-away

active users worldwide and 15 million annual active drivers worldwide. Of these, there are 377 million active users and 13 million active drivers in China. In the first quarter of 2021, Didi's China mobility business had 156 million monthly active users and an average of 25 million daily transactions. In terms of single and transaction volumes, Didi's global business saw an average daily transaction volume of 41 million orders in the 2021, with a total transaction volume of RMB 341 billion across the platform.[8]

Live streaming e-commerce helps resume work and production. Under the epidemic, the offline real economy has been hit hard, and the stagnation of human flow, logistics, and capital flow has generated a crisis in many industries. E-commerce live streaming has injected new momentum into the resumption of work and production and also brought possibilities for exploring digital transformation and expanding the operating radius of the real economy. It has become a fulcrum to leverage the recovery of the market, and the pressure of decreasing passenger flow has also been diverted into online live streaming. At the personal level, short video platforms expand employment opportunities by increasing the income of ordinary people, creating new positions, and improving the efficiency of employment matching through new forms such as live recruitment. Meanwhile, they break through the work restrictions of traditional industries and help disadvantaged groups obtain income and realize their value. At the regional level, the short video platform adds vitality to the traditional "sinking market" by developing characteristic resources and breaking space-time boundaries. At the same time, it also promotes rural revitalization and the development of the central and western regions through a series of actions such as the "Happy Village Leaders" program and reduces the gap between urban and rural areas and between the east and the west.

Live streaming e-commerce will help revitalize rural areas. In field of agriculture, live stream delivery will help open the sales chain of agricultural products and effectively help farmers in poor areas to lift themselves

Figure 14.8. China online shopping app active users. *Source*: Created by the author using data from Wind Database.

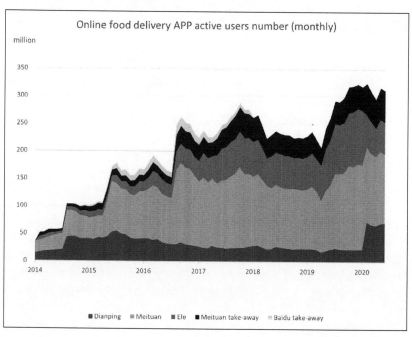

The Chinese Digital Revolution | 243

out of poverty and increase their incomes. The emergence of e-commerce live streaming of agricultural products with goods allows a comprehensive marketing of agricultural products, the leapfrogging of rural economy development, and the global promotion of a digital economy. In recent years, internet companies have assisted the transformation and upgrading of rural industries with industrial and technological advantages, and rural e-commerce has shown a trend of rapid development. Riding the wave of 5G technology and the internet, people can sell their meticulously crafted products across the country with just a smartphone. And selling goods via the 5G Live Show could improve people's lives. Data show that China's online retail sales of agricultural products will reach 422.1 billion yuan in 2021 and 529.3 billion yuan in 2022, a year-on-year growth of 25.4 percent, and this is expected to break through 800 billion yuan in 2025.[9] With the deep integration of modern information technologies such as big data, artificial intelligence, and the internet of things with all links of the whole agricultural industry chain, and the focus on industry to promote rural development, the potential of the rural digital economy will be rapidly released. With the acceleration of the integration of rural e-commerce systems and express logistics distribution systems, as well as the continuous innovation and implementation of content e-commerce, live stream e-commerce, and other modes, rural e-commerce shows a trend of rapid development. The consumption of agricultural products further shows an upgrading trend, and more and more users prefer online platforms with high-quality products.

The epidemic outbreak has further proved the importance of the internet and the digital economy. The outbreak spurred online social interaction, remote working, and online education, creating opportunities for China's technology and business model innovation. The digital economy has become an important engine for growth that is both sustainable and inclusive. It has helped to raise productivity in existing industries and given birth to new sectors, and integrated all aspects of business and society, helping to make our daily life more efficient and convenient while providing impetus and inspiration for socioeconomic development.

During the epidemic, the ability of digital technology to play a role was shown to the fullest. The emergence of the epidemic undoubtedly disrupted the supply and demand relationship in society. So as automation spreads, it is easy to be negative about employment prospects the world over. More labor will be diverted away from current roles and into those currently unaffected by automation. New jobs will need to be created and,

Figure 14.9. Digital application user comparison 2019–2020. *Source*: Created by the author using data from Wind Database.

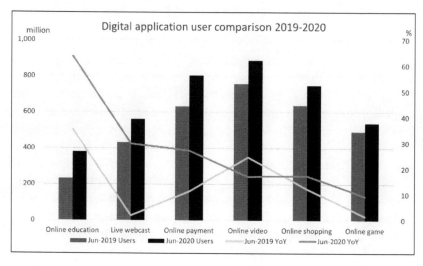

as well as taking jobs away, technology creates a platform for new jobs to emerge. Indeed, digitalization has eliminated some jobs in manufacturing sectors, but a growing number of people in China are turning to jobs in the digital-fueled new economy as the COVID-19 pandemic reshapes the world by accelerating a shift to online business. Despite the coronavirus impact, many digital platforms are ramping up efforts to hire talent. China's labor market has recovered significantly and became more vibrant during the spring recruitment season, and the new economy has become the key growth driver in the job market, said the report by a Chinese professional networking platform (Ouyang 2021). Artificial intelligence topped all other fields in terms of the ratio of the number of people with strong intentions to apply for jobs divided by the talent base number. That was followed by new entertainment and online education. Games, new life services, smart hardware, new education and training, and e-commerce are also among the fastest-growing job categories during the spring recruitment season. Furthermore, these online platforms might even be offering expanded employment opportunities for the 8.1 percent of respondents who identify as rural residents. In China, the development of digital labor platforms has occurred with significant government support, particularly from state-sponsored media, which has positioned labor platforms as both a market innovation and an employment opportunity. This development is viewed as particularly promising for young people who are tech-savvy and in need of paid work. Similar to the discourse in many Western countries, platform work is seen as a new avenue to promote freedom and flexibility of work and a better way to match workers' talents with market needs. This fits with the latest Future of Jobs Report from the World Economic Forum—which suggests a large share of "redundant" roles in the global labor market will be replaced by "new" roles in the coming few years (Saadia et al. 2020). At present, 4.55 million people are working in the digital economy in China, and this number will increase in the future (fig. 14.10). The digital information interaction of the internet quickly made up for the transmission of information and complemented the incongruity of supply and demand of social resources. The courier industry, take-away industry, distance education, and telecommuting field have all benefited from the efficient digital capability of information.

The epidemic has undoubtedly promoted the progress of social informatization. One person, one health code is the high-speed transmission, storage, processing, and presentation of information. China also finds diversified collaborations to actively assimilate into its innovation networks and create new ecosystems. Platforms such as Baidu and China Mobile use big data to monitor and analyze the pandemic situation in real time, reporting findings to governments for statistical decision-making. Similarly,

Figure 14.10. Number of digital economy employees in China. *Source*: Created by the author using data from Wind Database.

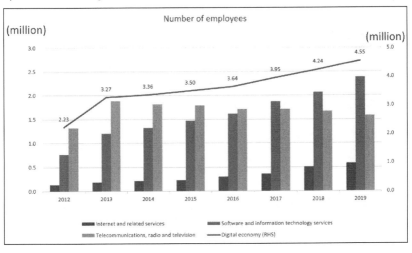

organizations such as Tencent, Huawei, and Alibaba Cloud have used AI and big data to track and judge capabilities to perform virus genetic testing, drug research and development screening, lung image analysis, and other scientific research activities, which help medical diagnosis and treatment. The use of intelligent systems, such as the infrared temperature sensor detection system developed by Megvii technology, the intelligent voice control system developed by iFlytek, and the question-answering robots in public places, contribute to community governance. Under the new normal, the use of digital technologies not only contains the spread of the pandemic but also promotes the rise of the digital economy. China is perhaps the first country to use digital mechanisms through mobile phones or social media apps such as WeChat and Alipay, or both, to monitor people's movements. It has now developed into a national Health QR Code System (Cheng et al. 2021). Many studies suggest that the health QR code had helped control the spread of COVID-19 in China. During the pandemic, Alibaba's mobile payment platform Alipay quickly added remote medical appointment features to the health code app, allowing local citizens to use the health code app instead of their medical insurance card to have online video appointments with doctors.

China has been able to promote effective control of the epidemic quickly because of the effective application of internet digitization. One person one code almost covers location information, identity information,

Figure 14.11. Government spending on AI. *Source*: Created by the author using data from Wind Database.

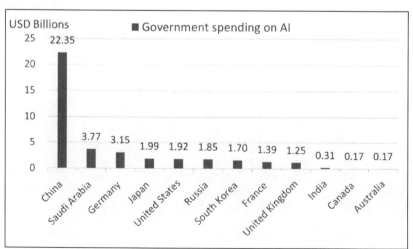

movement tracking, data interaction, data processing, data presentation, and many other related functions. A small two-dimensional code offers huge informational and analysis capability. And now Chinese customers are most confident that technologies can tackle the world's problems.

Looking ahead, continued digitization will provide new sources of growth, the impact of which will likely be an opportunity to reverse the gradual decline in potential growth in China. In China, the internet will become as much an ecological element as water and electricity, permeating every aspect of economic and social life. As you can see, the digital economy has permeated every aspect of our lives. Whether we are shopping online, reading news online, watching short videos or playing video games, we are all involved in the digital economy. It can be said that each of us is both a participant and an enabler of the digital economy. Through the digital economy, a cell phone, and a network, we can solve all the problems we need for food, clothing, housing, and transportation. The internet has memory, and every action we take on the platform generates data that leads to better iterations and a better user experience. In the information age, many resources are stored in the cloud. Books that used to be purchased in bookstores can now be viewed online. Information that needed to be found can also be easily obtained from the internet by searching for information and data. The digital economy has improved efficiency and

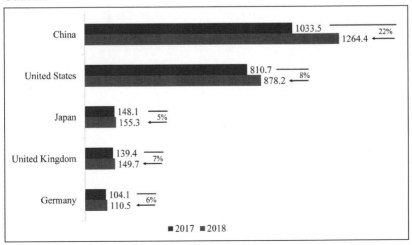

Figure 14.12. Top 5 fintech countries by digital payments transaction value in billion US$. *Source*: Created by the author using data from Statista Digital Market Outlook.

reduced human input. It is foreseeable that the digital economy will see rapid development in the future, and more imaginative spaces and application scenarios of the digital economy will be continuously developed, allowing more people to enjoy the development dividends in the digital wave and meet people's growing needs for a better life.

Future Challenges for China's Digital Society

While digital transformation brings new momentum to global economic and social development, it has also become a collective action challenge that needs to be built and shared among multiple actors in government, market, and society, facing a series of new challenges in the social field.

First, imbalances and inadequacies are increasingly prominent. Digital transformation has protected the sustained growth of the global economy, but the huge difference in the speed of transformation has also brought new development problems. The latest data show that, in comparison to developed countries and regions such as Europe and the United States, countries along the "Belt and Road" are generally lagging behind in digital transformation. Investment in digitalization in the global private economy has been climbing rapidly over the past twenty years, and investment opportunities in this emerging field will continue to grow by 2030. But as Nobel economics laureate Gunnar Myrdal has pointed out, the disorderly boundary entry of market forces may reinforce, rather than weaken, interregional imbalances.

The trend toward functional modularity and fragmentation of the division of labor in global value chains, augmented by technological forces, is increasingly evident, with value-added gains tending to flow to technological oligopolies. To promote the coordinated development of the digital society, it is necessary to strengthen the synergy and cooperation among different countries and between governments and markets to achieve higher quality, more equitable, and sustainable development based on open innovation, so that the fruits of digital transformation can truly benefit the people.

Second, holistic governance is not yet fully formed. With the innovative application of digital technology in social governance, strengthening digital government has become a common goal in the new round of global development, but the decentralized nature of technocracy also makes the theory of holistic governance face the challenge of fragmentation. Since the United States proposed the "Information Superhighway Initiative" in 1993, nearly one hundred digital policies and regulations have been formulated to encourage and protect liberal positions. Japan is striving to dovetail with the US and European digital governance models, promote cross-border data flows, and create a US-Europe-Japan "digital circulation circle." The global pandemic in 2020 has highlighted the importance of digital technologies, and the market value of digital platform companies has bucked the trend, becoming the brightest spot in the global economy.

However, the year 2020 also witnessed the increasing regulatory situation and policy changes of digital platforms in various countries. The United States has held intensive hearings on major platforms around different topics. The United Kingdom is preparing to set up a special regulatory agency, the Digital Markets Unit. France is exploring new policies in the field of digital taxation. And the focus issues around privacy protection, false information, media manipulation, algorithmic bias, and so forth have attracted global attention, and the value and responsibility of digital platforms are being reexamined. While technical barriers continue to fall, market competition and fragmentation are commonplace. How to form a consistent value orientation in the field of governance, gather a consensus, effectively curb the shortcomings of fragmentation and transformation, and truly realize people-oriented and holistic governance in the digital fields of health, employment, education, rights, and security, and so forth, which are related to people's livelihood, is still in urgent need of value-level clarification and recognition.

To govern the energetic yet nascent sector, particularly the platform economy, China has rolled out multiple regulatory measures, addressing problems such as data abuse and monopolistic market behavior. These measures guarantee a fair market environment and improve governance while maintaining the sector's vigor and innovation with high-speed growth. For example, China has taken a series of actions against the monopolistic and anticompetitive practices of internet titans in 2021. From December 2020 to April 2021, regulators fined over a dozen tech companies, including Alibaba, Tencent, and Baidu, for failing to seek antimonopoly approval for internet mergers and acquisitions, abusing market dominance, or forcing vendors or merchants to pick sides (namely, choosing between their services and those of their rivals). The country also sped up the pace of legislation. In February 2021, the top market regulator issued new antimonopoly guidelines for the platform economy to stop the monopolistic behaviors of platform companies. In November

2021, the closely watched draft amendment to the Anti-Monopoly Law was submitted to the country's legislative body for initial review and disclosed to the public for comments. The draft amendment stipulated that business operators should not exclude or limit market competition by abusing data, algorithms, technology, capital advantages, and platform rules.

On January 19, 2022, China published a slew of directives on regulating and guiding the "healthy and sustainable development" of the platform economy. The nineteen-point notice, which was issued by nine central government organs led by the National Development and Reform Commission, highlights strengthening financial regulations on platform companies, reining in monopolistic and improper practices of internet companies, and increasing their obligations regarding taxation. The notice defined the platform economy as "a new economic form" with internet platforms as the base and data as the driving force, supported by a new generation of information technology and internet infrastructure. Recognizing the increasingly prominent role of the platform economy in China's social and economic development, the directive aims to "establish and improve relevant rules and regulations and optimize the environment for the development of the platform economy." It suggested the clarification of the boundaries and responsibilities of internet companies and strengthening those of mega platforms. A compliance management system targeting platform companies should be put in place, along with an effective external supervision and evaluation system.

Third, the digital divide reveals new inequalities. The digital divide was once thought to be due to barriers to digital use caused by inadequate digital access, such as internet, mobile devices, or Wi-Fi signals, but as infrastructure continues to improve, it has been discovered that generational, income, educational, and geographic differences can further shape digital divides. For example, social costs worsen due to the lack of digital skills among the elderly, the lagging digital education in remote rural areas, and the increasingly frequently reported problem of internet addiction among teenagers, as well as the income gap caused by high and low digital literacy.

Digital transformation promotes economic prosperity, but it may also make the poor poorer and the weak weaker. For example, machine substitution and artificial intelligence take away jobs. A survey by the McKinsey Global Institute shows that 800 million jobs will be replaced by machines globally by 2030, and more than 300 million workers will need to be retrained in digital skills (Manyika et al. 2017). In addition, algorithmic errors could affect welfare policy and reshape poverty. As digital transformation rolls out across the board in epidemic prevention, retirement, disability, women and children, and health, there is also growing concern about whether the digitally disadvantaged, in the near future, will be punished for the lack of basic security in all areas of work life.

Last but not least, global competition has further intensified, and the US may implement a tougher crackdown policy. In January 2021, the U.S. Information Technology and Innovation Foundation released the report *A Grand Strategy for the U.S. Global Digital Economy*, which states that the rise of the digital economy over the past twenty years has further deepened and expanded global integration (Atkinson 2021). In the face of Chinese competition, the US needs an ambitious, comprehensive strategy to guide it and maintain US leadership in global technology. "Without such a strategy, the risk of the United States falling behind China increases significantly" (Atkinson 2021, 50). Further, the US is building a global plan to encircle China's digital economic development. For example, in June 2021, the US and the European Union established a Trade and Technology Council to promote digital transformation and cooperation on emerging technologies, to lead global digital economy and technology standards, and to move US-European digital coordination from strategic vision to practice.

China is not afraid of the competition and continues to improve to find its new development path. China's large domestic market offers powerful scale advantages that enable the rapid commercialization of digital technologies. Accounting for more than 40 percent of the value of worldwide transactions, China has the world's largest e-commerce market. The sheer size of the Chinese internet user base encourages continuous experimentation and enables digital players to achieve economies of scale quickly.

The digital economy is reshaping the world economic order, which stems from its naturally global competitive dynamics. This global nature is even more pronounced in the wake of the new coronavirus epidemic. With the normalization of epidemic prevention and control, more offline demand is being transformed into online demand. This has further accelerated the construction of a global economic and trade cyberspace, which led to the integration and optimization of the global innovation, industrial, and value chains, and played a role in promoting the reorganization of global factors and resources and the reshaping of the global economic structure.

Still, foreign companies, particularly those in the tech sector, have been pulling out of China. Reputable global firms, such as Amazon, Uber, and Airbnb, have gradually left the country, while their native counterparts—JD, Meituan, and Ctrip—continue to thrive. In addition, new legal measures also raise the costs of compliance and add to uncertainty for Western companies operating in China. Foreign investment in China's tech companies will get more complicated. For international corporations, accessing corporate data from China can become difficult in the near term. Foreign companies running platforms or apps in China must be more vigilant when collecting and using personal information amid a tighter regulatory environment. Facing both regulatory measures and competition from local companies, foreign tech firms encounter more challenges to expand operations and gain more customers. In the past few years, the development of China's digital economy is slowing down, and if this trend further intensifies, China's digital economy may be left behind by the technology giants represented by the US.

China has responded by seeking greater international cooperation in digital technology. In November 2021, China filed an application to join the Digital Economy Partnership Agreement, a new type of trade partnership agreement signed by Chile, New Zealand, and Singapore, which seeks to bolster digital trade. This application is in line with China's direction of further deepening domestic reform and opening up to strengthen digital economic cooperation with other countries. On another front, the country has also been actively sharing its digital knowledge by offering technology, equipment, and services to less developed countries. Chinese companies have participated in a number of submarine cable projects connecting Africa and Eurasia. In total, more than 200,000 kilometers of optical fiber has been laid, giving broadband internet access to six million households in Africa, according to official data. More than half of Africa's wireless sites and high-speed mobile broadband networks were built by Chinese companies.

Digital technology has become a key area of competition in relations between major powers, and China's traditional industries lack independent innovation and technology research and development capabilities. The dependence of key core technologies on foreign countries is high, especially in the manufacturing industry, mainly in original equipment manufacturer (OEM) and assembly, at the low end of the global value chain. In the case of semiconductors, for example, the United States has seven of the top ten firms, and no company from mainland China is on the list. This is related to the long-term low investment in basic research in China. Statistics show that China's basic research investment accounts for only 6 percent of R&D investment, far below the 15 percent to 25 percent level of developed countries such as the US, the UK, and France. Corporate basic research investment is also severely lacking, with corporate basic research spending accounting for about 28 percent of society as a whole in the US and only 2.9 percent in China.

Looking forward, the digital economy is not only reshaping the Chinese economy but also creating business opportunities for foreign companies. The strength of China's digital consumption goes beyond the advantages of scale. Nowadays, almost every aspect of people's lives is inseparable from digital technology, including education, health, information services, entertainment, finance, and e-commerce. This strong basis has enabled the expansion of services provided to consumers and has accelerated the commercialization of new products. Foreign companies can explore new and innovative services that can be incorporated into the existing digital ecosystem, even in the context of new and tighter regulations. Given the vast scope and size of China's digital economy, business opportunities still exist for foreign technology solution providers and are actively encouraged in areas such as industrial digital transformation, services, solutions for sustainable development, consumer products, and more, according to the Catalogue of Industries for Encouraging Foreign Investment (Zhou 2022). Potential industries for foreign investment include software development, information technology support management, and the maintenance of modern high-end equipment. In addition, the application of information technology also brings opportunities in other sectors, including healthcare, vehicle manufacturing, and energy transition. Doors are open for foreign investors in the research and exploration of new technologies to add to China's burgeoning digital sector.

Although China has shortcomings that need to be filled and faces considerable challenges in the development of the digital economy, as long as it plays to its unique strengths and stimulates its enormous potential, China's digital economy will lead the world in the future.

Notes

1. http://www.xinhuanet.com/english/2021-02/03/c_139717749.htm.
2. https://english.www.gov.cn/archive/statistics/202109/26/content_WS61|506f1cc6d0df57f98e0e46.html.
3. http://www.cnbayarea.org.cn/english/News/content/post_537379.html.

254 | Alessandro Teixeira Golombiewski and Zhenyu Jiang

4. https://mtt.macaotourism.gov.mo/201709/en/contents/3/735.html?1504669778.

5. https://www.ianbrown.tech/digital-competition-briefing-1/china/.

6. https://epaper.chinadaily.com.cn/a/202003/20/WS5e73fea2a310a2fabb7a3112.html.

7. https://china.usc.edu/online-education-china.

8. https://qz.com/2019750/chinese-tech-giant-didis-mega-ipo-filing-in-five-numbers/.

9. https://www.iimedia.cn/c400/84524.html.

15

Digital Futures and Global Power

Dynamics, Inequality, and Governance

MARCO CEPIK AND PEDRO TXAI LEAL BRANCHER

Since the beginning of the COVID-19 pandemic, digital technologies have become even more ubiquitous.[1] Smartphones, sensors, big data, algorithms, digital platforms, and cloud computing form a sociotechnical global assemblage that conditions the functioning of businesses, governments, and other social institutions. This chapter focuses on three related questions. First, what are the main properties and power dynamics that set the pace of the global digital era? Second, how do digital technologies affect the structural inequalities intrinsic to the capitalist mode of production? Third, how do states, private companies, and civil society interactions shape the digital global governance landscape?

In order to offer a preliminary answer to these questions, we divide this text into three sections. In the first section, we specify concepts and power dynamics. We argue that the digital age is now in its second phase. The first has been characterized by the emergence of microcomputers and the diffusion of the internet, and the second by the unfolding of exponential connectivity, cloud computing, artificial intelligence (AI), quantum computing, and platformization. In the second section, we look into how digital technologies exacerbate inequalities. Based on Ragnedda and Gladkova (2017), we discuss three levels of digital inequalities: (1) the divide between those who have and do not have access to the internet and the

Dynamics

necessary devices, (2) the differentials in how sociodemographic groups use data and digital technologies, and (3) the unequal capacities to create tangible and intangible benefits and outcomes from digital technologies. In the third section of this chapter, we delve into governance issues comprising the local, the national, and the international levels of cyberspace.

Dynamics

Conceptually, we define the digital era as a historically emerging global social formation distinguished by the growing centrality of digitized science, technology, and innovation systems for the production, circulation, and consumption of material and cultural value created by networked intellectual work (Cepik and Brancher 2022).

According to Rennstich (2008) and Brancher (2021), digitalization's historical roots date back to the 1970s, as technological advances in the areas of microelectronics (semiconductors and microprocessors), optoelectronics (fiber optic transmission), and computer programming (software and data sharing protocols) matured. Technological advances resulted from the efforts of the United States to win the Cold War against the Soviet Union. At the beginning of the twenty-first century, nearly a third of all capital invested in digital technologies was from the US government and American private companies (Rennstich 2008, 93). In this sense, the Cold War decisively contributed to creating *cyberspace*, an environment made by people, devices, infrastructure, information, and communication systems using the electromagnetic spectrum. More or less interconnected analog and digital networks define what is cyber. Therefore, cyberspace is a broader entity than the internet, both temporally and spatially (Kuehl 2009).

Since the end of the Cold War, the transnationalization of financial capital, the consolidation of global supply chains, particularly in East Asia, and the concentration of knowledge-intensive activities in the countries of the capitalist organic nucleus have changed the world economy (Arrighi 1994). Ideologically, the first phase of the digital age was driven by neoliberalism, which promoted the privatization of assets and institutions, the fragmentation of labor unions, and the compression of the working class share of the national income (Streeck 2016). In 2000, the so-called dot.com crisis clearly showed that cyberspace was not ready to sustain another round of expansion. However, China's development and a new wave of innovations in the twenty-first century have driven the digital era toward a new historical phase. Let us provide examples from four interconnected areas.

First, there was an exponential increase in global connectivity due to advances in fiber optic connections, 4G wireless diffusion, and the miniaturization of microchips, which enabled the development of advanced computing capabilities in devices with functional dimensions (smartphones, tablets, and sensors). At the beginning of 2001, there were 1.5 billion cell phones in use (equivalent to 19 percent of the world's population) and 600 million internet users. By January 2022, these figures had risen, respectively, to 5.31 billion (67.1 percent of the world's population) and 4.95 billion (62.5 percent of the world's population), a trend that is consistent and was reinforced even during the pandemic of COVID-19 that impacted health and the economy (Kemp 2022). Consequently, internet global traffic increased from 100 GB per day in 1992 to 46,600 GB per second in 2017. The volume of data created, captured, copied, and consumed worldwide increased from two zettabytes to ninety-four zettabytes between 2010 and 2022. In the most likely scenario, the rate of growth of global connectivity will accelerate over the next decade, with the installation of the enabling infrastructure for 5G networks and the emergence of the internet of things: the integration of sensors in everyday, industrial, and governmental activities (UNCTAD 2019; Brancher 2021; Sledziewska and Wloch 2021).

Second, the global connectivity growth is closely related to cloud computing services, a valuable way of sharing computing power and transforming fixed costs on infrastructure into variable costs arranged by contractual clauses. According to the US National Institute of Standards and Technology, cloud computing is a "model for enabling ubiquitous, convenient, on-demand network access to a shared pool of configurable computing resources (networks, servers, storage, applications, and services) that can be rapidly provisioned and released with minimal management effort or service provider interaction" (Mell and Grance 2011, 2). In terms of agility, "cloud computing services are very flexible since they can be scaled up and down as computational demand increases or decreases." Moreover, cloud computing became an enabling condition for the emergence of small companies with a high potential for innovation (start-ups), as it provided "resources for conventional data storage and processing but also more advanced digital technologies, such as quantum computing, blockchain technology, and artificial intelligence" (Lang 2021, 256). It is noteworthy that the cloud computing market is highly oligopolized, as Alphabet-Google, Amazon, Microsoft, Tencent, and Alibaba hold 75 percent of the global market (UNCTAD 2019).

Third, combined with the increase in global connectivity and the growing power of cloud computing, the second decade of the twenty-first century was characterized by an exponential strengthening of AI capacities to process and respond to the increasingly large fluxes of data. AI can be categorized into two significant subfields. First is machine learning, which "refers to a group of algorithms with the ability to learn without being explicitly programmed" (Lang 2021, 229). This type of algorithm evolves through unsupervised learning techniques. It "scans the input data for patterns and structures without predefined categories and iteratively identifies the statistically best categorization" (Lang 2021, 185). Exemplary applications of unsupervised learning are product recommendation, smart manufacturing, customer segmentation, and sentiment analysis. Second, deep learning is an area of research that "employs artificial neural networks to process digital information" (Lang 2021, 229). In this type of algorithm, data flows through hidden layers of interconnected artificial neural networks that have potentialized its capacities to recognize and classify even more complex features. Examples of deep learning applications are face and voice recognition, object detection for autonomous driving, diagnosing diseases from medical scans, and natural language processing.

AI and big data have a positive feedback relationship: the larger the datasets available, the greater the power of the machine and deep learning techniques to train algorithms to solve complex problems. Whenever someone uses a digital payment system, for example, they leave a "digital footprint," which might be used by tech companies to understand the customer's personal preferences, financial status, and social relations. With this kind of data, corporations can "engage in a number of economic activities by taking advantage of these newly gained insights, such as the direct sale of products, commercial advertisements, and financial risk assessment" (Huang, Qiu, and Wang 2021, 5). Therefore, although scientists are still far away from developing strong AI (machines whose cognitive capacities are indistinguishable from human intellectual capacities), contemporary intelligent algorithms are "more than enough to revolutionize the operational and business models of the companies" (Sledziewska and Wloch 2021, 22). According to McKinsey & Company, AI will be responsible for a $13 trillion GDP growth by 2030, primarily in noninternet sectors, such as manufacturing, energy, agriculture, and logistics (Bughin et al. 2018)

Fourth, there has been a steady growth in supercomputers' power and breakthroughs in quantum computing. In 2008, an IBM supercomputer achieved a performance of 1.026 quadrillion calculations per second (petaflop) for the first time. Two years later, a Chinese supercomputer (Tianhe-1A) reached 2.5 petaflops (Khosrow-Pour 2018; Warf 2018). In 2021, the Japanese supercomputer Fugaku recorded a performance of 442 petaflops. Hence, supercomputer applications have evolved from weather forecasting and aerodynamic research to code-breaking, 3D nuclear test simulations, and molecular dynamics simulations. As a new frontier, quantum computing refers to a computer that encodes information, not in binary bits but qubits, and processes them by quantum logic gates. This transition provides a gain in memory capacity, since a qubit can be both "0" and "1" at the same time, and in computational speed, since a "quantum computer employs superposition and entanglement to conduct multiple computational steps at the same time" (Lang 2021, 69). Quantum computers can be divided into three subcategories: (1) quantum annealers: which are fit to solve combinatorial optimization problems and sampling problems; (2) quantum simulators: which are mainly used in academia to explore quantum phenomena; and (3) universal quantum computers: which can solve all types of computational problems in quantum speeds (Lang 2021, 90). Quantum computing capacities are already commercially available for direct purchase or cloud computing services. Significant applications are being explored in automotive, aerospace and defense, chemicals, pharmaceuticals and healthcare, materials, finance, banking and insurance, electronics, energy, and cybersecurity (Lang 2021). Besides connectivity, cloud computing, AI, and quantum computing, the second phase of the digital age is also characterized by advances in general-purpose technologies such as blockchain, 3D printing, the internet of things, and 5G networks.

In sum, digital technologies have shown an exponential rate of innovation over the last decades, as predicted by three general quasi-laws that explain the general direction of this process. Moore's law states that processing units will double every eighteen months. Butter's law considers that the network communication speed doubles every nine months. Kryder's law predicts that storage capacity doubles every thirteen months (Lang 2021, 13). Thus, three general results define cyberspace as an emergent global social formation: datafication, networking, and platformization.

Datafication emerges from "the practical results of the virtuous circle between the growing amount of data and the growing application of intelligent algorithms" (Sledziewska and Wloch 2021, 23). An example of this trend is the concept of a digital twin, which refers to virtual models of a physical object or a system that is updated from real-time data, and can be used to perform simulations, study performance issues, and generate possible improvements (IBM 2022). As Fourcade and Healy (2017, 13) stated, "Modern organizations are now driven by a data imperative that demands the extraction of all data, from all sources by any means possible." As suggested by Sledziewka and Wloch (2021, 25), seeing data as capital and not as a commodity allows us to capture impressive properties: (1) "they are non-fungible—another cannot replace a single data," (2) "they have a non-rivalrous nature—a single data set can be used simultaneously by many algorithms or applications without losing its basic value," and (3) "the value of a data set is equal to the information it contains, and so this value can be assessed only after obtaining the information."

Free-of-scale networking refers to the exponential growth of ties (relationships) between many actors (nodes). In other words, "in the digital economy, networks are thicker because people and machines are connected all the time," and "there is no online or offline, but onlife" (Sledziewka and Wloch 2021, 27). From an economic perspective, the higher density of networks results in businesses having more knowledge about their customers' preferences, which in turn "enables more and more personalization in products and services, making the network even more beneficial from the point of view of consumers" (Sledziewka and Wloch 2021, 28).

At the operational level, datafication and free-of-scale networking are aggregated by digital platforms, which have become the dominant organizational form of firms and institutions in contemporary capitalism (Srnicek 2016). Platforms "provide the infrastructure for exchanges" in cyberspace (Sledziewka and Wloch 2021, 47). Thus, "the platform creates value by facilitating participants on one side, finding those on the other side, or mediating their interactions" (Tiwana 2014, 32). Platforms also develop reprogrammable software. Vast quantities of data and financial concentration allow for continuous updating of interfaces and algorithms and the emergence of decentralized novel applications from core components (Helmond 2015). In light of that, "the potential power of platform ecosystems comes from leveraging the unique expertise of many, diverse independent developers driven by market incentives on a scale that is impossible to replicate within a single organization" (Tiwana 2014, 5). The market capitalization value of the digital platform is not based on earnings, physical assets, or even scale and scope economies but on free-of-scale networking. In other words, the more users operate on the platform, the more valuable it becomes for the users themselves and the company since more personalized products and services can be generated (Cusumano, Gawer, and Yoffie 2019).

As discussed in the next section, the exponential growth of cyberspace in the digital age, compounded by datafication, networking, and platformization, produces unprecedented economic and power concentration.

Inequalities

In 2019, Facebook (now Meta) controlled 80 percent of the social media market through the Messenger, Instagram, and WhatsApp family of apps. Alphabet-Google, in addition to the search tool (Google Search), controls the operating platform (Android), web browser (Chrome), social network (Google+), application store (Google Play), payment platform (Google Wallet and Android Pay), internet video sharing platform (YouTube), georeferencing service (Google Maps and Google Earth), cloud computing systems (Google Cloud Platform), artificial intelligence (Deep Mind), and life science (Verify Science Life). Apple leads the production of devices (smartphones, tablets, and watches) that incorporate the company's iOS operating platform and the ecosystem's app store and streaming services (iCloud and iTunes). Amazon held one-third of the global cloud computing market and more than eighty hubs in various sectors: telemarketing, databases, and analytics (UNCTAD 2019). Finally, "Microsoft grew big on personal computer software in the 1980s and 1990s but has since shifted its focus to online service; LinkedIn and Microsoft Azure (cloud computing) are just two of over sixty platform services operated by the Seattle-based company" (Dijck, Poell, and de Waal 2018, 15). Five American technology corporations—Google-Alphabet, Apple, Facebook, Amazon, and Microsoft (GAFAM)—control the infrastructural platforms that other players rely on to develop their business models (Dijck, Poell, and de Waal 2018, 16).

Operationally, the Big Five's reach in the global platform ecosystem is disseminated through the strategic distribution of software development kits (SDK) and application programming interface (API): programming codes that allow external developers to interact with the resources and database of a specific platform. Through APIs and SDKs, for example, infrastructural platforms share "login identification services (FB ID, Google

ID, Amazon ID, Apple ID; WeChat ID), payment systems (Apple Pay, Google Pay, Alipay), payment e-mail and messaging (FB Messenger, Google Mail, BaiduMail, MS Mail, Skype, FaceTime), social networks (Weibo, Facebook, Instagram, WhatsApp, Youtube), search tools (Google Search, Bing, Baidu Search), services advertising (FB Ads, Google AD, Tencent AD), retail chains (Amazon Market Place, Alibaba) and app stores (Google Play, Apple)" (Djick 2020, 7). On the one hand, through APIs and SDK, infrastructure platforms make their data and programming environments available, allowing an ecosystem of connected applications to flourish. Not only do these companies increase their value with services built by third parties, but this computational integration expands their capabilities of structured data collection. These "two processes of decentralizing platform features and recentralizing platform ready data" is what Helmond (2015, 8) calls the double logic of platformization.

Since the beginning of the COVID-19 pandemic, there has been an enormous increase in online activities, measured by the number of new users, consumers, products, and services. Major platforms have concentrated even more capital and have entered into fierce competition among themselves and governments. The combined market capitalization value of the Big Five reached $8.7 trillion in January 2022. Consequently, GAFAM stock prices have sustained financial markets rentability during the pandemic period, as between October 2019 and January 2021, "the NYSE Composite Index increased by 17%" while "the growth rates of stock prices for the selected companies were at least three times larger: Facebook/Meta (55 percent), Alphabet (56 percent), Microsoft (64 percent), Amazon (90 percent), and Apple (144 percent)" (UNCTAD 2021, 25).

The dominance of GAFAM encountered an obstacle in China, where a dynamic and diversified national platform ecosystem has been formed, with at least three large corporations with a global reach: Baidu, Tencent, and Alibaba (collectively called BAT). Although foreign companies operate in China's cyberspace, the market environment is subjected to strict regulation and government strategic guidelines. The BATs have preferential access to a market that, in 2021, included 989 million users, more than three times the number of internet users in the US (SCMP 2021). The giant Chinese platforms constitute an essential element of the dual circulation strategy announced by Xi Jinping in 2020 (Arcesati et al. 2020). Without abdicating the integration of Chinese capital into the international economy, the dual circulation strategy aims to reduce China's vulnerabilities concerning the external environment by rebalancing the country's growth model toward domestic consumption and through efforts to obtain independence in semiconductor production (Javed, Tao, and Dong 2021).

Thus, differently from the former phase of the digital age, contemporary digitalization is embedded in an international system characterized by a new rivalry between great powers. Regarding connectivity, in 2020, China's national champion Huawei has become the world's leading supplier of 5G infrastructure, and while China's territory had 700,000 5G base stations, the US had only 50,000 (Allison et al. 2021, 10). Regarding AI, Chinese firms are leading in the speech technology, mobile payments, and facial recognition sectors. Beyond that, China overtook the US for overall AI citations. In the deep learning subfield, Chinese scientists registered six times more patent publications than Americans in 2020. However, as for human capital, although the number of bachelor's students in STEM in China increases four times more per year compared with the US, American companies still concentrate "half of the world's AI superstars" and "can recruit from all the world's 7.9 billion people, while inherent insularity restricts China to its own population" (Allison et al. 2021, 8). In quantum technology, while "China passed the U.S filing more than twice as many patents accounting for 52% of all quantum patents" in 2018, the US still leads in terms of quantum volume with the Honeywell system (Allison et al. 2021, 15–17).

It is too soon to tell if the emerging digital era will be characterized by more conflict or by cooperation between the United States and China. Likewise, it is not decided yet how the central governments of both countries will deal with giant national platforms. Nevertheless, what can be called "digital transformation with Chinese characteristics" seems to be more attentive to the potential roles of inequalities. Technological changes are not neutral but reflect the existing power relations and structured inequalities of the social systems in which they are embedded. Therefore, we should understand digital inequalities as part of a much more significant and persistent structural inequality intrinsic to capitalist dynamics. Since the beginning of the digital age, which correlates with the neoliberal turn of global capitalism, the income and wealth gap between social classes has widened, both in the periphery of the world economy and in developed countries (Piketty 2014). In 2021, while the global top 10 percent owned 76 percent of total household wealth and captured 52 percent of total income, the bottom 50 percent owned only 2 percent of global wealth and captured merely 8.5 percent of total income (Chancel 2022).

Digital inequalities add new layers to structural inequalities. According to Ragnedda and Gladkova (2017), we can talk about three levels of digital inequalities. The first level is a divide between those who have and those who do not have adequate access to the necessary devices and the internet. The second level relates to how different sociodemographic groups and individuals use digital technologies and data. The third level of the digital divide is related to unequal capacities to create tangible and intangible benefits and outcomes from digital technologies.

We should notice that the digital divide has a precise North-South dimension regarding the first level. For instance, in 2021, while more than 90 percent of the North American and Western European population had access to the internet, this percentage was 75 percent in South America, 24 percent in the Middle East and North Africa, 46 percent in South Asia, and 72 percent in Southeast Asia. In absolute terms, India had the most significant amount of unconnected population, with more than 740 million people excluded from the internet, followed by China (421 million), Pakistan (144 million), Bangladesh (114 million), and Nigeria (104 million).

Moreover, the international digital divide manifests in massive differences in mobile internet connection speeds. In 2021, whereas in the United Arab Emirates, Norway, and South Korea, the median download speeds were, respectively, 136.42, 116.66, and 104.98 megabytes per second, in Afghanistan, Palestine, and Venezuela, they were only 5.24, 5.68, and 5.76 megabytes per second (Kemp 2022). Finally, from a human development perspective, we can see that inequalities are much more significant for advanced technologies and more intensive information and communication technologies. For example, while the difference in mobile-cellular subscriptions per one hundred inhabitants from high human development countries to low human development ones is approximately 100 percent, the same score regarding fixed broadband subscription accounts for 3,537.5 percent (ITU UNESCO 2020).

At the second level, various barriers (economic, age, gender, linguistic, educational, cultural, and geographic) prevent or hinder individuals and groups from accessing relevant content and technologies. This level of digital exclusion is a significant problem in the Global South, particularly during the COVID-19 pandemic, where many services and activities have become available only online. Therefore, "those who need the most welfare policies are also those who are excluded from or have limited resources and skills to access the digital realm" (Ragnedda 2020, 18).

Although the gender digital divide has been narrowing in recent years, it is still significant in Africa and the Arab states, where the difference between male and female internet usage was more than 11 percent in 2020 (ITU 2021). Moreover, the literature suggests that women use the internet less frequently and underestimate their digital skills (Hargittai and Shaw 2015). From a geographic point of view, the urban-rural digital divide persists worldwide, with people in urban areas being twice as likely to use the internet as those in rural areas. The gap is consequential in Africa, where internet users in urban areas account for 50 percent of the population, compared with just 15 percent of the rural population (ITU 2021). In Latin America, while the median difference between urban and rural is only 25 percent, there are still significant gaps in countries such as Colombia, Mexico, Ecuador, Peru, Bolivia, and El Salvador (CEPAL 2021).

The distribution of the most commonly used languages on the internet at the content layer is an impressive way to capture second-level digital inequalities. A quantitative study with a sample of the top ten million websites by traffic rankings found that 60.4 percent of internet content is offered in English. At the same time, the share of the world population that speaks English is only 16.2 percent. On the other hand, while the share of the world population that speaks Chinese accounts for 14.3 percent, only 1.4 percent of internet content is recorded in Chinese. The same holds for Arabic, which is spoken by 3.5 percent of the world population but accounts only for 1.1 percent of the internet content (ITU 2021).

At the third level of digital inequalities, women, young, nonwhite, and older people are exposed to different levels of risk regarding unemployment, exploitation at work, school exclusion, and the violation of online rights (from privacy to moral and physical integrity). The concrete benefits from the digital economy are strongly intertwined with socioeconomic backgrounds and the historical accumulation of digital capital. This dynamic is emblematically visible in the functioning of gig platforms such as Uber, Rappi, and Ifood. These business models operationalize interfaces and algorithms to transfer costs and risks to workers subject to precarious labor rights, abusive commissions, extensive work journeys, and low average wages (Ragnedda 2020). On the other hand, the average technologist salary in the US reached U$104,566 in 2021, increasing 6.9 percent compared to 2020 (Dice 2022). Also, small businesses are increasingly left out of the digital economy because, as we noted in the previous section, the Big Five's grasp of the digital ecosystem is being reinforced by the funneling of data and by the enormous investments required in technologies such as AI, the internet of things, and quantum computing. In sum, the second digital age has been the stage of the emergence of a digital underclass and a digital oligarchy.

Another way to capture third-level digital inequalities is to look at the costs and consequences of algorithmic decision-making on social systems. According to Ragneda (2020), algorithmic-driven inequalities can be categorized in three dimensions: knowledge, databases, and treatment. The first dimension refers to the differential lack of awareness regarding the role of algorithms "in shaping our perception of the reality around us both in terms of filtering information we receive and see and reinforcing hegemonic ideals" (Ragneda 2020, 66). In this perspective, socially disadvantaged citizens are more vulnerable to algorithmic manipulation, lacking the skills to avoid being convinced "to buy or believe in something or act in predetermined ways" (Ragneda 2020, 68).

The second dimension points to the fact that "the data by which algorithms learn to judge candidates, situations, and predict behaviors contain a pre-existing set of beliefs" that are skewed in terms of race, wealth, gender, and disability (Ragneda 2020, 69; Fountain 2021). For instance, as reported by the *Guardian* (Kasperkevich 2015), the recently launched app "Google Photos" labeled the pictures of two black people as "gorillas." Moreover, Silva (2022) reported that the computational vision tools from Microsoft, IBM, and Face++ have a much lower accuracy rate for pictures of dark skinned women than for photos of white skinned men.

Finally, the third dimension of algorithm inequality works when these systems are "giving access or restriction to services only to certain social categories" while "monitoring and punishing certain categories more than others" (Ragnedda 2020, 73). Eubanks (2018, 15) reported that algorithms are used as poverty management tools. Predictive models tag poor and working-class people as risky investments, problematic parents, or unworthy of social benefits. Another example is the Correctional Offender Management Profiling for Alternative Sanctions, a software developed by Northpointe and used by US courts to predict the probability of a defendant becoming a recidivist. Silva (2022) reported that Correctional Offender Management Profiling for Alternative Sanctions risk scores have become highly biased, labeling blacks disproportionally as higher risk while making the opposite error toward whites. In sum, digital inequalities across different levels of analysis are pervasive intersectionally through the race, gender, and class structures of discrimination.

Governance

Digital governance is a working process concept. According to Welchman (2015, 8), it is "a discipline that focuses on establishing clear accountability for digital strategy, policy, and standards." The United Nations (2020, 4) comprehends digital governance as a "shared vision on digital cooperation and a digital future that show the full potential for beneficial technology usage." While addressing digital trust and security, this shared vision would "have the potential to accelerate the realization of the 2030 Agenda," contributing to issues ranging from women's empowerment to climate change. On the other hand, Ramanujam and Runden (2021) offer a more operational definition, considering that "global digital governance encompasses the norms, institutions, and standards that shape the regulation around the development and use of these technologies."

The definitions above recognize the complex array of actors, issues, institutions, spatial scales, and temporalities. Therefore, it seems appropriate to use the concept of multilevel governance when referring to cyberspace (Peters et al. 2022). To cite just a few examples of issues requiring governance, one could mention algorithm production norms, AI development strategies, investment policies, technical standards, digital trade, digital inequalities, digital government, information access, privacy, personal data protection, property rights, labor relations, human rights, and cybersecurity. Moreover, such issues cut across local, national, and international levels of analysis.

To assess global digital governance challenges, one might start by considering the oligopolist position held by GAFAM and BAT in their respective platform ecosystems. By controlling the infrastructural services that other actors must access to develop their own applications, these super platforms operate as intermediators between users, businesses, and governments, being able to set the parameters of digital interactions and to channel the data streams through their own databases.

Due to their technological preeminence and gatekeeping powers, this companies have become essential to governmental operations worldwide. During the COVID-19 pandemic, for example, the World Health Organization launched a Health Alert service on WhatsApp, owned by Facebook (Meta), as a tool to spread official information regarding preventive measures and debunking myths about vaccination (Storeng and Puyvallée 2021). In the United States, as of September 2021, twenty-six of the fifty states had developed and deployed exposure notification apps based on programming systems provided by Google and Apple (USA 2021). In China, the government enlisted the tech industry to supply data-driven solutions that ranged from movement tracing apps, facial recognition, and thermal imaging systems, "to AI models for communication, disease prediction and resource management in the healthcare sector" (Arcesati et al. 2020).

Notwithstanding these examples of complementarity among platforms and governments, the tension between corporate and state power has been exacerbated as platformization keeps entangling more sectors of society. A prominent transnational issue is taxation. That's because the ability to deliver services over the internet makes physical requirements less constraining, with major platforms holding their core intangible assets in low-tax jurisdictions. Moreover, most revenues with digital advertising in platforms such as Google and Facebook are not reported in the countries where they were earned, but only where they have a physical presence. This imbalance occurs due to the dual role taken by users in the digital economy: they not only consume the services provided by the platform but also generate the data used to feed the algorithms for targeted advertising (Köthenbürger 2020). Thus, in 2017, although Facebook earned 66 percent of its profits outside the US, it paid 92 percent of its taxes to the American government, leaving only 8 percent in other, mainly developed countries. As for Google, despite 61 percent of the company profits having been generated in foreign markets, it paid only 12 percent of its taxes abroad, and 88 percent in the United States (UNCTAD 2019, 95).

Several countries have unilaterally imposed digital service taxes. However, considering the global reach of digital platforms, national initiatives might not only prove ineffective to counter tax planning practices but also trigger a race to the bottom among states looking for investments. Internationally, the most advanced proposal is a two-pillar framework being negotiated by 130 countries under the leadership of the Organization for Economic Cooperation and Development. The first pillar would tackle the territorialization issue, allocating taxing rights to the markets where companies earn their profits, regardless of physical presence at the jurisdiction. The second pillar aims to establish a floor on competition over corporate income tax, defining a minimum rate of at least 15 percent, which would generate around US$150 billion in tax revenues annually (OECD 2021). However, with strong opposition from Republicans and lacking universal support from Democrats, the deal might not advance in the US Congress, stalling the development of a multilateral digital tax regime and propelling the proliferation of uncoordinated tax measures.

Cross-border data flows and data privacy are other subjects on which states and private platforms tend to collide. In this case, countries have been imposing different governance models, which are conditioned by security, political, and economic concerns.

In the US, for example, where Big Tech companies retain a dominant position in international markets and a deep reach in lobbying activities within Congress, a market-led approach has been articulated with the securitization of data flows abroad. On one hand, the country does not yet have a comprehensive federal law regarding data privacy, leaving each state to develop its own regulatory framework. As of 2022, four states—California, Colorado, Utah, and Virginia—had enacted data privacy laws with provisions such as the right to access and delete personal information, and to opt-out of a business's sale of personal information (NCSL 2022). Regarding digital trade, the US data policy is predicated on the use of "agreements to ensure its firm's unfettered access to foreign markets by, for example, favoring free data flows and banning practices such as data and server localization requirements" (UNCTAD 2021, 100).

On the other hand, the US government has "adopted strict localization policies for defense-related data, requiring that any company supplying cloud services to its Department of Defense must store its data domestically" (UNCTAD 2021, 100). In 2018, the US Congress approved the Clarifying Lawful Overseas Use of Data Act, which established that American law enforcement can compel US companies providing cloud services to give access to data stored on their servers whether they are on US territory or not. Furthermore, the bans on foreign digital companies (e.g., Huawei, TikTok, and Grindr) reveal another layer of ambiguity in the American approach, as the US would be "advocating for a free data flow policy for its companies around the world" whereas "imposing a policy of preventing foreign data-driven companies to enter the United States" (UNCTAD 2021, 102).

In China, where Big Tech companies rely on the huge domestic market to remain globally competitive, the Communist Party exercises a supervision role on the platform ecosystem, promoting a state-led approach that emphasizes cybersovereignty and political stability. Enacted in 2017, the Cybersecurity Law defined that companies considered critical information infrastructures operators (CIIOs) are obliged to store data collected in mainland China locally and must also undergo a security assessment in order to send any data overseas (Junck et al. 2021). In 2021, the Data Security Law came into force. The law expanded the requirements for the protection of any data involved in national security, people's welfare, or the public interest, prohibited CIIOs and non-CIIOs from providing any data stored in China to foreign law enforcement agencies, and increased the maximum penalties to 10 million yuan (Haldane 2021). Also in 2021, the Personal Information Protection Law was enacted. The law demands that companies obtain clear consensus from the data subjects before collecting personal information, that personal data shall be deleted once the collection purpose has been completed, and prohibits discriminatory pricing based on algorithms (Junck et al. 2021).

China also launched the digital component of the Belt and Road Initiative in 2015, an integrated effort to internationalize China's connectivity hardware and digital platforms. Moreover, through the "China Standards 2035" initiative, China is expanding its presence on international standards bodies such as the ISO (International Organization for Standardization), IEC (International Electrotechnical Commission), and ITU (International Telecommunication Union), particularly on the ITU-T (ITU Telecommunication Standardization Sector), the branch of the ITU responsible for information and communication technology standards, in which Beijing has more management team positions than any other country (Bruyère 2022, 58). In 2019, China submitted 830 technical documents to the ITU, "more than the next three countries—South Korea, USA, and Japan—combined" (Krempl 2021). In the next year, during the China Internet Governance Forum, Beijing proposed the Global Initiative on Data Security, which has garnered support from Russia, Tanzania, Pakistan, Ecuador, the Arab League, and countries in the Association of Southeast Asian Nations (Park 2022).

As for the European Union (EU), which is mainly a consumer of digital services from GAFAM, the regulation of the digital economy and data flows has been enacted in a reactive manner. In 2015, aiming to guarantee the scalability of its digital ecosystem, the European Commission released the Digital Single Market Agenda, which provided a framework for the elimination of roaming charges, the enhancement of portability for online content services, and a set of transparency measures for platform-to-business transactions. In 2018, the General Data Protection Regulation came into force, setting extensive requirements for the transfer of personal data outside the region. While the General Data Protection Regulation makes no explicit restrictions regarding cross-border transfers of personal data within the EU, it only allows data transfers to a specific group of countries that the European Commission has considered as having frameworks equivalent to the regulation. Also, it establishes safeguards against AI decision-making processes, ensuring the right for the "data subject to obtain human intervention, express his or her point of view, and contest decisions" (De Gregorio 2021, 64).

In 2022, the European Commission approved the Digital Markets Act, which specifically targets the monopolistic powers of GAFAM's business models. Under the Digital Markets Act, companies with at least 7.5 billion euros in annual turnover or a market capitalization of at least 75 billion euros, that provide services in at least 3 EU countries, and have 45 million monthly active EU individual users and 10,000 active EU business users will be appointed as gatekeepers. Among other things, gatekeepers will be obliged to guarantee the interoperability between messaging services, offer fair and nondiscriminatory terms to commercial users that use online sales platforms for application software, and allow commercial users to freely conclude contracts with their customers outside the gatekeeper platform. Moreover, gatekeepers will be prohibited from giving preferential treatment to their own products, aggregating data collected across different platform services without consent, and commercial users will be prevented from exposing their products on third-party platforms. If gatekeepers violate some of these rules, they may be subject to fines of more than 10 percent of their global annual turnover (Schmalenberger and Nagel 2022).

This nonexhaustive list of examples illustrates a diversified and socially embedded global digital governance landscape. Additionally, it is essential to remember that global digital transformation is inseparable from class conflicts shaping the distributive effects of platformed business models.

Exemplary of this dynamic is the collective organization of Brazilian workers who perform microtasks in the Amazon Mechanical Turk (AMT) marketplace. An AMT worker, who is commonly referred to as a turker, is responsible for digital tasks that AI is inefficient at or incapable of performing, such as describing images, transcribing text, finding information on the web, and answering surveys. Turkers are accessed by programmers through the use of an API, which represents them as an impersonal string of characters. The requesters have complete freedom to set the value paid per task and it is very common to see tasks that pay only 0.01 cents for minutes of work. In the case of Brazilian turkers, Amazon does not make a transfer to their bank account but pays them in credits that must be used on the US Amazon website. Therefore, "the turkers in Brazil find themselves at the bottom of an unregulated market" (Moreschi, Pereira, and Cozman 2020, 61).

Despite these dehumanizing and precarious conditions of work, Moreschi, Pereira, and Cozman (2020) found evidence that Brazilian turkers develop ways to support each other and self-organize to fight for worker protections in AMT. By applying multimethod research composed of a seventy-two-question survey with a sample of 149 Brazilian turkers and a six-month digital ethnography on the "MTurk" WhatsApp Group, the authors discovered that the workers exchange information daily on "the best tasks of the day, tips on how to deal when their work is rejected by requesters, dealing with the bureaucracies of the system" (Moreschi, Pereira, and Cozman 2020, 60). Beyond that, the group articulated strategies to circumvent Amazon's form of payment, and to send collective emails to the company asking to allow Brazilians to receive payments into their bank accounts. Thus, even though "this mobilization is still fragile, and doesn't necessarily change the labor conditions of the AMT, it offers some hope that, although digital platform labor attempts to isolate workers from each other, forms of mobilization and self-organization can still exist" (Moreschi, Pereira and Cozman 2020, 61).

Conclusion

In the digital age, the growing contradictions between the new productive forces, the inherited social relations, and the natural environment are at least as radical as the processes experienced in the modern age. Firms and governments will dispute emerging general-purpose technologies sustaining datafication and networks (e.g., blockchain, cloud computing, artificial intelligence, robotics, semiconductors, 3D printing, the internet of things, 5G mobile, and quantum computing). Along with bio, energy, and space technologies, digital techs will profoundly impact economics, society, and security in the decades ahead (UNCTAD 2019; Allison et al. 2021).

The digital transformation of global capitalist society will continue to advance, as much as the social and international conflicts inherent in such processes. Therefore, the future of humanity and the planet depend on the global working class's strategic struggle to transform the digital age into a more democratic, equal, and sustainable system (*Gesellschaftsformation*).

Note

1. The authors would like to thank Professor Aaron Schneider, the Lula Institute, the Brazilian National Council for Scientific and Technological Development (Conselho Nacional de Pesquisa Científica—CNPq), and the research assistance of Francisco Fabris of PROBIC (Programa Institucional de Bolsas de de Iniciação Científica, Scientific Initiation Program), CNPq, and UFRGS (Universidade Federal do Rio Grande do Sul, Federal University of Rio Grande do Sul).

16

Conclusion

AARON SCHNEIDER

This book has outlined the major issues facing the Global South and working classes as a result of digitalization. To make sense of the digital transition, the book includes chapters grouped according to three broad themes: historical dimensions of technological change, the formation of new collective identities around and as a result of digitalization, and shifting challenges and responses from states and the international system.

The central concept at the heart of digitalization is data. Investments in technologies to generate, capture, store, analyze, and commodify data have renewed capital accumulation after the crisis of 2008–2009, the stagnation of the 2010s, and the collapse of COVID-19. Digitalization interacts with the two other major changes to the international system, declining unipolarity and climate crisis, to define the digital age. Yet, with quasi-monopolistic firms mostly originating in the Global North controlling vast amounts of data and concentrating the benefits of new technologies, working classes and developing countries face the possibility of falling further behind.

This conclusion will focus on a concept that emerges from the previous chapters, appearing explicitly in some and hanging collectively in the background of all of them: the state in a digital age. In a digital age, developing country catch-up, the national and international regimes governing new technologies, and working class and popular sector access

276 | Aaron Schneider

to the wealth and control of new technologies requires states capable of digital statecraft.

The State in a Digital Age

Digitalization comes after decades of neoliberal erosion of state capacities, yet the digital age demands significant recuperation of capabilities and state-building projects. State-building is something that occurs not just at the initial foundation of nations or at a single historical moment, but rather is something that must happen repeatedly, with each epochal shift in the operation of the world system and each insertion of countries in the global political economy (Schneider 2012). As digitalization coincides and interacts with the geopolitical rise of China and ecological crisis, it represents the most significant change to the international system of recent decades. This poses new challenges to Global North and South, and the current volume provides detail on the "digital statecraft" required to compete.

The first such task is regulation. Data localization requirements and data protection appear in the toolkit of actions that serve goals such as security, serving local economic activities, and advancing popular interests. Yet, in the absence of international standards and best practices, countries are left to determine regulations on their own, with familiar differences across more and less powerful countries, with some racing to the bottom to liberalize furthest.

Still, even the more expansive European regulations on the use of data limit themselves to a focus on individual rights over data. While individual rights are clearly important to liberal polities, data takes its shape and generates value when gathered among individuals and across societies. As indicated in attempts to reconceptualize collectivities in this volume, states and societies have to reconceptualize the bearers of data, protecting the collective rights of communities and nations as they produce the information contained in their data. Some call for data nationalization, aggregating data at the national level and giving states power to protect national identity, culture, and access to rents, even as they facilitate the creation of markets, productive activity, and domestic innovation.

Given evident inequalities between countries, especially between North and South, data nationalization is not sufficient. Larger developing countries, such as Brazil, India, Indonesia, and China, may have a degree of state capacity and market leverage to effectively regulate and negotiate

Conclusion | 277

with powerful multinational corporate actors, but other developing country governments will surely require regional coordination and the creation of international institutions guarding national sovereignty over data. Only a few great powers have the capacity for extraterritorial authority over data, and even they lack a conceptualization of sovereignty over information living on servers and in the ether. We need a new conceptualization of territory, perhaps borrowing the concept of "interiority" from design, providing structure and regulation to experiences in external spaces (Teston 2020). For all developing countries, international coordination is important, especially in terms of South-South partnership to force northern countries and their firms to facilitate domestic development and more inclusive futures for the Global South.

A final form of regulation and tool for states to shape digitalization is available in terms of taxation. After decades of a globalized race to the bottom, the decision by a coalition of Organization for Economic Cooperation and Development and G20 countries to support a minimum global corporate tax rate[1] potentially changes calculations for digital firms. They had amassed power by controlling property rights over innovation and investments essential for development, but alternative tax regimes can both secure revenues for investment in education and research and development and reorganize positions in the international division of labor, capturing some of the rents from digitalization for home economies.

Finally, beyond mere regulation, state subsidy and investments in the activities that generate wealth and power in digital capitalism will be an important part of state action in a digital age. Investments in education and research and development remain at the center of policies to enhance popular and state sovereignty, especially as economic activities increasingly cross borders. Core-periphery dynamics are now more functionally oriented than territorially oriented and organized, producing unbalanced growth and accumulation within territories. Clusters of digitech, such as Silicon Valley and Shenzhen, are more integrated with each other than to nearby regions not in the same global value chains. The challenge to developing countries is to form clusters and capture the productivity gains of agglomeration, and to extend the developmental impact of these clusters to other areas and sectors.

Future Research

This project places the digital age in its historical context. Thinkers such as Fernand Braudel and Immanuel Wallerstein have understood world history in terms of epochal shifts in the way capitalism, geopolitics, and societies operate and interact (Wallerstein 1974; Braudel 1992). From early beginnings in long-distance trade within a relatively circumscribed and Eurasian territory of limited political organization, the world capitalist system has evolved into globally integrated chains of value that organize production, distribution, and consumption across multiple jurisdictions (Cox 1987). Digitalization should be studied as the latest phase, displacing, but not resolving, the crises associated with excessive financialization, destruction of the environment, weakening democracy, and rising inequality (Harvey 2005).

Yanis Varoufakis pessimistically observes that new technologies have defied the predictions of leftists who presumed capitalism would evolve into a more egalitarian and humane system. Instead, he observes a regression into "technofeudalism." If capitalism is defined by wage labor and competition within the market, digitalization has produced a system in which labor is done to create data with little or no pay and a few quasi-monopolistic firms exert overwhelming control while destroying competition. By creating new ways to establish and extract rents at the same time as it disrupted older social relations, digitalization has sent us backwards in historical time, rather than forwards (Varoufakis 2021).

We need further study into digitalization as an epochal shift, with a critical eye to the ways in which it reshapes capitalism, and not in healthy directions. New technologies reshape the structural conditions of surplus—the way surplus is produced, distributed, and redeployed—and Leo Panitch and Greg Albo remind us that capitalism is always about accumulating surplus. Digitalization itself results from the accumulated surplus extracted from workers and invested in fixed capital, experienced as technological innovations (Albo and Panitch 2021). Some, but not all, of these innovations raise levels of productivity, releasing ever greater surplus available for distribution and consumption, even as they evade or undermine the political, social, and economic mechanisms that previously regulated control and redistributed some of that surplus. The result has been rapidly accelerating inequality and increasing threats to employment, wages, and working class organization (UNCTAD 2021).

Workers' ability to secure a wage and consume what they need to reproduce themselves is increasingly mediated through digital platforms (Hua and Ray 2021; Atanasoski and Vora 2019; Noble 2018). Technological innovations have given capital new power over labor, forcing workers into flexible employment, automating production processes, and using

Conclusion | 279

data, artificial intelligence, and robotics to increase precarity. The result is increasing levels of poverty, inequality, and exploitation (Chandler and Fuchs 2019; Frey 2019). Moreover, there is evidence that platform-mediated jobs and services might induce neoliberal and authoritarian behavior at the individual level.[2]

A further avenue for research lies in the paradox of ecological crisis. Digitalization both accelerates and presents itself as a solution to ecological crisis. This crisis, as argued by John Bellamy Foster and others, is inherent in capitalist modernity, in which nature is viewed as an unlimited resource, available to be commodified for the purpose of capital accumulation (Bellamy Foster 2020). Despite claims of a green future, the digital age is as hungry as ever for energy and raw materials, forcing open frontiers in lithium and rare minerals, often under highly exploitative and environmentally damaging conditions (Chan, Selden, and Ngai 2020; Pappas 2022). Climate change and global inability to manage the destruction of the natural environment are only the latest indications that a new relationship between man and nature is necessary, something that people like Nick Estes have argued is possible only in a postcapitalist world (Estes 2019).

Changes to the international order are both accelerated by and symptomatic of the rise of new technologies. The post–World War II regime and the hegemonic moment of US unipolarity appear to have passed and attempts to regain dominance through a renewed investment in technology, finance, and militarism have further undermined the international norms and institutions meant to handle international problems, including climate change, migration, economic development, conflict, and equity (Robinson 2020b). An increasing number of observers worry about the relationship between digitalization and conflict, finding in new technologies both encouragement to polarization and conflict and the tools of conflict (Leonard 2021).

The link between digitalization and a changing global order has particularly been evident in the area of security, as major powers seek to control and deploy new technologies in ways that will shut out their rivals. An increasing host of voices in the US focus on cybersecurity as a new arena of great power conflict, lamenting the advance of China and urging rules governing new technologies that will privilege the US and its allies and contain rivals (Allison et al. 2021). At the same time, middle powers and poorer countries increasingly find themselves forced to navigate these issues without institutional constraints on great powers

280 | Aaron Schneider

nor their own capacity to control their insertion in global digital networks (Kovacs and Ranganathan 2019; Basu 2021).

Finally, we need additional research into digitalization and the functioning of democracy. Fake news, artificial intelligence, and algorithms have demonstrated the potential to exacerbate polarization, distort elections, and push voters toward certain candidates and policy positions or away from others. Democracy ceases to function if Google, Amazon, Facebook, Apple, and Microsoft (GAFAM), which control our data, can make use of it to push our decisions in one direction or another (Taplin 2017).

Worse, the combination of cultural breakdown, economic distress, and manipulation of democratic processes is especially favorable to the rise of fascist and antidemocratic forces. In the current moment of crisis, individual dissatisfaction is completely valid, but antidemocratic actors can use digital technologies to nudge people toward fascistic solutions. Terry Lee has demonstrated the way in which digital technologies facilitate direct communication between leaders and supporters, unmediated by parties, unions, and traditional social organizations (Lee 2019). This kind of connection is of particular utility to right-wing populists, who have proliferated and found success in democratic elections under the digital age.

Our current historical moment is characterized by economic stagnation, social disruption, ecological crisis, and war. Yet the defining characteristics of the digital age have not been set. There is still the potential for a more equitable, peaceful, sustainable, and democratic world, but it will require foregrounding the role of labor and the Global South. By focusing on labor and the Global South in a digital age, this volume attempts to map a way forward.

Notes

1. https://www.reuters.com/business/g20-leaders-endorse-global-minimum-corporate-tax-deal-2023-start-2021-10-30/.

2. https://www.bath.ac.uk/announcements/new-project-investigates-links-between-precarious-work-and-authoritarian-politics-in-global-south/.

Contributors

Aaron Schneider, Editor, is Leo Block Chair and Professor at the University of Denver. His books include State-Building and Tax Regimes in Central America (2012) and Renew Orleans? Globalized Development and Working Class Resistance in New Orleans (2018). Contact: aaron.schneider@du.edu.

Tássio Acosta is Professor at Santa Cecilia University. He has a PhD in education from the State University of Campinas, a master's in education from the Federal University of São Carlos (UFSCar), and is a specialist in ethics, values, and citizenship at the University of São Paulo (USP), a historian, and pedagogist. Contact: tassioacosta@gmail.com.

Neda Atanasoski is Professor and Chair of the Harriet Tubman Department of Women, Gender and Sexuality Studies at the University of Maryland. She is the author of Humanitarian Violence: The U.S. Deployment of Diversity (2013) and Surrogate Humanity: Race, Robots, and the Politics of Technological Futures (2019). She is also the coeditor of a 2017 special issue, "Postsocialist Politics and the Ends of Revolution," of the journal Social Identities. Contact: natanaso@umd.edu.

Pedro Txai Leal Brancher is Associate Professor of the Department of Foreign Languages at Sichuan University of Science and Engineering (SUSE). He also leads the institution's International Affairs Office. He completed his postdoctoral research at the Federal University of Rio Grande do Sul and the National Institute of Science and Technology on public policies, strategies, and development. Contact: brancherpedro022@gmail.com.

282 | Contributors

Marco Cepik is Professor, Department of Economics and International Relations, Federal University of Rio Grande do Sul, and director of the Brazilian Intelligence Agency's Intelligence School. His areas of study include international security, digital governance, and comparative politics. Publications available: http://professor.ufrgs.br/marcocepik. Contact: mcepik@gmail.com.

Henrique Estides Delgado is a PhD candidate in the Josef Korbel School of International Studies at the University of Denver and in the Department of Economics at the University of Chieti-Pescara. His research interests are the politics and the economics of development, with a focus on the institutions that mediate technological upgrading in different societies, the role of international flows, and the evolution of ideas in international political economy. Contact: henrique.estidesdelgado@du.edu.

Vashishtha Doshi is a PhD student in the Department of Political Science at the University of California, Santa Barbara. His research interests include currency internationalization, politics of sovereign debt, and the geopolitics of finance and technology. His dissertation focuses on the tools available to middle powers to enhance their autonomy in a hierarchically structured world of technology and finance. Contact: vdoshi@ucsb.edu.

Sílvio Gallo is Full Professor at the School of Education of the State University of Campinas (Unicamp) and researcher at the National Council for Scientific and Technological Development (CNPq), both in Brazil. His interests concern contemporary French philosophy as tools for politically thinking educational problems. Contact: silvio.gallo@gmail.com.

Benjamin Goldfrank is Professor at Seton Hall University's School of Diplomacy and International Relations. His research interests focus on the comparative analysis of Latin American politics, and especially democratic experiments like participatory budgeting. Contact: benjamin.goldfrank@shu.edu.

Rafael R. Ioris is Professor of Modern Latin America at the University of Denver, with a special focus on modern Brazilian political, diplomatic, cultural, and intellectual histories. His latest book, Transforming Brazil: A History of National Development in the Postwar Era, examines the political and cultural debates involved in the promotion of fast-paced, state-led programs of development in Brazil in the aftermath of World War II. Contact: rafael.ioris@du.edu.

Zhenyu Jiang is PhD candidate in the School of Public Policy and Management, Tsinghua University, and received a master's in engineering from Shandong University. His research interests are in environmental policy and global value chains. He has published in IEEE Access, Energy Economics, and PLoS. He is currently studying the digital economy and intellectual property rights protection within global value chains. Contact: zhenyujiang@126.com.

Andre Isai Leirner holds an Advanced Architecture Design Research Laboratory (AADRL) degree (Honors) and a Fundação Getulio Vargas (FGV) master's degree in public administration. He is currently a researcher at the Brazilian Center of Analysis and Planning (CEBRAP) and Director at INDX Design Brasil and Priorize.net. Contact: indx.design@gmail.com.

P. Locatelli is Educator at the Southern Regional Municipal Health School, doctor in sciences and doctoral student in public health from the University of São Paulo (USP), and graduated in dentistry. Contact: paulo.campi35@gmail.com.

Lizzie O'Shea is a lawyer and writer focused on law, technology, and human rights. Her writing has appeared in the New York Times, the Guardian, and the Sydney Morning Herald, among others, and she is the author of Future Histories (2019). She is founder of Digital Rights Watch, which advocates for human rights online, and was named a 2019 Human Rights Hero by Access Now. Contact: lizze.oshea@gmail.com.

Ivan da Costa Marques is retired full professor at the Federal University of Rio de Janeiro, and founded and is the president of the Brazilian Association of Social Studies of Sciences. He is editor of the journal Engineering Studies and works as an ad hoc advisor to several academic journals and government agencies. Contact: imarques@nce.ufrj.br.

Claudia Nociolini Rebechi led the Fairwork team, including Marcos Aragão de Oliveira, Tatiana López Ayala, Jonas C. L. Valente, Rafael Grohmann, Julice Salvagni, Roseli Aparecida Figaro Paulino, Rodrigo Carelli, Victória Mendonça da Silva, Ana Flávia Marques da Silva, Camilla

284 | Contributors

Voigt Baptistella, Jackeline Cristina Gameleira Cerqueira da Silva, Helena Rodrigues da Farias, Mark Graham, and Kelle Howson. Fairwork (https://fair.work) highlights practices in the emerging platform economy. Centrally coordinated by the Oxford Internet Institute and the WZB Berlin Social Science Centre, Fairwork operates through a global network of research teams reaching thirty-eight countries across the world. Contact: claudiarebechi@utfpr.edu.br.

William I. Robinson is Professor of Sociology at the University of California, Santa Barbara, affiliated with the Latin American and Iberian Studies Program, and with the Global and International Studies Program. He is the author of Into the Tempest: Essays on the New Global Capitalism, Global Police State, and Global Capitalism and the Crisis of Humanity. Contact: w.i.robinson1@gmail.com.

Benjamin Selwyn is Full Professor of International Relations and International Development in the Department of International Relations, University of Sussex, UK. His publications include The Struggle for Development (2017), The Global Development Crisis (2014), and Workers, State and Development in Brazil: Powers of Labor, Chains of Value (2012). Contact: b.selwyn@sussex.ac.uk.

Parminder Jeet Singh is Executive Director at IT for Change currently focused on internet governance, e-governance, the digital economy, the geopolitics of the digital world, democracy in the digital age, and technical governance of the internet. He is considered a key contributor in shaping a southern discourse on global internet governance, and a positive, rights-centered approach to the internet and digital policies. In 2001, he authored a book on Governance@Net: New Governance Opportunities for India. Contact: parminder@itforchange.net.

Alessandro Teixeira Golombiewski is a National Thousand Talent–Professor of Public Policy at the School of Public Policy and Management at Tsinghua University, Professor of International Business at Tsinghua Schwartzman College, and Professor at Tsinghua Berkley Graduate School in Shenzhen China. He is also Chief Economist of the New Development Bank and was previously Chief Minister of Tourism in Brazil, and Executive and Minister of Development, Industry and Foreign Trade. Contact: ag@mail.tsinghua.edu.cn.

Yanina Welp is Research Fellow at the Albert Hirschman Centre on Democracy, Graduate Institute (Geneva). She holds a PhD in political and social sciences from the Pompeu Fabra University (Spain) and two bachelor's degrees in social communication and political science from the University of Buenos Aires (Argentina). Her last book is The Will of the People: Populism and Citizen Participation in Latin America (2022). Contact: yanina.welp@graduateinstitute.ch.

References

Abers, Rebecca. 2000. *Inventing Local Democracy: Grassroots Politics in Brazil.* Boulder, CO: Lynne Rienner.

Abílio, L. C. 2020. "Digital Platforms and Uberization: Globalization of an Administered South?" *Contracampo* 39 (1): 12–26.

Abílio, L. C., R. Grohmann, and H. C. Weiss. 2021. "Struggles of Delivery Workers in Brazil: Working Conditions and Collective Organization during the Pandemic." *Journal of Labor and Society* 24 (4): 598–616.

Abudheen K, Sainul. 2017. "Alibaba to Facilitate Cross-Border E-Commerce Trade between Malaysia and China." *e27*. https://e27.co/alibaba-facilitate-cross-border-e-commerce-trade-malaysia-china-20170512/.

Acemoglu, Daron, and Pascual Restrepo. 2017. *Robots and Jobs: Evidence from US Labor Markets.* Working Paper 23285. Cambridge: National Bureau of Economic Research.

Acemoglu, Daron, and Pascual Restrepo. 2019. "Automation and New Tasks: How Technology Displaces and Reinstates Labor." *Journal of Economic Perspectives* 33 (2): 3–30.

Acersati, Rebeca. 2022. *E-Government and Covid-19: Digital China Goes Global.* https://merics.org/en/short-analysis/e-government-and-covid-19-digital-china-goes-global.

Acosta, T., and S. Gallo. 2020. "A educação em disputa no Brasil contemporâneo: Entre os estudos de gênero, a dita ideologia de gênero e a produção de uma 'ideologia de gênesis.'" *Educação* 45 (1): 1–28.

Albo, Gregory, and Leo Panitch. 2021. *Beyond Digital Capitalism.* New York: Monthly Review Press.

Alizadeh, Tooran, and Deepti Prasad. 2023. "The Right to the Smart City in the Global South: A Research Agenda." *Urban Studies* (May): 1–19.

Allcott, H., and M. Gentzkow. 2017. "Social Media and Fake News in the 2016 Election." *Journal of Economic Perspectives* 31: 211–36.

Allison, Graham, Kevin Klyman, Karina Barbesino, and Hugo Yen. 2021. *The Great Tech Rivalry: China vs. the US.* Boston: Belfer Center for Science and International Affairs, Harvard University.

288 | References

Alston, Philip. 2019. *Report of the Special Rapporteur on Extreme Poverty and Human Rights*. New York: United Nations.

Alter, Adam. 2017. *Irresistible: The Rise of Addictive Technology and the Business of Keeping Us Hooked*. New York: Penguin.

Anderson, Benedict R. 1991. *Imagined Communities*. London: Verso.

Andersson Schwartz, J. 2017. "Platform Logic: An Interdisciplinary Approach to the Platform-Based Economy." *Policy & Internet* 9 (4): 374–94.

Anduiza, Eva, Michael Jensen, and Laia Jorba, eds. 2012. *Digital Media and Political Engagement Worldwide: A Comparative Study*. Cambridge: Cambridge University Press.

Arcary, Valerio. 2021. "Is Bolsonaro a Neofascist?" *Historical Materialism*, April. https://www.historicalmaterialism.org/blog/bolsonaro-neofascist.

Arcesati, Rebecca, Anna Holzmann, Yishu Mao, Manlai Nyamdorj, Kristin Shi-Kupfer,

Kai von Carnap, and Claudia Wessling. 2020. "China's Digital Platform Economy: Assessing Developments towards Industry 4.0." *Merics Report*. Berlin: Mercator Institute for China Studies.

Arendt, Hannah. 1973. *Origins of Totalitarianism*. New York: Harcourt Brace.

Armijo, L. E., and S. N. Katada. 2014. "Theorizing the Financial Statecraft of Emerging Powers." *New Political Economy* 20 (1): 42–62.

Arrighi, Giovanni. 1994. *The Long Twentieth Century*. New York: Verso.

Associação Brasileira de Emissoras de Rádio e Televisão (Brazilian Association of Radio and TV Broadcasters). 2021. *Violações à liberdade de expressão: Relatório anual 2021*. São Paulo: ABERT.

Atanasoski, Neda, and Kalindi Vora. 2019. *Surrogate Humanity*. Durham: Duke University Press.

Athique, Adrian. 2013. *Digital Media and Society: An Introduction*. Hoboken, NJ: John Wiley and Sons.

Atkinson, Robert D. 2021. *A U.S. Grand Strategy for the Global Digital Economy*. Policy report. Washington, DC: Information Technology and Innovation Foundation.

Avritzer, L. 2009. *Experiências nacionais de participação social*. Rio de Janeiro: Cortes.

Azzi, Diego, et al. 2020. "A política externa bolsonarista e o agravamento de um Brasil insustentável." In *A política externa de Bolsonaro na pandemia*, edited by Diego Araujo Azzi, Gilberto Marcos Antonio Rodrigues, and Ana Tereza Lopes Marra de Sousa. São Bernardo do Campo, SP: Observatório Politica Externa Brasileira and Friedrich Ebert Stiftung.

Babic, M., J. Fichtner, and E. M. Heemskerk. 2017. "States versus Corporations: Rethinking the Power of Business in International Politics." *International Spectator* 52 (4): 20–43.

Baker, S. 2016. "Theresa May's Plan to Put Workers on Boards Is Borrowed from Germany and France." *Independent*, July 12. https://www.independent.co.uk/

References | 289

news/business/news/theresa-may-board-corporate-plan-germany-france-productivity-economics-a7132221.html.

Balderacchi, Claudio. 2015. "Participatory Mechanisms in Bolivia, Ecuador and Venezuela: Deepening or Undermining Democracy?" *Government and Opposition* 52 (1): 131–61.

Barbosa, B., H. Martins, and J. Valente. 2022. "Combate à desinformação não pode depender apenas das plataformas." *LeMonde Diplomatique Brasil,* March 3.

Barney, Darin, Gabriella Coleman, Christine Ross, Jonathan Sterne, and Tamar Tembeck, eds. 2016. *The Participatory Condition in the Digital Age.* Minneapolis: University of Minnesota Press.

Barrero, Jose Maria, Nick Bloom, and Steven J. Davis. *COVID-19 Is Also a Reallocation Shock.* Working Paper No. 2020–59. Chicago: Becker Friedman Institute, University of Chicago. https://www.nber.org/papers/w27137.

Barstow, S., and R. Stein. 2005. "Under Bush, a New Age of Prepackaged TV News." *New York Times,* March 13.

Bastani, A. 2019. *Fully Automated Luxury Communism.* London: Verso Books.

Basu, A. 2021. "Sovereignty in a 'Datafied' World." *ORF Issue Brief No. 501.* New Delhi: Observer Research Foundation.

Bauerlein, Mark. 2011. *The Digital Divide: Arguments for and against Facebook, Google, Texting, and the Age of Social Networking.* London: Penguin.

Baxter, Hugh. 1987. "System and Life-World in Habermas's Theory of Communicative Action." *Theory and Society* 16 (1): 39–86.

BBC. 2020. "Singapore Approves Lab-Grown 'Chicken' Meat." *BBC News,* December 2. https://www.bbc.co.uk/news/business-55155741.

Bebbington, J., J. Brown, and B. Frame. 2007. "Accounting Technologies and Sustainability Assessment Models." *Ecological Economics* 61 (2–3): 224–36.

Bejarano, Ana María, and Renata Segura. 2013. "Constituent Assemblies and Democracy: A Critical Reading of the New Constitutionalism in the Andes." *Colombia Internacional* 79: 19–48.

Bellamy Foster, John. 2020. *The Return of Nature: Socialism and Ecology.* New York: Monthly Review Press.

Belli, L. 2022. "Structural Power as a Critical Element of Social Media Platforms' Private Sovereignty." In *Constitutionalising Social Media,* edited by E. Celeste, A. Heldt, and C. Keller. New York: Hart Publishers.

Benanav, Aaron. 2019. "Automation and the Future of Work." *New Left Review* 119.

Benjamin, Ruha. 2019. *Race after Technology.* New York: Polity.

Bennett, Lucy, Bertha Chin, and Bethan Jones, eds. 2015. *Crowdfunding the Future: Media Industries, Ethics, and Digital Society.* Bern, Switzerland: Peter Lang.

Berry, David M. 2015. *Critical Theory and the Digital.* New York: Bloomsbury.

Beyes, Timon, Martina Leeker, and Imanuel Schipper, eds. 2017. *Performing the Digital: Performance Studies and Performances in Digital Cultures.* Bielefeld, Germany: Transcript-Verlag.

290 | References

BFAWU. 2021. *The Right to Food Report*. https://www.bfawu.org/wp-content/uploads/2021/09/BFAWU-Right-to-Food-Report.pdf.

Bhagat, S., and J. A. Brickley. 1984. "Cumulative Voting: The Value of Minority Shareholder Voting Rights." *Journal of Law and Economics* 27 (2): 339–65.

Bijsmla, Like, Wouter Deen, Udo Garritzmann, Christoph Grafe, Dick van den Heuvel, Marcel Musch, Ivan Nio, Lara Schrijver, and Mechthild Stuhlmacher. 2000. *Network Urbanism*. Amsterdam: Sun Publishers.

Binfield, Kevin, ed. 2004. *Writings of the Luddites*. Baltimore: Johns Hopkins University Press.

Birch, K., D. Cochrane, and C. Ward. 2021. "Data as Asset? The Measurement, Governance, and Valuation of Digital Personal Data by Big Tech." *Big Data & Society* 8 (1): 1–15.

Blum, Christian, and Christina Isabel Zuber. 2016. "Liquid Democracy: Potentials, Problems, and Perspectives." *Journal of Political Philosophy* 24 (2): 162–82.

Boeri, Stefano. 2007. *USE—Uncertain States of Europe*. Vienna: Springer.

Brakarz, J., M. Greene, and E. Rojas. 2002. *Cities for All: Recent Experiences with Neighborhood Upgrading Programs*. Washington, DC: Inter-American Development Bank.

Brancher, Pedro Txai. 2021. *Hegemonia financeira na era digital: O grupo empresarial XP no contexto de transição global*. Rio de Janeiro: State University of Rio de Janeiro (UERJ).

Braudel, Fernand. 1992. *Civilization and Capitalism. Vol. 3*. Berkeley: University of California Press.

Braz, M. V. 2021. "Heteromation and Microwork in Brazil." *Sociologias* 23 (57): 134–72.

Breuer, Anita, and Yanina Welp, eds. 2014. *Digital Technologies for Democratic Governance in Latin America*. New York: Routledge.

Briceño, Héctor. 2014. "Los consejos comunales y la democracia participativa en Venezuela." In *Venezuela under Chavez's Administration*, edited by Aki Sakaguchi, 1–44. Tokyo: IDE.

Brigatti, F. 2022. "Trabalho por aplicativo deve ser regulado, dizem 87% dos paulistanos." *Folha de S. Paulo*, April 30.

Bringel, B., and R. V. S. Varella. 2016. "A pesquisa militante na América Latina hoje: Reflexões sobre as desigualdades e as possibilidades de produção de conhecimentos." *Revista digital de direito administrativo* 3 (3): 474–89.

Brozek, B., and B. Janik. 2019. "Can Artificial Intelligences Be Moral Agents?" *New Ideas in Psychology* 54: 101–6.

Bruner, C. M. 2008. "States, Markets, and Gatekeepers: Public-Private Regulatory Regimes in an Era of Economic Globalization." *Michigan Journal of International Law* 30 (1): 125–76.

Brynjolfsson, Erik, and Andrew McAfee. 2014. *The Second Machine Age*. New York: W.W. Norton.

References | 291

Buckley, Peter J., and Roger Strange. 2015. "The Governance of the Global Factory: Location and Control of World Economic Activity." *Academy of Management Perspectives* 29 (2): 237–49.

Bufacchi, V. 2020. "What's the Difference between Lies and Post-Truth in Politics? A Philosopher Explains." *The Conversation*, January 24.

Bughin, Jacques, Jeongmin Seong, James Manyika, Michael Chui, and Raoul Joshi, et al. 2018. *Notes from the AI Frontier: Modeling the Impact of AI on the World Economy*. www.mickinsey.com/featured-insight/artificial-intelligence/notes-from-the-ai-frontier-modeling-the-impact-of-ai-on-the-world-economy.

Bunz, Mercedes, and Graham Meikle. 2017. *The Internet of Things*. Hoboken, NJ: John Wiley and Sons.

Burkhalter, Stephanie, John Gastil, and Todd Kelshaw. 2002. "A Conceptual Definition and Theoretical Model of Public Deliberation in Small Face-to-Face Groups." *Communication Theory* 12 (4): 398–422.

Butler, P. 2022. "More Than 2m Adults in UK Cannot Afford to Eat Every Day, Survey Finds." *Guardian*, May 9. https://www.theguardian.com/society/2022/may/09/more-than-2m-adults-in-uk-cannot-afford-to-eat-every-day-survey-finds.

C4AI 2022—Mesa Redonda. *AI em Foco: Accountability algorítmica e políticas públicas*. https://www.youtube.com/watch?v=URrRl3Owm4Y&list=PL4w4y EaOWuOYq0Bn54kvr3VTUvfZ01q9r.

Cafezeiro, I., I. da Costa Marques, F. Severo, and H. Cukierman. 2021. "Informática é Sociedade." In *Série Informática na Educação, V. 4*, edited by E. O. Santos, F. F. Sa.mpaio, and M. Pimentel. Porto Alegre: Sociedade Brasileira de Computação.

Calil, Gilbero Grassi. 2021. "A negação da pandemia: Reflexões sobre a estratégia bolsonarista." *Serviço Sociedade* 140: 30–47.

Calo, Ryan, and Alex Rosenblat. 2018. "The Taking Economy: Uber, Information, and Power." *Columbia Law Review* 117: 6.

Camargo, A. 2022. "Estado, quantificação e agência: Uma análise genealógica." *Dados* 65.

Cameron, Maxwell, Eric Hershberg, and Kenneth Sharpe. 2012. *New Institutions for Participatory Democracy in Latin America: Voice and Consequence*. Basingstoke: Palgrave Macmillan.

Cant, C. 2019. *Riding for Deliveroo*. Cambridge: Wiley.

Cardenas, J., J. Graf, and P. O'Dogherty. 2003. *Foreign Banks Entry in Emerging Market Economies: A Host Country Perspective*. CGFS Working Group on FDI in the Financial Sector. Geneva: Bank of International Settlements.

Carrington, D. 2018. "Global Food System Is Broken, Say World's Science Academies." *Guardian*, November 28. https://www.theguardian.com/environment/2018/nov/28/global-food-system-is-broken-say-worlds-science-academies.

Carrington, D. 2019. "UK Has Biggest Fossil Fuel Subsidies in the EU, Finds Commission." *Guardian*, January 23. https://www.theguardian.com/environment/2019/jan/23/uk-has-biggest-fossil-fuel-subsidies-in-the-eu-finds-commission.

292 | References

Carsten, Paul, and John Ruwitch. 2015. "Still an Underdog, but China Government Deals Help Alibaba's Cloud Ambitions." *Reuters*, June 18. https://www.reuters.com/article/us-alibaba-cloud/still-an-underdog-but-chinagovernment-deals-help-alibabas-cloud-ambitions-idUSKBN0OY2TC20150619.

Cartwright, M. 2020. "Internationalising State Power through the Internet: Google, Huawei and Geopolitical Struggle." *Internet Policy Review* 9 (3).

Carvalho, Bruno Leal Pastor de. 2016. "História pública e redes sociais na internet: Elementos iniciais para um debate contemporâneo." *Transversos: Revista de História* 7 (7): 743–61.

Casonato, C. 2021. "AI and Constitutionalism: The Challenges Ahead." In *Reflections on Artificial Intelligence for Humanity*, edited by Bertrand Braunschweig and Malik Ghallab. Cham, Switzerland: Springer.

Castells, Manuel. 2009. *Communication Power*. New York: Oxford University Press.

Castells, Manuel. 2015. *Networks of Outrage and Hope: Social Movements in the Internet Age*. Hoboken, NJ: John Wiley and Sons.

Casteltrione, Isidoropaolo. 2015. "The Internet, Social Networking Web Sites and Political Participation Research: Assumptions and Contradictory Evidence." *First Monday* 20 (3): 181–202.

Cenamor, Javier, David Sjodin, and V. Parida. 2017. "Adopting a Platform Approach in Servitization: Leveraging the Value of Digitalization." *International Journal of Production Economics* 192.

CEPAL. 2021. *Dados y hechos sobre la transformacion digital*. Santiago: Comisión Económica para América Latina y el Caribe.

Cepik, M., and P. T. Brancher. 2022. "A nova competição estratégica dos Estados Unidos com a China: Condicionantes, viabilidade, alternativa." In *De Trump a Biden Partidos, políticas, eleições e perspectivas*, edited by Sebastião Velasco e Cruz and Neusa Maria Pereira Bojikian. São Paulo: Editora UNESP.

Chambers, Sarah. 2021. "Truth, Deliberative Democracy, and the Virtues of Accuracy: Is Fake News Destroying the Public Sphere?" *Political Studies* 69 (1): 147–63.

Chami, Nandini, and Shreeja Sen. 2023. "Data Act Ignores Citizen Rights." *Datasyn*, August. New Delhi: It For Change. https://itforchange.net/data-act-ignores-citizen-rights.

Chan, Jenny, Mark Selden, and Pun Ngai. 2020. *Dying for an iPhone*. Chicago: Haymarket Books.

Chancel, L., lead author. 2022. *World Inequality Report 2022*. World Inequality Lab. wir2022.wid.world.

Chand, Ramesh. 2016. "E-Platform for National Agricultural Market." *Economic & Political Weekly* 51 (28). http://www.epw.in/journal/2016/28/commentary/e-platform-national-agricultural-market.html.

Chandler, David, and Christian Fuchs, eds. 2019. *Digital Objects, Digital Subjects: Interdisciplinary Perspectives on Capitalism, Labor and Politics in the Age of Big Data*. London: University of Westminster Press.

Chavunduka, C., K. Chikuku, and M. Chivenge. 2021. "Stocktaking Participatory and Inclusive Land Readjustment in Africa." In *Land Issues for Urban Governance in Sub-Saharan Africa*, edited by R. Home. Cham, Switzerland: Springer.

Chayko, Mary. 2017. *Superconnected: The Internet, Digital Media, and Techno-Social Life*. Thousand Oaks, CA: Sage.

Cheney-Lippold, John. 2017. *We Are Data: Algorithms and the Making of Our Digital Selves*. New York: NYU Press.

Cheng, Zhangkai Jason, Zhiqing Zhan, Mingshan Xue, Peiyan Zheng, Jiali Lyu, Jing Ma, Xiaohua Douglas Zhang, Wenting Luo, Huimin Huang, and Yong Zhang. 2021. "Public Health Measures and the Control of Covid-19 in China." *Clinical Reviews in Allergy & Immunology* 17 (4): 1–16.

Cher, Benjamin. 2017. "Alibaba Signs Agreement with Malaysian and Chinese Governments to Encourage Ecommerce and SME Growth." *Drum*, May 15. http://www.thedrum.com/news/2017/05/15/alibabasigns-agreement-with-malaysian-and-chinese-governments-encourage-ecommerce.

Chevré, Cecile. 2019. "GAFA vs BATX: To Rule Them All." *Leaders League*. https://bit.ly/32X3gq6.

Chibber, K. 2014. "American Cultural Imperialism Has a New Name: GAFA." *Quartz*, December 1. http://qz.com/303947/us-cultural-imperialism-hasa-new-name-gafa/.

China Academy of Information and Communications Technology. 2022. *Report on the Development of China's Digital Economy 2022*. Beijing: CAICT.

Chourabi, Hafedh, Taewoo Nam, Shawn Walker, J. Ramon Gil-Garcia, Sehl Mellouli, Karine Nahon, Theresa A. Pardo, and Hans Jochen Scholl. 2012. "Understanding Smart Cities: An Integrative Framework." In *45th Hawaii International Conference on System Sciences*. Maui, HI: IEEE. https://ieeexplore.ieee.org/document/6149291.

Chun, Wendy Hui Kyong. 2017. *Updating to Remain the Same: Habitual New Media*. Cambridge, MA: MIT Press.

Clapp, J., P. Newell, and Z. Brent. 2018. "The Global Political Economy of Climate Change, Agriculture and Food Systems." *Journal of Peasant Studies* 45 (1): 80–88.

Clutterbuck, C. 2017. *Bittersweet Brexit*. Chicago: University of Chicago Press.

Cohen, B. J. 2000. *The Geography of Money*. Ithaca: Cornell University Press

Cohen, B. J. 2019. *Currency Statecraft*. Chicago: University of Chicago Press.

Cohen, Jean L., and Andrew Arato. 2000. *Sociedad civil y teoría política*. México City: Fondo de Cultura Económica.

Collinson, P. 2018. "How Do Deliveroo and Uber Workers Cope with Precarious Pay?" *Guardian*, October 20. https://www.theguardian.com/business/2018/oct/20/deliveroo-uber-workers-pay-gig-economy.

Cooper, A., K. Nossal, and R. Higgott. 1993. *Relocating Middle Powers*. Vancouver: UBC Press.

294 | References

Cox, Robert. 1987. *Production, Power and World Order*. New York: Columbia University Press.

Crasnic, L., N. Kalyanpur, and A. Newman. 2017. "Networked Liabilities: Transnational Authority in a World of Transnational Business." *European Journal of International Relations* 23 (4): 906–29.

Crichton, T. 2013. "Scottish Land Owners Accused of Being Country's Greediest Benefit Claimants over £40m Tax Avoidance Schemes." *Daily Record*, July 12.

Crivelenti e Castro, L. 2022. "Brazilian Dependent Capitalism under the Hegemony of Financialized Capital." *Latin American Perspectives* 49 (2): 39–55.

Cubitt, Sean. 2016. *Finite Media: Environmental Implications of Digital Technologies*. Durham, NC: Duke University Press.

Cunha, J. 2022. "What Holds App Delivery Man at Home Is Gasoline Price, Not Omicron, Says Expert." *Folha de S. Paulo*, January 15.

Cusumano, M., A. Gawer, and D. Yoffie. 2019. *The Business of Platforms: Strategy in the Age of Digital Competition, Innovation, and Power*. New York: HarperCollins.

da Costa Marques, I. 2013. "A guerra das digitais: Identidades, hierarquias e corpos." *Universitas Humanística* 76: 349–69.

da Costa Marques, I., H. L. Cukierman, P. S. P. Mendes, and P. R. Erber. 2004. "The War of the Fingerprints." In *Public Proofs: Science, Technology and Democracy—Preuves Publiques: Science, Technologie et Démocratie*. Proceedings from August 25–28 conference of the Society for Social Studies of Science and European Association for the Study of Science and Technology. Paris: Centre de Sociologie de l'Innovationn.

Dagnino, Evelina, Alberto Olvera, and Aldo Panfich. 2006. "Para uma outra leitura da disputa pela construção democrática na América Latina." In *A disputa pela construção democrática na América Latina*, edited by Evelina Dagnino, Alberto Olvera, and Aldo Panfichi, 13–91. São Paulo: Paz e Terra; Campinas: Unicam.

Daley, Bruce. 2015. *Where Data Is Wealth: Profiting from Data Storage in a Digital Society*. Rancho Cordova, CA: Play Technologies.

Datafolha. 2022. *Pesquisa Eleitoral BR-05166/2022*. São Paulo: Datafolha.

Daugareilh, I., C. Degryse, and P. Pochet. 2019. *The Platform Economy and Social Law: Key Issues in Comparative Perspective*. ETUI Research Paper-Working Paper. Brussels: European Trade Union Institute.

Davis, Angela. 1983. *Women, Race, and Class*. New York: Penguin Press.

D'Cruz, C., and P. Mudimu. 2013. "Community Savings That Mobilize Federations, Build Women's Leadership and Support Slum Upgrading." *Environment and Urbanization* 25 (1): 31–45.

De Faria, Flavia. 2020. "Epistemologia emancipatória de coletivos políticos." *Simbiótica: Revista Eletrônica* 7 (3): 33–48.

De França Filho, G. C., J. T. S. Junior, and A. S. Rigo. 2012. "Solidarity Finance through Community Development Banks as a Strategy for Reshaping Local

Economies: Lessons from Banco Palmas." *Revista de Administração* 47 (3): 500–515.

De Goede, M. 2021. "Finance/Security Infrastructures." *Review of International Political Economy* 28 (2): 351–68.

De Gregorio, Giovanni. 2021. "The Rise of Digital Constitutionalism in the European Union." *International Journal of Constitutional Law* 19 (1): 41–70.

De la Bruyere, Emily. 2022. "Setting the Standards: Locking in China's Technological Influence." In *China's Digital Ambitions: A Global Strategy to Supplant the Liberal Order*, edited by Emily de La Bruyère, Doug Strub, and Jonathon Marek. New York: National Bureau of Asian Research.

Delfanti, Alessandro. 2019. "Machinic Dispossession and Augmented Despotism: Digital Work in an Amazon Warehouse." *New Media and Society* 23 (1): 39–55.

De Miranda Grilli, Natalia, Luciana Yokoyama Xavier, Pedro Roberto Jacobi, and Alexander Turra. 2019. "Integrated Science for Coastal Management: Discussion on a Local Empirical Basis." *Ocean & Coastal Management* 167: 219–28.

De Souza, F. 2009. *Métodos de planejamento urbano: Projetos de land readjustment e redesenvolvimento urbano.* São Paulo: SP Comunicação.

De Souza, F. F., and H. Koizumi. 2020. *Land Readjustment in Denpasar, Indonesia: Effects on Land Management, the Spatial Distribution of Land Prices, and the Sustainable Development Goals.* June. ADBI Working Paper Series No. 1148. Tokyo: Asian Development Bank Institute. https://www.adb.org/sites/default/files/publication/612531/adbi-wp1148.pdf.

De Stefano, V., and A. Aloisi. 2019. "Fundamental Labor Rights, Platform Work and Human Rights Protection of Non-standard Workers." In *Research Handbook on Labor, Business and Human Rights Law*, edited by Janice R. Bellace and Beryl ter Haar. London: Edward Elgar.

Dey, Adrija. 2018. *Nirbhaya, New Media and Digital Gender Activism.* London: Emerald Group Publishing.

Dias, Nelson, Sasil Enríquez, and Simone Júlio. 2019. *Participatory Budgeting World Atlas.* Lisbon: Epopeia y Oficina.

Dice. 2022. *The Dice Tech Salary Report.* New York: Dice Group.

D'Ignazio, Catherine, and Lauren Klein. 2020. *Data Feminism.* Cambridge: MIT Press.

Dijck, J. 2020. "Seeing the Forest for the Trees: Visualizing Platformization and Its Governance." *New Media & Society* 23 (9): 2801–19.

Dijck, J. V., T. Poell, and M. de Waal. 2018. *The Platform Society.* Oxford: Oxford University Press.

DiPippo, G., I. Mazzocco, and S. Kennedy. 2022. *Red Ink: Estimating Chinese Industrial Policy Spending in Comparative Perspective.* Washington, DC: Center for Strategic and International Studies.

Dixon, Jane. 2009. "From the Imperial to the Empty Calorie: How Nutrition Relations Underpin Food Regime Transitions." *Agriculture and Human Values* 264 (4): 321–33.

296 | References

Dooley, K. 1997. "A Complex Adaptive Systems Model of Organization Change." *Nonlinear Dynamics, Psychology, and Life Sciences* 1: 69–97.

Dourish, Paul, and Genevieve Bell. 2011. *Divining a Digital Future: Mess and Mythology in Ubiquitous Computing.* Cambridge, MA: MIT Press.

Dupuy, Gabriel. 2008. *Urban Networks—Network Urbanism.* Amsterdam: Techne Pr.

Ehret, M., and J. Wirtz. 2017. "Unlocking Value from Machines: Business Models and the Industrial Internet of Things." *Journal of Marketing Management* 33: 111–30.

Ekbia, Hamid. 2009. "Digital Artifacts as Quasi-Objects: Qualification, Mediation, and Materiality." *Journal of the American Society for Information Science and Technology* 60 (12): 2554–66.

Eloranta, Ville, and Taija Turunen. 2016. "Platforms in Service-Driven Manufacturing: Leveraging Complexity by Connecting, Sharing, and Integrating." *Industrial Marketing Management* 55: 178–86.

Emirbayer, M., and A. Mische. 1998. "What Is Agency?" *American Journal of Sociology* 103 (4): 962–1023.

Esping-Andersen, G. 1990. *The Three Worlds of Welfare Capitalism.* Princeton: Princeton University Press.

Estes, Nick. 2019. *Our History Is the Future.* London: Verso.

Eubanks, Virginia. 2018. *Automating Inequality: How High-Tech Tools Profile, Police, and Punish the Poor.* New York: St. Martin's.

European Parliament. 2020. "Digital Sovereignty for Europe." *EPRS Ideas Paper.* https:// www.europarl.europa.eu/RegData/etudes/BRIE/2020/651992/EPRS_BRI (2020)651992_EN.pdf.

Evans, D. S., and R. Schmalensee. 2016. *Matchmakers.* Cambridge: Harvard Business Review Press.

Fairlie, S. 2009. 'Can Britain Feed Itself?' *Land Magazine* 7 (Summer).

Fairwork. 2020. *Fairwork 2020 Annual Report.* https://fair.work/wp-content/ uploads/sites/131/2020/12/9943-Fairwork-annual-report-2020.JP_v5-1.pdf.

Fairwork. 2021. *Fairwork Cloudwork Report.* https://fair.work/wp-content/uploads/ sites/131/2021/06/Fairwork-cloudwork-2021-report.pdf.

Fairwork. 2022a. *Fairwork Brazil Ratings 2021.* https://fair.work/wp-content/ uploads/sites/131/2022/03/Fairwork-Report-Brazil-2021-EN.pdf.

Fairwork. 2022b. *Fairwork Argentina Ratings 2022.* https://fair.work/wp-content/ uploads/sites/131/2022/05/Fairwork_Report_Argentina-2022-EN.pdf.

Fairwork. 2022c. *Fairwork Colombia Ratings 2012.* https://fair.work/wp-content/ uploads/sites/131/2022/06/Fairwork_Report_Colombia-2022-EN.pdf.

Falcão, Paula, and Aline Batista Souza. 2021. "Pandemia de desinformação: As fake news no contexto da Covid-19 no Brasil." *Reciis* (Revista Eletrônica de Comunicação, Informação & Inovação em Saúde) (Rio de Janeiro) 15 (1): 55–71.

Fanon, Frantz. 1965. *A Dying Colonialism.* Boston: Grove Press.

Fanon, Frantz. 2009. "The Fact of Blackness." In *Theories of Race and Racism*, edited by Les Back and John Solomos. London: Routledge.

Farrell, H., and A. L. Newman. 2019. "Weaponized Interdependence: How Global Economic Networks Shape State Coercion." *International Security* 44 (1): 42–79.

Federal Reserve Bank of St. Louis. 2020. "Private Fixed Investment in Information Processing Equipment and Software." *Economic Research*, US Bureau of Economic Analysis. https://fred.stlouisfed.org/series/A679RC1Q027SBEA.

Federici, Silvia. 1975. *Wages against Housework.* Bristol: Power of Women Collective and Falling Water Press.

Fichtner, J. 2016. "Perpetual Decline or Persistent Dominance? Uncovering Anglo-America's True Structural Power in Global Finance." *Review of International Studies* 43 (1): 3–28.

Fichtner, J., and E. M. Heemskerk. 2020. "The New Permanent Universal Owners: Index Funds, Patient Capital, and the Distinction between Feeble and Forceful Stewardship." *Economy and Society* 49 (4): 493–515.

Fidler, Stephen. 2015. "Europe Seeks a Model to Repel U.S. Internet Giants." http://www.commoditiescontrol.com/commodity-market/dowjones commoditiesnews/europe-seeksa-model-to-repel-us-internet-giants-201505 21DN011950.html.

Financial Times. 2019. "Can British Farmers Achieve Net Zero Emissions by 2050." July 22, 2019.

Finchelstein, Federico. 2020. *Uma breve história das mentiras fascistas.* São Paulo: Vestígio.

Font, J., M. Wojcieszak, and C. J. Navarro. 2015. "Participation, Representation and Expertise: Citizen Preferences for Political Decision-Making Processes." *Political Studies* 63: 153–72.

Food and Land Use Commission. 2019. *Growing Better Report 2019.* https://www.foodandlandusecoalition.org/global-report/.

Ford, Martin. 2015. *Rise of the Robots: Technology and the Threat of a Jobless Future.* New York: Basic Books.

Fotopoulou, Aristea. 2017. "From Egg to Fertility Apps: Feminist Knowledge Production and Reproductive Rights." In *Feminist Activism and Digital Networks: Between Empowerment and Vulnerability.* London: Palgrave Macmillan.

Foucault, Michel. 2008. *Segurança, território, população: Curso no College de France (1977–1978).* São Paulo: Editora WMF Martins Fontes.

Foucalt, Michel. 2010. *Em defesa da sociedade: Curso no College de France (1975–1976).* São Paulo: Editora WMF Martins Fontes.

Foucault, Michel. 2013. *L'origine de l'herméneutique de soi—conférences prononcées à Dartmouth College, 1980.* Paris: Vrin.

Foucault, Michel. 2015. *A sociedade punitiva: Curso no College de France (1972–1973).* São Paulo: Editora WMF Martins Fontes.

298 | References

Fountain, J. 2021. "The Moon, the Ghetto and Artificial Intelligence: Reducing Systemic Racism in Computational Algorithms." *Government Information Quarterly*. Amsterdam: Elsevier.

Fourcade, M., and K. Healy. 2017. "Seeing Like a Market." *Socio-Economic Review* 15 (1): 41–70.

Freitas, Christiana Soares, Victor Cardoso, and Soraya Andrade. 2019. "Democracy and e-Participation in Latin America and the Caribbean." *GIGAPP Estudios Working Papers* 6 (131): 353–67.

Frey, Carl. 2019. *The Technology Trap*. Oxford: Oxford University Press

Frias Filho, Otavio. 2018. "O que e falso do fake news." *Revista USP* (São Paulo) 116: 39–44.

Friedman, Thomas. 2005. *The World Is Flat: A Brief History of the Twenty-First Century*. New York: Farrar, Straus and Giroux.

Frigotto, Gaudêncio. 2017. *Escola "sem" partido*. Rio de Janeiro: State University of Rio de Janeiro (UERJ).

Fuchs, Christian. 2010. "Labor in Informational Capitalism and on the Internet." *Information Society* 26 (3): 23–49.

Fuchs, Christian, and Vincent Mosco. 2016. "Marx in the Age of Digital Capitalism." *Studies in Critical Social Sciences* 80.

Fukuyama, Francis. 1992. *The End of History and the Last Man*. New York City: Free Press.

Fung, A. 2007. *Deliberation, Participation and Democracy*. London: Palgrave Macmillan.

Gallo, Sílvio. 2019. "Entre Édipos e o Anti-Édipo: Estratégias para uma vida não-fascista." In *Para uma vida não-fascista*, edited by Margareth Rago and Alfredo Veiga-Neto. Belo Horizonte: Editora Autêntica.

Garcia Guadilla, María Pilar. 2008. "La praxis de los consejos comunales en Venezuela: ¿Poder popular o instancia clientelar?" *Revista Venezolana de Economía y Ciencias Sociales* 14 (1): 125–51.

Garthwaite, K. 2016. "Stigma, Shame and 'People Like Us': An Ethnographic Study of Foodbank Use in the UK." *Journal of Poverty and Social Justice* 24 (3): 277–89.

Gartzke, E., and D. Rohner. 2011. "The Political Economy of Imperialism, Decolonization and Development." *British Journal of Political Science* 41 (3): 525–56.

Gastil, J., and L. Black. 2007. "Public Deliberation as the Organizing Principle of Political Communication Research." *Journal of Public Deliberation* 4 (1): 19–37.

Gauthier, Caroline, Julie Bastianutti, and Meyer Haggege. 2018. "Managerial Capabilities to Address Digital Business Models: The Case of Digital Health." *Digital Business Models* 27 (2): 173–80.

Gershgorn, Dave. 2017. "China Is Funding Baidu to Take on the US in Deep-Learning Research." *Quartz*, February 22. https://qz.com/916738/china-is-funding-baidu-to-take-on-the-united-states-in-deep-learningresearch/.

References | 299

Gerster-Bentaya, M., C. Rocha, and A. Barth. 2011. *The Food Security System of Belo Horizonte—a Model for Cape Town?* Fact-Finding Mission for an Urban Food and Nutrition Security System in Cape Town. https://www.worldfuturecouncil. org/wp-content/uploads/2016/01/2009_Feasibility_Study_Cape_Town.pdf.

Giusti, Serena, and Elisa Piras. 2021. "In Search of Paradigms: Disinformation, Fake News, and Post-Truth Politics." In *Democracy and Fake News: Information Manipulation and Post-Truth Politics*, edited by Serena Giusti and Elisa Piras. London: Routledge.

Gjesvik, Lars. 2022. "Private Infrastructure in Weaponized Interdependence." *Review of International Political Economy* 2 (May): 1–25.

Gladkova, A., and M. Ragnedda, eds. 2017. *Digital Inequalities in the Global South.* New York: Palgrave Macmillan.

Góes, Ana Lúcia Barbosa. 2021. Por que investir em pesquisa, ciência, tecnologia e inovação (C&T) no Brasil? *Revista Pesqui Fisioter* 11 (4): 627–30.

Goldfrank, Benjamin. 2011. *Deepening Local Democracy in Latin America: Participation, Decentralization, and the Left.* University Park: Pennsylvania State University Press.

Goldfrank, Benjamin. 2020. "Participatory Democracy in Latin America? Limited Legacies of the Left Turn." In *Legacies of the Left Turn in Latin America: The Promise of Inclusive Citizenship*, edited by Manuel Balán and Françoise Montambeault. Notre Dame, IN: University of Notre Dame.

Goldfrank, Benjamin. 2021. "Inclusion without Power? Limits of Participatory Institutions." In *The Inclusionary Turn in Latin American Democracies*, edited by D. Kapiszewski, S. Levitsky, and D. Yashar. Cambridge: Cambridge University Press.

Goldfrank, Benjamin, and Sveinung Legard. 2021. "The Systemic Turn and Participatory Budgeting: The Case of Rio Grande do Sul." *Journal of Latin American Studies* 53 (1): 161–87.

Goldfrank, Benjamin, and Carmen Pineda. 2022. "El presupuesto participativo digital y la cuestión de la deliberación: El caso de Decide Madrid." *Revista del CLAD Reforma y Democracia* 82.

González-Bailón, Sandra. 2017. *Decoding the Social World: Data Science and the Unintended Consequences of Communication.* Cambridge, MA: MIT Press.

Goodman, Marc. 2015. *Future Crimes: Inside the Digital Underground and the Battle for Our Connected World.* New York: Anchor Books.

Goodspeed, Robert, Raja Sengupta, Marketta Kyttä, and Christopher Pettit, eds. 2023. *Intelligence for Future Cities: Planning through Big Data and Urban Analytics.* Cham, Switzerland: Springer Nature.

Goraya, Hannah, Ann Light, and Simeon Yates. 2012. "Contact Networks and the Digital Inclusion of Isolated Community Members." *Digital Divide 2011 Yearbook*, 32

Gordon, Eric, and Paul Mihailidis. 2016. *Civic Media: Technology, Design, Practice.* Cambridge, MA: MIT Press.

300 | References

Gorissen, Leen, Karl Vrancken, and Saskia Manshoven. 2016. "Transition Thinking and Business Model Innovation—Towards a Transformative Business Model and New Role for the Reuse Centers of Limburg, Belgium." *Sustainability* 8 (2): 112. https://www.mdpi.com/2071-1050/8/2/112.

Grabel, Ilene. 2017. *When Things Don't Fall Apart.* Cambridge: MIT Press.

Graham, Mark, and William Dutton, eds. 2014. *Society and the Internet: How Networks of Information and Communication Are Changing Our Lives.* Oxford: Oxford University Press.

Graham, M., and F. Ferrari. 2022. *Digital Work in the Planetary Market.* Cambridge: MIT Press.

Graham, M., J. Woodcock, R. Heeks, P. Mungai, J. P. Van Belle, D. du Toit, and S. M. Silbermann. 2020. "The Fairwork Foundation: Strategies for Improving Platform Work in a Global Context." *Geoforum* 112: 100–103.

Graham, Roderick S. 2014. *The Digital Practices of African Americans: An Approach to Studying Cultural Change in the Information Society.* Bern, Switzerland: Peter Lang.

Green, D., R. King, and M. Miller-Dawkins. 2010. *The Global Economic Crisis and Developing Countries.* London: Oxfam International.

Greenwald, G., and E. MacAskill. 2013. "NSA Prism Program Taps in to User Data of Apple, Google and Others." *Guardian,* June 6. https://www.theguardian.com/world/2013/jun/06/us-tech-giants-nsa-data.

Gregory, A. 2021. "Childhood Obesity in England Soars during Pandemic." *Guardian,* November 16. https://www.theguardian.com/society/2021/nov/16/childhood-obesity-in-england-soared-during-pandemic.

Grohmann, Rafael, Gabriel Pereira, Abel Guerra, Ludmila Costhek Abílio, Bruno Moreschi, and Amanda Jurno. 2022. "Platform Scams: Brazilian Workers' Experiences of Dishonest and Uncertain Algorithmic Management." *New Media & Society* 24 (7). https://doi.org/10.1177/14614448221099225.

Groshek, Jacob. 2009. "The Democratic Effects of the Internet, 1994–2003: A Cross-National Inquiry of 152 Countries." *International Communications Gazette* 71: 115–36.

Grunewad, Adam. 2019. "A Gig Economy Solution to Boost Employment in Africa." March 20. https://www.brookings.edu/articles/a-gig-economy-solution-to-boost-employment-in-africa/.

Habermas, Jürgen. 1989. *The Structural Transformation of the Public Sphere.* Cambridge: MIT Press.

Haider, Asad. 2020. "Pessimism of the Will." *Viewpoint Magazine,* May 28. https://viewpointmag.com/2020/05/28/pessimism-of-the-will/.

Haldane, Matt. 2021. *What China's New Data Laws Are and Their Impact on Big Tech.* https://www.scmp.com/tech/policy/article/3147040/what-chinas-new-data-laws-are-and-their-impact-big-tech?module=perpetual_scroll_0&pg-type=article&campaign=3147040.

References | 301

Hanna, Nagy K., ed. 2016. *Mastering Digital Transformation: Towards a Smarter Society, Economy, City and Nation*. Bingley, UK: Emerald Group Publishing.

Hardt, Michael, and Antonio Negri. 2004. *Multitude: War and Democracy in the Age of Empire*. New York: Penguin.

Hargittai, E., and A. Shaw. 2015. "Mind the Skills Gap: The Role of Internet Know-how and Gender in Differentiated Contributions to Wikipedia." *Information Communication and Society* 18 (4): 71–91.

Harris, J. 2018. "We'll Have Space Bots with Lasers, Killing Plants." *Guardian*, October 20. https://www.theguardian.com/environment/2018/oct/20/space-robots-lasers-rise-robot-farmer.

Harris, T. 2019. *Humane: A New Agenda for Tech*. Center for Humane Technology. https://humanetech. com/newagenda.

Harvey, David. 2005. *A Brief History of Neoliberalism*. New York: Oxford University Press.

Harvey, David. 2020. *Automação, revolução e pós-capitalismo*. São Paulo: TV Boitempo.

Hasselblatt, Mathias, Tuomas Huikkola, Marko Kohtamaki, and David Nickell. 2018. "Modeling Manufacturer's Capabilities for the Internet of Things." *Journal of Business & Industrial Marketing* 33 (6): 822–36.

Head, B. W., and J. Alford. 2015. "Wicked Problems: Implications for Public Policy and Management." *Administration & Society* 47 (6): 711–39.

Heeks, Richard. 2017. *Information and Communication Technology for Development (ICT4D)*. New York: Routledge.

Heeks, Richard. 2019. "How Many Platform Workers Are There in the Global South?" *ICT4DBlog*, January 29. https://ict4dblog.wordpress.com/2019/01/29/how-many-platform-workers-are-there-in-the-global-south/.

Helleiner, E. 2019. "Still an Extraordinary Power after All These Years: The US and the Global Financial Crisis of 2008." In *Susan Strange and the Future of Global Political Economy*, edited by R. Germain. New York: Routledge.

Helmond, A. 2015. "The Platformization of the Web: Making Web Data Platform Ready." *Social Media + Society*: 1–11. https://doi.org/10.1177/2056305115603080.

Helsper, Ellen Johanna. 2012. "A Corresponding Fields Model for the Links between Social and Digital Exclusion." *Communication Theory* 22 (4): 403–26.

Hernes, T., and T. Bakken. 2003. "Implications of Self-Reference: Niklas Luhmann's Autopoiesis and Organization Theory." *Organization Studies* 24 (9): 1511–35.

Herzog, C. 2020. "Automating Morals—on the Morality of Automation Technology, Ironies of Automation and Responsible Research and Innovation." *IFAC-PapersOnLine* 53 (2): 17457–62.

Higgott, R. 1998. "The Asian Economic Crisis: A Study in the Politics of Resentment." *New Political Economy* 3 (3): 333–56.

Hill, A. 2020. "Coronavirus: 4.5m People in UK Forced to Become Unpaid Carers." *Guardian*, June 19.

302 | References

Himma-Kadakas, Marju. 2017. "Alternative Facts and Fake News Entering Journalistic Content Production Cycle." *Cosmopolitan Civil Societies* 9 (2): 115–33.

Hirschman, Albert. 1980. *National Power and the Structure of Foreign Trade.* Berkeley: University of California Press.

Ho, T. H. 2021. "Moral Difference between Humans and Robots: Paternalism and Human-Relative Reason." *AI & SOCIETY* 1 (2): 1–11.

Hochuli, A. 2021. "The Brazilianization of the World." *American Affairs* 5 (2): 93–115.

Holbraad, C. 1986. *Middle Powers in International Politics.* London: Macmillan.

Holland, J. H. 1992. "Complex Adaptive Systems." *Daedalus* 121 (1): 17–30.

Holmes, Michael, Jr., Shaker A. Zahra, Robert E. Hoskisson, Kaitlyn DeGhetto, and Trey Sutton. 2016. "Two-Way Streets: The Role of Institutions and Technology Policy in Firms' Corporate Entrepreneurship and Political Strategies." *Academy of Management Perspectives* 30 (3).

Homma, T. 2022. *Contemporary Agenda on Industrial Development and Policy Support to Developing Countries.* Tokyo: JICA Ogata Sadako Research Institute for Peace and Development.

Hong, Lu, and Scott Page. 2009. "Interpreted and Generated Signals." *Journal of Economic Theory* 144 (5): 2174–96.

Hu, Tung-Hui. 2015. *A Prehistory of the Cloud.* Cambridge, MA: MIT Press.

Hua, Julietta, and Kasturi Ray. 2021. *Spent behind the Wheel: Driver's Labor and the Uber Economy.* Minneapolis: University of Minnesota Press.

Huang, Y., H. Qiu, and J. Wang. 2021. *Digital Technology and Economic Impacts of COVID-19.* Shanghai: Asian Development Bank Institute.

Huws, Ursula. 2014. *Labor in the Global Digital Economy: The Cybertariat Comes of Age.* New York: Monthly Review Press.

IBGE. 2015. *Demografia das empresas.* Rio de Janeiro: Estatísticas de Empresas, Cadastros e Classificações.

IBGE. 2021. *Unemployment Drops to 12.6% in the Third Quarter and Reaches 13.5 Million People.* https://agenciadenoticias.ibge.gov.br/agencia-noticias/2012-agencia-de-noticias/noticias/32362-desemprego-recua-para-12-6-no-terceiro-trimestre-e-atinge-13-5-milhoes-de-pessoas.

IBM. 2022. *What Is a Digital Twin?* https://www.ibm.com/topics/what-is-a-digital-twin.

Ignatiev, Noel. 1995. *How the Irish Became White.* New York: Routledge.

Ignatow, Gabe, and Laura Robinson. 2017. "Pierre Bourdieu: Theorizing the Digital." *Information, Communication and Society* 20 (7): 950–66.

ILO. 2020. "COVID-19 and the World of Work: Concept Note." https://www.ilo.org/wcmsp5/groups/public/---dgreports/---dcomm/documents/meetingdocument/wcms_747931.pdf.

ILO. 2021. *World Employment and Social Outlook.* Geneva: International Labour Organization.

Indurkhya, B. 2019. "Is Morality the Last Frontier for Machines?" *New Ideas in Psychology* 54: 107–11.

IPCC. 2019. "Climate Change and Land." In *IPCC Special Report on Climate Change*. Geneva: Intergovernmental Panel on Climate Change.

IPEA. 2022. "Gig Economy Panel in Brazil's Transport Sector: Who, Where, How Many and How Much They Earn." *Carta de conjuntura* 55 (2): 25–49.

Isunza, E., and A. Gurza, eds. 2018. *Controles democráticos no electorales y regímenes de rendición de cuentas en el Sur Global*. Bern, Switzerland: Peter Lang UK.

ITU. 2021. *Measuring Digital Development: Facts and Figures*. Geneva: International Telecommunication Union.

ITU UNESCO. 2020. *The State of Broadband: Tackling Digital Inequalities*. Geneva: International Telecommunication Union.

Jacobi, P. R., and I. Giatti. 2014. "What Is Post-Normal in the Relations between the Environment and Society?" *Ambiente & Sociedade* 17: 1–4.

Jacobi, P. R., and S. N. Sulaiman. 2016. "Governança ambiental urbana em face das mudanças climáticas." *Revista USP* 109: 133–42.

James, Carrie. 2014. *Disconnected: Youth, New Media, and the Ethics Gap*. Cambridge, MA: MIT Press.

Javed, Saad Ahmed, Liangyan Tao, and Wenjie Dong. 2021. "The 'Dual Circulation' Development Model of China: Background and Insights." *Rajagiri Management Journal* 17 (1): 1–19.

Jenkins, H., S. Ford, and J. Green. 2013. *Cultura da conexão: Criando valor e significado por meio da mídia propagável*. Aleph: São Paulo.

Johnson, Clay. 2015. *The Information Diet: A Case for Conscious Consumption*. Sebastopol, CA: O'Reilly Media.

Johnson, David, and David Post. 1996. "Law and Borders—the Rise of Law in Cyberspace." *Stanford Law Review* 48: 1367–75.

Johnson, J. 2018. "157 of World's 200 Richest Entities Are Corporations, Not Governments." https://inequality.org/research/richest-entities-corporations-governments/.

Jordaan, E. 2003. "The Concept of a Middle Power in International Relations: Distinguishing between Emerging and Traditional Middle Powers." *Politikon* 30 (1): 165–81.

Juma, Calestous. 2017. "How Africa Can Negotiate an Effective Continental Free Trade Area Agreement." *African Independent*. https://www.tralac.org/news/article/12407-how-africa-can-negotiate-an-effective-continental-free-trade-area-agreement.html.

Junck, Ryan D., Bradley A. Klein, Akira Kumaki, Ken D. Kumayama, Steve Kwok, Stuart D. Levi, James S. Talbot, Eve-Christie Vermynck, and Siyu Zhang. 2021. *China's New Data Security and Personal Information Protection Laws: What They Mean for Multinational Companies*. https://www.

304 | References

skadden.com/Insights/Publications/2021/11/Chinas-New-Data-Security-and-Personal-Information-Protection-Laws.

Kalpokas, Ignas. 2019. *Algorithmic Governance: Politics and Law in the Post-Human Era*. London: Palgrave.

Karp, J. A., A. Nai, and P. Norris. 2018. "Dial 'F' for Fraud: Explaining Citizens' Suspicions about Elections." *Electoral Studies* 53: 11–19.

Kasperkevich, Jana. 2015. "Google Says Sorry for Racist Auto-Tag in Photo App." *Guardian*, July 1.

Kelsey, Jane. 2017. "The Risks for ASEAN of New Mega-Agreements that Promote the Wrong Model of e-Commerce." Economic Research Institute for ASEAN and East Asia. http://www.eria.org/publications/discussion_papers/DP2017-10.html.

Kember, Sarah, and Joanna Zylinska. 2012. *Life after New Media: Meditation as a Vital Process*. Cambridge, MA: MIT Press.

Kemp, Simon. 2022. *Digital 2022: Global Overview Report*. https://datareportal.com/reports/digital-2022-global-overview-report.

Khan, L. 2017. "Amazon's Antitrust Paradox." *Yale Law Journal* 126 (3): 710–805. https://www.yalelawjournal.org/pdf/e.710.Khan.805_zuvfyyeh.pdf.

Khosrow-Pour, Mehdi, ed. 2018. *Encyclopedia of Information Science and Technology*. Hershey, PA: IGI Global.

KiKUU. 2016. "KiKUU, Quietly Positioning Itself to Become Africa's First Mobile Commerce Unicorn." *Cision PR Newswire*. https://www.prnewswire.com/news-releases/kikuu-quietly-positioning-itself-to-become-africas-first-mobile-commerce-unicorn-300358163.html.

Kittur, Aniket, Jeffrey V. Nickerson, Michael S. Bernstein, Elizabeth M. Gerber, Aaron Shaw, John Zimmerman, Matthew Lease, and John J. Horton. 2013. *The Future of Crowd Work*. http://hci.stanford.edu./publications/2013/CrowdWork/futureofcrowdwork-cscw2013.pdf.

Klein, Naomi. 2020. "Screen New Deal." *Intercept*, May 8. https://theintercept.com/2020/05/08/andrew-cuomo-eric-schmidt-coronavirus-tech-shock-doctrine/.

Köthenbürger, Marko. 2020. "Taxation of Digital Platforms." *EconPol Working Paper*, No. 41. Munich: Leibniz Institute for Economic Research.

Kovacs, A., and N. Ranganathan. 2019. "Data Sovereignty, of Whom? Limits and Suitability of Sovereignty Frameworks for Data in India." *Working Paper No. 3*. Data Governance Network.

Kranzberg, Melvin. 1986. "Presidential Address, Technology and History: 'Kranzberg's Laws.'" *Technology and Culture* 27 (3): 544–70.

Krempl, Stefan. 2021. *China: A Developing Global Power in Standardization*. https://www.kan.de/fileadmin/Redaktion/Dokumente/KAN-Brief/en/21-2-en.pdf

Krotov, Vlad. 2017. "The Internet of Things and New Business Opportunities." *Business Horizons* 60 (6): 831–41.

References | 305

Kücklich, J. 2005. "Precarious Playbour: Modders and the Digital Games Industry." *Fibreculture Journal* 5.

Kuehl, Daniel T. 2009. "From Cyberspace to Cyberpower: Defining the problem." *Cyberpower and National Security* 30.

Kvedar, Joseph C., Carol Colman, and Gina Cella. 2017. *The New Mobile Age: How Technology Will Extend the Healthspan and Optimize the Lifespan*. Boston, MA: Partners Connected Health.

Lake, D. A. 2007. "Escape from the State of Nature: Authority and Hierarchy in World Politics." *International Security* 32 (1): 47–79.

Lake, D. A. 2011. *Hierarchy in International Relations*. Ithaca: Cornell University Press.

Landemore, Hélène. 2017a. "Beyond the Fact of Disagreement? The Epistemic Turn in Deliberative Democracy." *Social Epistemology* 31 (3): 277–95.

Landemore, Hélène. 2017b. *Democratic Reason: Politics, Collective Intelligence, and the Rule of the Many*. Princeton: Princeton University Press.

Landes, D. S. 1969. *The Unbound Prometheus: Technological Change and Industrial Development in Western Europe from 1750 to the Present*. Cambridge: Cambridge University Press.

Lang, T. 2020. *Feeding Britain: Our Food Problems and How to Fix Them*. London: Penguin.

Lang, T., and M. Heasman. 2015. *Food Wars*. Abingdon, UK: Routledge.

Lang, Volker. 2021. *Digital Fluency: Understanding the Basics of Artificial Intelligence, Blockchain Technology, Quantum Computing, and Their Applications for Digital Transformation*. Wilmington, DE: SSBM Finance.

Latour, B. 1989. "Pasteur e Pouchet: Heterogênese da história das ciências." In *Elementos para uma História das Ciências III: De Pasteur ao computador*, edited by Michel Serres, 49–76. Lisbon: Terramar.

Latour, B. 1991. *Nous n'avons jamais été modernes: Essai d'anthropologie symétrique*. Paris: Editions La Dâecouverte.

Latour, B. 1994. *Jamais fomos modermos—ensaio de antropologia simétrica*. Rio de Janeiro: Editora 34.

Latour, B. 2004. "How to Talk about the Body: The Normative Dimension of Science Studies." *Body & Society* 10 (2–3): 205–29.

Lavalle, A., M. C. Albuquerque, A. Leirner, and F. P. Rodrigues. 2021. "A voz das comunidades: Construção de problemas e propostas nos territórios ao longo do tempo." In *Desastre e Desgoverno no Rio Doce Atores e instituições na governança do desastre*, edited by Adrian Gurza Lavalle and Euzenaia Carlos. Rio de Janeiro: Garamond.

Lavalle, A., A. Leirner, M. Do Carmo Albuquerque, and F. Rodrigues. 2019. "As dificuldades da participação: Desencontro de interesses na recuperação do rio doce." *Revista Psicologia Política* 19 (1): 121–45.

Law, John. 1992. "Notes on the Theory of the Actor-Network: Ordering, Strategy, and Heterogeneity." *Systems Practice* 5 (4): 379–93.

306 | References

Lazer, D. M. J., M. A. Baum, Y. Benkler, A. J. Berinsky, K. M. Greenhill, and F. Menczer. 2018. "The Science of Fake News." *Science* 359: 1094—96.

Leary, John Patrick. 2017. "The Poverty of Entrepreneurship: The Silicon Valley Theory of History." *New Inquiry*, June 9. https://thenewinquiry.com/the-poverty-of-entrepreneurship-the-silicon-valley-theory-of-history/.

Leary, John Patrick. 2020. "The Slippery Definition of an 'Essential' Worker." *New Republic*, May 1. https://newrepublic.com/article/157544/slippery-definition-essential-worker-coronavirus-pandemic.

Lee, Terry. 2019. "The Global Rise of 'Fake News' and the Threat to Democratic Elections in the USA." *Public Administration and Policy* 22 (1): 15–24.

Legard, Sveinung, and Benjamin Goldfrank. 2021. "The Systemic Turn and Participatory Budgeting: The Case of Rio Grande do Sul." *Journal of Latin American Studies* 53 (1): 161–87.

Le Guin, Ursula. 1986. "The Carrier Bag Theory of Fiction." https://otherfutures.nl/uploads/documents/le-guin-the-carrier-bag-theory-of-fiction.pdf.

Lehdonvirta, V., O. Kassi, I. Hjorth, H. Barnard, and M. Graham. 2019. "The Global Platform Economy: A New Offshoring Institution Enabling Emerging-Economy Micro Providers." *Journal of Management* 45 (2): 567–99.

Leirner, Andre, and M. Alves. 2009. "Elementos para a construção de um modelo de voz pública." *XIV Congreso del CLAD*. Salvador, Bahia: CLAD.

Leonard, Mark. 2021. *The Age of Unpeace*. London: Transworld.

Lessig, L. 1999. *Code and Other Laws of Cyberspace*. New York: Basic Books.

Levine, Yasha. 2018. *Surveillance Valley*. New York: Public Affairs.

Levy, David M. 2016. *Mindful Tech: How to Bring Balance to Our Digital Lives*. New Haven: Yale University Press.

Lewandowsky, S., K. H. E. Ulrich, and J. Cook. 2017. "Beyond Misinformation: Understanding and Coping with the 'Post-Truth' Era." *Journal of Applied Research in Memory and Cognition* 6 (4): 353–69.

Lima, Cristiano. 2022. "Ukraine War Highlights Limits of Facebook Board." *Washington Post*, March 15. https://www.washingtonpost.com/politics/2022/03/15/war-ukraine-highlights-limits-facebooks-oversight-board/.

Lindgren, Simon. 2017. *Digital Media and Society*. Thousand Oaks, CA: Sage.

Lissidini, Alicia. 1998. "Una mirada crítica a la democracia directa: El origen y las prácticas de los plebiscitos en Uruguay." *Perfiles Latinoamericanos* 12: 169–200.

Lissidini, Alicia. 2012. "Direct Democracy in Uruguay and Venezuela: New Voices, Old Practices." In *New Institutions for Participatory Democracy in Latin America: Voice and Consequence*, edited by Maxwell Cameron, Eric Hershberg, and Kenneth Sharpe. Basingstoke: Palgrave Macmillan.

Llorens, F., and J. Del Castillo. 2002. "Estudios de caso de desarrollo económico local en América Latina." *Serie de informes de buenas prácticas del Departamento de Desarrollo Sostenible*. Washington, DC: Interamerican Development Bank.

Loveless, Matthew. 2021. "Information and Democracy: Fake News as an Emotional Weapon." In *Democracy and Fake News*, edited by Serena Giusti and Elisa Piras. London: Routledge.

Luo, Yadong, Jinyun Sun, and Stephanie Lu Wang. 2011. "Emerging Economy Copycats: Capability, Environment, and Strategy." *Academy of Management Perspectives* 25 (2): 37–56.

Lupton, Deborah. 2016. "The Diverse Domains of Quantified Selves: Self-Tracking Modes and Dataveillance." *Economy and Society* 45 (1): 101–22.

Lynch, Michael. 2017. *The Internet of Us*. New York: Liveright.

Machado, Jorge, and Richard Miskolci. 2019. "Das jornadas de junho à cruzada moral: O papel das redes sociais na polarização política brasileira." *Sociologia & Antropologia* 9 (3): 945–70.

MacKensie, D. 1990. *Inventing Accuracy—A Historical Sociology of Nuclear Missile Guidance*. Cambridge: MIT Press.

MacKensie, D., and G. Spinardi. 1996. *Knowing Machines—Essays on Technical Change*. Cambridge: MIT Press.

Macrotrends. 2018. "Alphabet Market Cap 2006–2020." *Macrotrends*. https://www.macrotrends.net/stocks/charts/GOOGL/alphabet/market-cap.

Madison, James. 1787. *Excerpts from Federalist No. 10*. https://founders.archives.gov/documents/Madison/01-10-02-0178.

Malcolm, Jeremy, and Maira Sutton. 2015. "Release of the Full TPP Text after Five Years of Secrecy Confirms Threats to Users' Rights." Electronic Frontier Foundation. https://www.eff.org/deeplinks/2015/11/release-fulltpp-text-after-five-years-secrecy-confirms-threats-users-rights.

Mansfield, Edwin. 1983. "Long Waves and Technological Innovation." *American Economic Review* 73 (2): 141–45.

Manyika, James, Susan Lund, Michael Chui, Jacques Bughin, Jonathan Woetzel, Parul Batra, Ryan Ko, and Saurabh Sanghvi, et al. 2017. *Jobs Lost, Jobs Gained: What the Future of Work Will Mean for Jobs, Skills, and Wages*. New York: McKinsey Global Institute.

March, J. G. 1995. "The Future, Disposable Organizations and the Rigidities of Imagination." *Organization* 2 (3–4): 427–40.

Margalho, M. G. 2015. *O pensamento social de Valentim Fernandes Bouças: Organização e ação política, 1930–1940*. XXVIII Simpósio Nacional de História, Florianópoli, SC, ANPUH.

Marois, Thomas. 2017. "TiSA and the Threat to Public Banks." https://www.tni.org/en/publication/tisa-and-the-threat-to-public-banks.

Maru, Pankaj Maru. 2017. "How Ashok Leyland Built Its Digital Marketplace to Create New Revenue Stream." https://cio.economictimes.indiatimes.com/news/corporatenews/.

Marx, Karl. 1856. *Speech at Anniversary of the People's Paper*. marxists.org.

Mason, L., D. Krutka, and J. Stoddard. 2018. "Media Literacy, Democracy, and the Challenge of Fake News." *Journal of Media Literacy Education* 10 (2): 1–10

308 | References

Mason, P. 2015. *PostCapitalism*. London: Allen Lane.

Maturana, H. R., and F. J. Varela. 2012. "Autopoiesis and Cognition: The Realization of the Living." *Springer Science & Business Media* 42: 118–37.

Mayka, Lindsay. 2019. *Building Participatory Institutions in Latin America: Reform Coalitions and Institutional Change*. New York: Cambridge University Press.

Mbembe, Achille. 2018. *Necropolítica*. São Paulo: N-1 Edições.

McElroy, Erin. 2019. "Unbecoming Silicon Valley: Techno Imaginaries and Materialities in Postsocialist Romania." PhD diss., University of California at Santa Cruz.

McMichael, P. 2009. "A Food Regime Genealogy." *Journal of Peasant Studies* 36 (1): 139–69.

McNulty, Stephanie. 2019. *Democracy from Above? The Unfulfilled Promise of Nationally Mandated Participatory Reforms*. Palo Alto: Stanford University Press.

Mekouar, D. 2020. "Here's Where the Internet Actually Lives." https://www.voanews.com/usa/all-about-america/heres-where-internet-actually-lives#:%7E:text=An%20Amazon%20data%20center%20across,known%20as%20Data%20Center%20Alley.

Melamed, Jodi. 2015. "Racial Capitalism." *Critical Ethnic Studies* 1(1): 76–85.

Mell, M., and T. Grance. 2011. *NIST Definition of Cloud Computing*. https://csrc.nist.gov/publications/detail/sp/800-145/final.

Mezzaroba, G. 2020. "Adrian Lavalle: No exercício da Democracia: Interview. *Pesquisa* 288 (February). https://revistapesquisa.fapesp.br/adrian-lavalle-no-exercicio-da-democracia/.

Miklós, S., and J. Simons. 2021. "How Orbán Won? Neoliberal Disenchantment and the Grand Strategy of Financial Nationalism to Reconstruct Capitalism and Regain Autonomy." *Socio-Economic Review* 20 (4): 1625–51.

Mintz, S. 1986. *Sweetness and Power*. London. Penguin.

Miskolci, Richard. 2021. *Batalhas morais: Política identitária na esfera pública técnico-midiatizada*. Belo Horizonte: Autêntica Editora.

Mohani, Vishwa. 2017. "India to Set Up Cloud-Based Digital Platform to Provide Agriculture Solutions to Farmers at Their Doorsteps." *Times of India*, August 30. https://timesofindia.indiatimes.com/india/india-toset-up-cloud-based-digital-platform-to-provide-agriculture-solutions-to-farmers-at-theirdoorsteps/articleshow/60296401.cms.

Monbiot, G. 2017. "The Meat of the Matter." https://www.monbiot.com/2017/10/06/the-meat-of-the-matter/.

Monbiot, G., R. Grey, T. Kenny, K. Macfarlane, A. Powell-Smith, G. Shrubsole, and B. Stratford. 2019. *Land for the Many*. London: Labor Party.

Monteiro, Carlos Augusto, Jean-Claude Moubarac, Renata Bertazzi Levy, Daniela Silva Canella, Maria Laura da Costa Louzada, and Geoffrey Cannon. 2018. "Household Availability of Ultra-Processed Foods and Obesity in Nineteen European Countries." *Public Health Nutrition* 21 (1): 18–26.

Morel, Ana P. M. 2021. "Negacionismo da Covid-19 e educação popular em saúde: Para além da necropolítica." *Trabalho, Educação e Saúde* 19.

Moreschi, B., G. Pereira, and F. Cozman. 2020. "The Brazilian Workers in Amazon Mechanical Turk." *Contracampo: Brazilian Journal of Communication* 39 (1): 19–42.

Morini, C., and A. Fumagalli. 2010. "Life Put to Work: Towards a Life Theory of Value." *Ephemera* 10 (3–4): 234–52.

Morozov, Eugeny. 2009. "The Brave New World of Slacktivism." *Foreign Policy*, May 19. https://www.foreignpolicy.com/2009/05/19/the-brave-new-world-of-slacktivism/.

Mosco, Vincent. 2005. *The Digital Sublime*. Cambridge: MIT Press.

Mosco, Vincent. 2017. *Becoming Digital: Toward a Post-Internet Society*. Bingley, UK: Emerald Group Publishing.

Mueller, Gavin. 2021. *Breaking Things at Work: The Luddites Are Right about Why You Hate Your Job*. New York: Verso.

Mueller, Milton. 2010. *Networks and States: The Global Politics of Internet Governance*. Cambridge, MA: MIT Press.

Murau, S., F. Pape, and T. Pforr. 2021. *The Hierarchy of the Offshore US-Dollar System: On Swap Lines, the FIMA Repo Facility and Special Drawing Rights*. Boston: Global Development Policy Center, Boston University.

Namatame, A., and S. Iwanaga. 2004. "Efficiency and Equity in Collective Systems of Interacting Heterogeneous Agents." In *Collectives and the Design of Complex Systems*, edited by Kagan Tumer and David Wolpert. New York: Springer-Verlag.

Narlikar, A. 2021. "Must the Weak Suffer What They Must?" In *The Uses and Abuses of Weaponized Interdependence*, edited by D. Drezner, H. Farrell, A. Newman. Washington, DC: Brookings Institution.

National Bureau of Statistics of China. 2022. *National Economy Continued to Recover with Expected Development Targets Well Achieved in 2021*. https://www.stats.gov.cn/english/PressRelease/202201/t20220117_1826409.html.

National Food Service. 2022. *I'm Creating A National Food Service*. https://nationalfoodservice.uk/.

NCSL. 2022. *State Laws Related to Digital Privacy*. https://www.ncsl.org/research/telecommunications-and-information-technology/state-laws-related-to-internet-privacy.aspx.

Nemer, David. 2019. "WhatsApp Is Radicalizing the Right in Bolsonaro's Brazil." *Huffington Post*, August 16. https://www.huffpost.com/entry/brazil-jair-bolsonaro-whatsapp_n_5d542b0de4b05fa9df088ccc.

Newton, Casey. 2022. "How Facebook Undercut the Oversight Board." *Verge*, May 12. https://www.theverge.com/23068243/facebook-meta-oversight-board-putin-russia-ukraine-decision.

Noble, Safiya. 2018. *Algorithms of Oppression*. New York: NYU Press.

310 | References

Norman, D. 2014. *Things That Make Us Smart: Defending Human Attributes in the Age of the Machine.* Boston: Diversion Books.

Norris, Pippa. 2003. "Preaching to the Converted? Pluralism, Participation and Party Websites." *Party Politics* 9 (1): 21–45.

Norris, Pippa, and Ron Inglehart. 2019. *Cultural Backlash: Trump, Brexit and Authoritarian Populism.* New York: Cambridge University Press.

Nugent, Ciara. 2022. "Brazil's Most Popular President Returns from Political Exile with a Promise to Save the Nation." *Time Magazine*, May 4. https://time.com/6172611/brazil-president-lula-interview.

Oatley, T., W. K. Winecoff, A. Pennock, and S. B. Danzman. 2013. "The Political Economy of Global Finance: A Network Model." *Perspectives on Politics* 11 (1): 133–53.

OECD. 2021. *Bridging Digital Divides in G20 Countries.* OECD Report for the G20 Infrastructure Working Group. https://www.oecd-ilibrary.org/docserver/35c1d850-en.pdf?expires=1702925176&id=id&accname=guest&checksum=FE08795FEFC6DFBA28DFC22536C7FA9C.

OECD/CAF. 2022. *The Strategic and Responsible Use of Artificial Intelligence in the Public Sector of Latin America and the Caribbean.* Paris: OECD Public Governance Reviews, OECD Publishing.

Oettinger, Günther. 2015. "Europe's Future Is Digital." European Commission. https://ec.europa.eu/commission/commissioners/2014-2019/oettinger/announcements/speechhannover-messe-europes-future-digital_en.

Ohmae, Kenichi. 1990. *The Borderless World.* New York: HarperCollins.

Oliveira, M. A. 2022. *Conceptos interseccionais para o Direito do Trabalho.* São Paulo: Editora Dialética.

Ollman, Bertell. 2005. "The Utopian Vision of the Future (Then and Now): A Marxist Critique." *Monthly Review* 57 (3) (July–August). https://monthlyreview.org/2005/07/01/the-utopian-vision-of-the-future-then-and-now-a-marxist-critique/.

Olsen, J. P. 2015. "Democratic Order, Autonomy, and Accountability." *Governance* 28 (4): 425–40.

Osborne, C. 2019. *NSA Surveillance of Foreign Nationals Surges.* ZDNET, May 1. https://www.zdnet.com/article/nsa-surveillance-of-foreign-nationals-surges.

O'Shea, Lizzie. 2021. "Future Histories: How Social Movements Can Shape a Sustainable Digital Future." Keynote speech, University of Alberta's International Week. https://lizzieoshea.com/future-histories-social-movements-can-shape-a-sustainable-digital-future/.

Ouyang, Shijia. 2021. *Jobs of Digital Economy Grow in Popularity.* Beijing: China Daily.

Oxfam. 2015. *Wealth: Having It All and Wanting More.* https://oi-files-d8-prod.s3.eu-west-2.amazonaws.com/s3fs-public/file_attachments/ib-wealth-having-all-wanting-more-190115-en.pdf.

References | 311

Page, B. 1996. "The Mass Media as Political Actors." *PS: Political Science and Politics* 29 (1): 20–24.

Panitch, Leo, and Gregory Albo. 2021. *Beyond Digital Capitalism.* London: Merlin Press.

Pappas, Nikolaos. 2022. *The Age of Information.* New York: Cambridge University Press

Paraná, E. 2020. *Bitcoin: A utopia tecnocrática do dinheiro apolítico.* São Paulo: Hucitec.

Parida, Vinit, David Sjodin, Sambit Lenka, and Joakim Wincent. 2015. "Developing Global Service Innovation Capabilities: How Global Manufacturers Address the Challenges of Market Heterogeneity." *Research Technology Management* 58 (5): 35–44.

Pariser, E. 2012. *The Filter Bubble.* New York: Penguin.

Park, Chaeri. 2022. "Knowledge Base: China's 'Global Data Security Initiative' 全球数据安全倡议." DigiChina. https://digichina.stanford.edu/work/knowledge-base-chinas-global-data-security-initiative/.

Parsons, Clark, Amelie Drünkler, and Roland Berger. 2019. "Democracy and Digital Disinformation: How Europe Can Protect Its People without Endangering Free Speech." https://www.ie.foundation/en/blog/ief-demokratie-und-digitale-desinformation.

Pascoe, Bruce. 2018. "Dark Emu." ABC Education. https://www.abc.net.au/education/aboriginal-ingenuity-ch-14-aquaculture-machine/13585670.

Pateman, Carole. 2012. "Participatory Democracy Revisited." *Perspectives on Politics* 10 (1): 7–19.

Pauwelyn, Joost. 2005. "The UNESCO Convention on Cultural Diversity, and the WTO: Diversity in International Law-Making?" https://www.asil.org/insights/volume/9/issue/35/unesco-convention-cultural-diversity-and-wto-diversityinternational-law.

Peck, Jamie, and Nik Theodore. 2015. *Fast Policy: Experimental Statecraft at the Thresholds of Neoliberalism.* Minneapolis: University of Minnesota Press.

Perold, Colette. 2020. "IBM's World Citizens: Valentim Bouças and the Politics of IT Expansion in Authoritarian Brazil." *IEEE Annals of the History of Computing* 42 (3): 38–52.

Peters, B. Guy, Jon Pierre, Eva Sørensen, and Jacob Torfing. 2022. "Bringing Political Science Back into Public Administration Research." *Governance* 35 (4): 962–82.

Petry, J., J. Fichtner, and E. Heemskerk. 2019. "Steering Capital: The Growing Private Authority of Index Providers in the Age of Passive Asset Management." *Review of International Political Economy* 28 (1): 152–76.

Piasna, A. 2020. "Counting Gigs: How Can We Measure the Scale of Online Platform Work?" ETUI Research Paper-Working Paper. Brussels: European

312 | References

Trade Union Institute. https://www.etui.org/sites/default/files/2020-09/Counting%20gigs_2020_web.pdf.

Picon, Antoine. 2015. *Smart Cities: Spatialized Intelligence.* New York: Wiley and Sons.

Piketty, Thomas. 2014. *Capital in the Twenty-First Century.* Cambridge: Harvard University Press.

Pogrebinschi, Thamy. 2021. *LATINNO Dataset.* Berlin: WZB.

Pohle, J., and T. Thiel. 2020. "Digital Sovereignty." *Internet Policy Review* 9 (4). https://policyreview.info/concepts/digital-sovereignty.

Polanyi, K. 2001. *The Great Transformation: The Political and Economic Origins of Our Time.* Boston: Beacon Press.

Pomar, Marcelo. 2013. "Não foi um raio em céu azul." In *Vinte centavos*, edited by E. Judensnaider, L. Lima, and P. Ortellado. São Paulo: Editora Veneta.

Portes, A., M. Castells, and L. A. Benton. 1989. *The Informal Economy: Studies in Advanced and Less Developed Countries.* Baltimore: Johns Hopkins University Press.

Portes, J., H. Reed, and A. Percy. 2017. "Social Prosperity for the Future: A Proposal for Universal Basic Services." In *Agroecology: Science and Politics*, edited by P. Rosset and M. Altieri. Warwickshire, UK: Practical Action Publishing.

Prahalad, C. K., and V. Ramaswamy. 2000. "Co-Opting Customer Competence." *Harvard Business Review* (January–February).

Prashad, Vijay. 2008. *The Darker Nations.* New York: New Press.

Prassl, J. 2018. *Humans as a Service.* Oxford: Oxford University Press.

Press Trust of India. 2017. "India's Data Protection Law Will Set Global Benchmark: Ravi Shankar Prasad." *Mint*, September 9. http://www.livemint.com/Politics/shkot8Pd24QprSzs4mQvQM/Indias-data-protectionlaw-will-set-global-benchmark-Ravi.html.

Quijana, Aníbal. 2005. *Coloniality of Power, Eurocentrism and Latin America.* Buenos Aires: CLACSO.

Rachinger, Michael, Romana Rauter, Christiana Muller, Wolfgang Vorraber, and Eva Schirgi. 2018. "Digitalization and Its Influence on Business Model Innovation." *Journal of Manufacturing Technology Management* 30 (8): 1143–60.

Ragnedda, Massimo. 2018. "Conceptualizing Digital Capital." *Telematics and Informatics* 35 (8): 2366–75.

Ragnedda, Massimo. 2020. *Enhancing Digital Equity: Connecting the Digital Underclass.* Cham, Switzerland: Springer Nature.

Ragnedda, Massimo, and Anna Gladovka. 2020. *Digital Inequalities in the Global South.* Cham, Switzerland: Palgrave Macmillan.

Ragnedda, Massimo, and Maria Laura Ruiu. 2017. "Social Capital and the Three Levels of Digital Divide." In *Theorizing Digital Divides*, edited by M. Ragnedda and W. Muschert, 27–40. New York: Routledge

Rago, Margareth. 2019. "Dizer sim à existência." In *Para uma vida não-fascista*, edited by Margareth Rago and Alfredo Veiga-Neto. Belo Horizonte: Editora Autêntica.

Ramanujam, S., and Runde, D. 2021. "Global Digital Governance: Here's What You Need to Know." Washington, DC: Center for Strategic and International Studies.

Rand, A. 1991. *A virtude do egoismo*. Porto Alegre: Editora Ortiz.

Rapoza, Kenneth. 2020. "Some 42% of Jobs Lost in Pandemic Are Gone for Good." *Forbes*, May 15. https://www.forbes.com/sites/kenrapoza/2020/05/15/some-42-of-jobs-lost-in-pandemic-are-gone-for-good/#d371c7c50ab9.

Rashotte, Nicole. 2020. "10 Top Technology Stocks by Market Cap." *Investing News*, February 11. https://investingnews.com/daily/tech-investing/top-technology-stocks/.

Raventós, Ciska. 2018. *Mi corazón dice No: El movimiento de oposición al TLC en Costa Rica*. San José: Editorial UCR.

Recuero, Raquel, and Anatoliy Gruzd. 2019. "Cascatas de Fake News Políticas: Um estudo de caso no Twitter." *Galaxia* 41: 31–47.

Rennstich, Joachim. 2008. *The Making of a Digital World*. New York: Palgrave Macmillan.

Resse, H. 1994. "Teleology and Teleonomy in Behavior Analysis." *Behavior Analyst* 1: 75–91.

Rezende, Fernando. 2002. "Por qué reformas administrativas falham?" *Revista Brasileira de Ciências Sociais* 17: 123–42.

Rezende, Fernando. 2008. "The Implementation Problem of New Public Management Reforms." *International Public Management Review* 9 (2): 40–65.

Rheingold, Howard. 2012. *Net Smart: How to Thrive Online*. Cambridge, MA: MIT Press.

Rhodes-Purdy, Matthew. 2015. "Participatory Populism: Theory and Evidence from Bolivarian Venezuela." *Political Research Quarterly* 68 (3): 415–27.

Robinson, William I. 2014. *Global Capitalism and the Crisis of Humanity*. New York: Cambridge University Press.

Robinson, William I. 2018. "The Next Economic Crisis: Digital Capitalism and Global Police State." *Race & Class* 60 (1): 11–34.

Robinson, William I. 2020a. "Global Capitalist Crisis Deadlier Than Coronavirus." *Arena*, April 28.

Robinson, William I. 2020b. *The Global Police State*. London: Pluto Press.

Rocha, C., and I. Lessa. 2009. "Urban Governance for Food Security: The Alternative Food System in Belo Horizonte, Brazil." *International Planning Studies* 14 (4): 389–400.

Romão Netto, J. V., and S. Cervellini. 2021. "Minipublicos e inovação democrática: O caso do Jardim Lapenna." *Revista Brasileira de Ciências Sociais* 36.

314 | References

Romão, Wagner de Melo, Adrián Gurza Lavalle, and Gisela Zaremberg. 2017. "Political Intermediation and Public Policy in Brazil: Councils and Conferences in the Policy Spheres of Health and Women's Rights." In *Intermediation and Representation in Latin America: Actors and Roles beyond Elections*, edited by Gisela Zaremberg, Valeria Guarneros-Meza, and Adrián Gurza Lavalle. Basingstoke, UK: Palgrave Macmillan.

Rossman, P. 2012. "Food Workers' Rights as a Path to a Low Carbon Agriculture." In *Trade Unions in the Green Economy*, edited by N. Räthzel and D. Uzzell. Abingdon, UK: Routledge.

Rudder, Christian. 2014. *Dataclysm: Who We Are (When We Think No One's Looking)*. New York City: Crown.

Ruth-Lovell, Saskia, Laurence Whitehead, and Yanina Welp, eds. 2017. *Let the People Rule? Direct Democracy in the Twenty-First Century*. Colchester: ECPR Press.

Saadia, Zahidi, Vesselina Ratcheva, Guillaume Hingel, and Sophie Brown. 2020. *The Future of Jobs Report 2020*. Geneva: World Economic Forum. https://www3.weforum.org/docs/WEF_Future_of_Jobs_2020.pdf.

Sadowski, J. 2019. "When Data Is Capital: Datafication, Accumulation, and Extraction." *Big Data & Society*: 1–12. https://doi.org/10.1177/2053951718820549.

Sadowski, Jathan. 2021. "I'm a Luddite, You Should Be One Too." *The Conversation*, August 9.

Sampaio, Rafael Cardoso. 2011. "Instituições participativas online: Um estudo de caso do Orçamento Participativo Digital." *Revista Política Hoje* 20 (1): 467–512.

Santos, Francisco Coelho dos, and Cristina Petersen Cypriano. 2014. "Redes sociais, redes de sociabilidade." *Revista Brasileira de Ciências Sociais* 29 (85).

Santos, L., A. Galdeano, and M. Cardoso. 2019. "Por uma tecnologia crítica, reflexiva e engajada com o público." *Revista Psicologia Política* 19: 199–221.

Saravalle, E. 2021. "The Watchful Eye of the U.S. Dollar." *Alchemist*, May 19. https://www.alchemistmag.com/past-editions/the-watchful-eye-of-the-us-dollar.

Sartoretto, P. 2015. "Becoming a Circumstantial Media Activist: Brazilian Landless Workers Movement Struggle to Construct Arenas for Communication." Presented at the 65th International Communication Association conference, San Juan, Puerto Rico, May 21–25.

Satterthwaite, D. 2001. "From Professionally Driven to People-Driven Poverty Reduction: Reflections on the Role of Shack/Slum Dwellers International." *Environment and Urbanization* 13 (2): 135–38.

Schmalenberger, Alexander, and Stephan Nagel. 2022. "The Digital Markets Act—a New Regulation for Digital Markets." https://www.taylorwessing.com/en/insights-and-events/insights/2022/04/the-digital-markets-act.

Schmid, B. 2019. "Degrowth and Postcapitalism: Transformative Geographies beyond Accumulation and Growth." *Geography Compass* 13 (11): 24–70.

Schneider, Aaron. 2012. *State-Building and Tax Regimes in Central America*. New York: Cambridge University Press.

Schneier, Bruce. 2015. *Data and Goliath: The Hidden Battles to Collect Your Data and Control Your World*. New York: W.W. Norton.

Schwab, Klaus. 2016. *The Fourth Industrial Revolution*. Geneva: World Economic Forum.

Schwarcz, Lilia Moritz. 2019. *Sobre o autoritarismo brasileiro*. São Paulo: Companhia das Letras.

Schwartz, H. 2019a. "American Hegemony: Intellectual Property Rights, Dollar Centrality, and Infrastructural Power." *Review of International Political Economy* 26 (3): 490–519.

Schwartz, H. 2019b. "Strange Power over Credit; or the Enduring Strength of US Structural Power." In *Susan Strange and the Future of Global Political Economy*, edited by R. Germain. New York: Routledge.

SCMP. 2021. *China Internet Report*. Hong Kong: SCMP Research.

Segovia, Joselin, Nicola Pontarollo, and Mercy Orellana. 2021. "Discontent with Democracy in Latin America." *Cambridge Journal of Regions, Economy and Society* 14: 417–38.

Selwyn, B. 2021. "A Green New Deal for Agriculture: For, within, or against Capitalism?" *Journal of Peasant Studies* 48 (4): 778–806.

Sen, A. 1999. "The Possibility of Social Choice." *American Economic Review* 89 (3): 349–78.

Shand, W., and S. Colenbrander. 2018. "Financing the Inclusive City: The Catalytic Role of Community Savings." *Environment and Urbanization* 30 (1): 175–90.

Shearer, E., and J. Gottfried. 2017. "News Use across Social Media Platforms." Pew Research, September 7. https://www.pewresearch.org/journalism/2017/09/07/news-use-across-social-media-platforms-2017/.

Shen, H., A. Cabrera, A. Perer, and J. Hong. 2022. *Public(s)-in-the-Loop: Facilitating Deliberation of Algorithmic Decisions in Contentious Public Policy Domains*. Mimeo. Cornell University, Computer Science Department.

Shrubsole, G. 2018. *How the Extent of County Farms Has Halved in 40 Years*. https://whoownsengland.org/2018/06/08/how-the-extent-of-county-farms-has-halved-in-40-years/.

Shrubsole, G. 2019. *Who Owns England?* London: HarperCollins UK.

Silva, André Luiz Reis da. 2020. *Bolsonaro e o coronavírus: O custo do isolamento diplomático num momento de crise*. Porto Alegre: Faculdade de Ciências Econômicas, Universidade Federal do Rio Grande do Sul.

Silva, Eduardo. 2017. "Reorganizing Popular Sector Incorporation: Propositions from Bolivia, Ecuador, and Venezuela." *Politics & Society* 45 (1): 91–122.

Silva, Tarcízio. 2022. *Racismo algorítmico: Inteligencia artificial e discriminação nas redes digitais*. São Paulo: Edições Sesc.

Simon, Herbert. 1990. *Utility and Probability*. London: Palgrave Macmillan.

316 | References

Singh, P. J. 2020. *Economic Rights in a Data-Based Society*. Bonn: Friedrich-Ebert-Stiftung.

Sivanandan, A. 1998. "Heresies and Prophecies: Social Fallout of the Technological Revolution." *Race and Class* 37 (4). https://doi.org/10.1177/030639689603700401.

Skocpol, Theda. 1992. *Protecting Soldiers and Mothers: The Political Origins of Social Policy in the United States*. Cambridge: Belknap Press of Harvard University Press.

Sledziewska, K., and R. Wloch. 2021. *The Economics of Digital Transformation*. New York: Routledge.

Sonnier, Paul. 2017. *The Fourth Wave: Digital Health*. https://storyofdigitalhealth.com/.

Srnicek, N. 2016. *Platform Capitalism*. Cambridge: Polity.

Standing, Guy. 2011. *Precariat: The New Dangerous Class*. London: Bloomsbury.

Stanley, Jason. 2018. *Como funciona o fascismo: A política do "nós" e "eles."* Porto Alegre: L&PM.

Starrs, S., 2013. "American Economic Power Hasn't Declined—It Globalized! Summoning the Data and Taking Globalization Seriously." *International Studies Quarterly* 57 (4): 817–30.

Statista. 2022. "Market Share of Grocery Stores in Great Britain from January 2017 to April 2022." https://www.statista.com/statistics/280208/grocery-market-share-in-the-united-kingdom-uk/.

Steiner-Adair, Catherine, and Teresa H. Barker. 2013. *The Bog Disconnect: Protecting Childhood and Family Relationships in the Digital Age*. New York: HarperCollins.

Storeng, K., and A. Puyvallée. 2021. "The Smartphone Pandemic." *Global Public Health* 16: 8–9.

Strange, S. 1987. "The Persistent Myth of Lost Hegemony." *International Organization* 41 (4): 551–74.

Streeck, Wolfgang. 2016. *How Will Capitalism End? Essays on a Failing System*. London: Verso.

Sun, Yu, Ling Li, Hui Shi, and Dazhi Chong. 2020. "The Transformation and Upgrade of China's Manufacturing Industry in Industry 4.0 Era." *Systems Research and Behavioral Science* 37: 734–40.

Sunstein, Cass. 2014. "Nudges.gov: Behavioral Economics and Regulation." In *The Oxford Handbook of Behavioral Economics and the Law*, edited by Eyal Zamir and Doron Teichman. Oxford: Oxford University Press.

Taplin, Jonathan. 2017. *Move Fast and Break Things: How Facebook, Google, and Amazon Cornered Culture and Undermined Democracy*. New York: Little, Brown and Company.

Tapscott, Don, and Alex Tapscott. 2018. *Blockchain Revolution: How the Technology behind Bitcoin and Other Cryptocurrencies Is Changing the World*. New York: Portfolio-Penguin.

Terranova, Tiziana. 2000. "Free Labor: Producing Culture for the Digital Economy." *Social Text* 63 (18): 2: 33–58.

Teston, Liz. 2020. "On the Nature of Public Interiority." *Interiority* 3 (1): 61–82.

Theocharis, Y., and J. W. Van Deth. 2018. "The Continuous Expansion of Citizen Participation: A New Taxonomy." *European Political Science Review* 10 (1): 139–63.

Tiwana, A. 2014. *Platform Ecosystems: Aligning Architecture, Governance, and Strategy.* Waltham, MA: Morgan Kaufmann.

Tony Blair Institute. 2022. *Making It Work: Understanding the Gig Economy's S hortcomings and Opportunities.* London: Tony Blair Institute for Social Change.

Toussaint, Eric. 2020. "No, the Coronavirus Is Not Responsible for the Fall of Stock Prices." *CADTM*, March 5.

Treacy, M. 2022. "Dependency Theory and the Critique of Neodevelopmentalism in Latin America." *Latin American Perspectives* 49 (1): 218–36.

Trentesaux, D., and S. Karnouskos. 2022. "Engineering Ethical Behaviors in Autonomous Industrial Cyber-Physical Human Systems." *Cognition, Technology & Work* 24 (1): 113–26.

Tribunal Superior Eleitoral. 2014. *Eleições no Brasil.* Brasília: Tribunal Superior Eleitoral.

Tribunal Superior Eleitoral. 2016. *Urna eletrônica: 20 anos a favor da democracia.* Brasília: Tribunal Superior Eleitoral.

Tribunal Supremo Eleitoral (TSE). 2022. RESPOSTAS AO OFÍCIO n° 001. https://www.tse.jus.br/++theme++justica_eleitoral/pdfjs/web/viewer.html?file=https://www.tse.jus.br/comunicacao/noticias/arquivos/respostas-as-forcas-armadas-em-relacao-ao-processo-eleitoral-16-02-2022/@@download/file/TSE-Respostas-%C3%A0s-For%C3%A7as-Armadas-16-02-2022.pdf.

Trussell Trust. 2022. *Stats.* https://www.trusselltrust.org/news-and-blog/latest-stats/.

Tuesta Soldevilla, Fernando, and Yanina Welp. 2020. *El diablo está en los detalles: Referéndum y poder político en América Latina.* Lima: Pontifical Catholic University of Peru.

Turkle, Sherry. 2011. *Alone Together: Why We Expect More from Technology and Less from Each Other.* New York: Basic Books.

Turow, Joseph. 2017. *The Aisles Have Eyes: How Retailers Track Your Shopping, Strip Your Privacy, and Define Your Power.* New Haven: Yale University Press.

UK Health Security Agency. 2021. "Patterns and Trends in Excess Weight among Adults in England." https://ukhsa.blog.gov.uk/2021/03/04/patterns-and-trends-in-excess-weight-among-adults-in-england/.

UNCTAD. 2017. *Information Economy Report 2017: Digitalization, Trade and Development.* New York: UNCTAD.

UNCTAD. 2019. *Digital Economy Report 2019: Value Creation and Capture: Implications for Developing Countries.* New York: UNCTAD.

318 | References

UNCTAD. 2021a. *Digital Economy Report 2021: Cross-Border Data Flows and Development: For Whom the Data Flow*. New York: UNCTAD.

UNESCO. 2016. "Diversity of Cultural Expressions Facing the Digital Challenge." https://en.unesco.org/news/diversity-cultural-expressions-facing-digital-challenge.

UN-Habitat. 2022. *World Cities Report 2022: Envisaging the Future of Cities*. New York: UN-Habitat. https://unhabitat.org/sites/default/files/2022/06/wcr_2022.pdf.

United Nations. 2019. *Report of the Special Rapporteur on Extreme Poverty and Human Rights, 2019*. New York: Office of the High Commissioner for Human Rights.

United Nations. 2022. *Universal Declaration of Human Rights*. https://www.un.org/en/about-us/universal-declaration-of-human-rights.

United Nations General Assembly. 2020. *Declaration on the Commemoration of the Seventy-Fifth Anniversary of the United Nations*. September, A/RES/75/1.

Uscinski, J. E., ed. 2018. *Conspiracy Theories and the People Who Believe Them*. Oxford: Oxford University Press.

U.S. Government Accountability Office. 2021. *Technology Assessment: Exposure Notifications. Benefits and Challenges of Smartphone Applications to Augment Contact Tracing*. Washington, DC: GAO.

U.S. Trade Representative. 2016. *The Digital 2 Dozen*. Washington, DC: USTR.

Vaidhyanathan, S. 2018. *Antisocial Media: How Facebook Disconnects Us and Undermines Democracy*. Oxford: Oxford University Press.

Valente, J. C. L. 2021. *From Online Platforms to Digital Monopolies: Technology, Information and Power*. Leiden: Brill.

Van Dijck, José. 2013. *The Culture of Connectivity: A Critical History of Social Media*. Oxford: Oxford University Press.

Van Dijk, Jan. 2005. *The Deepening Divide: Inequality in the Information Society*. Thousand Oaks, CA: Sage.

Van Doorn, N. 2017. "Platform Labor: On the Gendered and Racialized Exploitation of Low-Income Service Work in the 'On-Demand' Economy." *Information, Communication & Society* 20 (6): 898–914.

Varoufakis, Yanis. 2020. "From an Economics without Capitalism to Markets without Capitalism." https://www.yanisvaroufakis.eu/2021/01/28/from-an-economics-without-capitalism-to-markets-without-capitalism-tubingen-university-talk/.

Varoufakis, Yanis. 2021. "Technofeudalism Is Taking Over." *Project Syndicate*, July 28.

Veen, A., T. Barratt, and C. Goods. 2019. "Platform-Capital's 'Appetite' for Control: A Labor Process Analysis of Food-Delivery Work in Australia." *Work, Employment and Society* 34 (3): 388–406.

Veiga-Neto, Alfredo. 2019. "O currículo e seus três adversários: Os funcionários da verdade, os técnicos do desejo, o fascismo." In *Para uma vida não-fas-*

cista, edited by Margaeth Rago and Alfredo Veiga-Neto. Belo Horizonte: Editora Autêntica.

Verhulst, Stefaan. 2018. "Where and When AI and CI Meet: Exploring the Intersection of Artificial and Collective Intelligence towards the Goal of Innovating How We Govern." *AI & SOCIETY* 33 (2): 293–97.

Verhulst, Stefaan, Laura Sandor, and Julia Stamm. 2023. "The Urgent Need to Reimagine Data Consent." *Stanford Social Innovation Review*, July 26. https://ssir.org/articles/entry/the_urgent_need_to_reimagine_data_consent.

Viciano Pastor, Roberto, and Rubén Martínez Dalmau. 2011. "El nuevo constitucionalismo latinoamericano: Fundamentos para una construcción doctrinal." *Revista General de Derecho Público Comparado* 9: 1–24.

Vincent, J. 2018. "Google 'Fixed' Its Racist Algorithm by Removing Gorillas from Its Image-Labeling Tech—Nearly Three Years after the Company Was Called Out, It Hasn't Gone beyond a Quick Workaround." *Verge*, January 12. https://www.theverge.com/2018/1/12/16882408/google-racist-gorillas-photo-recognition-algorithm-ai.

Vir, Aaryaman, and Rahul Sanghi. 2021. "The Internet Country: How India Created a Digital Blueprint for the Economies of the Future." *Tigerfeathers* (blog), January 14. https://tigerfeathers.substack.com/p/the-internet-country.

Voon, Tania. 2006. "UNESCO and the WTO: A Clash of Cultures?" *International and Comparative Law Quarterly* 55 (3): 633–51.

Wade, Robert. 2013. "The Art of Power Maintenance." *Challenge* 56 (1): 5–39.

Walker, J. 2018. "What We Mean When We Say 'Conspiracy Theory.'" In *Conspiracy Theories and the People Who Believe Them*, edited by J. E. Uscinski. Oxford: Oxford University Press.

Wallerstein, Immanuel. 1974. *The Modern World-System*. Vol. 1. Berkeley: University of California Press.

Wallerstein, Immanuel. 1976. "Semi-Peripheral Countries and the Contemporary World Crisis." *Theory and Society* 3 (4): 461–83.

Walsham, Geoff. 2017. "ICT4D Research: Reflections on History and Future Agenda." *Information Technology for Development* 23 (1): 18–41.

Wampler, Brian, and Benjamin Goldfrank. 2022. *The Rise, Spread, and Decline of Brazil's Participatory Budgeting: The Arc of a Democratic Innovation*. Cham, Switzerland: Palgrave Macmillan.

Wampler, Brian, Stephanie McNulty, and Michael Touchton. 2021. *Participatory Budgeting in Global Perspective*. Oxford: Oxford University Press.

Wampler, Brian, Natasha Sugiyama, and Michael Touchton. 2020. *Democracy at Work: Pathways to Well-Being in Brazil*. Cambridge: Cambridge University Press.

Warf, Barney, eds. 2018. *The Sage Encyclopedia of the Internet*. Thousand Oaks, CA: Sage.

320 | References

Weis, T. 2007. *The Global Food Economy: The Cattle for the Future of Farming*. London: Zed Books.

Welchman, Lisa. 2015. *Managing Chaos: Digital Governance by Design*. New York: Rosenfeld Media.

Welp, Yanina. 2021. "Deliberation in the Constitutional Reform Process: Cuba in Comparative Context." In *Social Policies and Institutional Reform in Cuba Post Covid*, edited by Bert Hoffmann. Opladen, Germany: Verlag Barbara Budrich.

Welp, Yanina, and Alejandra Marzuca. 2016. "Presencia de partidos políticos y diputados en Internet en Argentina, Paraguay y Uruguay." *Perfiles Latinoamericanos* 24 (47): 199–224.

Welp, Yanina, and Francisco Soto. 2021. "Digital Participation in Chilean 'Citizenry Dialogues' (2015)." *International Journal of Electronic Governance* 13 (2): 192–207.

Weyland, Kurt. 2012. "The Arab Spring: Why the Surprising Similarities with the Revolutionary Wave of 1848?" *Perspectives on Politics* 10 (4): 917–34.

White, Andrew. 2014. *Digital Media and Society: Transforming Economics, Politics and Social Practices*. New York: Springer.

Wilkins, J. 2005. "Eating Right Here: Moving from Consumer to Food Citizen." *Agriculture and Human Values* 22 (3): 269–73.

Williams, E. 2014. *Capitalism and Slavery*. Chapel Hill: University of North Carolina Press.

Wilson, B. 2021. "We Need to Break the Junk Food Cycle: How to Fix Britain's Failing Food System." *Guardian*, November 30.

Winecoff, W. K. 2015. "Structural Power and the Global Financial Crisis: A Network Analytical Approach." *Business and Politics* 17 (3): 495–525.

Wise, Carol. 2020. *Dragonomics: How Latin America Is Maximizing (or Missing Out on) China's International Development Strategy*. New Haven: Yale University Press.

Wolpert, David H., and Kagan Tumer. 1999. *An Introduction to Collective Intelligence*. arXiv preprint cs/9908014.

Wood, A., M. Graham, A. Lehdonvirta, and I. Hjorth. 2019. "Good Gig, Bad Gig: Autonomy and Algorithmic Control in the Global Gig." *Work, Employment, and Society* 33 (1): 56–75.

Wood, E. M. 2002. *The Origin of Capitalism: A Longer View*. London: Verso.

Woodcock, J. 2020. "The Algorithmic Panopticon at Deliveroo: Measurement, Precarity, and the Illusion of Control." *Ephemera* 20 (3): 67–95.

Woodcock, J., and Mark Graham. 2019. *The Gig Economy: A Critical Introduction*. Cambridge: Polity.

Wu, Tim. 2017. *The Attention Merchants: The Epic Scramble to Get Inside Our Heads*. New York: Vintage.

Yates, Simeon J., John Kirby, and Eleanor Lockley. 2015. " 'Digital-by-Default': Reinforcing Exclusion through Technology." In *Defence of Welfare 2*, edited by L. Foster, A. Brunton, C. Deming, and T. Haux. Cambridge, UK: Polity Press.

Yates, Simeon, and Eleanor Lockley. 2018. "Social Media and Social Class." *American Behavioral Scientist* 62 (9): 1291–1316.

Young, Iris M. 2002. *Inclusion and Democracy*. Oxford: Oxford University Press.

Zaremberg, Gisela, Valeria Guarneros-Meza, and Adrián Gurza Lavalle, eds. 2017. *Intermediation and Representation in Latin America: Actors and Roles beyond Elections*. Cham, Switzerland: Palgrave Macmillan.

Zaremberg, Gisela, and Yanina Welp. 2020. "Más allá de enfoques utópicos y distópicos sobre innovación democrática: Beyond Utopian and Dystopian Approaches to Democratic Innovation." *Recerca: Revista de Pensament i Anàlisi* 25 (1): 71–94.

Zenglein, Max J., and Anna Holzmann. 2019. *Evolving Made in China 2025: China's Industrial Policy in the Quest for Global Tech Leadership*. MERICS Papers on China, no. 8 (July): 1–80.

Zhang, Longmei, and Sally Chen. 2019. *China's Digital Economy: Opportunities and Risks*. Washington, DC: International Monetary Fund.

Zhang, Weiwei. 2012. *China Wave: The Rise of a Civilizational State*. Hackensack, NJ: World Century Publishing.

Zhang, Weiwei. 2018. "The Three 'Genetic Defects' of the Western Model." *CGTN*, March 13. https://news.cgtn.com/news/3345444d796b7a6333566d54/share_p.html?fbclid=IwAR3_WYWmsHzAJN4f6WnH7OxlJ5vTdiQoGbVCcLGW55HbYR0vIiKGq0QZ1A0—.

Zhou, Qian. 2022. *China Releases Draft 2022 Encouraged Catalogue, Signals New Opportunities*. China Briefing, May 12. https://www.china-briefing.com/news/china-proposes-to-expand-encouraged-industries-for-foreign-investment-the-draft-2022-catalogue/.

Zuboff, Shoshana. 2015. "Big Other: Surveillance Capitalism and the Prospects of an Information Civilization." *Journal of Information Technology* 30 (1): 75–89.

Zuboff, Shoshana. 2019. *The Age of Surveillance Capitalism: The Fight for a Human Future at the New Frontier of Power*. New York: Public Affairs.

Index

5G, 29, 58, 61n, 229, 243, 257, 259, 263, 272

Algorithm, 4–5, 8, 13, 25, 26–27, 38, 40, 46, 54, 66–67, 69, 71–72, 75, 77, 87–88, 102–3, 117, 121, 131–33, 135, 136n6, 136n18, 180, 232, 249–51, 255, 258, 260, 265–68, 270, 280

Algorithmic bias, 5, 55, 249, 266

Artificial Intelligence (AI), 4, 55, 72, 100–1, 104, 117–18, 121–22, 135, 173, 177, 180, 182, 230, 232, 234–35, 237, 240, 243–44, 250, 255, 257, 261, 272, 279–80

Automation, 31, 103, 174, 181, 243

Blockchain, 229–30, 232–33, 237, 257, 259, 272

Bolsonaro, Jair, 2, 35, 42–43, 61n, 92, 94–95, 138

Brazil, 1–2, 12–14, 35, 42–43, 45–59, 60n, 61n, 65–76, 79–80, 81n, 83–96, 97n, 117–19, 121–22, 140, 143–44, 146, 148–52, 165, 170, 185–86, 193, 197–203, 206n, 271–72, 273n, 276

Brexit, 35

Capital, 5, 7–9, 11–14, 38, 42, 48, 55, 67, 101–2, 109–13, 124, 134, 135n, 157–58, 162, 165, 170, 173, 175–80, 188–89, 192, 196, 200, 202, 210, 213, 215, 229, 234, 237, 241, 250, 256, 260, 262–63, 265, 275, 278–79; Capitalism, 1–3, 8–9, 12, 20–21, 76–77, 101, 105, 108, 112, 123, 156–58, 173–74, 176, 183, 263, 278; Capitalist crisis, 175; Print capitalism, 37; Racial capitalism, 100–1, 104–6; Racial technocapitalism, 13, 100–1, 103; Surveillance capitalism, 25–26, 28, 101, 104

Catch-up, 234, 275

Chile, 68, 76, 143–44, 152–53, 252

China, 14, 58–60, 67, 92, 216, 218, 223, 227–54, 256, 262–64, 268–70, 276, 279

Citizenship, 10, 84, 120, 235

Class, 6–14, 26, 31, 48, 72–73, 99–100, 115, 145, 150, 155–56, 158, 160, 163–65, 168–70, 174, 176–77, 179–83, 256, 263, 266, 271–72, 275, 278

Cloud, 4, 6, 58, 66, 68, 72, 80n, 104, 174, 177–78, 186–87, 193, 202, 204n, 206n, 211, 215, 219–20, 224n, 233, 235, 237, 239–40, 246–47, 255, 257–59, 261, 269, 272

Collective identities, 5–6, 12, 27, 53–57, 70, 75, 85–86, 88, 96, 117,

324 | Index

Collective identities *(continued)*
125, 128, 129–32, 134–35, 136n,
138, 152, 212, 271, 275–76
Commons, 209–10, 221
Consumer, 6, 54, 66, 73, 79, 106, 111,
157, 160, 162, 185–88, 192, 195–97,
199, 201–3, 210, 232, 253, 260, 262,
270
Costa Rica, 145–47
COVID-19, 2, 68, 70, 72–73, 92,
103–4, 137, 151–52, 155–56,
160–61, 168, 184n, 189, 228, 232,
238–39, 244, 246, 255, 257, 262,
264, 267, 275; Pandemic 2–3, 14,
32, 68, 70, 72–73, 92, 103–5, 137,
151, 155–56, 160–61, 173, 175–77,
179, 181–82, 233, 239, 244–46, 249,
255, 257, 262, 264, 267
Crisis, 2, 46–49, 89, 93, 149, 155–56,
160–61, 163, 168, 170, 175–77, 183,
189, 196, 228, 241, 256, 275–76,
279–80
Cuba, 143–44

Data, 4–10, 12–13, 20, 24–28, 42, 46,
48–49, 51, 53–56, 58, 60n, 67–68,
70, 72, 75, 79, 86, 93, 95, 102–4,
114, 117, 120–21, 123–25, 128,
130–35, 141, 153, 163, 174–77,
180, 182, 186–87, 189, 193–94,
202, 204n–5n, 207n, 209–11,
213–15, 219–24, 224n–25n, 229,
233–37, 239–40, 243, 245–50, 252,
255–60, 262, 264, 266–71, 275–80;
Collection, 4, 26, 75, 127, 129–30,
174, 193, 221, 225n, 229, 262, 270;
Commons, 209–10, 221; Data flows,
175, 193–94, 219–24, 224n–25n,
232, 234, 248–49, 258, 269–70; Data
Infrastructure, 3–4, 48–49, 58, 66,
183, 185–86, 196, 206n, 210–11,

213–15, 223–24, 233, 237, 250,
256–57, 260, 262–63, 269; Data
protection, 67, 193, 207n, 220, 224,
236, 249, 267, 270, 276; Datafication,
259–61, 272; Localization, 189,
202, 221, 269, 276; Monetization,
193; Personal data, 25, 54, 193–94,
214, 221–22, 225n, 236, 252, 267,
269–70; Public data infrastructure,
214; Storage, 4, 7, 174, 193, 245,
257, 259
Democracy, 2–3, 10, 12–14, 33, 36,
39, 41–44, 50, 59, 83, 89, 93, 95–96,
102, 117, 122–23, 132, 135, 136n,
137–39, 141–42, 145, 148–51, 153–
54, 278, 280; Deliberation, 36–39,
41–44, 128, 131–32, 136n, 139–40,
142–44, 151–54; Democratic
governance, 11–12, 121–22, 130,
135, 140–41; Democratic decline,
95
Developing countries, 1, 3, 6–8, 14,
42, 185–86, 188–90, 193, 196,
198, 201, 209–14, 216–17, 219–20,
222–24, 233, 275–77
Digital, 1–15, 15n, 19–23, 24–29,
31–32, 36–37, 42, 44, 46, 55–56, 60,
65–69, 71–73, 76–80, 99–101, 103,
108–10, 121–22, 124, 137–42, 144–
45, 147, 149–53, 154n, 156–57, 162,
166, 173–75, 177–82, 185, 192–94,
196–19, 205n–7n, 209–24, 227–30,
232–38, 240–41, 243–53, 255–61,
263–72, 275–80; Digital Age, 1–3,
7–9, 11–15, 20–21, 28, 37, 42, 60,
108, 138, 140, 151, 194, 255–56,
259, 261, 263, 266, 272, 275–77,
279–80; Digital capital, 5, 229, 265;
Digital citizenship, 141, 152, 266;
Digital divide, 5–6, 151, 237, 250,
264–65; Digital trade, 210, 217,

220–23, 224n, 251–52, 267, 269; Digitalization, 3–14, 99, 138–39, 142, 144, 151, 153, 173–75, 177, 179–82, 209, 212–13, 219, 224n, 229–30, 232–34, 244, 248, 256, 263, 275–80; Governance, 11–12, 14, 28, 45, 53, 56, 60, 83–85, 96, 100, 118–22, 125, 130, 135, 140–41, 196, 214, 235–36, 238, 240, 246, 248–49, 255–56, 267, 269–71; Industrial policy, 194, 209–10, 217, 219; Labor platforms, 66–68, 76–77, 180, 244; Public digital infrastructure, 66, 185, 224; Regime, 12, 14, 86, 96, 121, 124, 166, 220, 222, 268, 275, 277, 279; Start-up, 22, 210–13, 257; Statecraft, 14, 191, 195–96, 276; Traditional sectors, 3, 212–13, 229

Disinformation, 83, 86, 88, 97n, 138, 204n

E-commerce, 174, 199–201, 203, 207n, 210, 215, 217–19, 222–23, 224n, 232, 235, 241–44, 251, 253

Economy, 2, 6, 9, 21, 25, 28, 30, 65–67, 71–72, 75, 77, 79–80, 84, 99–103, 108–10, 112, 118, 133–35, 156, 164, 169–70, 173–75, 177–78, 180, 182, 186–90, 193–95, 198, 201, 203, 205n, 207n, 209–12, 214, 216–19, 221–24, 227–38, 241, 243–53, 256–57, 260, 262–63, 265, 268, 270, 276

Ecuador, 68, 76, 142–45, 147, 152, 265, 270

Effects, 49, 52, 68, 76, 119, 124–25, 138–39, 141, 147, 153–54, 185–86, 188, 190, 192, 195, 198, 201, 203, 235, 271; Intended, 185, 195, 198, 201–3; Spillover, 185–86, 188, 195–98, 201–3

Elections, 11, 41–42, 54, 88–90, 94–95, 139, 146–47, 280

Employment, 54, 69, 73, 77, 107, 111, 127, 156, 158, 181, 184n, 200, 242–45, 249, 278

Environment, 3, 6, 10, 13–14, 23, 38, 118, 120, 129, 135, 148, 155, 157, 159, 162, 164, 169, 221, 228, 231, 235 (smart environment), 272, 278–79; Green technology, 235

Exchange, 10, 47, 66, 99, 102–3, 112, 134, 157, 159, 196, 218, 224, 237, 260

Extraction, 13, 22, 104, 110–13, 177, 193, 222, 260

Fake news, 12–13, 35, 39–43, 83–94, 96, 97n, 138, 280; Journalistic narratives, 86; Propagation, 85–88, 96; Viral, 86–88, 97n

Fanon, Frantz, 12, 27–29

Fairwork framework, 67–68, 69–71, 73, 76–79, 80n; Fairwork Brazil, 68, 70–71, 73, 75, 79; Fairwork Latin America 65, 68, 76–80

Fascism, 84–85, 90–91, 95–96, 104–5, 280

Financialization, 177, 278

Food systems, 13, 155–58, 163–66, 169–70; Capitalist food system, 156–58, 164, 170; Democratic socialist food system, 13, 156; Decommodification of food, 13, 165, 167; Food inequality, 155, 157, 160, 162; Food poverty, 155, 160–61, 164, 168; Right to food, 156–57, 163–64, 170

Fraud, 27, 89, 95

G20, 277, 280n

326 | Index

Gender, 10, 13, 75, 90–92, 96, 99–100, 103, 105, 107, 111–12, 138, 156, 158, 160, 163, 165, 264–66
Geopolitics, 3, 195, 276, 278
Global, 1–3, 6–12, 14, 27, 33, 36, 38, 41–42, 46, 49, 66–69, 72, 76–78, 80, 99–101, 103, 118–19, 129, 137, 139, 156–60, 173–78, 180–83, 184n, 186, 188–89, 192–94, 196, 204n–7n, 209–10, 212, 214–24, 228–33, 235, 241, 243, 245, 248–52, 255–59, 261–64, 267–68, 270–72, 275–77, 279–80, 280n; Global Police State, 173, 178, 182–83; Global South, 1, 3, 8–12, 14, 36, 42, 76–77, 80, 99–101, 103, 118–19, 139, 156, 158, 264, 275, 277, 280; Global value chain (GVC), 6, 188, 224, 231, 248, 252, 277; Globalization, 3, 173–74, 176–77, 185, 187, 219, 232; South-South, 217, 277
Governance, 11–12, 14, 28, 45, 53, 56, 60, 83–85, 96, 100, 118–22, 125, 130, 135, 140–41, 196, 214, 235–36, 238, 240, 246, 248–49, 255–56, 267, 269–71; Governmentalize, 83

Hegemony, 84, 186, 192, 194; Digital hegemony, 194; Hegemonic action, 185–87, 190–91, 195, 197–98, 201–2; United States Hegemony, 186, 192
Hua, Julietta, 99–101, 105–6, 112–13, 278

India, 14, 27, 100, 182, 185–86, 193, 196–203, 204n, 206n–8n, 211–15, 220, 224n–25n, 264, 276
Information, 5–6, 24–27, 36, 39–41, 43, 46–49, 54–55, 58, 60n, 70, 79, 84, 86–87, 102, 120–21, 124, 126, 129–34, 140–41, 143–44, 147, 152–54, 173–74, 190, 193, 209, 229, 232–37, 243, 245–47, 249–53, 256, 258–60, 264, 266–67, 269–72, 276–77
Information and communication technology (ICT), 6, 270
Innovation, 4, 6, 8, 10, 19, 31, 35–36, 38, 42, 46, 93, 99, 106, 109, 121, 139, 152, 166, 191, 205n, 212–13, 237, 243–45, 248–49, 251–52, 256–57, 259, 276–78
Intellectual property, 188–89, 209, 217
Internet of things (IOT), 4, 102, 174–75, 237, 243, 257, 259, 266, 272

Jobs, 2, 6, 13, 67, 74, 77, 107, 110, 163, 179–81, 184n, 188, 227, 232, 243–45, 250, 279
Journalism, 39, 94

Labor, 2–3, 6–10, 12, 30–31, 54, 66–73, 75–80, 99–100, 102–3, 105–15, 136n, 156–60, 162–63, 170, 175, 179–82, 231, 236–37, 243–45, 248, 256, 265, 267, 272, 277–78, 280; Labor market, 66, 71, 112, 244–45; Labor platforms, 66–68, 76–77, 180, 244; Labor regulation, 77, 80, 107; Feminization of labor, 105, 110, 112; Gendered labor, 99–100, 103, 105, 111–12, 158; Gig/gigging/gigged worker, 8, 22, 31, 66, 78, 100, 104–10, 112, 114–15, 180; Invisible work, 8, 10, 106; Unpaid labor, 8–9, 67, 110–11, 158, 160, 163, 167
Latin America, 2, 11, 13, 46, 50, 60n, 65, 67–68, 76–80, 122, 137–39, 141–45, 147–48, 150–52, 189, 196, 265
Leapfrog, 6, 100, 243
Libertarianism, 42, 57

Location-based, 194
L'Ouverture, Toussaint, 21–22
Lula, 2, 15n, 91, 92, 95, 97n; Luiz
    Inácio "Lula" da Silva, 2
Luddites, 12, 29–33
Lyft, 99, 101–3, 106–10, 113–15, 115n

Machine learning, 174, 258
Market volatility, 185–87, 189–90,
    192, 195–96, 202
Media, 3–5, 8, 19, 26, 28, 35, 37–41,
    43–44, 56, 59, 72, 90–92, 94,
    99, 138, 141, 144, 146–47, 161,
    178, 193, 206n, 244, 246, 249,
    261; Media control, 40; Media
    manipulation, 249; New media, 35,
    37–38, 40; Social media, 8, 19, 26,
    28, 38, 40–41, 43–44, 56, 59, 72, 91,
    138, 193, 206n, 246, 261
Middle powers, 14, 185–86, 191–92,
    195, 201, 203, 279
Monopoly, 7, 187, 199, 209,
    221, 236(antimonopoly),
    249–50(antimonopoly); Market
    power, 187, 235
Monopoly corporations, 2–3, 11–12,
    14, 38, 45, 48, 50, 53–56, 99, 108,
    134, 160, 162, 177, 179–81, 193,
    201, 207n, 209, 214, 216, 221–22,
    252, 258, 261–62; Alibaba, 57, 176,
    210, 213, 215, 218, 235, 239, 246,
    249, 258, 262; Amazon, 20, 24, 26,
    32, 54, 56, 72, 102–5, 176, 178,
    187, 193, 199, 200, 204n–8n, 210,
    213, 251, 258, 261–62, 271–72,
    280; Apple, 54, 56, 102, 176, 178,
    187, 193, 205n, 239, 261–62, 268,
    280; Baidu, 57, 213, 245, 249, 262;
    BATX, 57; Facebook, 4, 24–25,
    54, 56, 60n, 102, 138, 176, 178,
    187, 193, 195, 204n, 206n, 261–62,
    267–68, 280; GAFAM, 261–62, 267,

270–71, 280; Google, 24–26, 32,
    54–57, 102, 176, 178, 187, 193, 195,
    204n–6n, 213, 239, 258, 261–62,
    266, 268, 280; Huawei, 57–58,
    61n, 206n, 246, 263, 269; IBM,
    45–50, 56, 60n, 240, 259–60, 266;
    Microsoft, 26, 56, 176, 178, 187,
    193, 206n, 258, 261–62, 266, 280;
    Tencent, 57, 176, 239, 246, 249,
    258, 262; Xiaomi, 57
Multitude, 7

Neoliberalism, 2, 9, 13, 88, 96, 182,
    188, 256, 263, 276, 279
Network, 3–4, 6, 19–20, 29, 40–41,
    54, 56, 68, 76, 80, 85–88, 90–91,
    96, 118–19, 121, 123, 141, 153, 160,
    169, 190, 192–93, 195, 197–99, 203,
    205n–7n, 212, 235, 237, 239–40,
    244–45, 247, 252, 256–62, 272, 280
New media, 35, 37–38, 40

Objectivism, 57
Open source, 134

Participation, 4, 7, 10, 13, 37, 49,
    84, 89–90, 102, 117, 120–25,
    127, 130, 132–35, 136n, 137–47,
    149–54, 154n, 157, 168, 239; citizen
    initiatives, 147, 153; communal
    councils, 140, 148–49; deliberative
    constitution making, 142, 145, 153–
    54; digital participation, 7, 13, 120,
    123, 130, 137, 138–39, 140, 142,
    151–53, 154n; mechanisms of direct
    democracy, 142, 145; participatory
    budgeting, 139–40, 142, 150,
    153–54; planning councils, 148;
    public policy councils, 122, 140,
    142, 147–48, 153–54; referendums,
    139–40, 142, 144–47, 153
Peru, 68, 145, 152–53, 265

328 | Index

Platform capitalism, 66, 101, 103
Popular sovereignty, 1–2, 7, 9, 11–12, 14, 37, 100, 139, 142, 150, 154
Populism, 84–85, 140, 280
Precariat, 8
Privacy, 4–5, 24–25, 27–28, 51, 54, 104, 207n, 214, 220, 224n, 249, 265, 267, 269
Public, 4–5, 11, 13–14, 19–20, 26, 35–39, 41, 43–44, 49, 51, 59, 65, 70, 73–74, 79–80, 84, 88, 90–94, 96, 117–19, 121–25, 128, 130, 133–35, 136n, 139–42, 145, 147, 150–53, 159, 162, 164, 166, 168–69, 175, 178, 194–97, 206n, 210–11, 213–16, 220–21, 223–24, 236, 239, 246, 250, 270

Ray, Kasturi, 99–101, 105–6, 107–10, 112, 114, 278
Regulation, 5–6, 42, 44, 55, 77, 80, 107, 123, 146, 153, 157, 169, 199, 207n, 214–15, 220–22, 224, 236–37, 249–50, 253, 262, 267, 270–71, 276–77
Rents, 187, 222, 224n, 276–78
Reproductive labor, 8–9, 105–6, 110–11, 113
Robotics, 4, 102, 174, 232, 272, 279

Science, 4–5, 13, 22, 26–27, 45, 50, 53, 55–57, 59–60, 68, 85–86, 90–91, 92–93, 105, 121, 125, 236, 256, 258, 261, 273
Services, 8, 10, 14, 26–27, 50, 54, 56, 66, 71–72, 74, 80, 99, 102–3, 105, 108–11, 113–14, 118–22, 124, 135, 135n, 151, 162, 164, 169, 174–75, 178, 181, 186–88, 190, 193–94, 196–97, 199, 201, 204n, 206n, 209–11, 215, 217–21, 224n, 234–36,

238, 240, 244, 249, 252–53, 257, 259–62, 264, 266–71, 279
Sharing economy, 9, 99, 102, 174, 237
Sovereignty, 1–3, 7, 9, 11–12, 14, 37, 54, 58, 93, 99–100, 139, 142, 150, 154, 185, 192, 194, 225n, 269, 277; Digital sovereignty, 185, 192, 194, 269 ("cybersovereignty"); Popular sovereignty, 1–2, 7, 9, 11–12, 14, 37, 100, 139, 142, 150, 154
State, 3, 5–6, 9, 11, 13–14, 37–38, 44–46, 48–50, 53–57, 59–60, 83, 85–86, 90–91, 96, 101, 105, 115, 122–23, 125, 133–34, 141, 148, 157–59, 164, 168–69, 173, 175–78, 182–83, 189–90, 192–96, 203, 204n–5n, 215, 222, 227, 244, 255, 268–69, 275–77; Digital Statecraft, 14, 276; Nation-building, 276; State-building, 37

Technology, 2, 5–6, 11, 14, 19–20, 22–24, 27–33, 37, 45, 53, 81n, 93, 103–6, 115, 120, 123, 130, 132–34, 137, 141, 145, 149, 155–56, 160, 162, 166, 173–74, 177–79, 181, 185–88, 190, 192–95, 198–99, 203, 205n, 207n, 209, 212, 216, 219–20, 224, 224n, 229–30, 233–40, 243–44, 246, 248, 250–53, 256–57, 261, 263, 267, 270, 279; Technological innovation, 4, 6, 8, 31, 35–36, 38, 46, 93, 106, 109, 121, 139, 212, 237, 251, 256, 259, 278; Fourth industrial revolution, 1, 101, 173–74, 180, 182–83
Techno-feudalism, 278
Trump, 35, 40, 43, 57, 60n–61n, 138
Trust, 43, 46, 91, 93–96, 121, 133, 139, 141, 267; Distrust/Mistrust, 91, 93, 94–96, 139

Index | 329

Uber, 9, 26, 32, 57, 68, 71, 74, 78, 81n, 99, 101–3, 106–10, 112–15, 115n, 162–63, 169, 210, 240, 251, 265

United Kingdom (UK), 13, 26–27, 67, 155–57, 159–64, 166–70, 229, 249, 253

Uruguay, 145–46, 152

Venezuela, 140, 142–46, 148–50, 191, 264

Weaponized interdependence, 185, 190, 192, 194–95, 206n

West, 50, 57–60, 189–90, 196, 230, 240, 245, 252, 264

WhatsApp, 42–43, 70, 86–88, 96, 138, 198, 261–62, 267, 272

Working class, 6–7, 9, 11–14, 72, 99–100, 150, 160, 165, 169–70, 179, 181, 256, 266, 272, 275, 278

Workers' Party (PT), 2, 84, 165

Web–based, 100